*SCHAUM'S OUTLINE OF*

# THEORY AND PROBLEMS

of

# PROGRAMMING
# with
# PASCAL

•

## BYRON S. GOTTFRIED, Ph.D.
*Professor of Industrial Engineering*
*Engineering Management and Operations Research*
*University of Pittsburgh*

•

## SCHAUM'S OUTLINE SERIES
### McGRAW-HILL, INC.

New York   St. Louis   San Francisco   Auckland   Bogotá   Caracas   Hamburg
Lisbon   London   Madrid   Mexico   Milan   Montreal   New Delhi   Paris
San Juan   São Paulo   Singapore   Sydney   Tokyo   Toronto

BYRON S. GOTTFRIED is Professor of Industrial Engineering, Engineering Management, and Operations Research at the University of Pittsburgh. He received his Ph.D. from Case-Western Reserve University (1962), and has been a member of the Pitt faculty since 1970. His primary interests are in the development of complex technical and business applications of computers. Dr. Gottfried is the author of several textbooks, including *Introduction to Engineering Calculations* and *Programming with BASIC* in the Schaum's Outline Series.

Schaum's Outline of Theory and Problems of
PROGRAMMING WITH PASCAL

7 8 9 10 BAW 9 8 7 6 5 4 3 2 1 0

ISBN 0-07-023849-9

Sponsoring Editor, Jeff McCartney
Editing Supervisor, Marthe Grice
Production Manager, Nick Monti
Cover design by Amy E. Becker.


**Library of Congress Cataloging in Publication Data**

Gottfried, Byron S.
    Schaum's outline of theory and problems of programming
with PASCAL.

    (Schaum's outline series)
    Includes index.
    1. PASCAL (Computer program language)     I. Title.
QA76.73.P2G68   1984       001.64'24       84-10032
ISBN 0-07-023849-9

# Preface

Pascal has taken the world by a storm since its introduction in the early 1970s. Within a few short years it has become the standard language for serious programming students in most major colleges and universities, and it is now being taught in many high schools and junior colleges. Many computer professionals are also turning to Pascal, in preference to other languages that may be more readily accessible. Clearly, no other programming language has had so great an influence on the computing community in so short a period of time.

Why all the interest in Pascal? For several reasons. First, because Pascal is a language with style. In fact, Pascal was specifically designed to promote a disciplined, stylized approach to computer programming. Its use therefore encourages the development of programs that are well organized, clearly written, and relatively free of errors. Moreover, the language is available for practically any computer, whether it be a large mainframe or a small, inexpensive microcomputer. And it can be used effectively in any programming environment, ranging from batch processing to highly interactive computing. Thus, Pascal offers a number of desirable characteristics that are relatively unattainable with other programming languages.

This book offers instruction in computer programming using the features of standard (ISO) Pascal. The GOTO statement is included in the discussion of control structures, though its use is discouraged. Some additional, nonstandard features are also discussed, the most notable being the passing of variable-length array parameters (conformant array parameters) to procedures and functions.

The book continues in the tradition of other programming texts in the Schaum's Outline Series. Thus, the book presents complete and understandable explanations of all of Pascal's principal features, supplemented by a large number of illustrative examples. In addition, the book presents a contemporary approach to programming, stressing the importance of clarity, legibility and efficiency in program development. The reader is therefore exposed to the principles of good programming practice as well as the specific rules of Pascal.

The style of writing has been kept elementary, so that the book can be used by a wide reader audience ranging from high-school students to practicing professionals. The book is particularly well suited for advanced secondary or beginning college-level students, either as a textbook for an introductory programming course, as a supplementary text, or as an effective self-study guide.

For the most part, the required mathematical level does not go beyond high-school algebra. Much of the material requires no mathematical background at all.

The material is presented in such a manner that the reader can write complete, though elementary, Pascal programs almost immediately. It is very important that the reader write such programs and run them concurrently with reading the text material. This will greatly enhance the beginning programmer's self-confidence and stimulate his or her interest in the subject. (It should be recognized that computer programming is a skill, much like creative writing or playing a musical instrument. Such skills cannot be acquired simply by reading a textbook!)

# PREFACE

A large number of examples are included as an integral part of the text. These include several comprehensive programming examples as well as simple drill-type problems. Additional programming exercises are illustrated in the solved problems that appear at the end of most chapters. These examples and solved problems should be studied carefully as the reader progresses through each chapter and begins to write his or her own programs.

With two exceptions, the programming examples were all solved on an IBM Personal Computer using the original Pascal Compiler supplied by IBM. Examples 8.10 and 9.32 were executed on a Digital Equipment VAX-750, using the Pascal compiler supplied by DEC for use with their VMS operating system.

The programming examples were also solved using Borland International's Turbo Pascal wherever possible. Most of the programming examples ran under Turbo Pascal, though some required slight modification. Those programs that had to be modified, or would not run at all, are listed and discussed at the end of this book, in Appendix H.

Sets of review questions, supplementary problems and programming problems are also included at the end of each chapter. The review questions enable the reader to test his or her recall of the material presented within each chapter. They also provide an effective chapter summary. Most of the supplementary problems and programming problems require no special mathematical or technical background. The student should solve as many of these problems as possible. (Answers to many of the problems are provided at the end of the text.) When using this book in a programming course, the instructor may wish to supplement the programming problems with additional programming assignments that reflect particular disciplinary interests.

The principal features of the language are summarized in Appendixes A–G at the end of the book. This material should be used frequently for ready reference and quick recall. It will be particularly helpful when writing or debugging a new program.

The readers who complete this book will have had a solid exposure to general programming concepts as well as the specific rules of Pascal. From this, they should have acquired some realistic understanding of the capabilities and limitations of computers. They should also be able to program a computer to carry out specific tasks of their own choosing. And they may very well experience some of the excitement and exhilaration of being a part of the current computer revolution, which appears to be a major factor in the reshaping of modern post-industrial societies.

In closing, I wish to express my thanks to my daughter Sharon, who solved many of the programming problems and provided the answers to the programming problems at the end of the book.

Byron S. Gottfried

# Contents

CONTENTS

CONTENTS

# Complete Programming Examples

Italic numbers in parentheses refer to the page where the example appears.

# Chapter 1

# Introductory Concepts

This book offers instruction in computer programming using a disciplined, structured programming language called *Pascal*. We will see how a problem that is initially described in vague terms can be analyzed, outlined and finally transformed into a well-organized Pascal program. These concepts are demonstrated in detail by the many sample problems that are included in the text.

## 1.1 INTRODUCTION TO COMPUTERS

Today's computers come in a variety of shapes, sizes and costs. Huge, general-purpose computers are used by many large corporations, universities, hospitals and government agencies to carry out sophisticated scientific and business calculations. These computers are generally referred to as *mainframes*. They are very expensive (some cost millions of dollars), and they require a carefully controlled environment (temperature, humidity, etc.). As a rule, they are not physically accessible to the scientists, engineers and corporate accountants that use them.

Mainframes have been available since the early 1950s, but very few people had any opportunity to use them, particularly in the earlier years. Thus it is not surprising that computers were viewed mysteriously and with some suspicion by the general public.

The late 1960s and early 1970s saw the development of smaller, less expensive *minicomputers*. Many of these machines offer the performance of earlier mainframes at a fraction of the cost. Many business and educational institutions that could not afford mainframes acquired minicomputers as they became increasingly available.

By the mid-1970s, advances in integrated-circuit technology (silicon "chips") resulted in the development of still smaller and less expensive computers called *microcomputers*. These machines are built entirely of integrated circuits and are therefore not much larger (or more expensive) than a conventional office typewriter. Yet they can be used for a wide variety of personal, educational, commercial and technical applications. Their use tends to complement rather than replace the use of mainframes. In fact, many large organizations utilize microcomputers as terminals or workstations that are connected to a mainframe computer (or a series of mainframes) through a communications network.

Of particular interest is the development of the *personal computer*—a small, inexpensive microcomputer that is intended to be used by only one person at a time (see Fig. 1-1). Many of these machines approach a minicomputer in computing power. Moreover, their performance continues to improve dramatically as their cost continues to drop. Personal computers are now used in many schools and small businesses, and it appears likely that they will soon become a common household item.

## 1.2 COMPUTER CHARACTERISTICS

All digital computers, regardless of their size, are basically electronic devices that can transmit, store and manipulate information (i.e., data). There are basically two different types of data: numerical data and character-type data (names, addresses, etc.). Scientific and technical applications primarily require the processing of numerical data, whereas business applications usually involve the processing of both numerical and character data. Some computers are used only to process textual-type character data (letters, book manuscripts, etc.); this is known as *word processing*.

In order to process a particular set of data, the computer must be given an appropriate set of instructions, called a *program*. These instructions are entered into the computer and then stored in a portion of the computer's memory.

1

**Fig. 1-1**

A stored program can be *executed* at any time. This causes the following things to happen.

1. A set of information, called the *input data*, will be entered into the computer (from a terminal, card reader, etc.) and stored in another portion of the computer's memory.

2. The input data will then be processed to produce certain desired results, known as the *output data*.

3. The output data (and perhaps some of the input data) will be printed onto a sheet of paper or displayed on a *monitor* (i.e., a video-type display device).

This three-step procedure can be repeated many times if desired, thus causing a large quantity of data to be processed in rapid sequence. It should be understood, however, that each of these steps, particularly steps 2 and 3, can be lengthy and complicated.

**EXAMPLE 1.1**

A computer has been programmed to calculate the area of a circle using the formula $A = \pi r^2$, given a numerical value for the radius $r$ as input data. The following steps are required:

1. Read the numerical value for the radius of the circle.

2. Calculate the value of the area, using the above formula. (This value will be stored, along with the input data, in the computer's memory.)

3. Print (display) the values of the radius and the corresponding area.

4. Stop.

Each of these steps will require one or more instructions in a computer program.

The foregoing discussion illustrates two important characteristics of a digital computer: memory and capability to be programmed. Other important characteristics are its speed and reliability. We will say more about memory, speed and reliability in the next few paragraphs. The subject of programmability will be discussed at length throughout the remainder of this book.

## Memory

Every piece of information that is stored within the computer's memory is encoded as some unique combination of zeros and ones. These zeros and ones are called *bits* (*bi*nary dig*its*). Each bit is represented by an electronic device that is, in some sense, either "off" (zero) or "on" (one).

Most small computers have memories that are organized into 8-bit multiples called *bytes*. Normally 1 byte will represent a single character (i.e., a letter, a single digit or a punctuation symbol); an instruction may occupy 1, 2 or 3 bytes, and a single numerical quantity may occupy anywhere from 2 to 8 bytes, depending on the precision and type of number.

The size of a computer's memory is usually expressed as some multiple of $2^{10} = 1024$ bytes. This is referred to as 1$K$. Small computers have memories whose sizes typically range from 64K to 1024K (1M) bytes.

## EXAMPLE 1.2

The memory of a small personal computer has a capacity of 64K bytes. Thus, as many as $64 \times 1024 = 65,536$ characters and/or instructions can be stored in the computer's memory. If the entire memory is used to represent character data, then about 800 names and addresses can be stored within the computer at any one time (assuming 80 characters for each name and address).

If the memory is used to represent numerical data rather than names and addresses, then about 16,000 individual quantities can be stored at any one time (assuming 4 bytes per number).

Large computers have memories that are organized into *words* rather than bytes. Each word will consist of a relatively large number of bits, typically 32 or 36. This allows one numerical quantity, or a small group of characters (typically four or five) to be represented within a single word of memory. Large computer memories are usually expressed as some multiple of 1K (i.e., $2^{10} = 1024$) words. A large computer may have several million words of memory.

## EXAMPLE 1.3

The memory of a large general-purpose computer has a capacity of 2048K, which is equivalent to $2048 \times 1024 = 2,097,152$ words. If the entire memory is used to represent numerical data, then roughly 2 million numbers can be stored within the computer at any one time.

If the memory is used to represent characters rather than numerical data, then about 8 million characters can be stored at any one time. This is more than enough memory to store the contents of an entire book.

Most computers also employ *auxiliary memory devices* (e.g., magnetic tapes, disks, solid-state memory devices) in addition to their primary memories. These devices typically range from a few hundred thousand bytes (for a small computer) to several million words (for a larger computer). Moreover, they allow for the permanent recording of information, since they can be physically mounted or dismounted from the computer and stored when not in use. However the access time (i.e., the time required to store or retrieve information) is considerably greater for these auxiliary devices than for primary memory.

## Speed and Reliability

Because of its extremely high speed, a computer can carry out calculations in just a few minutes that would require months—perhaps even years—if carried out by hand. Simple tasks, such as adding two numbers, can be carried out in a fraction of a microsecond (1 $\mu s = 10^{-6}$ s). On a more practical level, the end-of-semester grades for all students in a large university can typically be processed in just a few minutes of computer time.

This very high speed is accompanied by an equally high level of reliability. Thus a computer practically never makes a mistake of its own accord. Highly publicized "computer" errors, such as a person's receiving a monthly bill of over a million dollars from a local department store, are virtually always the result of a programming error or an error in data transmission rather than an error caused by the computer itself.

## 1.3 MODES OF OPERATION

There are two different ways that a digital computer facility can be utilized. These are the batch mode and the interactive mode. Both are very common. Each has its own advantages for certain types of problems.

### Batch Processing

In the early days of computing, all jobs were processed via batch processing. This mode of operation is still in use, though it is much less common than it once was.

In *batch processing* a number of jobs are read into the computer, stored internally, and then processed sequentially. (A *job* refers to a computer program and its associated sets of input data that are to be processed.) Classical batch processing requires that the program and the data be recorded on punched cards. This information is read into the computer by means of a mechanical card reader and then processed. After the job is processed, the output, along with a listing of the computer program, is printed on large sheets of paper by a high-speed printer.

Modern batch processing is generally tied into a timesharing system (see below). In this system the program and the data are typed into the computer via a timesharing terminal or a microcomputer. The information is then stored within the computer's memory and processed in its proper sequence. This form of batch processing is preferable to classical batch processing, since it eliminates the need for punched cards and allows the input information (program and data) to be edited while it is being entered.

Large quantities of information (both programs and data) can be transmitted into and out of the computer very quickly in batch processing. Furthermore, the user need not be present while the job is being processed. Therefore, this mode of operation is well suited to jobs that require large amounts of computer time or are physically lengthy. On the other hand, the total time required for a job to be processed in this manner may vary from several minutes to several hours, even though the job may have required only a second or two of actual computer time. (The job must wait its turn before it can be read, processed, and printed out.) Thus batch processing can be undesirable when it is necessary to process many small, simple jobs and return the results as quickly as possible.

### EXAMPLE 1.4

A student has 1000 different values for the radius of a circle and would like to calculate an area for each radius. To do so, he or she might execute a computer program similar to the one described in Example 1.1. The calculations will now be carried out 1000 times, however, once for each value of the radius. (The program will have to be

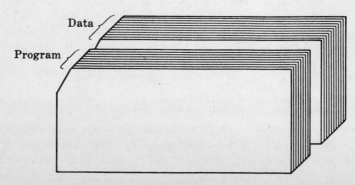

**Fig. 1-2**

modified to run repetitively.) Batch processing will be used, since all the calculations are to be carried out in rapid succession. Let us assume that the program and the data are recorded on punched cards.

To process the data, the student will read the deck of cards into the computer. The first part of the deck will contain the program. Following the program will be 1000 data cards, each of which will contain a single value for the radius. The card deck is illustrated in Fig. 1-2.

After the deck of cards has been read into the computer, there may be a delay of several hours before the program is executed and the input data processed. Once the computation has been completed, the results will be printed on a large sheet of paper. In this case the student will receive a listing that contains the actual program followed by 1000 pairs of numbers. Each pair of numbers will represent a value for the radius and its corresponding area. A portion of the computer-generated output is shown in Fig. 1-3.

| RADIUS | AREA |
|--------|------|
| 1 | 3.141593 |
| 2 | 12.566372 |
| 3 | 28.274337 |
| 4 | 50.265488 |
| 5 | 78.5398251 |
| 6 | 113.097348 |
| 7 | 153.938057 |
| 8 | 201.061952 |
| 9 | 254.469033 |
| 10 | 314.1593 |
| 11 | 380.132753 |
| 12 | 452.389392 |
| 13 | 530.929217 |
| 14 | 615.752229 |
| 15 | 706.858425 |
| 16 | 804.247808 |
| 17 | 907.920378 |
| 18 | 1017.87613 |
| 19 | 1134.11507 |
| 20 | 1256.6372 |

Fig. 1-3

## Interactive Computing

*Interactive computing* is carried out either with a personal computer, such as that shown in Fig. 1-1, or with a computer terminal, as illustrated in Fig. 1-4. In either case the user provides the computer with input information through a keyboard, which resembles an ordinary typewriter. The corresponding output information is then either printed onto large sheets of paper or displayed on a video-type monitor. (Printed output may be more desirable for some types of applications, since it provides a "hard copy" of the interactive session; however, the use of a monitor is usually more convenient.) Interactive computer terminals are often referred to as *consoles*.

A significant feature of interactive computing is that the user and the computer are able to converse with each other during the computational session. Thus the user may periodically be asked to provide certain information that will determine what subsequent actions are to be taken by the computer.

### EXAMPLE 1.5

A student wishes to use a personal computer to calculate the radius of a circle whose area has a value of 100. A program is available which will calculate the area of a circle, given the radius. (Note that this is just the opposite of what the student wishes to do.) This program is not exactly what is needed, but it does allow the student to proceed by trial and error. The procedure will be to guess a value for the radius and then calculate a corresponding area. This trial-and-error procedure continues until the student has found a value for the radius that yields an area sufficiently close to 100.

Once the the desired program has been entered, the message

```
RADIUS=?
```

**Fig. 1-4**

will be printed. The student then enters a value for the radius. Let us assume that the student enters a value of 5 for the radius. The computer will respond by printing

    AREA= 78.5398

    DO YOU WISH TO REPEAT THE CALCULATION?

The student then types either "yes" or "no." If the student types "yes" then the message

    RADIUS=?

will again by printed, and the entire procedure is repeated. If the student types "no" then the message

    GOODBYE

is printed and the computation is terminated.

In Fig. 1-5 we see the information that is printed during a typical interactive session, using the program described above. The information typed by the student has been underlined. An approximate value of $r = 5.6$ was determined after only three calculations.

Notice the manner in which the student and the computer appear to be conversing with one another. Also, note that the student waits until he or she sees the calculated value of the area before deciding whether or not to carry out another calculation. If another calculation is initiated, the new value for the radius that the student supplies will depend on the previously calculated results.

```
RADIUS=? 5
AREA= 78.5398

DO YOU WISH TO REPEAT THE CALCULATION? YES

RADIUS=? 6
AREA= 113.097

DO YOU WISH TO REPEAT THE CALCULATION? YES

RADIUS=? 5.6
AREA= 98.5204

DO YOU WISH TO REPEAT THE CALCULATION? NO

GOODBYE
```

**Fig. 1-5**

Programs that are designed for interactive-type applications are sometimes said to be *conversational* in nature. Computerized games, such as Adventure, checkers, and chess, are excellent examples of such interactive applications. So are the fast-action, graphical arcade games, such as Space Invaders, Pac-Man and Defender.

### Timesharing

*Timesharing* is a form of interactive computing in which many different users are able to use a single computer simultaneously. Each user communicates with the computer through a terminal, such as that shown in Fig. 1-4, or through a microcomputer (see Fig. 1-1). The terminals may be wired directly to the computer, or they may be connected to the computer over telephone lines or a microwave circuit. Thus a timesharing terminal can be located far away—perhaps several hundred miles away—from its host computer.

Since a computer operates much faster than a human sitting at a terminal, one computer can support a large number of terminals at essentially the same time. Therefore each user will be unaware of the presence of other users and will seem to have the entire computer at his or her own disposal.

Timesharing is best-suited for processing relatively simple jobs that do not require extensive data transmission or large amounts of computer time. Many of the computer applications that arise in schools and commercial offices have these characteristics. Such applications can be processed quickly, easily, and at minimum expense using timesharing.

### EXAMPLE 1.6

A large university has a computer timesharing capability consisting of 100 timesharing terminals located at various places around the campus. These terminals are connected to a large computer via telephone lines. Each terminal transmits data to or from the computer at a maximum speed of 120 characters per second. All the terminals can be used simultaneously, even though they are interacting with a single computer.

In addition, 20 remote terminals are connected to the computer. Fifteen of these are located at five high schools in the area, and the remaining five terminals are stationed at a government research laboratory. All 120 terminals can be (and frequently are) used at the same time. By sharing the computer in this manner, each institution (and each individual user) is able to utilize the services of a large computer at a reasonable cost.

Certain features of batch processing and timesharing can be combined if desired. For example, it is possible to enter a set of input data directly from a terminal and then proceed to process the data in the batch mode, as described earlier. Another possibility is to use a card reader (batch processing) to enter a program and a set of data and then edit (modify) the program and process the data in the timesharing mode. Such "hybrid" operations have become increasingly common in recent years.

## 1.4 TYPES OF PROGRAMMING LANGUAGES

There are many different languages that can be used to program a computer. The most basic of these is *machine language*, a collection of very detailed, cryptic instructions that control the computer's internal circuitry. This is the natural dialect of the computer. Very few computer programs are actually written in machine language, however, for two significant reasons: first, because machine language is very cumbersome to work with, and second, because most computers have their own unique instruction sets. Thus a machine-language program written for one type of computer cannot be run on another type of computer without significant alterations.

Usually, a computer program will be written in some *high-level language*, whose instruction set is more compatible with human languages and human thought processes. Most of these high-level languages are *general-purpose* languages such as Pascal. (Other commonly used general-purpose languages are BASIC, Cobol, Fortran and PL/1.) There are also various high-level *special-purpose* languages whose instruction sets are specifically designed for some particular type of application.

As a rule, a single instruction in a high-level language will be equivalent to several instructions in machine language. Moreover, a program that is written in a high-level language can generally be run on many different computers with little or no modification. Therefore the use of a high-level language offers us some very significant advantages over the use of machine language, namely, simplicity, uniformity, and portability (i.e., machine independence).

A program that is written in a high-level language must, however, be translated into machine language before it can be executed. This is known as *compilation* or *interpretation*, depending on how the translation is carried out. (Most versions of Pascal are compiled rather than interpreted.)

It is generally more convenient to develop a new program using an interpreter rather than a compiler, though compiled programs execute much faster than interpreted programs. (The reasons for this are beyond the scope of our present discussion.) In either case, however, the translation is carried out automatically within the computer. In fact, an inexperienced programmer may not even be aware that this procedure is taking place, since he or she typically sees only the original program, the input data and the resulting output data.

The compiler or interpreter is itself a computer program that accepts a high-level program as input data and generates a corresponding machine-language program as output. Accordingly, the original high-level program is called the *source* program, and the resulting machine-language program is called the *object* program. Every computer must have its own compiler or interpreter for a given high-level language. It is this use of compilers and interpreters that allows us to achieve uniformity and machine independence with high-level languages such as Pascal.

## 1.5 INTRODUCTION TO PASCAL

Pascal is a general-purpose, high-level programming language that has been derived from Algol-60. Its instructions are made up of algebralike expressions and certain English words such as BEGIN, END, read, write, IF, THEN, REPEAT, WHILE, DO. In this respect Pascal resembles many other high-level languages. Pascal also contains some unique features, however, that have been specifically designed to encourage the use of *structured programming*—an orderly, disciplined approach toward programming that promotes clear, efficient, error-free programs. For this reason, many educators and professional programmers favor the use of Pascal over other general-purpose languages.

Pascal was named in honor of Blaise Pascal (1623–1662), the brilliant French scientist and mathematician whose many accomplishments include the invention of the world's first mechanical calculating machine.

### History of Pascal

Pascal was originally developed in the early 1970s by Niklaus Wirth at the Technical University in Zurich, Switzerland. Wirth's original purpose was to develop a disciplined, high-level language for teaching structured programming. Wirth's original language definition is sometimes referred to as *standard Pascal* or *standard Pascal as defined by Jensen and Wirth*.[1] There is, however, some ambiguity in the term "standard Pascal," as there are now several different standards.

Most actual implementations of Pascal differ somewhat from Wirth's original definition. A European standard has recently been proposed by the International Standards Organization (ISO/DIS 7185). At the time of this writing, an American standard is under joint development by the American National Standards Institute (ANSI committee X3J9, draft BSR X3.97-198X) and the Institute of Electrical and Electronic Engineers (IEEE). It appears that the American standard will differ only slightly from its European counterpart.

Pascal is now widely used in the United States and Europe, both as a teaching language and as a powerful general-purpose language for a variety of different applications. Its use is becoming increasingly common for both large and small computers. In fact, Pascal has become very popular among serious users of personal computers, and there is some speculation that it may replace BASIC as the dominant microcomputer language within the next few years.

This book is primarily oriented toward the use of ISO/ANSI standard Pascal, though a few commonly used, nonstandard features (e.g., conformant array parameters) are also discussed. This material provides the basis for virtually all commercial implementations of Pascal. Thus, the reader who has mastered his material will have very little difficulty learning specific versions of the language.

### Structure of a Pascal Program

Every Pascal program contains a header and a block. The *header* begins with the word PROGRAM, followed by some additional required information. This part of the program is only one line long.

The *block* has two main parts, the declaration part and the statement part. The *declaration part* defines the various data items that are used within the program. The *statement part* contains the actual statements that cause actions to be taken. At least one statement must be present in every Pascal program. This overall program structure is outlined below in greater detail.

1. Header
2. Block
   - (*a*) Declarations
        - Labels
        - Constants
        - Type definitions
        - Variables
        - Procedures and functions
   - (*b*) Statements

Each of these program components will be discussed in much greater detail later in this book. Only the overview is important for now. It should be pointed out that all components of the declaration part need not be present in any single Pascal program. If present, however, these components must appear in the order shown above.

### EXAMPLE 1.7

**Area of a Circle.** Here is an elementary Pascal program called `circle` that reads in the radius of a circle, calculates its area and then writes out both the radius and the area.

```
PROGRAM circle(input,output);        (* HEADER *)

VAR area,radius : real;              (* VARIABLE DECLARATION *)

BEGIN
    read(radius);                    (* STATEMENT *)
    area := 3.14159*sqr(radius);     (* STATEMENT *)
    write(radius,area)               (* STATEMENT *)
END.
```

[1] Jensen, K. and N. Wirth, "Pascal User Manual and Report," 2nd edition, Springer-Verlag, 1974.

The principal components of this program have been separated and labeled in order to emphasize the overall program organization. Normally a program will not look like this. Rather, it might appear as shown below.

```
PROGRAM circle(input,output);
(* PROGRAM TO CALCULATE THE AREA OF A CIRCLE *)
VAR area,radius : real;
BEGIN
    read(radius);
    area := 3.14159*sqr(radius);
    write(radius,area)
END.
```

The following features should be pointed out in the above program.

1. Some of the words are capitalized. These are *reserved words* (or *keywords*) that have special predefined meanings. (More about this later.)

2. The first line contains the program name (circle) as well as some additional information that will be described in the next section. This is the program header.

3. The second line is a *comment* which identifies the purpose of the program. Comments can always be recognized because they are enclosed in special symbols, such as (* . . . *).

4. Notice the three lines that are indented between BEGIN and END. These are the program *statements*. They cause a value of the radius to be entered into the computer, a value of the area to be calculated and the values of the radius and the area to be written out. The indentation of these statements is not essential but is strongly recommended as a matter of good programming practice. (This is the type of disciplined program development that Pascal is designed to encourage.)

5. The numerical values for the radius and the area are represented by the symbolic names radius and area. These symbolic names are called *variables*. They are defined (declared) in the third line.

6. The symbolic name sqr in line 6 is a *standard function* that is used to compute the square of the radius.

7. Finally, notice the punctuation at the end of each line. Most lines end with semicolons; some have no punctuation and the last line ends with a period. This is a part of Pascal's syntax. We will say more about punctuation in later sections of this book.

## 1.6  DESIRABLE PROGRAM CHARACTERISTICS

Before concluding this chapter let us briefly examine some important charactistics of well-written computer programs. These characteristics apply to programs that are written in *any* programming language, not just Pascal. They can provide us with a useful set of guidelines later in this book, when we start writing our own Pascal programs.

1. *Integrity* refers to the accuracy of the calculations. It should be clear that all other program enhancements will be meaningless if the calculations are not carried out correctly. Thus, the integrity of the calculations is an absolute necessity in any computer program.

2. *Clarity* refers to the overall readability of the program, with particular emphasis on its underlying logic. If a program is clearly written, it should be possible for another programmer to follow the program logic without undue effort. (It should also be possible for the original author to follow his or her own program after being away from the program for an extended period of time.) One of the objectives in the design of Pascal is the development of clear, readable programs through a disciplined approach to programming.

3. *Simplicity*. The clarity and accuracy of a program are usually enhanced by keeping things as simple as possible, consistent with the overall program objectives. In fact, it may be desirable to sacrifice a certain amount of computational efficiency in order to maintain a relatively simple, straightforward program structure.

4. *Efficiency* is concerned with execution speed and effective memory utilization. These are generally important goals, though they should not be obtained at the expense of clarity or simplicity. Many complex programs require a trade-off between these characteristics. In such situations, experience and common sense are key factors.

5. *Modularity*. Most large programs can be broken down into a series of identifiable subtasks. It is good programming practice to implement each of these subtasks as a separate program module. (In Pascal, such modules are referred to as *procedures* and *functions*.) The use of a modular programming structure enhances the accuracy and clarity of a program, and it facilitates future program alterations.

6. *Generality*. Usually we will want a program to be as general as possible, within reasonable limits. For example, we may design a program to read in the values of certain key parameters rather than placing fixed values into the program. As a rule, a considerable amount of generality can be obtained with very little additional programming effort.

## *Review Questions*

**1.1**   What is meant by a mainframe computer? Where can mainframes be found? What are they generally used for?

**1.2**   What is a minicomputer? How do minicomputers differ from mainframes?

**1.3**   What is a microcomputer? How do microcomputers differ from mainframes and minicomputers?

**1.4**   Name two different types of data.

**1.5**   What is meant by a computer program?

**1.6**   What, in general, happens when a computer program is executed?

**1.7**   What is a computer memory? What kinds of information are stored in a computer's memory?

**1.8**   What is a bit? What is a byte?

**1.9**   What is the difference between a byte and a word of memory?

**1.10**  What terms are used to describe the size of a computer's memory? What are some typical memory sizes?

**1.11**  Name some typical auxiliary memory devices. How does this type of memory differ from the computer's main memory?

**1.12**  What time unit is used to express the speed with which elementary tasks are carried out by a computer?

**1.13**  What is the difference between the batch mode and the interactive mode? What are their advantages and disadvantages?

**1.14**  What is meant by a console?

**1.15**  What is meant by timesharing? For what types of applications is timesharing best suited?

**1.16**    What is machine language? How does it differ from high-level languages?

**1.17**    Name some commonly used high-level languages.

**1.18**    What are the advantages in the use of high-level languages?

**1.19**    What is meant by compilation? What is meant by interpretation? How do these two processes differ?

**1.20**    What is a source program? An object program? Why are these concepts important?

**1.21**    What is meant by structured programming?

**1.22**    Who was Blaise Pascal? For what was he noted?

**1.23**    By whom was the Pascal language first developed? What was its original purpose?

**1.24**    Summarize the current state of standardization in Europe and the United States.

**1.25**    What two major program components must be present in every Pascal program? What is the purpose of each component?

**1.26**    What are the two main parts of the block? What is the purpose of each part?

**1.27**    What are reserved words (or keywords)?

**1.28**    What are standard functions?

**1.29**    Why are some of the statements within a Pascal program indented?

**1.30**    Summarize the meaning of each of the following program characteristics: integrity, clarity, simplicity, efficiency, modularity and generality. Why is each of these characteristics important?

# Problems

**1.31**    Determine the purpose of each of the following Pascal programs.

```
(a)   PROGRAM greeting(output);
      BEGIN
          writeln('Welcome to the Wonderful');
          writeln;
          writeln('World of Computing!')
      END.
```

(*b*)
```
PROGRAM payroll(input,output);
CONST rate = 0.14;
VAR gross,tax,net : real;
BEGIN
    read(gross);
    tax := rate*gross;
    net := gross-tax;
    write(gross,tax,net)
END.
```
(*c*)
```
PROGRAM order(input,output);
VAR a,b : integer;
BEGIN
    read(a,b);
    IF a <= b THEN write(a,b) ELSE write (b,a)
END.
```

**1.32**  Refer once again to the Pascal programs presented in the previous problem. Determine as best you can the purpose of each line within each of the programs.

# Chapter 2

# Pascal Fundamentals

This chapter is concerned with the basic elements used to construct simple Pascal statements. These elements include the Pascal character set, reserved words, identifiers, numbers, strings, constants, variables and expressions. We will see how these basic elements can be combined to form simple but complete Pascal statements. Some attention will also be given to the different kinds of statements that are available, their constituent elements and their respective purposes.

Some of this material is rather detailed and therefore somewhat difficult to absorb, particularly by an inexperienced programmer. Remember, however, that the present purpose of this material is to introduce certain basic concepts and provide some necessary definitions for the topics that follow in the next few chapters. Therefore, when reading this chapter for the first time, you need only acquire a general familiarity with the individual topics. A more detailed understanding will come later, from repeated references to this material in subsequent chapters.

## 2.1 THE PASCAL CHARACTER SET

Pascal uses the letters A to Z (both upper- and lowercase), the digits 0 to 9, and certain special symbols as building blocks to form basic program elements (numbers, identifiers, expressions, etc.). The special symbols are listed below.

| | | | |
|---|---|---|---|
| + | . | < | ( |
| - | : | <= | ) |
| * | ; | > | [ |
| / | , | >= | ] |
| := | ' | <> | { |
| = | ^ | .. | } |

On some computers the symbols (* and *) are used instead of { and }. Also, the symbols (. and .) may be used in place of [ and ], and @ may replace ^.

Note that some of the special symbols are comprised of two separate, consecutive characters (e.g., <=, :=, ..).

## 2.2 RESERVED WORDS

There are certain reserved words that have a standard, predefined meaning in Pascal. They are

| | | | |
|---|---|---|---|
| AND | END | NIL | SET |
| ARRAY | FILE | NOT | THEN |
| BEGIN | FOR | OF | TO |
| CASE | FUNCTION | OR | TYPE |
| CONST | GOTO | PACKED | UNTIL |
| DIV | IF | PROCEDURE | VAR |
| DO | IN | PROGRAM | WHILE |
| DOWNTO | LABEL | RECORD | WITH |
| ELSE | MOD | REPEAT | |

14

These reserved words can be used only for their intended purpose, they cannot be arbitrarily redefined by the programmer.

It is customary to display the reserved words within a Pascal program in either boldface or uppercase letters. We will use uppercase letters throughout this text.

## 2.3  IDENTIFIERS

An *identifier* is a name that is given to some program element, such as a constant, a variable, a procedure or a program. Identifiers are comprised of letters or digits, in any order, except that *the first character must be a letter*. Both upper- and lowercase letters are permitted, and are considered to be indistinguishable. We will use only lowercase letters for identifiers, however, in order to distinguish them from reserved words (which are shown in uppercase).

Some versions of Pascal also allow certain other characters, such as the underscore (__).

### EXAMPLE 2.1

The following names are valid identifiers.

```
      x         y12        sum         temperature

      names     area       taxrate     table1
```

The following names are *not* valid identifiers for the reasons stated.

| | |
|---|---|
| c_max | Characters other than letters and digits are not allowed. (In some versions of Pascal, this identifier would be valid.) |
| 4th | The first character must be a letter. |
| array | ARRAY is a reserved word (see Sec. 2.2). |
| last word | Blank spaces are not allowed (remember that a blank space is a character). |

An identifier can be arbitrarily long, although some implementations of Pascal recognize only the first eight characters. In such situations the remaining characters are carried along for the convenience of the programmer.

### EXAMPLE 2.2

The identifiers `filemanager` and `filemanagement` are both grammatically valid. The computer may be unable to distinguish between them, however, because the first eight letters are the same for each identifier. Therefore, only one of these identifiers should be used in a single Pascal program (unless, of course, it is known that this particular implementation of Pascal has no restriction on significant identifier length).

As a rule, an identifier should contain enough characters so that its meaning is readily apparent. On the other hand, an excessive number of characters should be avoided.

### EXAMPLE 2.3

A Pascal program is being written to calculate the future value of an investment. The identifiers `value` or `futurevalue` would probably be appropriate symbolic names. However, `v` or `fv` would probably be too brief, since the intended purpose of these identifiers is not clear. On the other hand, the identifier `futurevalueofaninvestment` would be unsatisfactory because it is too long and cumbersome.

## 2.4  STANDARD IDENTIFIERS

Pascal contains a number of standard identifiers that have certain predefined meanings. These standard identifiers are

| abs | false | pack | sin |
|---|---|---|---|
| arctan | get | page | sqr |
| boolean | input | pred | sqrt |
| char | integer | put | succ |
| chr | ln | read | text |
| cos | maxint | readln | true |
| dispose | new | real | trunc |
| eof | odd | reset | unpack |
| eoln | ord | rewrite | write |
| exp | output | round | writeln |

Some implementations of Pascal include additional standard identifiers. The reader should determine exactly what standard identifiers are available for his or her particular version of the language.

In contrast to reserved words (which can never be redefined), standard identifiers *can* be redefined by the programmer. This is accomplished by means of appropriate declarations and definitions, as explained later in this text. In most situations, however, it is good practice to use the standard identifiers only for their predefined purposes. This is particularly true of programs written by beginning programmers. Thus, standard identifiers should be treated in the same manner as reserved words in elementary programming situations.

## 2.5 NUMBERS

Numbers can be written several different ways in Pascal. In particular, a number can include a sign, a decimal point and an exponent (or scale factor) if desired. The following rules apply to all numbers.

1. Commas and blank spaces cannot be included within the number.
2. The number can be preceded by a plus (+) or a minus (−) sign if desired. If a sign does not appear the number will be assumed to be positive.
3. Numbers cannot exceed specified maximum and minimum values. These values depend upon the type of number, the particular computer and the particular compiler being used.

### Integer Numbers

An *integer number* contains neither a decimal point nor an exponent. Thus an integer number is simply a sequence of digits, preceded (optionally) by a sign.

**EXAMPLE 2.4**

Several valid integer numbers are shown below.

| 0 | 1 | +1 | −1 |
|---|---|---|---|
| 743 | −5280 | 60000000 | −999999 |

The following integer numbers are written incorrectly for the reasons stated.

| 123,456 | Commas are not allowed. |
|---|---|
| 36. | A decimal point cannot appear in an integer number. |
| 10 20 30 | Blank spaces are not allowed. |

The magnitude of an integer number can range from zero to some maximum value that varies from one computer (and one compiler) to another. A typical maximum value on a microcomputer is 32767, though some computers allow integer numbers that are much larger. (The maximum value is specified by the standard identifier maxint, as discussed in Sec. 3.5.) The reader should determine the appropriate maximum value at his or her particular installation.

### Real Numbers

A *real number* must contain either a decimal point or an exponent (or both). *If a decimal point is included, it must appear between two digits*. Thus, a real number cannot begin or end with a decimal point.

### EXAMPLE 2.5

Several valid real numbers are shown below.

|  |  |  |  |
|---|---|---|---|
| 0.0 | 1.0 | -0.2 | 827.602 |
| 50000.0 | -0.000743 | 12.3 | -315.0066 |

The following are *not* valid real numbers, for the reasons stated.

| | |
|---|---|
| 1. | A digit must be present on each side of the decimal point. |
| 1,000.0 | Commas are not allowed. |
| .333333 | A digit must be present on each side of the decimal point. |
| 50 | Either a decimal point or an exponent must be present. |

An exponent (scale factor) can be included to shift the location of the decimal point. (If a decimal point is not included within the number, it is assumed to be positioned to the right of the last digit.) This is essentially the same as scientific notation except that the base 10 is replaced by the letter E (or e). Thus, the number $1.2 \times 10^{-3}$ would be written as 1.2E-3 or 1.2e-3. The exponent itself must be either a positive or a negative integer.

### EXAMPLE 2.6

The quantity $3 \times 10^{10}$ could be represented in Pascal by any of the following real numbers.

|  |  |  |  |
|---|---|---|---|
| 3.0E+10 | 3.0E10 | 3e+10 | 3E10 |
| 0.3E+11 | 0.3e11 | 30.0E+9 | 30e9 |

Similarly, the quantity $-5.026 \times 10^{-17}$ can be represented by any of the following real numbers.

| | | | |
|---|---|---|---|
| -5.026E-17 | -0.5026E-16 | -50.26e-18 | -0.0005026e-13 |

### EXAMPLE 2.7

The following are valid real numbers with exponents.

| | | | |
|---|---|---|---|
| 2E-8 | -0.006e-5 | 1.6667E+8 | +0.12121212e12 |

The following real numbers are *not* valid for the reasons stated.

| | |
|---|---|
| `3.E+10` | A digit must be present on each side of the decimal point. |
| `8e2.3` | The exponent must be an integer (it cannot contain a decimal point). |
| `.3333e-3` | A digit must be present on each side of the decimal point. |
| `3E 10` | Blank spaces are not allowed. |

Real numbers have a much greater range than integer numbers. Typically, the magnitude of a real number might range from a minimum value of approximately 1E–38 to a maximum of approximately 1E+38. (These values will vary from one computer (one compiler) to another.) In addition, the number 0.0 (which is less than 1E–38) is also a valid real number. The reader should determine the appropriate values for his or her particular computer.

The number of significant figures in a real number will vary from one version of Pascal to another. Most versions allow seven or eight significant figures, which is adequate for most applications. The reader should determine how many significant figures are available at his or her particular installation.

### Numerical Precision

It should be understood that integer numbers are exact quantities whereas real numbers are approximations. Thus, the real number 1.0 might actually be represented within the computer's memory as 0.99999999..., even though it might appear as 1.0 on the monitor or on a printout. Therefore real numbers cannot be used for certain purposes, such as counting, indexing, etc., where exact values are required. We will discuss these restrictions as they arise, in later chapters of this book.

### 2.6  STRINGS

A *string* is a sequence of characters (i.e., letters, digits and special characters) enclosed by apostrophes. Both uppercase and lowercase letters can be used.

### EXAMPLE 2.8

Several valid strings are shown below.

| | | |
|---|---|---|
| `'GREEN'` | `'Washington, D.C. 20005'` | `'270-32-3456'` |
| `'$19.95'` | `'THE CORRECT ANSWER IS:'` | `'2*(I+3)/J'` |

The maximum number of characters that can be included in a string will vary from one version of Pascal to another. Most versions allow maximum string lengths of at least 255 characters, which is adequate for most purposes.

If a string includes an apostrophe, the apostrophe must be entered twice. Only one apostrophe will appear, however, when the string is printed out or displayed. Thus, a single apostrophe is interpreted as a *string delimiter*, whereas a repeated apostrophe is interpreted as a single apostrophe within the string.

### EXAMPLE 2.9

A Pascal program contains the following string.

`'PLEASE DON''T VERB YOUR NOUNS'`

(Notice the repeated apostrophe in the word "don't.") If the program causes the string to be printed or displayed, however, it will appear as it should; namely,

`PLEASE DON'T VERB YOUR NOUNS`

Strings are normally used in write statements to label output. We will discuss this further in Chap. 4.

## 2.7  DATA TYPES

One of the most important and interesting characteristics of Pascal is its ability to support many different types of data. These include simple data types, structured data types and pointer data types.

*Simple-type data* are single items (numbers, characters, etc.) that are associated with single identifiers on a one-to-one basis. Actually there are several different simple data types. These include the four standard data types—integer, real, char and boolean—and the user-defined simple types, which include enumerated types and subrange types. The standard data types will be discussed thoroughly in the next chapter; user-defined data types will be considered in Chap. 8.

*Structured-type data* consist of multiple data items that are related to one another in some specified manner. Each group of data items is associated with a particular identifier. The individual data items within each group can also be associated with corresponding individual identifiers. There are four types of structured data in Pascal: arrays, records, files and sets.

*Pointer-type data* are used to construct dynamic structured data types. A simple description of their characteristics and use is beyond the scope of the present discussion (see Chap. 13).

The various data types are summarized below for the reader's convenience.

1.  Simple-type data
    (*a*)  Standard data types
        (*i*)     integer
        (*ii*)    real
        (*iii*)   char
        (*iv*)    boolean
    (*b*)  User-defined data types
        (*i*)     enumerated
        (*ii*)    subrange

2.  Structured-type data
    (*a*)  Arrays
    (*b*)  Records
    (*c*)  Files
    (*d*)  Sets

3.  Pointer-type data

For now we will be concerned only with simple-type data. Structured-type data and pointer-type data will be discussed in later chapters of this book.

## 2.8  CONSTANTS

It is often convenient to associate a simple data item, such as a numerical value or a string, with an identifier, thus providing a name for the data item. The identifier is called a *constant* if the data item is assigned permanently (i.e., if the value of the data item remains unchanged throughout the program).

A constant must always be defined before it can appear in a Pascal statement. This definition serves two purposes; it establishes that the identifier is a constant, and it associates a value with the constant. The type of the constant will implicitly be determined by the data item.

The general form of a constant definition is expressed as

```
CONST name = value
```

where *name* is an identifier that represents the constant name, and *value* is the actual data item that is assigned to *name*.

**EXAMPLE 2.10**

A Pascal program requires frequent use of the numerical value 0.1666667. It may therefore be convenient to introduce a constant called `fraction`, which can be used in place of the actual number. This constant can be defined by writing

```
CONST fraction = 0.1666667;
```

Subsequent references to the identifier `fraction` will be equivalent to referencing the actual number. Note that `fraction` is considered to be a real constant, since it is associated with a real number.

**EXAMPLE 2.11**

Now suppose that a Pascal program makes frequent use of the string

```
'The Super-Duper Computer Company'
```

in order to generate report headings. This string can conveniently be represented as a constant called `title`. To do so, we write

```
CONST title = 'The Super-Duper Computer Company';
```

at the beginning of the program. If we should want to print out the actual string at a later point in the program, we merely refer to the identifier `title` in the appropriate output statement. (Input/output operations will be discussed in Chap. 4.)

In this example `title` is considered to be a string-type constant, since it is associated with a string.

## 2.9 VARIABLES

An identifier whose value is allowed to change during the execution of a program is called a *variable*. Every variable must be individually declared (i.e., defined) before it can appear in a statement. The variable declaration establishes the fact that the identifier is a variable (rather than a constant, etc.), and specifies the type of the variable. Unlike a constant definition, however, a data item (e.g., a numerical value or a string) is *not* associated with a variable within a variable declaration.

The general form of a variable declaration is

```
VAR name : type
```

or, if there are several variables of the same type,

```
VAR name 1, name 2, . . . , name n : type
```

where *name 1*, *name 2*, etc. are identifiers that represent individual variable names, and *type* refers to the data type of the variables.

**EXAMPLE 2.12**

A Pascal program contains the integer variables `row` and `column`, the real variable `value`, and the char variable `flag`. The program would therefore contain the following declarations.

```
VAR row,column : integer;
    value : real;
    flag : char;
```

The appropriate data items would then be assigned to these variables at later points in the program.

**EXAMPLE 2.13**

Now suppose that the program contains the constants described in Examples 2.10 and 2.11 and the variables described in Example 2.12. Here is the complete list of declarations.

```
CONST fraction = 0.1666667;
      title = 'The Super-Duper Computer Company';
VAR row,column : integer;
    value : real;
    flag : char;
```

Remember that the declarations and definitions must appear in a certain order, and that the constant definitions must precede the variable declarations. (See Sec. 1.5.)

## 2.10  EXPRESSIONS

An *expression* is a collection of *operands* (i.e., numbers, constants, variables, etc.) joined together by certain operators to form an algebralike term that represents a value (i.e., a simple data item). There are two types of expressions in Pascal: numerical expressions and boolean expressions. A *numerical expression* represents a numerical value, whereas a *boolean expression* represents a logical condition which is either true or false.

**EXAMPLE 2.14**

A typical numerical expression is shown below.

```
(b*b-4*a*c)/(2*a)
```

The identifiers a, b and c and the numbers 4 and 2 are called *operands*; and the symbols *, − and / are the corresponding *operators* (which represent multiplication, subtraction and division, respectively). The parentheses are used to specify the order in which the operations are carried out. The entire expression represents a number. Thus, if a, b and c represent the values 1, 2 and 3, respectively, the expression will represent the value −4.

When constructing numerical expressions, care must be taken to distinguish between integer and real quantities. This is true of the operators and operands as well as the expression itself. We will say more about this in the next chapter.

**EXAMPLE 2.15**

Here is an example of a boolean (logical) expression.

```
pay < 1000.0
```

In this expression pay is a variable of type real, 1000.0 is a real number and the symbol < is a boolean operator. (Note that pay and 1000.0 are operands in this boolean expression.) The expression will have the value true if pay represents a value that is less than 1000.0; otherwise the expression will have the value false.

Boolean expressions are used in various control structures, such as the IF–THEN structure shown below.

```
IF pay < 1000.0 THEN writeln(employeenumber);
```

This structure will cause the value of the variable employeenumber to be written out if the value of pay is less than 1000.0.

We will discuss the use of boolean expressions within control structures in much greater detail in Chap. 6.

All expressions must satisy the following general conditions.

1.  Two successive operators are not permitted. However, parentheses can be used to separate two successive operators. (Remember that parentheses must always be used in pairs.)

2.  An expression can consist of a single identifier that is used as a constant or a variable.

3.  A function name (i.e., a function reference) can be used in place of a constant or variable identifier within an expression (more about this in Sec. 2.12).

## 2.11   STATEMENTS

A Pascal *statement* is an instruction, or a group of instructions, that causes the computer to carry out certain actions. There are two basic types of statements in Pascal: simple and structured. *Simple* statements are essentially single, unconditional instructions that perform one of the following tasks.

1.  Assign a data item to a variable. (This is called an *assignment* statement.)
2.  Access a self-contained computational module, called a *procedure*.
3.  Transfer program control unconditionally to another part of the program (the GOTO statement).

### EXAMPLE 2.16

A typical assignment statement is shown below.

```
tax := 0.14*gross;
```

In this example it is assumed that tax and gross are both variables of type real, and that a real value has been assigned to gross. (This value may have been read into the computer, or it may have been calculated earlier in the program.) The assignment statement causes the value of gross to be multiplied by 0.14 and the product assigned to the variable tax.

Notice that the symbol which is used for assignment is := (not =, as in most other programming languages). Also, note that the right-hand side of the statement (i.e., 0.14*gross) is a numerical expression, as described in the previous section.

### EXAMPLE 2.17

Here is a typical GOTO statement.

```
GOTO 100;
```

Thus, the next statement to be executed will be the statement that is labeled 100.

Use of the GOTO statement is discouraged in Pascal. We will say more about this in Chap. 6.

We will say more about simple statements that access procedures in the next section. Pascal recognizes several different types of structured statements. These include

1.  Compound statements, which consist of a sequence of two or more consecutive statements
2.  Repetitive statements, which involve the repeated execution of several simple statements
3.  Conditional statements, in which one or more simple statements are executed only if some specified logical condition is satisfied

### EXAMPLE 2.18

A typical compound statement, taken from Example 1.7, is shown below.

```
BEGIN
    read(radius);
    area := 3.14159*sqr(radius);
    write(radius,area)
END
```

Note that the simple statements that comprise the compound statement are enclosed within the keywords BEGIN and END. Also, notice that the simple statements are separated from one another by semicolons.

### EXAMPLE 2.19

Here is a typical repetitive statement.

```
FOR count := 1 TO 100 DO write(count);
```

This statement will be executed 100 times. Each time the statement is executed the current value of the variable count will be printed out or displayed. Thus, the statement will cause the values

       1   2   3   . . .   100

to appear on the output device.

**EXAMPLE 2.20**

A typical conditional statement is shown below.

```
IF pay < 1000.0 THEN write('group 1') ELSE write('group 2');
```

This statement causes the message group 1 to appear on the output medium if the variable pay represents a value that is less than 1000.0. If pay has a value that is greater than or equal to 1000.0, however, then the message group 2 will appear instead.

Structured statements will be discussed in much greater detail in Chap. 6. For now the reader should be concerned only with an overview of the general concepts.

## 2.12  PROCEDURES AND FUNCTIONS

Procedures and functions are self-contained program elements, sometimes referred to as *modules*, that carry out designated actions. These modules can be accessed from anywhere within a program. Moreover, if the same module is accessed from several different points, the module can be given different information (i.e., different values for the required data items) at each access point.

When a module is accessed, the information provided is processed by the action statements within the module. Usually, this will cause new information to be generated. This information is then returned to the point at which the module was last accessed, and the program continues to execute from that point.

The information that is passed to a module is provided as a list of data items (i.e., constants, variables, expressions, etc.), called *parameters*. These parameters are separated by commas and enclosed in parentheses, immediately after the module name. Certain of the parameters may also be used to represent new information that is generated within the module. Thus, the parameters may represent information being returned by a module as well as information supplied to the module.

Pascal supports both standard and user-defined procedures and functions. We will be concerned only with standard procedures and standard functions for the time being. These program elements are included in the Pascal library, which is a part of the language. A complete discussion of user-defined procedures and functions will be presented in Chap. 7.

All *procedures* have the following general characteristics.

1. A procedure is accessed by a simple statement consisting of the procedure name followed by an (optional) list of parameters.

2. The parameters may represent information supplied to the procedure or, under certain conditions, information returned by the procedure.

3. Any number of data items can be transferred between a procedure and its reference point (i.e., the statement that accesses the procedure).

**EXAMPLE 2.21**

The write statement is actually a reference (i.e., an access) to a standard Pascal procedure. Thus, the statement

```
write(a,b,c);
```

will cause the values of the parameters a, b and c to be printed out or displayed.

Note that the parameters in this example all represent information being supplied *to* the procedure; no new information is returned.

Now suppose that a Pascal program contained the following two write statements.

```
write(a,b,c);
    .
    .
    .
write(x,y,z);
```

The first statement would cause the values of the variables a, b and c to be written out, whereas the second statement (which is identical to the first except for the parameters) would output the values of the variables x, y and z.

All *functions* have the following general characteristics.

1.  A function is accessed by specifying its name within an expression, as though it were an ordinary variable, followed by an (optional) list of parameters.

2.  The function name can be followed by an (optional) list of parameters. These parameters are used only to transfer information to the function from its reference point.

3.  The function will return a single data item. This data item will be represented by the function name itself.

4.  A function must be of the correct data type for the expression in which it is accessed.

**EXAMPLE 2.22**

Consider once again the statement

```
area := 3.14159*sqr(radius);
```

The right-hand side is a numerical expression in which the value of the variable radius is passed to the standard function sqr. This function returns the value of the radius squared. The value of the radius squared is then multiplied by 3.14159, and the result is assigned to the variable area.

Note that radius is a parameter that represents a data item supplied to the standard function. The data item that is returned by the function is represented by the function name sqr. Also, note that the type of the function is numeric (specifically, real); this is necessary if the function is to be used in a numerical expression.

We will say much more about procedures and functions in Chap. 7. For now we need only be concerned with the general information presented above. This information will allow us to understand the material that is discussed in the next chapter.

## 2.13  PASCAL SYNTAX DIAGRAMS

Before leaving this chapter it is appropriate to discuss a method that is commonly used to represent the *syntactical* (i.e., the grammatical) constructs in Pascal. This involves the use of syntax diagrams, such as that shown in the following example.

**EXAMPLE 2.23**

Figure 2-1 shows a Pascal syntax diagram which explains the manner in which an identifier can be constructed. This diagram shows that an identifier must begin with a letter, as indicated by the leftmost box containing the word "letter." Following this box is a straight path with two optional return loops. Each loop

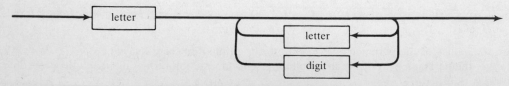

**Fig. 2-1**  Identifier.

contains a box representing a type of character that can be included as a part of the identifier name. Since the topmost box contains the word "letter" and the bottom box contains the word "digit," we conclude that an identifier must begin with a letter, followed by any number of letters and digits.

These syntax diagrams can become quite complex, even for relatively simple constructs. Therefore many beginners choose not to use them. Once the reader has acquired some familiarity with Pascal, however, these diagrams appear much more understandable.

A complete list of Pascal syntax diagrams is included in App. F. The reader is encouraged to refer to these diagrams frequently.

## Review Questions

**2.1**    What does the Pascal character set consist of?

**2.2**    What are the Pascal reserved words? How can the reserved words be identified within this textbook?

**2.3**    What are Pascal identifiers? What is an identifier comprised of?

**2.4**    How many characters can be included in an identifier? Are all of these characters equally significant?

**2.5**    What is meant by a standard identifier?

**2.6**    How do standard identifiers differ from reserved words?

**2.7**    Summarize the general rules for writing numbers in Pascal.

**2.8**    What special rules apply to integer numbers?

**2.9**    How can the largest permissible integer number be determined for each particular computer?

**2.10**    Describe two different ways that real numbers can be written. Summarize the rules that apply in each case.

**2.11**    What is the purpose of the exponent in a real number?

**2.12**    Describe the differences between real and integer numbers. Under what circumstances should each type of number be used?

**2.13**    What is a string? What characters can be included within a string?

**2.14**    What restrictions apply to maximum string length?

**2.15**    How can an apostrophe (') be included within a string?

**2.16**    Name three different types of data that are supported by Pascal.

**2.17**    What is meant by simple-type data?

**2.18**    What are the four standard simple data types?

**2.19**    What is meant by user-defined simple types? How do these data types differ from the standard data types?

**2.20**    What is meant by structured-type data? How do structured-type data differ from simple-type data?

**2.21**    Name four different structured data types.

**2.22**    What is meant by a constant? What must be done before a constant can appear in a Pascal statement?

**2.23**    How is the type of a constant determined?

**2.24**    What is meant by a variable? In what way does a variable differ from a constant?

**2.25**    Summarize the rules for declaring the data types of variables.

**2.26**    What is an expression? What types of expressions are supported by Pascal? How do they differ?

**2.27**    What is an operand? What is an operator? How are operands and operators used in an expression?

**2.28**    Summarize the general conditions that must be satisfied by all expressions.

**2.29**    What is a statement? What are the two basic types of statements in Pascal? How do they differ?

**2.30**    Name three different tasks that can be performed by simple statements.

**2.31**    What is the purpose of the assignment statement? What kind of statement is this?

**2.32**    Name three different types of structured statements.

**2.33**    What is a procedure? What is a function? How do procedures and functions differ from each other?

**2.34**    What is a module? What is the relationship between a module, a procedure and a function?

**2.35**    What happens when a module is accessed?

**2.36**    What is meant by parameters? What is their purpose?

**2.37**    Name two general classes of procedures and functions.

**2.38**    Summarize the general characteristics of procedures.

**2.39**   Summarize the general characteristics of functions.

**2.40**   What is the significance of a function name? How does this differ from a procedure name?

**2.41**   What is meant by a syntactical construct? How are syntactical constructs represented in Pascal?

# Solved Problems

**2.42**   Determine which of the following are valid identifiers.

| | |
|---|---|
| record_number | Characters other than letters and digits are not allowed. (Some versions of Pascal accept the underscore. Hence this example may be valid.) |
| identifier1 | Valid. |
| identifier2 | Valid, though possibly indistinguishable from identifier1 (longer than eight characters). |
| 1pointer | The first character must be a letter. |
| first record | Characters other than letters and numbers are not allowed. |
| to | TO is a reserved word. |
| total | Valid. |

**2.43**   Determine which of the following are valid numbers. If a number is valid, specify whether it is integer or real.

| | |
|---|---|
| -666 | Valid, integer. |
| -666. | A digit must appear on each side of the decimal point. |
| -666.0 | Valid, real. |
| -6.66e2 | Valid, real. |
| 483,500 | Commas are not allowed. |
| 166667e -6 | Blank spaces are not allowed. |

**2.44**   Determine which of the following are valid strings.

| | |
|---|---|
| 'Visit beautiful, sunny Pittsburgh!' | Valid. |
| 'The price is $56.50' | Valid. |
| 'It's terribly cold out there!' | Invalid (a single apostrophe cannot appear inside of a string) |

**2.45**   Show how the following identifiers can be associated with their respective constant values.

| Identifier | Constant Value |
|---|---|
| count | 3 |
| offset | −2 |
| fraction | 0.333333 |
| color | blue |

```
CONST count = 3;
      offset = -2;
      fraction = 0.333333;
      color = 'blue';
```

Note that these are constant *definitions*.

**2.46**  Show how the following identifiers can be associated with their respective data types.

| Identifier | Data Type |
|------------|-----------|
| index      | integer   |
| cmax       | real      |
| cmin       | real      |
| code       | char      |
| status     | boolean   |

```
VAR index : integer;
    cmax,cmin : real;
    code : char;
    status : boolean;
```

Note that these are variable *declarations*.

**2.47**  Identify the type of each of the following expressions.

(a)  `2*x+7`              numerical

(b)  `count >= 100`       boolean

(c)  `sqr(value+3)/5`     numeric

(d)  `value = 666`        boolean

(e)  `test`              numeric or boolean, depending on the data type associated with test.

**2.48**  Several Pascal statements are shown below. Identify which are simple and which are structured.

(a)  `area := length*width;`                          simple (assignment statement)

(b)  `IF count = 100 THEN write(a,b,c);`              structured (conditional)

(c)  `GOTO 200;`                                      simple (unconditional transfer)

(d)  `read(length,width);`                            simple (procedure access)

(e)  ```
     BEGIN
         read(length,width);
         area := length*width;
         write(length,width,area)
     END
     ```                                              structured (compound)

(f)  `FOR index := 100 DOWNTO 1 DO write(index);`    structured (repetitive)

(g)  `mean := sqrt(sqr(a)+sqr(b)+sqr(c));`           simple (assignment)

**2.49**  Which statements in Prob. 2.48 access procedures? Which include function references?

Procedures are accessed in Probs. 2.48(*b*), (*d*), (*e*) and (*f*). Functions are referenced (accessed) in Prob. 2.48(*g*).
     ```

# Supplementary Problems

**2.50**   Determine which of the following are valid identifiers.

| | |
|---|---|
| (a) record1 | (e) name and address |
| (b) file2 | (f) employee_number |
| (c) file | (g) 123-45-6789 |
| (d) name | |

**2.51**   Determine which of the following are valid numbers. If a number is valid, specify whether it is integer or real.

| | | |
|---|---|---|
| (a) 0.5 | (d) -4.083e-67 | (g) 12E12 |
| (b) 27,822 | (e) 1. | (h) 131072 |
| (c) +93e12 | (f) 40-55 | (i) 1.31072e5 |

**2.52**   Determine which of the following are valid strings.

| | |
|---|---|
| (a) '8:15 P.M.' | (d) 'Chapter 3 (Cont''d)' |
| (b) "red, white and blue" | (e) '1.30172e5' |
| (c) 'Name: | (f) 'NEW YORK, NY 10020' |

**2.53**   Associate each of the following identifiers with its respective constant value.

| Identifier | Constant Value |
|---|---|
| month | july |
| fica | 123-45-6789 |
| price | $95.00 |
| gross | 2500.00 |
| partno | 48837 |
| bound | 0.00391 |

**2.54**   Write a declaration that will associate each of the following identifiers with its respective data type.

| Identifier | Data Type |
|---|---|
| period | char |
| terminal | boolean |
| status | char |
| index | integer |
| row | integer |
| clearance | real |

**2.55**   Specify the type of each of the following expressions. Identify any expression that is not written correctly.

| | |
|---|---|
| (a) counter := 87 | (e) 2*-x+y |
| (b) value | (f) factor1*(sum1+sum2)/factor2 |
| (c) sqr(first+second+third) | (g) color = 'blue' |
| (d) cost <= maximum | |

**2.56**  Specify which of the following statements are simple and which are complex. Identify the type of each statement.

(*a*)  `net := gross-(fedtax+statetax+citytax);`

(*b*)  ```
BEGIN
    tax := fedtax+statetax+citytax;
  net := gross-tax
END
```

(*c*)  `FOR counter := start TO finish DO write(counter);`

(*d*)  `IF counter < finish THEN counter := counter+1;`

(*e*)  `root := sqrt(a+b+c+d);`

(*f*)  `write('root=',root);`

(*g*)  `GOTO 17;`

(*h*)  `new := new+old;`

**2.57**  Which statements in Problem 2.56 access procedures? Which include function references?

**2.58**  Explain the meaning of each of the following Pascal syntax diagrams.

(*a*)

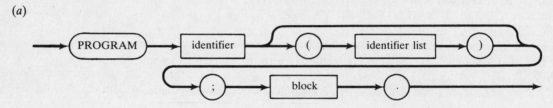

**Fig. 2-2**  Program.

(*b*)

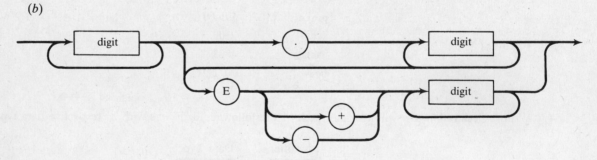

**Fig. 2-3**  Unsigned real.

(*c*)

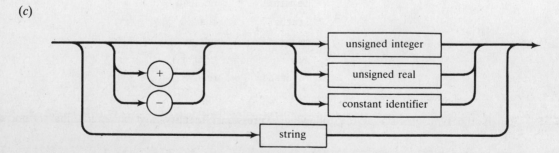

**Fig. 2-4**  Constant.
```

# Chapter 3

## Simple-Type Data

Now that the reader is familiar with certain fundamental concepts in Pascal, we can consider applications of simple-type data in greater detail. In particular, we will consider the uses of the standard (or built-in) simple data types that are included as a part of the Pascal language. These data types include integer, real, char and boolean data. The operators and standard functions that can be used with each of the standard data types will be discussed in detail. The chapter also includes additional information on expressions and their use in assignment statements.

Three of the standard data types, integer, char and boolean, are often referred to as *ordinal* data types, since the data items that comprise each of these data types are members of an ordered, finite set. User-defined simple-type data (i.e., enumerated and subrange data) also fall into this category. Note, however, that real-type data cannot be classified in this manner and are therefore not included within this category.

### 3.1 INTEGER-TYPE DATA

Integer-type data are whole-number (integer) quantities. Included within this category are integer-type constants, variables, functions and expressions. We have already discussed the rules for writing integer numbers and for defining or declaring integer constants and variables. Let us now concentrate on the operators that can be used with integer-type data and then consider the rules for writing integer-type expressions.

Collectively, the operators that are used to carry out numerical-type operations are called *arithmetic operators*. There are six arithmetic operators that can be used with integer-type operands. Five of these will produce an integer-type result (i.e., an integer-type *resultant*); the sixth will produce a quantity of type real. These operators are summarized below.

| Arithmetic Operator | Purpose | Type of Operands | Type of Resultant |
|:---:|---|---|---|
| + | addition | integer | integer |
| – | subtraction | integer | integer |
| * | multiplication | integer | integer |
| / | division | integer | real |
| DIV | truncated division | integer | integer |
| MOD | remainder after division | integer | integer |

Notice that the division operator (/) will result in a real quantity, even though the operands are integer. Also notice that there is no exponentiation operator (Pascal does not support an exponentiation operator).

**EXAMPLE 3.1**

Suppose that a and b are integer-type variables that have been assigned the values 13 and 5, respectively. Several simple integer expressions and their resulting values are shown below.

| Expression | Value |
|------------|-------|
| a+b | 18 |
| a-b | 8 |
| a*b | 65 |
| a DIV b | 2 |
| a MOD b | 3 |
| a/b | 2.6 |

There are certain rules that must be observed when using these operators to form numerical expressions. Some of the more common rules, which apply to expressions involving only two integer operands, are given below (others will be discussed in Sec. 3.7).

1.  The resultant will be positive if both operands are of the same sign. Otherwise, the resultant will be negative.

2.  The two division operators (/ and DIV) and the MOD operator require that the second operand be nonzero.

3.  Use of the DIV operator with a negative operand will result in truncation toward zero; i.e., the resultant will be smaller in magnitude than the true quotient.

4.  According to the ISO standard, the second operand cannot be negative when using the MOD operator. However, many implementations of Pascal do allow this operand to be negative. In such cases the sign of the resultant will be determined so that the condition

$$a = (a \ DIV \ b)*b + (a \ MOD \ b)$$

is always satisfied, regardless of the signs of the individual operands.

**EXAMPLE 3.2**

Suppose that i and j are integer-type variables whose assigned values are 11 and −3, respectively. Several integer expressions and their corresponding values are given below.

| Expression | Value |
|------------|-------|
| i+j | 8 |
| i-j | 14 |
| i*j | −33 |
| i DIV j | −3 |
| i MOD j | 2 (nonstandard) |
| i/j | −3.6666667 |

If i had been assigned a value of −11 and j had been assigned 3, then we would have

| Expression | Value |
|------------|-------|
| i DIV j | −3 |
| i MOD j | −2 |
| i/j | −3.6666667 |

Finally, if i and j were both assigned negative values (−11 and −3, respectively), then we would obtain

| Expression | Value |
|------------|-------|
| i DIV j | 3 |
| i MOD j | −2 (nonstandard) |
| i/j | 3.6666667 |

Note that the (nonstandard) condition

    i = (i DIV j)*j + (i MOD j)

is satisfied in each of the above situations.


## 3.2  REAL-TYPE DATA

Real-type data refers to data items that represent real numerical quantities. This includes real-type constants, variables, functions and expressions.

There are four arithmetic operators that can be used with real-type operands. They are

| Arithmetic Operator | Purpose | Type of Operands | Type of Resultant |
|---|---|---|---|
| + | addition | real | real |
| − | subtraction | real | real |
| * | multiplication | real | real |
| / | division | real | real |

Notice that these operators can also be used with integer-type operands, but the integer operators DIV and MOD cannot be used with real-type data. (We again remark that there is no exponentiation operator in Pascal.)

### EXAMPLE 3.3

Suppose that v1 and v2 are real-type variables whose assigned values are 12.5 and 0.5, respectively. Several simple real expressions, and their resulting values, are shown below.

| Expression | Value |
|---|---|
| v1+v2 | 13.0 |
| v1−v2 | 12.0 |
| v1*v2 | 6.25 |
| v1/v2 | 25.0 |

There are certain rules that must be followed when forming numerical expressions with real-type data. Three of the most common rules, which apply to expressions containing only two operands, are summarized below. (Several other rules are presented in Sec. 3.7.)

1. The resultant will be positive if both operands are of the same sign. Otherwise the resultant will be negative.
2. The division operator (/) requires that the second operand be nonzero.
3. If one operand is of type integer and the other is of type real, then the resulting value will always be of type real.

### EXAMPLE 3.4

Let r1 and r2 be real variables whose assigned values are −0.66 and 4.50. Several real expressions and their corresponding values are given below.

| Expression | Value |
|---|---|
| r1+r2 | 3.84 |
| r1−r2 | −5.16 |
| r1*r2 | −2.97 |
| r1/r2 | −0.1466667 |

**EXAMPLE 3.5**

Suppose that i is an integer-type variable that has been assigned a value of −2, and r is a real-type variable that has been assigned a value of 1.2. Then the expression

        3∗i∗r

will represent the real value −7.2, since $3 \times (-2) \times 1.2 = -7.2$.

## 3.3  CHAR-TYPE DATA

Char-type data are single-character strings; i.e., single characters enclosed in apostrophes. This data type includes single-character constants, identifiers that represent single-character constants, char-type variables and certain char-type functions.

**Table 3-1   A Portion of the ASCII Character Set**

| ASCII Value | Character | ASCII Value | Character | ASCII Value | Character |
|---|---|---|---|---|---|
| 032 | blank | 063 | ? | 093 | ] |
| 033 | ! | 064 | @ | 094 | ^ |
| 034 | " | 065 | A | 095 | — |
| 035 | # | 066 | B | 096 | ` |
| 036 | $ | 067 | C | 097 | a |
| 037 | % | 068 | D | 098 | b |
| 038 | & | 069 | E | 099 | c |
| 039 | ' | 070 | F | 100 | d |
| 040 | ( | 071 | G | 101 | e |
| 041 | ) | 072 | H | 102 | f |
| 042 | ∗ | 073 | I | 103 | g |
| 043 | + | 074 | J | 104 | h |
| 044 | , | 075 | K | 105 | i |
| 045 | − | 076 | L | 106 | j |
| 046 | . | 077 | M | 107 | k |
| 047 | / | 078 | N | 108 | l |
| 048 | 0 | 079 | O | 109 | m |
| 049 | 1 | 080 | P | 110 | n |
| 050 | 2 | 081 | Q | 111 | o |
| 051 | 3 | 082 | R | 112 | p |
| 052 | 4 | 083 | S | 113 | q |
| 053 | 5 | 084 | T | 114 | r |
| 054 | 6 | 085 | U | 115 | s |
| 055 | 7 | 086 | V | 116 | t |
| 056 | 8 | 087 | W | 117 | u |
| 057 | 9 | 088 | X | 118 | v |
| 058 | : | 089 | Y | 119 | w |
| 059 | ; | 090 | Z | 120 | x |
| 060 | < | 091 | [ | 121 | y |
| 061 | = | 092 | \ | 122 | z |
| 062 | > | | | | |

The complete set of characters that can be used with char-type data will vary from one compiler to another. In general, however, the letters A to Z (both upper- and lowercase), the digits 0 to 9 and the commonly available special characters $(+, -, =, \$,$ etc.) are all acceptable.

**EXAMPLE 3.6**

The following are acceptable char-type data items.

$$\text{'P'} \qquad \text{'5'} \qquad \text{'t'} \qquad \text{'*'} \qquad \text{' '} \qquad \text{''''}$$

(Note that the last data item represents a single apostrophe, as explained in Sec. 2.6.)

Most computers, and virtually all microcomputers, make use of the ASCII (American Standard Code for Information Interchange) character set in which each individual character is numerically encoded with its own unique 7-bit combination (hence a total of $2^7 = 128$ different characters). Thus the characters are ordered as well as encoded. In particular, the digits are ordered consecutively in their proper numerical sequence (0 to 9), and the letters are arranged consecutively in their proper alphabetical order. This allows char-type data items that represent ASCII characters to be compared with one another, based upon their relative order within the character set.

Table 3-1 contains a portion of the ASCII character set, showing the decimal equivalent of the 7 bits that represent each character. Notice that the digits precede the letters, and the uppercase letters precede the lowercase letters. Also, notice that there are small groups of special characters separating the digits, the uppercase letters and the lowercase letters.

**EXAMPLE 3.7**

Table 3-1 shows that the letter A is encoded as (decimal) 65 in the ASCII code, and the letter B is encoded as 66. Since 65 is less than 66, A is considered to precede B. Similarly, A precedes a because 65 is less than 97; and 0 precedes 1 because 48 is less than 49.

An important exception is found on the larger IBM computers, which use the EBCDIC (Extended Binary-Coded Decimal Interchange Code) character set. This is an 8-bit, 256-character encoding scheme (because $2^8 = 256$). The EBCDIC character set is independent from, and incompatible with, the ASCII code. A portion on the EBCDIC character code is shown in Table 3-2. Notice that the lowercase letters precede the uppercase letters in this character code, and the uppercase letters precede the digits. Also, there are "gaps" (discontinuities) in the sequence of encoded numbers. The letters and digits are still ordered in their proper respective sequences, however, so that EBCDIC-encoded characters can be compared on the basis of their relative order within the character set.

**EXAMPLE 3.8**

Table 3-2 shows that the letter A is encoded as (decimal) 193 in the EBCDIC character code, and the letter B is encoded as 194. Since 193 is less than 194, A is considered to precede B. Similarly, a precedes A because 129 is less than 193; and 0 precedes 1 because 240 is less than 241.

The reader should determine which character set is used at his or her particular installation. Also, it should be understood that char-type digits and integer quantities are represented altogether differently inside the computer. The beginning programmer should be careful not to confuse these two different types of data.

None of the arithmetic operators can be used with char-type data, since char-type data items do not represent numerical quantities. Char-type data can be compared, however, using the relational operators described in the next section.

**Table 3-2    A Portion of the EBCDIC Character Set**

| EBCDIC Value | Character | EBCDIC Value | Character | EBCDIC Value | Character |
|---|---|---|---|---|---|
| 064 | blank | 132 | d | 200 | H |
| 074 | ] | 133 | e | 201 | I |
| 075 | . | 134 | f | 209 | J |
| 076 | < | 135 | g | 210 | K |
| 077 | ( | 136 | h | 211 | L |
| 078 | + | 137 | i | 212 | M |
| 079 | ! | 145 | j | 213 | N |
| 080 | & | 146 | k | 214 | O |
| 090 | [ | 147 | l | 215 | P |
| 091 | $ | 148 | m | 216 | Q |
| 092 | * | 149 | n | 217 | R |
| 093 | ) | 150 | o | 226 | S |
| 094 | ; | 151 | p | 227 | T |
| 095 | ^ | 152 | q | 228 | U |
| 096 | - | 153 | r | 229 | V |
| 097 | / | 162 | s | 230 | W |
| 108 | , | 163 | t | 231 | X |
| 109 | % | 164 | u | 232 | Y |
| 110 | — | 165 | v | 233 | Z |
| 111 | > | 166 | w | 240 | 0 |
| 112 | ? | 167 | x | 241 | 1 |
| 122 | : | 168 | y | 242 | 2 |
| 123 | # | 169 | z | 243 | 3 |
| 124 | @ | 193 | A | 244 | 4 |
| 125 | ' | 194 | B | 245 | 5 |
| 126 | = | 195 | C | 246 | 6 |
| 127 | " | 196 | D | 247 | 7 |
| 129 | a | 197 | E | 248 | 8 |
| 130 | b | 198 | F | 249 | 9 |
| 131 | c | 199 | G | | |

## 3.4  BOOLEAN-TYPE DATA

Boolean-type data are truth values that are either true or false. This category includes boolean-type constants, variables, functions and expressions. The two values that apply to boolean-type data (true and false) represent an ordered set, with false preceding true. (Note that false is encoded as 0, and true is encoded as 1.)

Boolean-type expressions are formed by combining operands of the same type with *relational operators*. These operators represent various conditions of equality and/or inequality. There are seven relational operators in Pascal, though we will consider only six of them in this chapter. The six are

| Relational Operator | Meaning |
|:---:|:---|
| = | equal to |
| <> | not equal to |
| < | less than |
| <= | less than or equal to |
| > | greater than |
| >= | greater than or equal to |

The seventh relational operator, IN, will be discussed in Chap. 12.

These six operators can be used with operands of any type other than boolean. When used with nonnumerical operands, the inequalities refer to the order in which the operands are encoded.

Certain of these operators (namely =, <>, <= and >=) are also used in conjunction with set comparisons, as described in Chap. 12 (see Sec. 12.4).

**EXAMPLE 3.9**

Here are some simple boolean expressions involving numerical operands. (Within each expression, assume that both operands are of the same type.)

| Expression | Value |
|:---:|:---|
| 2 = 3 | false |
| 2 < 3 | true |
| 0.6 >= 1.5 | false |
| 0.6 >= -1.5 | true |
| -4 <> 4 | true |
| 1.7 <= -2.2 | false |

**EXAMPLE 3.10**

Suppose that i and j are integer-type variables that have been assigned the values of 3 and −5, respectively. Several boolean expressions involving the use of these variables are shown below.

| Expression | Value |
|:---:|:---|
| i <= 10 | true |
| i+j > 0 | false |
| (i-j) < (i+j) | false |
| i-3 = j+5 | true |
| 2*i >= i DIV 2 | true |
| (i DIV 2) > (j+6) | false |

Notice that the operands can be constants, variables or expressions.

**EXAMPLE 3.11**

Suppose that ch1 and ch2 are char-type variables that have been assigned the characters P and T, respectively. Several boolean expressions involving the use of these variables are shown below.

| Expression | Value |
|---|---|
| ch1 = ch2 | false |
| ch2 = 'T' | true |
| ch1 = 'p' | false |
| ch1 < ch2 | true (because P precedes T) |
| ch2 > 'A' | true (because T succeeds A) |
| 'W' <> ch1 | true |

Pascal also contains three logical operators. Two of these operators allow boolean-type operands to be combined to form boolean-type expressions; the third is used to *negate* (i.e., to *reverse*) the value of a boolean operand.

The logical operators are

| Operator | Meaning |
|---|---|
| OR | Expression will be true if either operand is true (or if both operands are true). |
| AND | Expression will be true only if both operands are true. |
| NOT | This operator is used as a *prefix* to negate a boolean operand. |

To avoid ambiguities in the order in which the logical operations are carried out, the boolean operands should be enclosed in parentheses.

**EXAMPLE 3.12**

Suppose that n is an integer-type variable that has been assigned a value of 10, and s is a char-type variable that represents the character A. Several boolean expressions involving the use of these variables are shown below.

| Expression | Value |
|---|---|
| (n > 0) AND (n < 20) | true |
| (n > 0) AND (n < 5) | false |
| (n > 0) OR (n < 5) | true |
| (n < 0) OR (n > 20) | false |
| (n = 10) AND (s = 'A') | true |
| (n <> 5) OR (s >= 'A') | true |

**EXAMPLE 3.13**

Suppose that the boolean expression j > 6 is true. Then the expression

    NOT (j > 6)

will be false. Also, the expression

    NOT (j <= 6)

will be true, since (j<=6) will be false.

**EXAMPLE 3.14**

Now suppose that the char-type variable ch represents the character G. Then the expression ch > 'A' will be true, and the expression

    NOT (ch > 'A')

will be false. Also, the expression ch = 'A' will be false, so that the expression

    NOT (ch = 'A')

will be true.

We will see how boolean expressions are used in Pascal programs when we reach Chap. 6.

## 3.5  STANDARD CONSTANTS

Pascal includes three standard identifiers that represent constants. They are maxint, false and true. The first of these, maxint, specifies the largest value that may be assumed by an integer-type quantity (see Sec. 2.5). The two remaining constants, false and true, represent the two values that may be assigned to a boolean-type data item. (The reader is again reminded that false and true represent an ordered set, with false preceding true.)

## 3.6  STANDARD FUNCTIONS

Pascal also contains a number of standard functions that are used with various simple data-types. (Standard functions are also referred to as *intrinsic* or *built-in* functions.) Some of these functions accept one type of parameter and return a value of the same type, while others accept a parameter of one type and return a value of a different type. Several of these functions are summarized below. (See also App. D.)

| Function | Purpose | Type of Parameter (x) | Type of Result |
|---|---|---|---|
| abs(x) | Compute the absolute value of x. | integer or real | same as x |
| arctan(x) | Compute the arctangent of x. | integer or real | real |
| chr(x) | Determine the character represented by x. | integer | char |
| cos(x) | Compute the cosine of x (x in radians). | integer or real | real |
| exp(x) | Compute $e^x$, where $e=2.7182818...$ is the base of the natural (Naperian) system of logarithms. | integer or real | real |
| ln(x) | Compute the natural logarithm of x (x > 0). | integer or real | real |
| odd(x) | Determine if x is odd or even. (Return a value of true if x is odd, false otherwise.) | integer | boolean |

(*continues on next page*)

| Function | Purpose | Type of Parameter (x) | Type of Result |
|---|---|---|---|
| ord(x) | Determine the (decimal) integer that is used to encode the character x. | char | integer |
| pred(x) | Determine the predecessor of x. | integer, char or boolean | same as x |
| round(x) | Round the value of x to the nearest integer. | real | integer |
| sin(x) | Compute the sine of x (x in radians). | integer or real | real |
| sqr(x) | Compute the square of x. | integer or real | same as x |
| sqrt(x) | Compute the square root of x (x >= 0). | integer or real | real |
| succ(x) | Determine the successor to x. | integer, char or boolean | same as x |
| trunc(x) | Truncate x (i.e., drop the decimal part of x). | real | integer |

There are two additional standard functions, eoln and eof, that are used with data files. These functions will be described in Chap. 4.

The purpose of most of the functions presented above should be readily apparent. There are a few, however, whose purpose may be less obvious. Their use is illustrated in the following examples.

**EXAMPLE 3.15**

The function abs(x) computes the absolute value of the number represented by the parameter x. Thus, if diff is a real-type variable that has been assigned a value of −0.003, then the function abs(diff) will return a value of 0.003 when it is accessed. (Note that diff is a parameter in the function access.)

**EXAMPLE 3.16**

The functions chr and ord are used to determine the relationship between any Pascal character and its corresponding integer code. Thus, if a computer uses the ASCII code,

```
chr(65)='A'          ord('A')=65

chr(112)='p'         ord('p')=112

chr(53)='5'          ord('5')=53
```

and so on. Note that

```
ord('A')=ord(chr(65))=65
```

and

```
chr(65)=chr(ord('A'))='A'
```

and so on.

**EXAMPLE 3.17**

Since integer-, char- and boolean-type data all represent ordered sets, we can determine the predecessor or successor of any data item within one of these sets (or in any user-defined ordered set) with the functions pred and succ. Thus,

| | | |
|---|---|---|
| pred(3)=2 | succ(3)=4 | (*integer-type data*) |
| pred('e')='d' | succ('e')='f' | (*char-type data*) |
| pred(true)=false | succ(false)=true | (*boolean-type data*) |

Also, note that the ASCII character set satisfies conditions such as

    pred('e')=chr(ord('e')-1)

and

    succ('e')=chr(ord('e')+1)

It should be understood that the functions pred and succ do not apply to real-type data.

**EXAMPLE 3.18**

The functions round and trunc can accept both positive and negative real-type numbers. Negative numbers are treated as though they were positive numbers, with the minus sign added after the rounding or truncation has been carried out. Thus,

| | |
|---|---|
| round(2.3)=2 | trunc(2.3)=2 |
| round(3.7)=4 | trunc(3.7)=3 |
| round(-1.8)=-2 | trunc(-1.8)=-1 |
| round(-6.1)=-6 | trunc(-6.1)=-6 |

Several of these standard functions can also be used with other (nonstandard, user-defined) data types. We will mention such applications as the need arises later in this text.

Finally, the reader is again reminded that the parameters in a function reference can be constants, variables, expressions or even references to other functions. The only restriction is that the parameters be of the proper type. We will say more about parameters in Chap. 7, where we consider the subject of procedures and functions in greater detail.

## 3.7  MORE ABOUT EXPRESSIONS

An expression can sometimes become quite complex, because of the presence of multiple operators within the expression. In such cases it becomes necessary to specify the order in which the various operations are carried out. This order may be determined by the natural *operator precedence* which is included within the Pascal language. The precedence groups are tabulated below, from highest to lowest.

| Precedence | Operator(s) | | | | | | |
|---|---|---|---|---|---|---|---|
| 1 (highest) | | | NOT | | | | |
| 2 | * | / | DIV | MOD | AND | | |
| 3 | | + | − | OR | | | |
| 4 (lowest) | = | <> | < | <= | > | >= | IN |

Within a given precedence group the operations are carried out as they are encountered, reading from left to right.

**EXAMPLE 3.19**

The numerical expression

    a-b/c*sqrt(d)

is equivalent to the algebraic formula $a - [(b/c) \times \sqrt{d}]$. Thus, if the variables a, b, c and d have been assigned the values 1, 2, 3 and 4, respectively, the expression would represent the value $-0.33333333$, since

$$1 - [(2/3) \times \sqrt{4}] = 1 - (4/3) = -1/3$$

Notice that the division is carried out first, since this operation falls within a higher precedence group than subtraction. The resulting quotient is then multiplied by $\sqrt{4}$ (left-to-right rule within a precedence group). Finally, this product is subtracted from the value of the first variable.

The natural operator precedence can be altered through the use of parentheses, thus allowing the operations within an expression to be carried out in any desired order. In fact, the parentheses can be *nested*, one pair within another. In such cases the innermost operations are carried out first, then the next innermost operations, and so on.

**EXAMPLE 3.20**

The numerical expression

```
(a-b)/(c*sqrt(d))
```

is equivalent to the algebraic formula

$$(a - b)/(c \times \sqrt{d})$$

Thus, if the variables a, b, c and d have been assigned the values 1, 2, 3 and 4, respectively, the expression would represent the value $-0.1666667$, since $(1 - 2)/(3 \times \sqrt{4}) = -1/6 = -0.1666667$. (Compare with the result obtained in Example 3.19.)

**EXAMPLE 3.21**

Consider the boolean expression

```
(x > 0) OR (y < 10)
```

where x and y are integer-type variables. This expression will be true if x has been assigned a value greater than zero or if y has been assigned a value less than 10 (or both). If neither condition has been satisfied, then the expression will be false.

Note that the parentheses are required within this expression. Without the parentheses, Pascal would first attempt to evaluate the expression

```
0 OR y
```

which is not meaningful (because the logical operator OR cannot be used with numeric operands).

**EXAMPLE 3.22**

Now consider the numerical expression

```
2*((a MOD 5)*(4+(b-3)/sqr(c+2)))
```

If the variables a, b and c have been assigned the values 8, 15 and $-4$, respectively, then the given expression would be evaluated as

```
2*((3)*(4+12/sqr(-2))) = 2*(3*(4+12/4)) = 2*(3*(4+3)) = 42
```

Sometimes it is a good idea to use parentheses to clarify an expression, even though the parentheses may not be required. On the other hand, the use of overly complex expressions should be avoided if at all possible, as such expressions are a frequent source of error (the last example contains an expression of this type).

Finally, the following grammatical rules (in addition to those stated in Secs. 3.1 and 3.2) must always be observed when constructing numerical and boolean expressions.

1.  Undefined identifiers cannot appear within an expression. (In other words, each identifier must be assigned a value before it can appear within an expression.)

2.  Preceding an identifier with a minus sign is equivalent to multiplication by $-1$. Thus, $-a*b$ is equivalent to $-1*a*b$.

3. Arithmetic operators cannot appear consecutively. Hence, the expression a*-b is not allowed, but a*(-b) is permitted.

4. Arithmetic operations cannot be implied. Thus, the expression 2(x+y) is incorrect, but the expression 2*(x+y) is valid.

5. Arithmetic operations cannot be carried out on char- or boolean-type data. Therefore expressions such as

    ```
    'A'+'B'
    ```

and

    ```
    (n > 0) + (n < 20)
    ```

are not allowed.

6. There cannot be an imbalance of parentheses. In other words, the number of left parentheses must be the same as the number of right parentheses.

## 3.8 THE ASSIGNMENT STATEMENT

We have already seen that the assignment statement is a type of simple statement that is used to assign a data item to a variable. This statement is written in the form

```
variable := data item
```

The data item can be a single item (e.g., a constant, another variable or a function reference), or it can be an expression. The data item must, however, be of the same *type* as the variable to which it is assigned. (There is one exception to this rule: an integer data item can be assigned to a real variable.)

**EXAMPLE 3.23**

A typical assignment is shown below.

```
area := 3.14159*sqr(radius);
```

This statement causes the value of the expression

```
3.14159*sqr(radius)
```

to be assigned to the variable area. Thus, if radius has been assigned a value of 10.0, area will be assigned a value of 314.159.

The semicolon at the end of the statement is actually not a part of the statement itself, but is a *separator* that distinguishes the end of the current statement from the beginning of the next statement. This use of the semicolon is used throughout Pascal; it is not restricted only to the assignment statement.

Numerical-type assignment statements frequently look like algebraic equations. This need not always be true, however, as illustrated in the next example.

**EXAMPLE 3.24**

Consider the assignment statement

```
count := count+1;
```

This statement causes the current value of the integer-type variable count to be increased by one. (This is called *incrementing*.) Algebraically, this statement would make no sense. It is entirely logical, however, when viewed in terms of its intended purpose.

Another way to accomplish the same thing is to write

```
count := succ(count);
```

where succ is a standard function, as described in Sec. 3.6.

Assignment statements need not be restricted to numerical data, as shown in the following examples.

**EXAMPLE 3.25**

Suppose that state is a char-type variable. The assignment

    state := 'S';

will cause the character s to be assigned to state.

**EXAMPLE 3.26**

Suppose that flag is a boolean variable, and x and y are integer variables. Then the statement

    flag := (x > 0) OR (y < 10);

will cause flag to be assigned either the value true or the value false, as determined by the boolean expression. Thus, flag will be assigned the value true if x is greater than zero or if y is less than 10 (or both); otherwise, flag will be assigned the value false.

# Review Questions

**3.1**    What do integer-type data represent?

**3.2**    What are arithmetic operators? Which arithmetic operators can be used with integer-type data? What is the purpose of each of these operators?

**3.3**    How does the division operator (/) differ from the truncated division operator (DIV) when using integer-type operands?

**3.4**    Summarize the rules for using an arithmetic operator with two integer-type operands. In particular, summarize the restrictions that apply to the use of the two division operators (/ and DIV) and the MOD operator.

**3.5**    What do real-type data represent?

**3.6**    Which arithmetic operators can be used with real-type data? What is the purpose of each of these operators?

**3.7**    Summarize the rules for using an arithmetic operator with two real-type operands.

**3.8**    What type of resultant is obtained if an arithmetic operator is used with one integer-type operand and one real-type operand?

**3.9**    What do char-type data represent? Which characters can be used with char-type data?

**3.10**   What is meant by the ASCII character set? How widely used is this character set?

**3.11**   In what general order are the characters arranged within the ASCII character set?

**3.12**   What is the EBCDIC character set? On what type of computers can this character set be found?

**3.13**    In what general order are the characters arranged within the EBCDIC character set?

**3.14**    What type of operations can be carried out on char-type data? Which operators are used?

**3.15**    What do boolean-type data represent?

**3.16**    How are boolean-type data items ordered?

**3.17**    What are relational operators? What is the purpose of each of these operators? With what types of operands can they be used? What type of resultant is obtained in each case?

**3.18**    What is the interpretation of an inequality-type relational operator (such as <) being used with char-type operands?

**3.19**    What are logical operators? What is the purpose of each of these operators? With what type of operand can they be used? What type of resultant is obtained?

**3.20**    What three standard constants are included in Pascal? What type of data item is each constant? What is the purpose of each constant?

**3.21**    What are standard functions? By what other names are they known?

**3.22**    What is the purpose of the abs function? With what types of parameters is it used? What type of resultant is obtained?

**3.23**    What is the purpose of the chr and ord functions? With what types of parameters are they used? What type of resultant is obtained in each case?

**3.24**    What is the purpose of the pred and succ functions? With what types of parameters are they used? What type of resultant is obtained in each case?

**3.25**    When using the ASCII character set, what relationships exist between the chr and ord functions and the pred and succ functions? Why are these relationships not valid for *all* character sets?

**3.26**    What is the purpose of the round and trunc functions? With what types of parameters are they used? What type of resultant is obtained in each case?

**3.27**    How are negative parameters treated by the round and trunc functions?

**3.28**    Explain what is meant by operator precedence and summarize its structure.

**3.29**    In what order are the operations within a precedence group carried out?

**3.30**    How can the natural operator precedence be altered?

**3.31**    In what order are the operations carried out within an expression that contains nested parentheses?

**3.32**   Under what circumstances should parentheses be included within an expression? Under what circumstances should they be avoided?

**3.33**   Summarize the rules that must be observed when constructing numerical and boolean expressions.

**3.34**   What is the purpose of the assignment statement? What restrictions apply to the *type* of data that is assigned to a variable?

**3.35**   What is the purpose of the semicolon that appears at the end of most assignment statements? Is the semicolon actually a part of the statement?

**3.36**   Is there a relationship between a numerical-type assignment statement and an algebraic equation?

# Solved Problems

**3.37**   Suppose that a, b, c and d are numeric-type variables that have been assigned the following values.

| Variable | Type | Value |
|----------|---------|-------|
| a | real | 5.7 |
| b | real | 8.2 |
| c | integer | 7 |
| d | integer | 4 |

These variables are used in the following numerical expressions. In each case, determine the type of the expression and the value that it represents.

| Numerical Expression | Type | Value |
|----------------------|---------|------------|
| sqr(a+b)/(c+d) | real | 17.5645 |
| 6*(c MOD d) | integer | 18 |
| 6.0*(c MOD d) | real | 18.0 |
| (c DIV d)+(c MOD d) | integer | 4 |
| (c MOD d)/2 | real | 1.5 |
| trunc(a-b) | integer | -2 |
| trunc(a-b) DIV c | integer | 0 |
| (c DIV d)/(-a) | real | -0.17543860 |

**3.38**   Several boolean expressions are shown below. Determine the value that is represented by each expression. Assume that the variables a, b, c and d have the same values as in Prob. 3.37 and that letter is a char-type variable that has been assigned the character w.

| Boolean Expression | Value |
|---|---|
| a < b | true |
| letter = '$' | false |
| 'q' < 'r' | true |
| abs(a-b) > 2.0 | true |
| (c <= d) OR (letter = 'Z') | false |
| NOT (5 = pred(6)) | false |
| 100*(c+d) = maxint | false |
| true | true |
| (c > 0) AND (c <> 7) | false |

**3.39** Several numerical and boolean expressions are presented below. Some are written incorrectly. Determine which are incorrect and identify all errors.

| Expression | Validity |
|---|---|
| 2*a*b/(c-1)-u/abs(3*(v-w)) | correct |
| 2*a*-b/(c-1)-u/abs(3*(v-w)) | incorrect (two consecutive operators) |
| 'a'+'b'+'c' | incorrect (arithmetic operators cannot be used with char-type data) |
| succ('E') = 'F' | correct |
| x > 0 AND x < 100 | incorrect (the boolean operands must be enclosed in parentheses) |
| (a+b+c) <= (c+d+e) | correct |
| 2*n+1 <> 'a' | incorrect (the operands are incompatible) |
| round(99.7) = 100 | correct |
| ((x-y)/3+(abs(u-v)) | incorrect (parentheses are not balanced) |
| (-5(x-y)/3+abs(u-v)) | incorrect (a multiplication operator is missing) |

## Supplementary Problems

**3.40** Suppose that a, b, c, d and e are numeric-type variables that have been assigned the following values.

| Variable | Type | Value |
|---|---|---|
| a | integer | 8 |
| b | integer | 5 |
| c | real | 4.3 |
| d | real | 0.8 |
| e | real | −2.2 |

These variables are used in the following numerical expressions. Determine the type of each expression and the value that it represents.

(a)  (b-a)/sqr(d-e)             (d)  (a-2*b)*trunc(3*c-d+2*e)

(b)  round((c+d)/e)             (e)  0.01*(a-b)

(c)  (a DIV b)/(a MOD b)        (f)  trunc(3*sqrt(abs(d+e)))

**3.41**  Several boolean expressions are shown below. Determine the value that is represented by each expression. Assume that the variables a, b, c, d and e have the same values as in the previous problem, and that y and n are char-type variables that have been assigned the characters Y and N, respectively.

(a)  c < d+e                    (e)  true OR false

(b)  (y = 'Y') AND (n = 'N')    (f)  NOT (y < 'z')

(c)  trunc(c+d) <= 10.0         (g)  (a >= 100) AND (b <= maxint)

(d)  (a = 8) OR (b = 8)         (h)  odd(a-b)

**3.42**  Evaluate each of the following expressions. Assume that the characters are members of the ASCII character set.

(a)  abs(-4.667)     (i)  succ(false)     (p)  trunc(2.2)

(b)  chr(67)         (j)  odd(10)         (q)  trunc(2.8)

(c)  ord('e')        (k)  odd(15)         (r)  trunc(-2.2)

(d)  pred(10)        (l)  round(2.2)      (s)  trunc(-2.8)

(e)  pred('e')       (m)  round(2.8)      (t)  chr(ord('8')+4)

(f)  pred(true)      (n)  round(-2.2)     (u)  ord(pred('A'))

(g)  succ(10)        (o)  round(-2.8)     (v)  chr(ord('g'))

(h)  succ(e)

**3.43**  Which of the answers in Prob. 3.42 would change if the EBCDIC character set were used?

**3.44**  Several numerical and boolean expressions are shown below. Some are written incorrectly. Determine which are incorrect and identify all errors.

(a)  sum DIV 0.005              (h)  slope <> m*x+b

(b)  200*sum                    (i)  sqrt(a+b) < succ('G')

(c)  '100'+'27'+440'            (j)  (a+abs(c1+c2)/((c1+c3)*(c2+c3))

(d)  true = false              (k)  2*maxint+3

(e)  (a-b)/(2g+7)              (l)  round(a*-b)

(f)  'D'=pred('E')             (m)  odd(12.82)-6.6

(g)  value = 0.0 OR count < 100 (n)  -b+sqrt(sqr(b)-4*a*c)/(2*a)

**3.45**  A Pascal program includes the following variables.

| Variable | Data Type |
| --- | --- |
| gross | real |
| net | real |
| tax | real |
| employee | integer |
| status | char |
| sex | char |
| exempt | boolean |

Show how these variables are declared within the program.

# Chapter 4

# Data Input and Output

This chapter is concerned with methods for reading data into the computer and writing data out of the computer. We will see that this can be accomplished quite easily, using the special input/output statements that are included within Pascal. Once we have learned how to carry out these input/output operations we will be able to write a variety of complete, though simple, Pascal programs.

## 4.1 INPUT AND OUTPUT FILES

Let us first consider the manner in which input data and output data are transferred into and out of the computer. For now we will consider a (noninteractive) mainframe computing environment.

The input data items must be placed in a separate file, called the *input file*, before the corresponding program is actually run. This file is most often created via a text editor, as described in Chap. 5 (see Section 5.3). However, it may also be entered into the computer via punched cards, using a keypunch machine and a card reader. In either case the data items will be stored sequentially, in the same order that they were entered. These individual data items will be grouped into logical *lines*, where each line corresponds to one line of typed data or one punched card.

Output data are transferred from the computer's memory to an *output file*, which is similar but opposite to the input file. Again the data items are stored sequentially, in the same order that they were written. The data items will again be grouped into logical lines, which will correspond to physical lines of output when the data are printed or displayed.

It should be understood that the input data file and the output data file are stored within the computer as separate entities; they are *not* a part of a Pascal program. These files are associated with a Pascal program, however, by naming them as parameters within the program header.

**EXAMPLE 4.1**

A Pascal program contains the following program header.

```
PROGRAM payroll(input,output);
```

The header specifies that the name of the program is payroll and that the program utilizes both input and output files.

A program need not utilize both an input and an output file, though most programs do so, since most programs require input data and generate output data when they are executed.

**EXAMPLE 4.2**

A Pascal program called primes is used to generate the first twelve prime numbers. This program includes the following header.

```
PROGRAM primes(output);
```

Notice that this program utilizes only an output file, since it does not require any input data. If the program were modified, however, so that it would generate the first $n$ prime numbers, where $n$ is an input quantity, then the program header would have to be changed to

```
PROGRAM primes(input,output);
```

Such a modification would be a good idea, since the program would then be much more general.

49

Finally, the reader is reminded that there are some interactive versions of Pascal that allow input/output operations to be carried out directly during program execution. Input and output files are not required in such situations. This is particularly common with microcomputers.

## 4.2   THE READ STATEMENT

The read statement is used to read data items from the input file and assign them to integer, real or char-type variables. The statement is written as

```
read(input variables)
```

where the input variables are separated by commas. (Note that boolean-type variables cannot be included in the list of input variables.)

### EXAMPLE 4.3

Here is a typical read statement.

```
read(a,b,c);
```

This statement causes three data items to be read from the input file and assigned to the variables a, b and c, respectively.

The data items are read from the input file and assigned to their respective variables in the same order that they are stored. Each variable must be of the same *type* as its corresponding data item. (*Exception*: An integer number can be assigned to a real-type variable.) Each data item can be read only once.

### EXAMPLE 4.4

A portion of a Pascal program is shown below.

```
VAR a,b : real;
    i,j : integer;
    p,q : char;
      .
      .
      .
read(a,b,i,j,p,q);
```

The read statement will cause two real numbers, two integer numbers and two single characters to be read from the input file and assigned to the variables a, b, i, j, p and q, respectively.

Some care must be given to the spacing of the input data items. Numerical data items must be separated from one another by blank spaces or by end-of-line designations. To be more precise, a numerical data item may be *preceded* by one or more blank spaces or end-of-line designations. Real numbers can be written with or without an exponent. Moreover, real numbers that represent integral quantities (e.g., 1.0) can be written as integers (i.e., 1). Any number may be preceded by a plus or a minus sign provided there is no space between the sign and the number.

Char-type data must be treated somewhat differently, since all characters are significant. In particular, a char-type data item must *not* be enclosed in apostrophes. Also, a char-type data item *cannot* be separated from the preceding data item by a blank space or an end-of-line designation, since the separator will be interpreted (incorrectly) as the data item. (An end-of-line designation will be interpreted as a blank space if assigned to a char-type variable.)

**EXAMPLE 4.5**

Consider once again the portion of the Pascal program shown in the last example, i.e.,

```
VAR a,b : real;
    i,j : integer;
    p,q : char;
      .
      .
      .
read(a,b,i,j,p,q);
```

Suppose that the variables are to be assigned the following values.

| Variable | Value |
|----------|-------|
| a | 12500 |
| b | −14.8 |
| i | 5 |
| j | −9 |
| p | X |
| q | Y |

The data items might be entered into the input file as follows.

```
12500.0 -14.8 5 -9XY
```

Alternatively, the data items might be entered as

```
12500 -14.8 +5 -9XY
```

or as

```
1.25e4 -1.48e1 5 -9XY
```

If one read statement is followed by another, then the second read statement begins where the first read statement ended. More precisely, the second read statement will begin by reading the data item following the last data item that was read by the previous read statement. Thus, a new read statement does not necessarily begin by reading a new line of data.

**EXAMPLE 4.6**

Let us again consider the the Pascal program described in Examples 4.4 and 4.5. Now suppose that the read statement is replaced by the following two statements.

```
read(a,b,i);
read(j,p,q);
```

The input file need not be changed, since the first read statement would read the first three values on the line, and the second read statement would read the last three values.

## 4.3  THE READLN STATEMENT

The readln statement, like the read statement, is used to read data items from the input file and assign them to integer, real or char-type variables. This statement is written in the form

```
readln(input variables )
```

The difference between the two statements is that the readln statement causes the *next* (not the current) read or readln statement to begin by reading a new line of data, whereas the read statement will allow the next read or readln statement to begin on the same line.

**EXAMPLE 4.7**

A portion of a Pascal program is shown below.

```
VAR p1,p2,p3,p4 : integer;
    .
    .
    .
read(p1,p2);
read(p3,p4);
```

Suppose that the input file contained the following eight numbers, arranged in two lines.

```
1  2  3  4
5  6  7  8
```

The read statements would cause the numbers 1, 2, 3 and 4 to be assigned to the variables p1, p2, p3 and p4, respectively.

If the read statements were replaced with readln statements, i.e.,

```
VAR p1,p2,p3,p4 : integer;
    .
    .
    .
readln(p1,p2);
readln(p3,p4);
```

then the variables p1 and p2 would still be assigned the values 1 and 2, but p3 and p4 would be assigned the values 5 and 6 (from the second line of input data).

Note that it is the *first* readln statement that causes the values for p3 and p4 to be read from the second line of input.

If a readln statement is preceded by a read statement, then the readln statement will begin where the previous read statement ended. Thus, the readln statement does not necessarily *begin* by reading a new line of data. (Note that the readln statement behaves the same as the read statement in this respect.)

**EXAMPLE 4.8**

Now suppose that the read statements in Example 4.7 are written as

```
read(p1,p2);
readln(p3,p4);
```

The variables p1, p2, p3 and p4 would be assigned the values 1, 2, 3 and 4, respectively, since the readln statement would begin by reading the third value in the first line of data. However, the next read or readln statement would begin by reading the 5 from the second line of input data.

The readln statement is convenient for reading data on a line-by-line basis, as is common in batch processing.

**EXAMPLE 4.9**

A Pascal program contains the following three readln statements.

```
readln(a,b);
readln(c,d);
readln(e,f);
```

Suppose that the variables are all of type integer, and the input file contains the numbers

```
1  2  3
4  5  6
7  8  9
```

Then the values 4 and 5 will be assigned to the variables c and d; the values 7 and 8 will be assigned to e and f.

It is not clear what values will be assigned to a and b, since it is not known where the first readln statement will begin. If the statement begins at the start of the line, then the values 1 and 2 will be assigned to a and b. On the other hand, if this statement is preceded by a read statement, e.g.,

```
read(x);
```

then x will be assigned the value 1, and a and b will be assigned the values 2 and 3, respectively.

## 4.4  THE EOLN AND EOF FUNCTIONS

Pascal includes two standard functions, eoln and eof, that are useful when reading input data. The first of these, eoln, returns the boolean value true if an end-of-line designation has been detected on the line being read. Otherwise it returns the value false.

The value of eoln is automatically reset to false whenever a new line of input is started, provided the new line is not empty (i.e., provided the new line contains at least one data item). Thus this function allows us to read an unspecified number of data items from any one line, by reading data from the same line until eoln returns the value true. We can then repeat this procedure for the next line of data, and so on. The exact manner in which this is accomplished will be illustrated later in this text (e.g., Examples 7.24, 9.7, 10.21).

The eof function is used to detect the end of an input file (i.e., an end-of-file designation). This function returns the boolean value true when an end-of-file designation has been detected; otherwise it returns the value false. Use of the eof function will be explained in Chap. 11 (see Sec. 11.5).

The eof function is often used in conjunction with the eoln function to read an unspecified number of data items from an input file. The end of each line can be detected by means of the eoln function, and the end of the file (i.e., the end of the last line) can be determined using the eof function. We will see how this is accomplished in Chap. 11 (see Sec. 11.8).

## 4.5  THE WRITE STATEMENT

The write statement is used to write data items to the output file. This statement is written as

```
write(output data items)
```

The output data items can be strings, numerical constants or the values of variables or expressions. They may be of type integer, real, char or boolean. (Each string must be enclosed within apostrophes, as described in Sec. 2.6.) The data items must be separated by commas if there are more than one.

### EXAMPLE 4.10

Here is a typical write statement.

```
write('x=',x);
```

This statement causes the value of the numeric-type variable x to be written to the output file, with a corresponding label. Thus, if x represents the value 123.456, then the following output will be written to the output file.

```
x= 1.2345600E+02
```

Similarly, the write statement

```
write('sum=',a+b);
```

causes the value of the numerical expression a+b to be written to the output file, with a corresponding label. Thus, if a and b represent the values 3 and −1, respectively, the write statement will produce the following output.

```
sum=      2
```

Real numbers can be displayed in a number of different ways, though the default (standard) format is scientific notation, as illustrated in the above example. Boolean data items will be represented by the standard identifiers true or false, depending on their values.

Most versions of Pascal utilize a standard *field width* (i.e., number of spaces) to represent integer, real and boolean data items. This field width will be different for each data type. Moreover, the field width that is used for a given type of data will vary from one version of Pascal to another. Typically, integer data might have a standard field width of 8, real data might have a standard field width of 14, with 7 digits to the right of the decimal point; and boolean data might have a standard field width of 6. If the field is wider than necessary (as is often the case), then the data item is placed within the right portion of the field. This results in one or more leading blank spaces, as illustrated in the previous example.

The standard field widths can easily be altered, thus allowing the programmer greater control over the appearance of the output items. The method for doing this is described in Sec. 4.7.

When string and char-type data items are written out the field width will be exactly equal to the number of characters in the data item. Hence there will be no leading or trailing blank spaces, unless they are included as a part of the actual data.

**EXAMPLE 4.11**

A Pascal program contains the following write statement.

```
write('RED',' WHITE',' BLUE');
```

This statement will generate the following line of output.

```
RED WHITE BLUE
```

Notice that the blank spaces separating the individual words are included within the last two strings. If the write statement had not included these blanks, i.e., if we had written

```
write('RED','WHITE','BLUE');
```

then the resulting output data would appear as an unbroken sequence of letters, i.e.,

```
REDWHITEBLUE
```

If one write statement is followed by another, then the second write statement will begin where the first one ended. In other words, the first data item written by the second write statement will begin on the current line, immediately after the last data item that was written by the previous write statement. Therefore a new write statement does *not* necessarily generate a new line of output data.

**EXAMPLE 4.12**

A portion of a Pascal program is shown below.

```
VAR a,b : real;
    i,j : integer;
    p,q : char;
    .
    .
    .
write(' a=',a,' b=',b,' i=',i);
write(' j=',j,' p=',p,' q=',q);
```

Suppose that the variables have been assigned the following values.

| Variable | Value |
|----------|-------|
| a | 12500.0 |
| b | −14.8 |
| i | 5 |
| j | −9 |
| p | X |
| q | Y |

Then the resulting output data would appear on one line, as

```
a= 1.2500000E+04 b=-1.4800000E+01 i=        5 j=        -9 p=X q=Y
```

## 4.6  THE WRITELN STATEMENT

The writeln statement is identical to the write statement, except that the writeln statement results in an end-of-line designation being written after the last data item. Therefore any *subsequent* write or writeln statement will begin a new line of output.

The statement is written as

```
writeln(output data items)
```

where the output data items can be strings, numerical constants or the values of variables or expressions of type integer, real, char or boolean.

### EXAMPLE 4.13

Suppose that the write statements in the last example are replaced with writeln statements, i.e.,

```
VAR a,b : real;
    i,j : integer;
    p,q : char;
    .

    .
    .
writeln(' a=',a,' b=',b,' i=',i);
writeln(' j=',j,' p=',p,' q=',q);
```

Then the following *two* lines of output would be generated.

```
a= 1.2500000E+04 b=-1.4800000E+01 i=        5

j=        -9 p=X q=Y
```

Notice that it is the *first* writeln statement that causes the original single line of output to be broken up into two lines. The *second* writeln statement has no effect on this output, though any *subsequent* output would begin on a new line. Therefore, the statements

```
writeln(' a=',a,' b=',b,' i=',i);
write(' j=',j,' p=',p,' q=',q);
```

would produce the same two lines of output shown above, but the statements

```
write(' a=',a,' b=',b,' i=',i);
writeln(' j=',j,' p=',p,' q=',q);
```

would generate the single line of output shown in Example 4.12.

An *empty* writeln statement can be used to generate a blank line, as illustrated in the next example.

**EXAMPLE 4.14**

Consider the following three writeln statements.

```
writeln('line one');
writeln;
writeln('line two');
```

These statements will generate three lines of output (including one blank line), as shown below.

```
line one

line two
```

If the empty writeln statement were not present the blank line would not appear, and the two printed lines would be spaced closer together, i.e.,

```
line one
line two
```

## 4.7  FORMATTED OUTPUT

Output data can usually be made more legible by altering the field widths associated with numerical and boolean-type data. This can easily be accomplished by adding certain *format* features within the write and writeln statements. In particular, each integer, real or boolean item in a write or writeln statement can be followed by a colon and a positive integer quantity which indicates the field width. This quantity can be expressed as a constant, a variable or an expression.

**EXAMPLE 4.15**

A Pascal program contains the following write statement.

```
write('The answer is',sum : 4);
```

Suppose that sum is an integer-type variable whose assigned value is −16. Then the value will be written out using a four-character field width, resulting in the following output.

```
The answer is -16
```

(Notice the blank space preceding the number. This is a part of the four-character field width.)

**EXAMPLE 4.16**

Now suppose that the write statement in the above example is changed to read

```
write('The answer is',sum : j+2);
```

If j is an integer-type variable that has been assigned the value 3, then the resulting field width associated with sum will be five characters, and the output will appear as

```
The answer is  -16
```

(Notice that two blank spaces now precede the number.)

The specified field width is interpreted as the *minimum* field width associated with the data item. If the field width is too large, then the data item is shifted to the right portion of the field, resulting in one or more leading blank spaces. On the other hand, additional space will automatically be added if the field width is too small, thus preventing a part of the data item from being "chopped off."

**EXAMPLE 4.17**

Returning to Example 4.15, suppose that sum had been assigned a value of 3. Then the output would appear as

```
The answer is   3
```

(Notice that the number has been placed within the right portion of the field, resulting in three leading spaces between "is" and "3.")

On the other hand, if sum had been assigned a value of 10000, then the output would appear as

```
The answer is 10000
```

Two additional spaces have now been added to the output field to accommodate the 5-digit number and its preceding sign.

Now suppose that the value −30000 had been assigned to sum. The resulting output would be

```
The answer is−30000
```

A real-type number can be written in a more conventional form (without the exponent) if a second format term is included. Thus the complete format designation for a real number is a colon, followed by an integer indicating the total field width, followed by another colon, followed by another integer indicating the number of places to the right of the decimal point. The decimal part of the number will automatically be rounded when appropriate.

**EXAMPLE 4.18**

Suppose that root is a real-type variable that has been assigned the value 17487.266. This number can be written out in several different ways, as shown below.

| Writeln Statement | Resulting Output |
|---|---|
| `writeln('root=',root);` | root= 1.7487266E+04 |
| `writeln('root=',root : 12);` | root= 1.74873E+04 |
| `writeln('root=',root : 18);` | root= 1.74872660000E+04 |
| `writeln('root=',root : 10 : 3);` | root= 17487.266 |
| `writeln('root=',root : 8 : 1);` | root= 17487.3 |

Pascal also includes the page statement. This is a standard procedure that causes the next printed output item to be displayed at the top of a new page.

**EXAMPLE 4.19**

Suppose a Pascal program contains the following three statements.

```
writeln(a,b,c);
page;
writeln(x,y,z);
```

These statements will cause the values of the variables a, b and c to be printed on one line, followed by the values of the variables x, y and z on another line. The page statement will cause the second line of output to appear at the top of a new page.

Many interactive systems that utilize video monitors do not recognize the page statement (it is simply ignored). With some interactive systems, however, the page statement causes the screen to be cleared.

Some computer systems interpret the first character of each line of output as a *printer-control* character. This character will not be printed but will be used to control the spacing of the line printer.

The following are commonly used printer-control characters.

| Character | Interpretation |
|---|---|
| blank space | Print immediately after the preceding line (single-spaced output). |
| ·0 | Skip one line, then begin to print (double-spaced output). |
| 1 | Skip to the top to the next page, then begin to print |
| + | Print over the previous line. |

**EXAMPLE 4.20**

A Pascal program includes the following writeln statements.

```
writeln(a,b,c);
writeln('1',x,y,z);
```

These statements will cause the values of the variables a, b and c to be printed on one line, followed by the values of the variables x, y and z on a second line. The second line will appear at the top of a new page, however, because of the presence of the printer-control character in the second writeln statement. Thus, the output will be displayed in the same manner as in the preceding example.

If the second writeln statement is altered to read

```
writeln('0',x,y,z);
```

then the two lines of output will appear on the same page, with one blank line in between (the output will be double-spaced).

It should be understood that these printer-control characters are not recognized by all versions of Pascal. The reader should determine whether this feature is available at his or her particular installation.

## 4.8   CLOSING REMARKS

Before leaving this chapter, there are a few general remarks that should be made about the read, readln, write, writeln and page statements.

First, these are actually *standard procedures* that are included as a part of the Pascal language. We have already discussed the use of the various standard procedures and the manner in which they are accessed in Secs. 2.11 and 2.12. The reader is again reminded that the access to a standard procedure is considered to be a type of simple statement. It is in this sense that we refer to the use of these procedures as statements.

Second, it should be understood that these statements actually represent a simple subset of Pascal's input/output capability. We will consider the topic of input/output operations in greater generality when we study files in Chap. 11.

Finally, the reader should appreciate that these simple input/output operations, together with the material that has been covered in earlier chapters, provide us with the ability to write complete, though simple, Pascal programs. The next chapter will contain instructions for organizing, writing and running such programs.

## *Review Questions*

**4.1**    What is an input file? How are data items entered into the input file?

**4.2**    What is an output file? What happens to data items that are entered into the output file?

**4.3**    How are the data items arranged within an input or an output file?

**4.4**    How are the input and output files referred to in a Pascal program?

**4.5**    What is the purpose of the read statement?

**4.6**    In what sense must the data items in the input file correspond to the variables in the read statement?

**4.7**    Summarize the rules for spacing numerical and char-type data items within the input file.

**4.8**    Can boolean-type data be processed with a read statement?

**4.9**    How are data items read from the input file when one read statement follows another?

**4.10**   What is the purpose of the readln statement? How does this statement differ from the read statement?

**4.11**   What happens when a readln statement is preceded by a read statement? What happens when a readln statement is preceded by another readln statement?

**4.12**   What is the purpose of the eoln function? What type of information is provided by this function?

**4.13**   What is the purpose of the eof function? What type of information is provided by this function? How does this function differ from the eoln function?

**4.14**   In general terms, how can the eoln and eof functions be used to read an unspecified number of data items from an input file?

**4.15**   What is the purpose of the write statement? What types of output items can be included in this statement?

**4.16**   Can strings be included within a write statement? Can numerical constants be included? Can expressions be included? Compare with the read statement.

**4.17**   How are real numbers normally displayed when written out by a write statement?

**4.18**   Can boolean-type data be processed with the write statement? Compare with the read statement.

**4.19**   What is meant by a field width? What are the default field widths at your particular installation?

**4.20**   Summarize the rules that apply to the spacing of output data items.

**4.21**   How are data items written to the output file when one write statement follows another?

**4.22**   What is the purpose of the writeln statement? How does this statement differ from the write statement?

**4.23**   What happens when a writeln statement is preceded by a write statement? What happens when a writeln statement is preceded by another writeln statement?

**4.24**   Why might an empty writeln statement be included in a Pascal program? What type of statement would the empty writeln statement most likely follow?

**4.25**   How can a field width be altered in the output file? To what types of data does this apply?

**4.26**   What happens if an output field is wider than necessary for a given data item? What happens if the output field is too narrow?

**4.27**   How can a real number be displayed in standard decimal form (i.e., without an exponent)?

**4.28**   Suppose that a real number is displayed in nonscientific form, and the field is not wide enough for the entire decimal part of the number. Will the decimal be rounded or truncated?

**4.29**   What is the purpose of the page statement? How is this statement interpreted by certain interactive computer systems?

**4.30**   Can printer-control characters be used at your particular computer installation? Which characters are available? What is the purpose of each character?

**4.31**   Has this chapter described *all* of the input/output procedures that are available in Pascal? Explain.

# Solved Problems

**4.32**   The skeletal outline of a complete Pascal program is shown below, with emphasis on the input/output features.

```
PROGRAM sample(input,output);
CONST factor = 12345;
      flag = 'entry point';
VAR i1,i2 : integer;
    r1,r2,r3 : real;
    c1,c2 : char;
    b1 : boolean;
```

(*Program continues on next page*)

```
BEGIN
   .
   .
   .
   readln(i1,i2,r1,r2,c1);
   .
   .
   .
   writeln(' I1=',i1:4, ' I2=',i2:4);
   writeln;
   writeln(' R1=',r1:10:2, ' R2=',r2:10:2, ' R3=',r3:12:4);
   writeln;
   write(' FIRST CHAR IS ',c1,' SECOND CHAR IS ',c2);
   write(' TEST STATUS: ',b1:5);
   .
   .
   .
END.
```

This program will read one line of data (five data items) from the input file and will write three lines of data to the output file. The output data items will be labeled and formatted, and the lines of output will be double-spaced.

**4.33** The following problem situations refer to the constants and variables defined in the preceding problem. Write an appropriate statement, or group of statements, for each situation.

(a) Read the values for i1, r3 and c2 from one line of data.

```
read(i1,r3,c2);
```
or
```
readln(i1,r3,c2);
```
or
```
read(i1);
read(r3);
read(c2);
```

(b) Read the values for i1, r1, r2 and c1 from one line, followed by the values of i2, r3 and c2 from another line.

```
readln(i1,r1,r2,c1);
readln(i2,r3,c2);
```

The second readln statement could be replaced by a read statement, i.e.

```
read(i2,r3,c2);
```

(c) Write the values for the two constants on one line, followed by the values for all of the variables on another line. Do not label the output, but leave a blank space between the two constants. Also, place two blank lines between the two lines of output (i.e., triple space the output).

```
writeln(factor,' ',flag);
writeln;
writeln;
writeln(i1,i2,r1,r2,r3,c1,c2,b1);
```

The last writeln statement could be replaced by a write statement, i.e.

```
write(i1,i2,r1,r2,r3,c1,c2,b1);
```

(d) Write the values of the two constants on one line, followed by the values of i1, r1, r2 and c1 on another line, followed by the values of i2, r3, b1 and c2 on another line. Begin at the top of a new page and double-space the output. Label all of the output items.

```
page;
writeln('Factor=',factor,' Flag=',flag);
writeln;
writeln('I1=',i1,' R1=',r1,' R2=',r2,' C1=',c1);
writeln;
writeln('I2=',i2,' R3=',r3,' B1=',b1,' C2=',c2);
```

If a version of Pascal is being used that supports printer-control characters, then the above statements could also be written as

```
writeln('1Factor=',factor,' Flag=',flag);
writeln('0I1=',i1,' R1=',r1,' R2=',r2,' C1=',c1);
writeln('0I2=',i2,' R3=',r3,' B1=',b1,' C2=',c2);
```

(e) Repeat the previous problem. This time do not label the output data, but format them as follows.

> integer: 5 characters
>
> real: 10 characters, with 3 digits to the right of the decimal point (no exponent)
>
> boolean: 7 characters

Also, precede each string or char-type data item with one blank space.

```
page;
writeln(factor:5,' ',flag);
writeln;
writeln(i1:5, r1:10:3, r2:10:3,' ',c1);
writeln;
writeln(i2:5, r3:10:3, b1:7,' ',c2);
```

It may be possible to rewrite these statements using printer-control characters, as follows.

```
writeln('1',factor:5,' ',flag);
writeln('0',i1:5, r1:10:3, r2:10:3,' ',c1);
writeln('0',i2:5, r3:10:3, b1:7,' ',c2);
```

**4.34** Suppose that an input file contains the following two lines of data.

```
10   0.005   4.66E12ABC

-817   2.7E-3   XYZ
```

What values will be assigned to the variables given in Prob. 4.33(b)?

```
i1=10    r1=0.005    r2=4.66E+12    c1=A

i2=-817    r3=2.7E-03    c2= (blank space)
```

**4.35** Suppose that an input file contains the following four lines of data.

```
10   0.005

4.66E12 ABC  -63  17.7

-75  33.9E  B

C
```

What values will be assigned to the variables given in Prob. 4.33(*b*)?

```
i1=10    r1=0.005    r2=4.66E+12    c1= (blank space)

i2=-75    r3=33.9    c2=E
```

**4.36**  Suppose that the variables listed in Prob. 4.32 have been assigned the following values.

| Variable | Value |
|----------|-------|
| i1 | −630 |
| i2 | 375 |
| r1 | 20.8 |
| r2 | −477300.0 |
| r3 | 0.000185 |
| c1 | $ |
| c2 | 5 |
| b1 | false |

Show how the data will appear in the output file if they are written out in accordance with the writeln statements given in Prob. 4.33(*c*).

```
12345 entry point
(blank line)
(blank line)
 -630     375 2.0800000E+01-4.7730000E+05 1.8500000E-04$5 false
```

**4.37**  Repeat Prob. 4.36, assuming that the output data have been written out in accordance with the writeln statements given in Prob. 4.33(*d*).

```
Factor=12345 Flag=entry point
(blank line)
I1=    -630 R1= 2.0800000E+01 R2=-4.7730000E+05 C1=$
(blank line)
I2=     375 R3= 1.8500000E-04 B1= false C2=5
```

**4.38**  Repeat Prob. 4.36, assuming that the output data have been written out in accordance with the writeln statements given in Prob. 4.33(*e*).

```
12345 entry point
(blank line)
 -630    20.800-477300.000 $
(blank line)
   375     0.000  false 5
```

**4.39**  Here is a portion of a Pascal program.

```
PROGRAM sample2(input,output);
VAR a,b,c,d : integer;
```

(*Program continues on next page*)

```
BEGIN
     .
     .
     .
   readln(a,b,c,d);
     .
     .
     .
   writeln(5*(a+b)/2 : c+2, 10*(a-b)/2 : c+d-1);
     .
     .
     .
END.
```

Suppose that the input file contains the following data.

3    5    4    1

What output will be generated by this program?

The two numerical values are 20 and $-10$, and the corresponding field widths are 6 and 4, respectively. Hence, the output will appear as

20 -10

with four spaces preceding the first number.

# Supplementary Problems

**4.40**    The skeletal outline of a complete Pascal program is shown below.

```
PROGRAM example(input,output);
CONST flag = 'red';
      factor = 0.005;
VAR i1,i2,i3 : integer;
    r1,r2 : real;
    c1,c2,c3,c4 : char;
    b1,b2 : boolean;
BEGIN
     .
     .
     .
   read(i1,i2);
   readln(i3,r1,r2);
   read(c1,c2,c3,c4);
     .
     .
     .
   page;
   writeln(flag,factor);
   writeln;
   write(i1,i2);
   writeln(i3,r1,r2);
   writeln;
   write(c1,c2,c3,c4);
   writeln(b1,b2);
     .
     .
     .
END.
```

In general terms, how must the input data items be entered? How will the output data items appear? Will the output items be separate and distinct from one another?

**4.41** Each of the following problems shows a set of data within an input data file. In each case, what values will be assigned to the variables in Prob. 4.40?

(a)　1　2　3　4.0　5.0

　　　blue　green

(b)　1
　　　2
　　　3
　　　4
　　　5
　　　b
　　　l
　　　u
　　　e

(c)　1　2　3　4.0　5.0　blue

(d)　1　2
　　　3　4
　　　5　blue
　　　green

**4.42** How will the output generated in Prob. 4.40 appear, assuming that the variables have been assigned the following values.

| Variable | Value |
|----------|-------|
| i1 | 100 |
| i2 | −200 |
| i3 | −300 |
| r1 | 400.444 |
| r2 | −500.555 |
| c1 | P |
| c2 | I |
| c3 | N |
| c4 | K |
| b1 | true |
| b2 | false |

**4.43** Suppose that the output statements in Prob. 4.40 are replaced with those shown below.

```
page;
writeln('flag=',flag,' factor=',factor:6:3);
writeln;
write('i1=',i1:4,' i2=',i2:4);
writeln('i3=',i3:4,' r1=',r1:6:1,' r2=',r2:6:1);
writeln;
write('color=',c1,c2,c3,c4);
writeln('b1=',b1:5,' b2=',b2:5);
```

How will the output appear, assuming that the variables are assigned the values shown in the preceding problem?

**4.44**  Now suppose that a version of Pascal is being used that supports the use of printer-control characters, and the output statements in Prob. 4.40 are replaced with those shown below.

```
writeln('1flag=',flag,' factor=',factor:6:3);
writeln('0i1=',i1:5,' i2=',i2:5,' i3=',i3:5);
writeln(' r1=',r1:8:2,' r2=',r2:8:2);
writeln('1color=',c1,c2,c3,c4);
writeln('0b1=',b1:6,' b2=',b2:6);
```

How will the output appear, assuming that the variables are assigned the values shown in Prob. 4.42?

**4.45**  The following problem situations refer to the constants and variables defined in Prob. 4.40. Write an appropriate statement, or group of statements, for each situation.

(a)   Read all of the input data items from one line of data.

(b)   Read the values of i1, r2, c3 and c4 from one line of data.

(c)   Read the integer data items from one line of data, the real data items from another line and the char-type data items from a third line.

(d)   Read each input data item from a separate line.

(e)   Write the values for the two constants and all of the variables on one line. Do not label the output, but place at least one blank space between each data item.

(f)   Repeat the previous problem, with the numerical and boolean data items formatted as follows.

  integer: 4 characters

  real: 8 characters, with 2 digits to the right of the decimal point (no exponent)

  boolean: 6 characters

(g)   Write the values for the two constants on one line, followed by the values of the char-type variables and the boolean-type variables on another line, followed by the the values of the numerical variables on a third line. Do not label the output, but place at least one blank space between each data item. Also, leave a blank line between each line of printed output (i.e., double-space the output).

(h)   Repeat the previous problem. This time label each constant, each numerical value and each boolean data item. Write the char-type data as successive characters, without intervening spaces. Precede these characters with a single label.

(i)   Write the values of flag, i1, r1, c1, c2 and b1 on one line, followed by the values of factor, i2, i3, r2, c3, c4 and b2 on another line. Do not label the output, but place at least one blank space between each data item. Start the first line at the top of a new page, and leave two blank lines between the printed lines of output.

(j)   Repeat the previous problem, with the numerical and boolean data formatted as follows.

  integer: 5 characters

  real: 7 characters, with 2 digits to the right of the decimal point (no exponent)

  boolean: 7 characters

(k)   Write the values for both constants and all of the variables. Begin at the top of a new page, and write each data item on a separate line. Label all of the data items. Format the data as follows.

  integer: 4 characters

  real: 12 characters, with an exponent

  boolean: 5 characters

**4.46**  A portion of a Pascal program is shown below.

```
PROGRAM example2(input,output);
VAR w,x,y,z : integer;
```

*(Program continues on next page)*

```
    BEGIN
      .
      .
      .
    readln(w,x,y,z);
      .
      .
    writeln('SUM=',x+y+z : w,' PRODUCT=',x*y*z : w+3);
      .
      .
      .
    END.
```

Suppose that the input file contains the following values.

3　　10　　20　　30

Show what the output will look like.

# Chapter 5

# Preparing and Running
# a Complete Pascal Program

By now we have learned enough about Pascal to write complete, though simple, Pascal programs. Let us therefore pause briefly from our coverage of new features and devote some attention to the planning, writing and execution of such programs. Moreover, we will consider some of the more subjective aspects of programming, such as logical program development and good programming style, as well as the mechanics of complete program development.

## 5.1 PLANNING A PASCAL PROGRAM

It is essential that the overall program strategy be completely mapped out before any of the detailed programming actually begins. This way the programmer can concentrate initially on the general program logic, without becoming bogged down in the syntactical details of the individual instructions. This overall planning process may then be repeated several times, with more programming detail added at each stage. Thus, the programmer can gradually shift his or her attention from the overall computational strategy to the details of the individual instructions. Such an approach is often referred to as "top-down" programming.

Top-down program organization is normally carried out by developing an informal outline, consisting of phrases (or sentences) that are part English and part Pascal. In its initial stages the amount of Pascal is minimal, consisting only of various keywords that define major program components (e.g., PROGRAM, BEGIN, END). The descriptive English material is then inserted between these keywords, often in the form of program comments. The resulting outline is sometimes referred to as *pseudo code*.

### EXAMPLE 5.1

**Selling Pizzas.** A pizza shop sells pizzas in three sizes: small (10-inch diameter), medium (12-inch diameter) and large (16-inch diameter). A pizza can be purchased plain (with sauce and cheese only), or with extra ingredients such as pepperoni, mushrooms or onions.

The shop owner wishes to develop a computer program that will calculate the selling price of a pizza, given its size and the number of ingredients. The selling price will be 1.5 times the total cost, which is determined by the area of the pizza and the number of ingredients. In particular, the total cost will include a fixed preparation cost, a variable base cost that is proportional to the size of each pizza and an additional variable cost for each extra ingredient. For simplicity, it will be assumed that each extra ingredient has the same cost per unit of area.

Now consider a pizza whose diameter is d, with n extra ingredients. The selling price of this pizza will be determined as

$$price = 1.5 * cost$$

where

$$cost = fixedcost + (basecost * area) + (n * extracost * area)$$

and

$$area = \frac{\pi d^2}{4}$$

Thus, the selling price of the pizza can easily be determined if the various costs are known and the size (i.e., the diameter) and the number of ingredients are specified.

Note that the cost components can either be read into the computer at the start of each problem, along with the size and the number of extra ingredients, or they can be defined as constants within the program. We will do the latter. The reason for this is the assumption that the program will be run many times, with different input values for the diameter and the number of ingredients, but with the same costs.

We can now write the following general program outline.

1.  Specify (define) the various cost components.

2.  Read in the size (diameter) of the pizza and the number of extra ingredients.

3.  Calculate the area of the pizza.

4.  Calculate the overall cost and the selling price.

5.  Write out the final answer (the selling price), along with enough of the input to identify the problem.

If we write this outline in the form of pseudo code, we might obtain

```
PROGRAM pizzas

(* define the cost components as program constants *)

BEGIN

    (* read the diameter and the number of extra ingredients *)

    (* calculate the area of the pizza, the overall cost and the selling price *)

    (* write out the input data and the selling price *)

END.
```

Since this problem is particularly simple the outline does not require any additional refinement. If this were a more complex problem, however, we might write a more detailed version of the pseudo code, showing a finer breakdown of the overall program logic.

Another method that is sometimes used when planning a Pascal program is the "bottom-up" approach. This method may be useful for those programs that make use of self-contained program modules (e.g., user-defined functions and procedures) that will be accessed from other parts of the program. The bottom-up approach is to first develop these program modules in detail, early in the overall planning process. Any subsequent program development can then be based upon the known characteristics of these program modules.

In practice we often use both approaches: bottom-up in developing modules before the main program block, but top-down with respect to the development of each module. The main block will also be developed using a top-down approach in most situations.

## 5.2  WRITING A PASCAL PROGRAM

Once an overall program strategy has been formulated and a program outline has been written, attention can be given to the detailed development of a working Pascal program. At this point the emphasis becomes one of translating each step of the program outline (or each portion of the pseudo code) into one or more equivalent Pascal instructions. This should be a straightforward activity provided the overall program strategy has been thought through carefully and in enough detail.

When writing a complete Pascal program there are, however, several points that must be kept in mind. First, the various declarations and definitions must be entered in the proper order. Second, some care must be given to the features that will be made available to the user (though some of these considerations should be included in the program planning phase). Finally, attention must be given to certain aspects of programming style that are concerned with program organization, clarity and legibility. Let us consider each of these topics in some detail.

In Sec. 1.5 we presented an outline showing the overall structure of a Pascal program. This outline is repeated below, followed by some explanatory comments.

1.  Header

2.  Block

    (*a*)  Declarations
           Labels
           Constants
           Type definitions
           Variables
           Procedures and functions

    (*b*)  Statements

Recall that the header is a one-line item, beginning with the word PROGRAM, followed by the program title and references to any input and output files. The file references are enclosed in parentheses and separated by commas.

The program block consists of a declarations part and an action-statement part. The declarations must be presented in the order given, though all of these various types of declarations need not appear in any single program. In fact, constants and variables are the only types of declarations that have been considered so far. For now, the important point to remember is that constant definitions must precede variable declarations.

Syntactically, considerable latitude is allowed in writing the action statements. The only firm requirement is that the action statements be embedded within one overall compound statement (i.e., BEGIN . . . END). Thus, every program must include one BEGIN . . . END sequence. Other compound statements can be embedded within this overall compound statement if desired. Each compound statement can include a variety of individual action statements or groups of statements. (More about this in the next chapter.)

Some care must be given to the matter of punctuation, particularly the use of the semicolon. The following rules apply.

1.  The semicolon is used as a *separator* (not a *terminator*) in Pascal. Hence it is used between successive statements and declarations, rather than as an ending for each particular statement or declaration.

2.  Special rules apply to BEGIN and END. These two items are actually *brackets* that indicate the beginning and end of a compound statement. Therefore BEGIN need not be followed by a semicolon, and END need not be preceded by a semicolon.

3.  An unnecessary semicolon (e.g., preceding an END bracket) will be interpreted as a *null statement* (i.e., an empty statement). Usually this will have no noticeable effect on the execution of the program, though there are certain situations in which the program logic could be unintentionally altered. Therefore unnecessary semicolons should be avoided.

4.  Every complete program must be terminated by a period. Thus, the final END bracket must be followed by a period.

The Pascal syntax diagrams at the end of this book should be consulted for precise information about the use of punctuation with specific statements.

**EXAMPLE 5.2**

**Selling Pizzas.** Suppose that the pizza pricing problem described in the preceding example makes use of the the following cost data.

$$\text{fixed cost} = \$0.75 \text{ per pizza}$$
$$\text{base cost} = \$0.01 \text{ per square inch}$$
$$\text{cost of each extra item} = \$0.0025 \text{ per square inch}$$

A primitive Pascal program which includes these cost figures is presented below.

```
PROGRAM pizzas(input,output);
CONST pi = 3.14159;
      fixedcost = 0.75;
      basecost = 0.01;
      extracost = 0.0025;
VAR n : integer;
    d,area,cost,price : real;
BEGIN
   readln(d,n);
   area := pi*sqr(d)/4;
   cost := fixedcost + basecost*area + n*extracost*area;
   price := 1.5*cost;
   writeln(d,n,price)
END.
```

Notice that the program includes both constant definitions and variable declarations, with the constant definitions preceding the variable declarations. Also, notice that the definitions, declarations and statements are separated by semicolons, with the semicolons appearing at the end of each line as needed. BEGIN is not followed by a semicolon and END is not preceded by a semicolon, since these two keywords serve as brackets which define the beginning and the end of the single compound statement. Finally, observe the period at the end of the program, as required.

The above program is complete, but it lacks certain desirable features. More complete (and more desirable) versions of this program will therefore be presented in the next two examples.

The reader should understand that there is more to writing a complete Pascal program than simply arranging the individual declarations and statements in the right order and then punctuating them correctly. Attention should also be given to the inclusion of certain subjective features that will improve the readability of the program and its resulting output. These features include the logical sequencing of the statements, the use of indentation, the use of comments and the generation of clearly labeled output.

The logical sequencing of the statements within the program is, to a large extent, determined by the underlying logic of the program. Often, however, there are several different ways to sequence certain statements without altering the program logic. This is particularly true of more complex programs that involve the use of conditional or repeated program segments. In such cases the sequencing of certain statements, or groups of statements, can have a major effect on the logical clarity of the program. Therefore it is important that the statements be sequenced in the most effective manner. We will say more about this in the next chapter, where we discuss the various types of conditional and repetitive features that are available in Pascal.

The use of indentation is closely related to the sequencing of groups of statements within a program. Whereas sequencing affects the order in which a group of operations is carried out, indentation illustrates the subordinate nature of individual statements within a group. The advantages of indentation are fairly obvious, even in the simple programs presented earlier in this book. This will become even more apparent later, as we encounter Pascal programs whose structure is more complex.

Comments should always be included within a Pascal program. If written properly, such comments can provide a useful overview of the general program logic. They can also delineate major segments of a program, identify certain key items within the program and provide other useful information about the program. (Comments of this type can be of great use to a programmer as well as to other persons trying to read and understand a program, since programmers sometimes forget the details of their own programs over a period of time. This is especially true of long, complicated programs.) Frequently, the comments that are placed within a program need not be extensive; a few well-placed comments can shed a great deal of light on an otherwise obscure program.

Another important characteristic of a well-written program is its ability to generate clear, legible output. Two factors contribute to this legibility. The first is labeling of the output data, as we discussed in Chap. 4. The second is the appearance of some of the input data along with the output, so that each set of input data (if there is more than one) can be clearly identified. The manner in which this is accomplished depends upon the environment in which the Pascal program will be executed.

In a noninteractive environment a certain amount of the input data should be written out, in addition to the desired output data. If the input is extensive, only a few key input items should be displayed, just enough to identify each particular problem (i.e., each set of output data).

**EXAMPLE 5.3**

We now present an improved version of the program for pricing pizzas presented in Example 5.2. The present version includes identifying comments and generates output data that are labeled and arranged more legibly than the output generated by the previous program. (Note that the previous program did include the use of indentation, and it did cause the input data to be printed along with the calculated output.)

We will assume that this program will be executed in a noninteractive environment. Therefore we will continue to print out the input data along with the calculated output, in order to identify each problem (in the event that the program is to be run for several different sets of input data).

```
PROGRAM pizzas(input,output);

(* This program calculates the selling price of a pizza,
        given the diameter and the number of extra items. *)

(* Non-interactive version *)

CONST pi = 3.14159;
      fixedcost = 0.75;
      basecost = 0.01;
      extracost = 0.0025;
VAR n : integer;
    d,area,cost,price : real;

BEGIN   (* action statements *)
   readln(d,n);
   area := pi*sqr(d)/4;
   cost := fixedcost + basecost*area + n*extracost*area;
   price := 1.5*cost;
   writeln(' Pizza size (diameter):', d:4:0,' inches');
   writeln(' Number of extra ingredients:', n:2);
   writeln;
   writeln(' The selling price is: $', price:5:2)
END.
```

In an interactive environment the input data will usually be displayed on the terminal at the time of data entry (during program execution). Hence the input data need not be written out again. However, the user may not know how to enter the input data when the program is executing (e.g., what data items are required? When are they entered? In what order?) Thus a well-written interactive program should generate *prompts* (i.e., requests for input data) at appropriate times during the program execution. This can be accomplished by including a number of write (or writeln) statements within the program, as illustrated in the following example.

**EXAMPLE 5.4**

Let us now consider an interactive version of the program presented in Example 5.3. In particular, we will include a set of prompts so that the user will know how to enter the input data during program execution. Also we will no longer write out the input data along with the calculated output, as this is not necessary in an interactive environment.

```
PROGRAM pizzas(input,output);

(* This program calculates the selling price of a pizza,
      given the diameter and the number of extra items. *)

(* Interactive version *)

CONST pi = 3.14159;
      fixedcost = 0.75;
      basecost = 0.01;
      extracost = 0.0025;
VAR n : integer;
    d,area,cost,price : real;

BEGIN   (* action statements *)
   page;
   write(' Enter the pizza size (diameter), in inches: ');
   readln(d);
   write(' Enter the number of extra ingredients: ');
   readln(n);
   area := pi*sqr(d)/4;
   cost := fixedcost + basecost*area + n*extracost*area;
   price := 1.5*cost;
   writeln;
   writeln(' The selling price is: $', price:5:2)
END.
```

The programs shown in the previous two examples were logically very straightforward. Thus we did not have to concern ourselves with alternate ways to sequence the statements. There are, however, some other desirable features that might have been included. For example, we might have chosen to write the various costs (i.e., the values of the constants) along with the calculated results. This information would be useful if the program were executed several times, using different cost data each time.

Another feature that might be quite useful is the ability to execute the program consecutively, for several different sets of input data. We will see how this can be accomplished in the next chapter.

## 5.3   ENTERING THE PROGRAM INTO THE COMPUTER

Once the program has been written it must be entered into the computer before it can be compiled and executed. This is usually accomplished by one of two possible methods, the most common being the use of an *editor*.

Practically all modern computer systems include some type of editor that can be used to enter text files (a *text file* can be a program, a textual document such as a letter, a data file, etc.). Some editors are *line-oriented*, while others are *character-oriented*. Character-oriented editors that are used with interactive video-display devices are often referred to as *screen editors*. Such editors are particularly convenient to use, since they allow large portions of the file to be displayed on the screen at any one time. A flashing *cursor* can easily be moved to any location on the screen, thus facilitating the entry, alteration and deletion of text.

A variety of editors are commonly available for virtually all types of computers. Any editor can be used to enter a Pascal program and its accompanying data files, though some Pascal systems include their own editor. Regardless of the type of editor in use, the procedure for entering the program is to type the Pascal program into the computer on a line-by-line basis. (This can be accomplished with both line-oriented and character-oriented editors.) The program is then assigned a file name and stored in the computer's memory or on an auxiliary storage device. Sometimes a suffix, such as PAS, is attached to the file name, thus identifying the file as a Pascal program. (Such suffixes are often called *extensions*.) The program will remain in this form until it is ready to be processed by the Pascal compiler.

The alternative to the use of an editor is to read a Pascal program into the computer from a deck of punched cards. This is actually a rather outmoded approach to program entry, though the procedure is still utilized on some older mainframe systems. The use of punched cards is less convenient than the use of an editor but is obviously better than nothing at all.

Many large mainframe systems support both batch processing and timesharing, with some form of on-line editing. This allows the user to choose whichever mode of operation is most convenient for the particular task at hand. For example, a new program and its accompanying data may be entered via an editor, but the calculated results (i.e., the contents of the output file) might be routed to a line printer.

The reader should determine what type of program-entry procedure is available at his or her particular installation. If an editor is available, the reader should obtain a manual or other set of instructions that describes exactly how the editor can be used.

## 5.4   COMPILING AND EXECUTING THE PROGRAM

Once a complete program has been correctly entered into the computer, it can then be compiled and executed. The compilation is usually accomplished automatically, in response to a single command (e.g., COMPILE). Sometimes it is also necessary to *link* the compiled object program to one or more library routines in order for the program to be executed. This is also accomplished automatically in most cases, simply by issuing a single command (e.g., LINK).

The successful compilation and linking of a Pascal program will result in an executable (machine language) object program that can now be executed in response to an appropriate system command (e.g., EXECUTE). The details of the execution will differ, however, depending on the type of environment. For example, in a noninteractive environment a separate input data file will be required. This file must be entered into the computer before the object program can be executed. Once the program is executed the input data will automatically be read from the data file and processed, resulting in a set of output data that are automatically stored in an output data file. This output file must then be printed or displayed as a separate operation, after the program execution has been completed.

### EXAMPLE 5.5

Suppose we wish to determine the selling price of a 10-inch pizza with three extra ingredients: mushrooms, pepperoni and onions. We will use the noninteractive Pascal program presented in Example 5.3.

We first type the program into the computer from a terminal using a text editor, being careful to correct any typing errors. The program must be given a recognizable file name, such as PIZZAS.PAS. We then enter the input data file, containing the following two values.

```
10.0   3
```

This file will be stored as a separate entity, under the name

```
INPUT.DAT.
```

We are now ready to compile and link the program. This can be accomplished by entering the single command

```
COMPILE PIZZAS.PAS
```

from the terminal. (The linking will be initiated automatically if the program is compiled successfully.) We will then have a new file, called PIZZAS.OBJ, which will contain the compiled object program. This will, of course, be in addition to the original file, PIZZAS.PAS, which contained the Pascal source program.

To execute the object program, we type the command

```
EXECUTE PIZZAS
```

from the terminal. (The extension .OBJ is not required.) The instructions contained in the original Pascal program will then be carried out, even though it is the object program rather than the original source program that is being executed. Thus, the following things will happen.

1.  The values of d and n will be read from the input file.

2.  The area, overall cost and selling price will be calculated.

3.  The values of d, n and price will be written to the output file.

This concludes the execution portion of the program. In order to see the calculated results, however, it will be necessary to display the output file. Thus, we issue the command

        TYPE OUTPUT.DAT

from the terminal. This will cause the following output to be displayed.

        Pizza size (diameter): 10. inches
        Number of extra ingredients: 3

        The selling price is: $ 3.19

Interactive Pascal programs are executed quite differently. In particular, input data files and output data files are not required. Rather, the input data are entered into the computer during program execution. Similarly, the output data are displayed as they are generated, during program execution. For most applications, this mode is much more convenient.

**EXAMPLE 5.6**

Let us repeat the problem presented in Example 5.5 using the interactive Pascal program presented in Example 5.4. The program will now be run on a personal computer with a software system that includes an editor and a Pascal compiler.

We again type the program into the computer using a text editor, being careful to correct any typing errors. The program is then stored as a text file under the name PIZZAS.PAS. Now, however, we need not bother with an input data file. Rather, we procede to compile and link the program by entering the commands

        COMPILE PIZZAS.PAS

        LINK PIZZAS

If the COMPILE and LINK commands are carried out successfully we will have generated an object program (PIZZAS.OBJ), and we can then proceed with the execution. Otherwise, it will be necessary to return to the source program (PIZZAS.PAS), make any necessary corrections (via the editor) and then begin all over again. (This repetitive procedure must, of course, be followed in noninteractive as well as interactive versions of Pascal.)

Now let us assume that the compilation and linking have been carried out successfully. To execute the program, we type the command

        EXECUTE PIZZAS

The instructions contained in the original Pascal program will then begin to be carried out. In particular, the computer will prompt for the pizza size by generating the following message on the console.

        Enter the pizza size (diameter), in inches:

The user then responds by typing the value 10.0. The computer will then prompt for the number of extra items by generating the message

        Enter the number of extra ingredients:

The user now enters the value 3 in response to this prompt.

All of the required input data have now been entered. Therefore the area, overall cost and selling price are calculated and the selling price is displayed as follows.

        The selling price is: $ 3.19

Notice that the final answer is displayed directly as it is calculated; there is no need for an output data file.

The entire interactive session is summarized below. The user's responses are underlined for clarity.

```
(program statements . . . entered via an editor)

COMPILE PIZZAS.PAS

LINK PIZZAS

EXECUTE PIZZAS

Enter the pizza size (diameter), in inches: 10.0
Enter the number of extra ingredients: 3

The selling price is: $ 3.19
```

The procedures shown in the above two examples are representative of those that are commonly used, though there may be some variation from one computer to another. For example, some Pascal systems support a single command (e.g., RUN) that will cause a Pascal source program to be compiled, linked and executed in succession. In such cases a given operation will be initiated only if the previous operations have been completed. The reader should determine the specific compilation, linking and execution commands that are available with his or her particular computer.

Finally, the reader is again reminded that the successful compilation, linking and execution of a Pascal program usually requires several attempts because of errors that are invariably present in most new programs. This is true of programs written by experienced programmers as well as by beginners. Thus the entire procedure may seem tedious, particularly to the beginning programmer. It should be understood, however, that the frequency of such errors will decrease as the programmer gains a modest amount of experience. Beginners are therefore cautioned against becoming unduly discouraged with their first few programs, as things really do get better.

## 5.5 ERROR DIAGNOSTICS

Programming errors often remain undetected until an attempt is made to compile the program. Once the COMPILE command has been issued, however, the presence of certain errors will become readily apparent, since these errors will prevent the program from being compiled successfully. Some particularly common errors of this type are improperly declared constants or variables, a reference to an undeclared variable and incorrect punctuation. Such errors are referred to as *syntactical* (or *grammatical*) errors.

Most versions of Pascal will generate a diagnostic message when a syntactical error has been detected. (The compiler will usually come to an abrupt halt when this happens.) These diagnostic messages are not always completely straightforward in their meaning, but they are nevertheless helpful in identifying the nature and location of the error.

**EXAMPLE 5.7**

Here is another version of the interactive Pascal program shown in Example 5.4 which calculates the selling price of a pizza, given the pizza size (diameter) and the number of extra ingredients. This program differs from the earlier version only in that the present version contains several syntactical errors.

When a compilation was attempted the following list of messages was obtained.

```
PROGRAM pizzas(input,output);

(* This program calculates the selling price of a pizza,
        given the diameter and the number of extra items.

(* Interactive version *)
```

(*Program continues on next page*)

```
           CONST pi = 3.14159
                 fixedcost = 0.75;
                              ^

****** ERROR 346 MISSING ;
                 basecost := 0.01;
                                ^

****** WARNING 149 := ASSUMED =
                 extracost = 0.0025;
             VAR n : integer;
                 d,area,cost,price = real;
                                   ^

****** WARNING 148 = ASSUMED :

           BEGIN   (* action statements *)
             page;
             write(' Enter the pizza size (diameter), in inches: );
                                                                 ^

****** WARNING 105 END OF STRING NOT FOUND

****** WARNING 169 INSERT )
             readln(d);
                 ^

****** ERROR 185 INVALID SYMBOL BEGIN SKIP
          ^

****** WARNING 164 INSERT ;
          ^

****** ERROR 186 END SKIP
          ^

****** ERROR 185 INVALID SYMBOL BEGIN SKIP
           ^

****** ERROR 186 END SKIP
             write(' Enter the number of extra ingredients: ');
             readln(n);
             area = pi*sqr(d)/4;
                 ^

****** WARNING 150 = ASSUMED :=
             cost := fixedcost + basecost*area + n*extracost*area
                                                                ^

****** WARNING 164 INSERT ;
             price := 1.5cost;
                 ^

****** ERROR 185 INVALID SYMBOL BEGIN SKIP
                ^

****** ERROR 186 END SKIP
             writeln;
             writeln(' The selling price is: $', price,5,2)
           END
          ^

****** ERROR 146 UNEXPECTED END OF FILE

****** FATAL PROGRAM ERRORS - COMPILER CANNOT CONTINUE!
```

Several points must be made. First, note that the error messages are often cryptic; some are difficult to understand. Second, notice that several of the errors are corrected automatically. These corrections are identified as WARNINGS rather than ERROR messages. Finally, note that the missing *) at the end of the first comment has gone undetected (the two comments are interpreted as one long comment containing embedded parentheses).

The specific error messages and warnings will vary from one version of Pascal to another. These are merely representative.

Syntactical errors are usually very obvious because of the diagnostics that they generate. Much more insidious, however, are *logical* errors. Here the program correctly conveys the programmer's instructions, free of syntactical errors, but the programmer has supplied the computer with a set of instructions that is logically incorrect.

Sometimes a logical error will result in a condition that can be recognized by the computer. Such a situation might result from the generation of an excessively large numerical quantity (exceeding the largest permissible number that can be stored in the computer), or from an attempt to compute the square root of a negative number, etc. Diagnostic messages will normally be generated in situations of this type, making it easy to identify and correct the errors. These diagnostics are sometimes called *execution* diagnostics, to distinguish them from the *compilation* diagnostics described earlier.

**EXAMPLE 5.8**

**Real Roots of a Quadratic Equation.** Suppose we want to calculate the real roots of the quadratic equation

$$ax^2 + bx + c = 0$$

using the quadratic formula

$$x = \frac{-b \pm \sqrt{b^2 - 4ac}}{2a}$$

Here is a Pascal program that will carry out these calculations.

```
PROGRAM realroots(input,output);

(* This program calculates the real roots of a quadratic equation *)

VAR a,b,c,d,x1,x2 : real;

BEGIN   (* action statements *)
   readln(a,b,c);
   d := sqr(b)-4*a*c;
   x1 := (-b+sqrt(d))/(2*a);
   x2 := (-b-sqrt(d))/(2*a);
   writeln(' a=',a,'   b=',b,'   c=',c);
   writeln;
   writeln(' x1=',x1,'   x2=',x2)
END.
```

This program is completely free of syntactical errors, but it is unable to accommodate negative values for sqr(b) − 4 a*c.

Furthermore, numerical difficulties may be encountered if the variable a has a very small or a very large numerical value, or if a = 0. An execution diagnostic will be generated in each case.

Suppose, for example, that the program is run with the following input values:

```
a=1.0      b=2.0      c=3.0
```

The program compiles without any difficulty. When the object program is executed, however, the following error message is generated.

```
? Error: SQRT of Negative Argument
   Error Code 2104
```

Everything then comes to a halt, since the program execution cannot continue beyond this point.

Similarly, suppose that the program is run with the input values

```
a=1E-30    b=1E+10    c=1E+36
```

The system now generates the error message

```
? Error: REAL Math Overflow
   Error Code 2101
```

when an attempt is made to execute the program.

## 5.6  LOGICAL DEBUGGING

We have just seen that syntactical errors and certain types of logical errors will cause diagnostic messages to be generated when compiling or executing a program. Errors of this type are easy to find and correct. Some types of logical errors can be much more difficult to detect, however, since the output resulting from a logically incorrect program may appear to be error-free. Moreover, logical errors are often hard to find even when they are known to exist (as, for example, when the computed output is obviously incorrect). Thus a good bit of detective work may be required in order to find and correct errors of this type. Such detective work is known as *logical debugging*.

### Detecting Errors

The first step in attacking logical errors is to find out if they are present. This can sometimes be accomplished by testing a new program with data that will yield a known answer. If the correct results are not obtained, then the program obviously contains errors. Even if the correct results are obtained, however, one cannot be absolutely certain that the program is error-free, since some errors cause incorrect results only under certain circumstances (as, for example, with certain values of the input data or with certain program options). Therefore a new program should receive thorough testing before it is considered to be debugged. This is especially true of complicated programs or programs that will be used extensively by others.

As a rule, a calculation will have to be carried out by hand, with the aid of a calculator, in order to obtain a known answer. For some problems, however, the amount of work involved in carrying out a hand calculation is prohibitive. (Remember, a calculation that requires a few minutes of computer time may require several weeks to solve by hand!) Therefore a sample calculation cannot always be developed to test a new program. The logical debugging of such programs can be particularly difficult, though an observant programmer can often detect the presence of logical errors by studying the computed results carefully to see if they are reasonable.

### Correcting Errors

Once it has been established that a program contains a logical error, some resourcefulness and ingenuity may be required to find the error. Error detection should always begin with a thorough review of each logical group of statements within the program. Armed with the knowledge that an error exists somewhere, the programmer can often spot the error by such careful study. If the error cannot be found, it sometimes helps to set the program aside for a while. (This is especially true if the programmer is experiencing some fatigue or frustration.) It is not unusual for an overly intent programmer to miss an obvious error the first time around.

If an error cannot be located simply by inspection, the program should be modified to print out certain intermediate results and then rerun. (This technique is sometimes referred to as *tracing*.) The source of error will often become evident once these intermediate calculations have been carefully examined. In particular, the programmer can usually identify the particular area within the program where things begin to go wrong. The greater the amount of intermediate output, the more likely the chances of pinpointing the source of error.

Sometimes an error simply cannot be located, despite the most elaborate debugging techniques. On such occasions beginning programmers are often inclined to suspect a problem that is beyond their control, such as a hardware error or an error in the compiler. In almost all cases, however, the problem turns out to be some subtle error in the program logic. Thus the beginning programmer should resist the temptation to simply blame the computer and not look further for that elusive programming error. (Hardware errors do occur on rare occasions, though they usually produce very bizarre results, such as the computer "dying" or the terminal spewing out random, unintelligible characters. Also, compiler errors occasionally crop up with a new compiler but are usually corrected after a compiler has been in use for a while.)

Finally, the reader should recognize the fact that some logical errors are inescapable in computer programming, though a conscientious programmer will make every attempt to minimize their occurrence. The programmer should therefore anticipate the need for some logical debugging when writing realistic, meaningful Pascal programs.

**EXAMPLE 5.9**

**Evaluating a Polynomial.** A student has written a Pascal program to evaluate the polynomial

$$y = \left(\frac{x-1}{x}\right) + \frac{1}{2}\left(\frac{x-1}{x}\right)^2 + \frac{1}{3}\left(\frac{x-1}{x}\right)^3 + \frac{1}{4}\left(\frac{x-1}{x}\right)^4 + \frac{1}{5}\left(\frac{x-1}{x}\right)^5$$

To simplify the programming the student has defined a new variable $u$ as

$$u = \left(\frac{x-1}{x}\right)$$

so that the formula becomes

$$y = u + \frac{u^2}{2} + \frac{u^3}{3} + \frac{u^4}{4} + \frac{u^5}{5}$$

Here is the student's complete Pascal program.

```
PROGRAM formula(input,output);

(* Program to evaluate an algebraic formula *)

VAR u,x,y : real;
BEGIN
   readln(x);
   u := x-1/x;
   y := u+sqr(u/2)+(u/3)*sqr(u/3)+sqr(u/4)*sqr(u/4)+(u/5)*sqr(u/5)*sqr(u/5);
   writeln(' x=',x,'      y=',y)
END.
```

The student knows that y should have a value of about 0.69 when x=2, but the output generated by the program appears as follows.

```
x= 2.0000000E+00     y= 2.2097050E+00
```

The student concludes, therefore, that the program contains logical errors, which must be found and corrected.

After careful inspection of the program the student realized that the first assignment statement is incorrect. This statement should have been written as

```
u := (x-1)/x;
```

The student then corrected the program and reran it, again using a value of x=2. The output,

```
x= 2.0000000E+00     y= 5.6738380E-01
```

indicates that a logical error is still present.

After some additional study the student discovered that the second assignment statement is also incorrect. This statement should appear as

```
y := u+sqr(u)/2+(u*sqr(u))/3+(sqr(u)*sqr(u))/4+(u*sqr(u)*sqr(u))/5;
```

The program was then modified and rerun, resulting in the correct answer (finally!), as indicated below.

```
x= 2.0000000E+00     y= 6.8854160E-01
```

## Review Questions

**5.1**     What is meant by top-down programming? What are its advantages? How is it carried out?

**5.2**     What is pseudo code?

**5.3**     What is meant by bottom-up programming? How does it differ from top-down programming?

**5.4**     Summarize the overall structure of a Pascal program.

**5.5**     How is the semicolon used in Pascal? Where must it appear?

**5.6**     What is the purpose of BEGIN and END? What punctuation is associated with these two keywords?

**5.7**     What special punctuation mark must appear at the end of every Pascal program?

**5.8**     How much flexibility does the programmer have in the logical sequencing of the statements within a Pascal program? Explain.

**5.9**     Why are some statements indented within a Pascal program? Is this indentation absolutely necessary?

**5.10**    What are the reasons for placing comments within a Pascal program? How extensive should these comments be?

**5.11**    Name two factors that contribute to the generation of clear, legible output data.

**5.12**    Explain how the programming environment (i.e., interactive vs. noninteractive) influences the particular input/output features that are included within the program.

**5.13**    What is a prompt? Under what conditions should the use of prompts be included in a Pascal program?

**5.14**    What is a text file?

**5.15**    What is the difference between a line-oriented editor and a character-oriented editor?

**5.16**    Cite two different ways for entering a Pascal program into the computer. Which method is preferable?

**5.17**    What is the difference between compilation and execution of a Pascal program?

**5.18**    What is meant by linking? How does linking differ from compilation?

**5.19**    Cite some major differences in the way that a Pascal program will be executed, depending on whether or not the computing environment is interactive.

**5.20**    What is meant by a syntactical error?

**5.21**   What is meant by a logical error? How do syntactical errors and logical errors differ from one another?

**5.22**   Name some common syntactical errors.

**5.23**   Name some common logical errors.

**5.24**   What are diagnostic messages?

**5.25**   What is the difference between compilation diagnostics and execution diagnostics? Name some situations in which each type of diagnostic message would be generated.

**5.26**   What is meant by logical debugging? Name some common debugging procedures.

**5.27**   What is meant by tracing? In what way is tracing useful?

# Problems

The following exercises are concerned with information gathering rather than actual problem solving.

**5.28**   If timesharing is used at your particular school or office, obtain answers to the following questions.

(a)   Are video-display terminals available? Are hard-copy terminals available?

(b)   How can a terminal be turned on and off?

(c)   How can a single character be deleted from a typed line before it has been sent to the computer? How can an entire line be deleted?

(d)   How can a typed line be transmitted to the computer?

(e)   Can a hard copy of your timesharing session be obtained? If so, how?

(f)   Is a telephone dialup required to establish a connection with the computer? If so, what is the dialup procedure?

(g)   Exactly how do you log on and log off of your computer?

(h)   Can your timesharing terminal be operated in a local mode (i.e., as a stand-alone device, independent of the computer)? If so, how is this done?

(i)   What editor or editors are available on your system? How are normal editing functions (i.e., insert, delete, etc.) carried out?

(j)   How can Pascal be accessed on your system? What procedures are required to compile, link and execute a Pascal program?

(k)   How much does it cost to use your particular computer?

**5.29**   If batch processing is used at your particular school or office, obtain answers to the following questions.

(a)   Are keypunch machines available? If so, how are they turned on and off? How are cards fed through the machines? How is a card punched? How can a card be reproduced?

(b)    Where is the card reader located? How can a deck of punched cards be read by the card reader?

(c)    What control cards are required at your particular installation?

(d)    How is the Pascal system accessed? What procedures are required to compile, link and execute a Pascal program?

(e)    How can a program or a datafile be stored in your system? How can a program or datafile be accessed? How can it be deleted?

(f)    Where is the line printer located? What does the printed output look like?

(g)    What does it cost to use your particular computer?

5.30    If personal computers are used at your particular school or office, obtain answers to the following questions.

(a)    Exactly what equipment is available (printers, auxiliary memory devices, etc.)?

(b)    How can the computer be turned on and off?

(c)    How can programs be saved, displayed and transferred from one memory device to another?

(d)    How can a single character be deleted from a typed line before it has been sent to the computer? How can an entire line be deleted?

(e)    How can a typed line be transmitted to the computer?

(f)    How is the editor accessed? How are normal editing functions (i.e., insert, delete, etc.) carried out?

(g)    How is the Pascal system accessed on your computer? What procedures are required to compile, link and execute a Pascal program?

(h)    What is the cost of your particular computer system?

## Programming Problems

5.31    Example 1.7 presents a Pascal program for calculating the area of a circle, given its radius. Enter this program into your computer. Be sure to correct any typing errors. List the program after it has been stored within the computer. When you are sure that it is correct, compile the program and then execute the object program using several different values for the radius. Verify that the computed answers are correct by comparing them with hand calculations.

5.32    Repeat Prob. 5.31 for one or more of the programs given in Prob. 1.31.

5.33    Examples 5.3 and 5.4 present two different versions of a Pascal program for determining the selling price of a pizza, given the size of the pizza and the number of extra ingredients. Choose the version of the program that is appropriate for your particular computing environment. Enter the program into the computer and save it; then run the program using several different sets of input data. Use the computed results to prepare a menu, such as you would expect to see in a pizza shop, showing the prices for each pizza size with different numbers of extra items.

5.34    Write a complete Pascal program for each of the following problem situations. Enter each program into the computer, being sure to correct any typing errors. Save and then list the program. When you are sure that it has been entered correctly, compile and then execute the program. Repeat as often as necessary in order to obtain an error-free program. Use conversational-style programming wherever appropriate.

(a)   Print HELLO! at the beginning of a line.

(b)   Have the computer print

HI, WHAT'S YOUR NAME?

on one line. The user then enters his or her name immediately after the question mark. The computer then skips two lines and prints

WELCOME (name)

LET'S BE FRIENDS!

on two consecutive lines. Assume the user's name is exactly six characters long (add trailing blanks if necessary).

(c)   Convert a temperature reading in Fahrenheit degrees to Celsius, using the formula

$$C = (5/9)*(F-32)$$

Test the program with the following values: 68, 150, 212, 0, $-22$, $-200$ (degrees Fahrenheit).

(d)   Determine how much money (in dollars) is in a piggy bank that contains $n_1$ half-dollars, $n_2$ quarters, $n_3$ dimes, $n_4$ nickels and $n_5$ pennies. Use the following values to test your program: $n_1 = 11$, $n_2 = 7$, $n_3 = 3$, $n_4 = 12$, $n_5 = 17$ (Answer: 8.32 dollars).

(e)   Calculate the volume and area of a sphere using the formulas

$$V = \frac{4\pi r^3}{3}$$

$$A = 4\pi r^2$$

Test the program using the following values for the radius: 6, 12.2, 0.2.

(f)   Calculate the mass of air in an automobile tire, using the formula

$$PV = 0.37m(T + 460)$$

where   $P$ = pressure, pounds per square inch
        $V$ = volume, cubic feet
        $m$ = mass of air, pounds
        $T$ = temperature, degrees Fahrenheit

The tire contains 2 cubic feet of air. Assume that the pressure is 32 pounds per square inch at room temperature.

(g)   Read a five-letter word into the computer, then encode the word on a letter-by-letter basis by subtracting 30 from the numerical value that is used to represent each letter. Thus if the ASCII character set is being used, the letter a (which is represented by the value 97) would become a C (represented by the value 67), and so on.

        Write out the encoded version of the word. Test the program with the following words: white, roses, Japan, zebra. *Hint*: Note that C=chr(ord(a)−30)

(h)   Read into the computer a five-letter word that has been encoded using the scheme described above. Decode the word by reversing the above procedure, then write out the decoded word.

# Chapter 6

# Control Structures

In all of the Pascal programs that we have encountered so far, each instruction was executed once and once only, in the same order that it appeared within the program. Programs of this type are unrealistically simple since they do not include any logical control structures, such as tests to determine if certain conditions are true or false, the repeated execution of groups of statements or the selection of one group of statements out of several different possibilities. Yet most programs that are of practical interest make extensive use of such features. Thus, we must learn to utilize logical control structures in our programs so that we can consider more interesting and realistic problem situations.

For example, many programs require that a group of consecutive instructions be executed repeatedly until some logical condition has been satisfied. Generally the required number of repetitions will not be known in advance. This type of repetition is known as *conditional looping*. A related operation is *unconditional looping* (or just plain *looping*), in which the execution of a group of consecutive instructions is repeated some specified number of times. Another situation that arises frequently is the need to carry out a logical test and then take some particular action which depends upon the outcome of that test. This is known as *conditional execution*. And finally, there is a special kind of conditional execution in which a particular group of statements is chosen from several available groups. This is sometimes referred to as *selection*.

All of these operations can easily be carried out in Pascal. We will see how this is accomplished in this chapter. The use of this material will open the door to a much broader and more interesting class of programming problems.

## 6.1 PRELIMINARIES

Before considering the details of the Pascal control structures, let us review certain concepts that were presented in Chaps. 2 and 3. These concepts must be used in conjunction with the control structures; hence their understanding is essential before we can proceed further.

First, recall that a boolean expression represents a condition that is either true or false (see Sec. 2.10). Boolean expressions are formed by combining operands of the same type (any type *other than boolean*) with one of the seven *relational operators*: =, <>, <, <=, >, >=, and IN (see Sec. 3.4). So far we have discussed only the first six relational operators; the seventh (IN) will be deferred until we reach Chap. 12.

**EXAMPLE 6.1**

Several boolean expressions are shown below.

```
count <= 100

sqrt(a+b+c) > 0.005

answer = 0

balance >= cutoff

ch1 < 'T'
```

The first four expressions involve numerical operands. Their meaning should be readily apparent.

In the last expression, ch1 is assumed to be a char-type variable. This expression will be true if the character represented by ch1 "comes before" T in the character set; i.e., if ord(ch1) < ord('T'). Otherwise, the expression will be false.

In addition to the relational operators, Pascal contains three *logical operators* (OR, AND and NOT) that are used with boolean operands (Sec. 3.4). The first two (OR and AND) are used to combine boolean operands to form logical expressions; the third (NOT) is a prefix that is used to negate a boolean operand.

### EXAMPLE 6.2

Here are some boolean expressions that illustrate the use of the logical operators.

```
(count <= 100) AND (ch1 <> '*')

(balance < 1000.0) OR (status = 'R')

(answer < 0) OR ((answer > 5.0) AND (answer < 10.0))

(pay >= 1000.0) AND (NOT single)
```

Note that ch1 and status are assumed to be char-type variables in these examples, and single is assumed to be boolean. The remaining variables are assumed to be numeric (either integer or real).

Also, notice that the boolean operands are enclosed in parentheses to avoid any ambiguities in the order in which the operations are carried out.

Recall also that there are two basic types of statements in Pascal—*simple* and *structured* (see Sec. 2.11). Simple statements refer to assignment statements, procedure references and the GOTO statement. We have already discussed assignment statements and procedure references in Secs. 2.11 and 2.12; the GOTO statement will be discussed at the end of this chapter.

Of greater importance at this time are structured statements, since most of the Pascal control structures fall into this category. We will present a detailed discussion of each of these control structures later in this chapter. For now, however, let us recall our earlier discussion of one type of structured statement, the compound statement.

A *compound statement* consists of a sequence of two or more consecutive statements enclosed within the keywords BEGIN and END and separated by semicolons. The individual statements that comprise the compound statement can themselves be simple or structured. Thus, individual structured statements (i.e., control structures) can be included within a compound statement. Moreover, one compound statement can be embedded within another.

### EXAMPLE 6.3

Here is an elementary compound statement which we have seen before.

```
BEGIN
    read(radius);
    area := 3.14159*sqr(radius);
    write(radius,area)
END
```

Here is a more complex compound statement.

```
BEGIN
    sum := 0;
    FOR count := 1 TO n DO
        BEGIN
            read(x);
            sum := sum+x
        END;
    write(' sum = ',sum)
END
```

Notice that the second compound statement includes the FOR control structure. (We will discuss the details of this control structure later in this chapter; see Sec. 6.4.) Also, notice that a smaller compound statement is embedded within the FOR control structure. Thus we see an example of a compound statement embedded within a control structure which is included within another compound statement.

The control structures presented in this chapter will make extensive use of both boolean expressions and compound statements.

## 6.2 THE WHILE—DO STRUCTURE

The WHILE—DO structure is a repetitive control structure that is used to carry out conditional looping. The general form of this structure is

        WHILE *boolean expression* DO *statement*

The statement part of the structure will be executed repeatedly, as long as the boolean expression remains true. This statement can be simple or structured, though it is usually a compound statement that includes some feature that can alter the value of the boolean expression.

Suppose, for example, that we wanted to write out the integer quantities 1, 2, . . . , 20, with one quantity on each line. This could be accomplished with the following WHILE—DO structure.

```
digit := 1;
WHILE digit <= 20 DO
    BEGIN
        writeln(digit);
        digit := digit + 1
    END;
```

where digit is assumed to be an integer-type variable. We therefore begin with a value of digit = 1. We proceed to write out the current value of digit, increase its value by 1 and then repeat the cycle. This process is continued as long as (i.e., WHILE) the value assigned to digit does not exceed 20.

The net effect of this WHILE—DO structure is that the process of writing and incrementing will be repeated 20 times, resulting in 20 successive lines of output. Each line will contain a successive integer value, beginning with 1 and ending with 20.

Similarly, suppose that we wanted to determine the sum of the first n integer quantities, where n is a known integer-type variable. This could be accomplished by writing

```
sum := 0;
digit := 1;
WHILE digit <= n DO
    BEGIN
        sum := sum + digit;
        digit := digit + 1
    END;
```

or, equivalently,

```
sum := 0;
digit := 1;
WHILE digit < n+1 DO
    BEGIN
        sum := sum + digit;
        digit := succ(digit)
    END;
```

where sum and digit (as well as n) are assumed to be integer-type variables.

In either case, we begin with a value of sum = 0, and then proceed to add successive values of digit to sum. The process of adding the current value of digit to sum and then increasing the value of digit by 1 will continue as long as (i.e., WHILE) the current value of digit is less than n + 1. At the conclusion of this process, sum will represent the sum of the first n integer quantities; i.e., $1 + 2 + 3 + \cdots + n$.

The WHILE—DO structure is used extensively in Pascal, as there are many programming applications that require this type of conditional looping capability. We will see many sample programs that utilize the WHILE—DO structure throughout this text.

**EXAMPLE 6.4**

**Averaging a List of Numbers.** Let us use the WHILE—DO structure to obtain the average of a list of n numbers. Our strategy will be based upon the use of a partial sum that is initially set equal to zero and is then updated as each new number is read into the computer. Thus, the problem very naturally lends itself to the use of repetition.

The actual calculations can be carried out in the following manner.

1. Assign a value of 1 to the integer variable count. (This variable will be used as a loop counter.)
2. Assign a value of 0 to the real variable sum.
3. Read in the value for n.
4. Do the following steps repeatedly, as long as the counter does not exceed n (i.e., while the value of count is less than n + 1).
   (a) Read in one of the numbers in the list. (Each number will be represented by the real variable x.)
   (b) Add the number to the value of sum.
   (c) Increase the value of count by 1.
5. Divide the value of sum by n to obtain the desired average.
6. Write out the calculated value for the average.

Here is the actual Pascal program.

```
PROGRAM average1(input,output);

(* This program calculates the average of n numbers
   using a WHILE - DO structure. *)

VAR n,count : integer;
    x,sum,average : real;

BEGIN   (* action statements *)
  count := 1;
  sum := 0;
  readln(n);
  WHILE count < n+1 DO
    BEGIN
      readln(x);
      sum := sum+x;
      count := count+1
    END;   (* count < n+1 *)
  average := sum/n;
  writeln(' The average is ',average)
END.
```

Notice that the WHILE—DO structure contains a compound statement which, among other things, causes the value of count to increase. Eventually, this will cause the boolean expression

```
count < n+1
```

to become false, thus terminating the loop.

Also, note that the loop will not be executed at all if n is assigned a value that is less than 1. Physically, of course, it would not make any sense to do this.

Finally, notice that the innermost compound statement is indented within the WHILE—DO structure. This causes the physical extent of the WHILE—DO structure to be readily identifiable.

## 6.3  THE REPEAT—UNTIL STRUCTURE

The REPEAT—UNTIL structure is another repetitive control structure that is used to carry out conditional looping. It is similar to the WHILE—DO structure, and in some respects these two control structures complement one another.

The general form of the REPEAT—UNTIL structure is

    REPEAT *sequence of statements* UNTIL *boolean expression*

The sequence of statements will be executed repeatedly until the boolean expression becomes true. Note that the sequence of statements will always be executed at least once, since the boolean expression is not tested until the *end* of the control structure. (This is in contrast to the WHILE—DO structure, where the boolean expression is tested at the *beginning* of the control structure. The WHILE—DO structure will not be executed at all if the boolean expression is initially false.)

Notice that this structure allows a *sequence* of statements to be included, whereas the WHILE—DO structure permits only one statement (though it can be compound). The sequence of statements within the REPEAT—UNTIL structure need *not* be included within BEGIN and END. Thus, the keywords REPEAT and UNTIL act as brackets that indicate the beginning and the end of the statement sequence. It is possible, of course, to include a compound statement or another control structure within this sequence. In addition, the sequence of statements will usually include some feature that will alter the value of the boolean expression.

To illustrate the use of the REPEAT—UNTIL structure, consider once again the problem of writing out the integer quantities $1, 2, \ldots, 20$, with one quantity on each line. We have already seen how this can be accomplished using the WHILE—DO structure (see Sec. 6.2). Now let us utilize the REPEAT—UNTIL structure for the same purpose.

```
digit := 1;
REPEAT
    writeln(digit);
    digit := digit + 1
UNTIL digit > 20;
```

Again, digit is assumed to be an integer-type variable.

We again begin with a value of digit = 1, and then proceed to write out the current value of digit, increase its value by 1 and then repeat the cycle. The process is continued UNTIL the current value of digit (which was just increased in value) exceeds 20.

The net effect of this REPEAT—UNTIL structure will be the same as the corresponding WHILE—DO structure presented in the last section. Thus, 20 successive lines of output will be generated, with each line showing a successive integer value.

Now let us consider the use of a REPEAT—UNTIL structure to determine the sum of the first n integer quantities, where n is a known integer-type variable (see Sec. 6.2). The required structure is

```
sum := 0;
digit := 1;
REPEAT
    sum := sum + digit;
    digit := succ(digit)
UNTIL digit > n;
```

Again, sum and digit (as well as n) are assumed to be integer-type variables.

In this case we begin with a value of sum = 0, and then proceed to add successive values of digit to sum. The process of adding the current value of digit to sum and then increasing the value of digit by 1 will continue UNTIL the current value of digit exceeds n. At this time, sum will represent the sum of the first n integer quantities; i.e., $1 + 2 + 3 + \cdots + n$.

The REPEAT—UNTIL structure, like the WHILE—DO structure, is used extensively in Pascal. Sometimes the choice of one structure over the other is simply a matter of personal preference. In other applications, however, the choice is influenced by the desirability of testing the boolean expression either at the beginning or at the end of the control structure.

**EXAMPLE 6.5**

**Averaging a List of Numbers.** Now let us use the REPEAT—UNTIL structure to obtain the average of a list of n numbers. This is the same problem that we considered in Example 6.4, using WHILE—DO. Our approach will therefore be similar to that used in Example 6.4, making allowances for the different control structure.

The actual calculations can be carried out as follows.

1. Assign a value of 1 to the integer variable count. (This variable will be used as a loop counter.)
2. Assign a value of 0 to the real variable sum.
3. Read in the value for n.
4. Repeat the following steps, until the counter exceeds n.
   (a) Read in one of the numbers in the list. (Each number will be represented by the real variable x.)
   (b) Add this number to the value of sum.
   (c) Increase the value of count by 1.
5. Divide the value of sum by n to obtain the desired average.
6. Write out the calculated value for the average.

Note the similarity between this outline and that presented in Example 6.4.

The corresponding Pascal program is shown below.

```
PROGRAM average2(input,output);

(* This program calculates the average of n numbers
   using a REPEAT - UNTIL structure. *)

 VAR n,count : integer;
     x,sum,average : real;

BEGIN   (* action statements *)
   count := 1;
   sum := 0;
   readln(n);
   REPEAT
      readln(x);
      sum := sum+x;
      count := count+1
   UNTIL count > n;
   average := sum/n;
   writeln(' The average is ',average)
END.
```

Notice that the sequence of statements contained within the REPEAT—UNTIL structure includes a statement that causes the value of count to increase. Eventually, this causes the boolean expression

```
count > n
```

to become true, thus terminating the loop.

It should be understood that this loop will always be executed at least once, since the value of the boolean expression is not tested until the end of the loop.

Finally, observe that the sequence of statements included within the REPEAT—UNTIL structure is indented so that the physical extent of the structure can easily be identified.

This example should be carefully compared with Example 6.4. Either structure (WHILE—DO or REPEAT—UNTIL) is equally valid for this particular problem. In many situations, however, the nature of the problem will suggest a preference for one of these two structures.

## 6.4  THE FOR STRUCTURE

The FOR structure is used to carry out unconditional looping in Pascal. That is, this structure allows some action to be repeated a specified number of times.

The FOR structure has two different forms. The more common form is

```
FOR control variable := value 1 TO value 2 DO statement
```

The statement part of the structure can be either simple or structured, though it is typically a compound statement that may include other control structures. This statement will be executed for each of several consecutive values assigned to the control variable. The number of values assigned to the control variable therefore determines the number of times the statement will be executed.

The control variable must be a simple-type variable of any type other than real. Typically, it will be either an integer variable or a user-defined variable. (We will discuss user-defined variables in Chap. 8. For now, we will confine our discussion to integer-type control variables.) Initially, the control variable is assigned the value specified by *value 1*. The control variable automatically takes on its next successive value each time the statement is repeated, until it finally takes on the value specified by *value 2*. If the control variable is an integer-type variable, then it will automatically increase by 1 each time the statement is executed; hence, the statement will be executed (*value 2– value 1*+1) times.

To illustrate the use of the FOR structure, let us again consider the problem of writing out the first 20 positive integers, with one integer on each line. (We have already seen how to do this using the WHILE—DO structure in Sec. 6.2 and with the REPEAT—UNTIL structure in Sec. 6.3.) We require only a single FOR—TO statement to carry out this task. In particular, we can write

```
FOR digit := 1 TO 20 DO writeln(digit);
```

where digit is assumed to be an integer-type variable.

In this example digit takes on the successive values $1, 2, \ldots, 20$, thus causing the loop to be executed 20 times. During each pass, the current value of digit will be written out on a separate line, as required.

Similarly, the problem of determining the sum of the first n integer quantities can be expressed as

```
sum := 0;
FOR digit := 1 TO n DO sum := sum + digit;
```

Here we begin by assigning a value of 0 to sum. Each pass through the loop then causes the current value of digit to be added to sum. Therefore, sum will represent the desired value $1 + 2 + 3 + \cdots + n$ after the loop has been executed n times.

Notice how much easier it has been to use the FOR structure than the WHILE—DO or the REPEAT—UNTIL structures for these problems (see Secs. 6.2 and 6.3). This is usually the case when the required number of passes through the loop is known in advance.

There are a few rules that must be adhered to when writing a FOR statement. Specifically, the values of *value 1* and *value 2* can be expressed as constants, variables or expressions. However, these values must be of the same data type as the control variable. Also, the value of *value 1* must be less than *value 2* if the statement is to be executed more than once. (If *value 1* and *value 2* are equal, the statement will be executed once only; if *value 1* is greater than *value 2*, the statement will not be executed at all.)

**EXAMPLE 6.6**

The use of the FOR structure is really less complicated than it first appears, as illustrated by the following examples.

(*a*)
```
sum := 0;
FOR count := 1 TO n DO BEGIN readln(x); sum := sum+x END;
writeln(' sum=',sum);
```

(*b*)
```
sum := 0;
FOR count := n TO (3*n+1) DO
    BEGIN
        readln(x);
        sum := sum+x
    END;
writeln(' sum=',sum);
```

The first example contains a compound statement that is executed n times. (Note that n is an integer-type variable whose value is assumed to be known, and that x is a real-type variable.) During each pass through the loop a new number (i.e., a new value for x) is read into the computer and added to sum. The sum of all n numbers is then written out, after the loop has been completed.

In the second example the initial and final values of the control variable are given by an integer-type variable and an integer-type expression, respectively. Notice that the compound statement is now spread out over several lines, with appropriate indentation. (This is the preferred format.)

The second form of the FOR structure is similar to the first, except for the use of the keyword DOWNTO in place of TO. Thus, the FOR structure can be written as

FOR *control variable* := *value 1* DOWNTO *value 2* DO *statement*

The action taken by this form of the FOR structure is similar to the first form, except that the control variable is evaluated backward rather than forward. Thus, if the control variable is an integer-type variable it will automatically *decrease* by 1, from *value 1* to *value 2*, during successive passes through the loop. Therefore *value 1* should be greater than *value 2*. (If the two values are equal, then the statement will be executed once only; and if *value 1* is less than *value 2*, then the statement will not be executed at all.)

**EXAMPLE 6.7**

Here is an illustration of the second form of the FOR structure.

```
FOR i := 0 DOWNTO -12 DO
    BEGIN
        z := 2*i+5;
        writeln(' i=',i,'   z=',z)
    END;
```

This example will cause 13 lines of text to be printed. Each line will contain the current value of the integer variable i, followed by the corresponding value of the formula $z = 2i + 5$. Notice that the successive values of i will decrease, from $i = 0$ on the first line to $i = -12$ on the last line.

It should be understood that *value 1* and *value 2* are evaluated only once, before the first pass through the loop. Therefore the reader should not attempt to change either of these values within the loop. Also, the reader is cautioned not to use the control variable after the FOR structure has terminated, since it will normally be undefined.

**EXAMPLE 6.8**

**Averaging a List of Numbers.** Let us return to the problem of averaging a list of numbers, which we considered in Examples 6.4 and 6.5. Now, however, we will use the FOR structure to carry out the looping action.

The calculations will be carried out in the following manner.

1. Assign a value of 0 to the real variable sum.
2. Read in the value for n.
3. Do the following steps n times (i.e., for successive values of the control variable count ranging from 1 to n).

   (a)  Read in the next number in the list. (Each number will be represented by the real variable x.)

   (b)  Add this number to the value of sum.
4. Divide the value of sum by n to obtain the desired average.
5. Write out the calculated value for the average.

Note the similarity between this outline and the two earlier outlines given in Examples 6.4 and 6.5.

The complete Pascal program is shown below.

```
PROGRAM average3(input,output);

(* This program calculates the average of n numbers
   using a FOR structure. *)

 VAR n,count : integer;
     x,sum,average : real;

BEGIN   (* action statements *)
   sum := 0;
   readln(n);
   FOR count := 1 TO n DO
      BEGIN
         readln(x);
         sum := sum+x
      END;
   average := sum/n;
   writeln(' The average is ',average)
END.
```

Notice that the control variable count is initially assigned a value of 1. This value increases by 1 each time the loop is executed, until count finally takes on a value of n. Thus, the loop will be executed exactly n times. Also, observe that the sequence of statements included within the FOR structure is indented. This permits the physical extent of the structure to be easily identified.

The reader should compare this approach to the problem with those given in Examples 6.4 and 6.5. The use of the FOR structure is better-suited to this particular problem than either the WHILE—DO structure or the REPEAT—UNTIL structure, since the number of passes through the loop is known in advance. There are many problems, however, for which this is not true (see Example 6.26 and Prob. 6.45 at the end of this chapter). In such cases the WHILE—DO or REPEAT—UNTIL structures may be more appropriate. Thus, the reader should not attempt to draw general conclusions about the relative utility of these control structures; each application must be evaluated on its own merits.

## 6.5  NESTED CONTROL STRUCTURES

Control structures can be *nested* (i.e., embedded), one within another. The inner and outer structures need not be of the same type. It is essential, however, that one structure be completely embedded within the other. In other words, there can be no overlap.

### EXAMPLE 6.9

**Repeated Averaging of a List of Numbers.** Suppose that we want to calculate the average of several consecutive lists of numbers. If we know in advance how many lists are to be averaged, then we can use a FOR structure to control the number of times the averaging loop is executed. The actual averaging can be accomplished using any one of the three repetition structures (WHILE—DO, REPEAT—UNTIL or FOR), as illustrated in Examples 6.4, 6.5 and 6.8.

Let us arbitrarily use the REPEAT—UNTIL structure to carry out the averaging, as in Example 6.5. Thus, we will proceed in the following manner.

1.  Read in a value for loopmax, an integer quantity that indicates the number of lists that will be averaged.

2.  Repeatedly read in a list of numbers and determine its average (i.e., calculate an average for successive values of the control variable loop ranging from 1 to loopmax). Follow the steps given in Example 6.5 to calculate each average.

Here is the actual Pascal program.

```
PROGRAM average4(input,output);

(* This program uses nested control structures
   to repeatedly calculate the average of n numbers *)

VAR loop,loopmax,n,count : integer;
    x,sum,average : real;

BEGIN   (* action statements *)
   readln(loopmax);
   FOR loop := 1 TO loopmax DO
      BEGIN
         count := 1;
         sum := 0;
         readln(n);
         REPEAT
            read(x);
            sum := sum+x;
            count := count+1
         UNTIL count > n;
         average := sum/n;
         writeln(' list number ',loop,'   The average is ',average)
      END   (* loop *)
END.
```

Notice the manner in which the REPEAT—UNTIL structure is nested within the FOR structure. (This is easy to see, because of the indentation.) Thus the entire averaging procedure will be completely executed during each pass through the outer loop.

Many applications require the use of nested FOR structures. In such situations each FOR structure must utilize a different control variable. (Remember also that each inner FOR structure must be completely embedded within the next outermost FOR structure.) This is illustrated in the next example.

### EXAMPLE 6.10

**Compound Interest Factors.** Suppose that a sum of money, $P$, is invested for $n$ years at an interest rate of $i$ percent, compounded annually. The amount of money that will have accumulated after $n$ years, $F$, can be determined by the well-known formula

$$F = P(1 + i/100)^n$$

(This is the so-called *law of compound interest*.)

The ratio $F/P$ is often tabulated as a function of the interest rate and the number of years. Let us write a progam that will generate a table of compound interest factors for interest rates of 5, 6, 7, 8, 9, 10, 11 and 12 percent, and for periods of 1 through 20 years. To do so, we will utilize a nested loop structure, with an outer loop to generate successive rows for $n = 1$ to 20, and an inner loop to generate the columns within each row for $i = 5, 6, \ldots, 12$.

We begin by defining the following variables.

factor = a real variable that represents the calculated value of $F/P$
     i = an integer variable that represents the interest rate, expressed as a percentage
     n = an integer variable that represents the number of years

The computation will proceed as follows.

1.  Write out a heading containing n and the various interest rates.

2.  Do the following for consecutive values of n ranging from 1 to 20.

    (*a*)  Write the current value of n.

    (*b*)  Within each row, do the following for consecutive values of i ranging from 5 to 12:
         (i)  Calculate the value of $F/P$ and assign it to factor.
        (ii)  Write out the current value of factor.

    (*c*)  Skip to the next line (with an empty writeln statement).

Here is the complete Pascal program.

```
PROGRAM compoundinterest(output);

(* This program generates a table of compound interest factors
    to calculate a future value, given a present value or vice versa *)

VAR i,n : integer;
    factor : real;

BEGIN  (* action statements *)
    write(' n      5%        6%          7%      8%');
    writeln('        9%       10%       11%      12%');
    writeln;
    FOR n := 1 TO 20 DO
        BEGIN                    (* generate successive rows *)
            write(n:3);
            FOR i := 5 TO 12 DO
                BEGIN                    (* generate entries within each row *)
                    factor := exp(n*ln(1+0.01*i));
                    write(factor:9:5)
                END;
            writeln
        END
END.
```

Note that this program does not require any input data. Also, notice the manner in which the program uses nested FOR-type structures. In particular, observe that the inner structure is completely embedded in the outer structure and that each structure has its own control variable.

## 6.6  THE IF STRUCTURE

The IF structure is a conditional control structure that allows some action to be taken only if a given logical condition has a specified value (either true or false).

This structure has two different forms. The simpler form is

```
IF boolean expression THEN statement
```

This structure is often referred to as the IF—THEN structure. The statement part of the structure will be executed if and only if the boolean expression is true. If the boolean statement is false, then the statement-part of the structure will be ignored. The statement itself can be either simple or structured, though it is often a compound statement.

### EXAMPLE 6.11

Some examples of the IF—THEN structure are shown below.

```
IF count <= 100 THEN count := count+1;

IF tag = '*' THEN
    BEGIN writeln(accountno); credit := 0 END;
```

(*continues on next page*)

```
IF test THEN BEGIN x := 100; test := false END;

IF (balance < 1000.0) OR (status = 'R') THEN writeln(balance);
```

In the first example, the integer variable count will be increased by 1 if its current value does not exceed 100. The second example causes the value of accountno to be written out, and a value of 0 to be assigned to credit if an '*' has been assigned to the char-type variable tag. Notice that this example includes a compound statement.

The third example includes both a boolean variable (test) and a compound statement. If test is originally true, then a value of 100 is assigned to x and test is set to false.

In the last example, the value of balance is written out if its value is less than 1000.0 or if the char-type variable status represents the character R (or if both conditions are true).

Finally, notice that there are no semicolons included in the IF—THEN structure, except within the compound statements.

The second form of the IF structure is

IF *boolean expression* THEN *statement 1* ELSE *statement 2*

This is frequently referred to as the IF—THEN—ELSE structure. In this case, *statement 1* will be executed if the boolean expression is true; otherwise, *statement 2* will be executed. Notice that one statement or the other is always executed (but never both statements). Again, the individual statements may be either simple or structured and are often compound statements.

Semicolons should not appear in an IF—THEN—ELSE structure, except as separators within a compound statement. Beginners sometimes make the mistake of placing a semicolon before the keyword ELSE. This should be avoided, as it will result in a compilation error.

**EXAMPLE 6.12**

Here are several examples illustrating the use of the IF—THEN—ELSE structure.

```
IF status='S' THEN tax := 0.20*pay ELSE tax := 0.14*pay;

IF tag = '*' THEN BEGIN writeln(accountno); credit := 0 END
             ELSE credit := 1000;

IF circle THEN BEGIN
                 readln(radius);
                 area := 3.141593*sqr(radius);
                 writeln(' Area of circle=',area)
             END
         ELSE BEGIN
                 readln(length, width);
                 area := length*width;
                 writeln(' Area of rectangle=',area)
             END;
```

In the first example the value of tax is determined in one of two possible ways, depending on the value that is assigned to the char-type variable status.

The second example looks for certain "tagged" accounts. If an account is tagged (i.e., if an '*' is assigned to the char-type variable tag), then the account number is written out and the credit limit is set to zero; otherwise the credit limit is set at 1000.

The third example shows how an area can be calculated for either of two different geometries. If the boolean-type variable circle is true, then the radius of a circle is read into the computer, the area is calculated and then written out. If circle is false, then the length and width of a rectangle are read into the computer, the area is calculated and then written out.

Notice once again that there are no semicolons in the IF—THEN—ELSE structure, except as separators in the compound statements.

IF structures can be nested within one another, just as any other control structure. Some of the forms that nested IF structures can take on are shown below.

The most general form of two-layer nesting is

```
IF be1 THEN IF be2 THEN s1 ELSE s2
        ELSE IF be3 THEN s3 ELSE s4
```

where $be1$, $be2$ and $be3$ represent boolean expressions, and $s1$, $s2$, $s3$ and $s4$ represent statements. In this situation, one complete IF—THEN—ELSE structure will be executed if $be1$ is true, and another will be executed if $be1$ is false. It is, of course, possible that $s1$, $s2$, $s3$ and $s4$ will contain other IF—THEN—ELSE structures. We would then have multilayer nesting.

Some other forms of two-layer nesting are

```
IF be1 THEN s1
        ELSE IF be2 THEN s2 ELSE s3
```

```
IF be1 THEN IF be2 THEN s1 ELSE s2
        ELSE s3
```

```
IF be1 THEN IF be2 THEN s1 ELSE s2
```

In each of the first two cases, the subordinate nature of the inner IF—THEN—ELSE structure is indicated by the line on which it is written. In the last case, however, it is not clear which boolean expression is associated with the ELSE clause. The answer is $be2$. Thus, this last example is equivalent to

```
IF be1 THEN
        BEGIN IF be2 THEN s1 ELSE s2 END
```

If we should want to associate the ELSE clause with $be1$ rather than $be2$, we could write

```
IF be1 THEN BEGIN IF be2 THEN s1 END
        ELSE s2
```

This type of nesting must therefore be carried out carefully in order to avoid possible ambiguities.


## EXAMPLE 6.13

**Encoding Characters.** Let us write a simple Pascal program that will read in an ASCII character and write out an encoded character in its place. If the character is a letter or a digit, then replace it with the next character in the sequence, except that Z should be replaced by A, z by a, and 9 by 0. Thus 1 becomes 2, C becomes D, p becomes q, and so on. Any character other than a letter or a digit should be replaced by an asterisk (*). Continue the computation until an asterisk is entered as the input character. (The asterisk should be interpreted as a stopping condition.)

In order to outline the program, let us define the following variables.

charin = a char-type variable that represents the input
        character

charout = a char-type variable that represents the output
        character

flag = a boolean variable that indicates whether or not
        to continue the looping action.

The computation will proceed as follows.

1.  Assign a value of true to flag.

2.  Repeat the following steps until the value of flag becomes false.

    (*a*)  Read in a value for charin.

    (*b*)  If charin represents an asterisk (*), set flag to false. Otherwise, determine if charin represents a letter or a digit.

        (*i*)  If charin represents a letter or a digit, set charout to its appropriate value.

(*ii*)  If charin represents some character that is not a letter or a digit, let charout represent an asterisk (∗).

(*iii*)  Write out the newly assigned value of charout.

The corresponding Pascal program is shown below.

```
PROGRAM charactercode(input,output);

(* THIS PROGRAM REPLACES INPUT CHARACTERS
   WITH EQUIVALENT ENCODED CHARACTERS *)

VAR charin,charout : char;
    flag : boolean;
BEGIN
   flag := true;
   REPEAT
     write(' Enter character: ');
     readln(charin);
     IF charin = '*'   (* stopping criterion *)
        THEN flag := false
        ELSE BEGIN      (* character replacement *)
                IF ((charin >= '0') AND (charin < '9')) OR
                   ((charin >= 'A') AND (charin < 'Z')) OR
                   ((charin >= 'a') AND (charin < 'z'))
                   THEN charout := succ(charin)
                   ELSE IF charin = '9'
                           THEN charout := '0'
                           ELSE IF charin = 'Z'
                                   THEN charout := 'A'
                                   ELSE IF charin = 'z'
                                           THEN charout := 'a'
                                           ELSE charout := '*';
                writeln('   New character: ',charout);
                writeln
             END
   UNTIL flag = false
END.
```

Notice that the program contains several IF—THEN—ELSE statements, with multiple levels of nesting. Also, notice that we have chosen to use the REPEAT—UNTIL structure to carry out the looping action. We could just as easily have selected WHILE—DO, though a FOR loop would be inappropriate in this case.

Execution of this program generates the following representative output. (The user's responses are underlined.)

```
Enter character: f
  New character: g

Enter character: z
  New character: a

Enter character: P
  New character: Q

Enter character: 5
  New character: 6

Enter character: 9
  New character: 0

Enter character: ?
  New character: *

Enter character: *
```

## EXAMPLE 6.14

**Solution of an Algebraic Equation.** For those of you who are mathematically inclined, this example illustrates how computers can be used to solve algebraic equations that cannot be solved by more elementary methods. Consider, for example, the equation

$$x^5 + 3x^2 - 10 = 0.$$

This equation cannot be rearranged to yield an exact solution for $x$. However, we can determine the solution by a repeated trial-and-error procedure (i.e., an *iterative* procedure) that successively refines an initially crude guess.

We begin by rearranging the equation into the form

$$x = (10 - 3x^2)^{1/5}$$

Our procedure will then be to guess a value for $x$, substitute this value into the right-hand side of the rearranged equation, and thus calculate a new value for $x$. If this new value is equal to the old value (or very nearly so), then we will have obtained the solution to the equation. Otherwise, this new value will be substituted into the right-hand side and still another value obtained for $x$, and so on. This procedure will continue until either the successive values of $x$ have become sufficiently close (i.e., until the computation has *converged*), or a specified number of iterations has been exceeded (thus preventing the computation from continuing indefinitely in the event that the computed results do not converge).

To see how the method works, suppose we choose an initial value of $x = 1.0$. Substituting this value into the right-hand side of the equation, we obtain

$$x = [10 - 3(1.0)^2]^{1/5} = 1.47577$$

We then substitute this new value of $x$ into the equation, resulting in

$$x = [10 - 3(1.47577)^2]^{1/5} = 1.28225$$

Continuing the procedure, we obtain

$$x = [10 - 3(1.28225)^2]^{1/5} = 1.38344$$
$$x = [10 - 3(1.38344)^2]^{1/5} = 1.33613$$

and so on. Notice that the successive values of $x$ appear to be converging to some final answer.

The success of the method depends on the value chosen for the initial guess. If this value is too large in magnitude, then the quantity in brackets will be negative, and a negative number cannot be raised to a fractional power. Therefore we should test for a negative value of $10 - 3x^2$ whenever we substitute a new value of $x$ into the right-hand side.

In order to write a program outline, let us define the following symbols.

count = an iteration counter (count will increase by
      one unit at each successive iteration)

guess = the value of $x$ substituted into the right-hand
      side of the equation

root = the newly calculated value of $x$

test = the quantity $(10 - 3x^2)$

error = the absolute difference between root and guess

flag = a boolean variable that signifies whether or not to
      continue the iteration

We will continue the computation until one of the following conditions is satisfied.

1. The value of error becomes less than 0.00001 (in which case we will have obtained a converged solution)
2. Fifty iterations have been completed (i.e., count = 50)
3. The variable test takes on a negative value (in which case the computation cannot be continued)

Let us monitor the progress of the computation by writing out each successive value of root.

We can now write the following program outline.

1. Initialize the variables flag and count (assign true to flag and 0 to count).
2. Read in a value for the initial guess (guess).
3. Carry out the following looping procedure, while flag remains true.
   (*a*)  Increment the counter (increase its value by 1).
   (*b*)  Assign false to flag if the new value of the counter equals 50. (This signifies the last pass through the loop.)
   (*c*)  Evaluate test. If this value is positive, proceed as follows.
       (*i*)  Calculate a new value for root; then write out the current value for count, followed by the current value for root.
       (*ii*)  Evaluate error (the absolute difference between root and guess). If this value is greater than 0.00001, then assign the value of root to guess and proceed with another iteration. Otherwise write out the current values of root and count, and set flag to false (the current value of root will be considered to be the desired solution).
   (*d*)  If the value of test is not positive, then the computation cannot proceed. Hence, write an appropriate error message ("numbers out of range") and set flag to false.
4. Upon completion of the looping action, write an appropriate error message ("convergence not obtained") if count has a value of 50 and the value of error is greater than 0.00001.

Now let us express the program outline in the form of pseudo code, in order to simplify the transition from a general outline to a working Pascal program.

```
PROGRAM equation(input,output);

(* variable declarations *)

BEGIN

(* initialize flag and count *)

(* read guess *)

WHILE flag DO
   BEGIN

      (* increment count *)

      IF count = 50 THEN flag := false;

      (* evaluate test *)

      IF test > 0 THEN BEGIN (* another iteration *)

                 (* evaluate root *)

                 (* write count and root *)

                 (* evaluate error *)

                 IF error > 0.00001 THEN guess := root;
                         ELSE BEGIN
                                   flag := false;

                                   (* write final answer -
                                   root and count *)

      END

END
```

(*Program continues on next page*)

```
                                ELSE BEGIN
                                        flag := false;
                                        (* write error message *)
                                    END
            END;
        IF (count = 50) AND (error > 0.00001) THEN
                                        (* write error message *)

END.
```

Here is the complete Pascal program.

```
    PROGRAM equation(input,output);

    (* THIS PROGRAM DETERMINES THE ROOTS OF AN ALGEBRAIC EQUATION
        USING AN ITERATIVE PROCEDURE *)

    VAR count : integer;
        guess,root,test,error : real;
        flag : boolean;
    BEGIN
        flag := true;   (* Initialize *)
        count := 0;
        write(' Initial guess= ');   (* Begin input routine *)
        readln(guess);
        writeln;
        WHILE flag DO   (* Begin main loop *)
            BEGIN
                count := count+1;
                IF count = 50 THEN flag := false;
                test := 10-3*sqr(guess);
                IF test > 0
                    THEN BEGIN   (* Another iteration *)
                            root := exp(0.2*ln(test));
                            write(' Iteration number ',count:2);
                            writeln('   x= ',root:7:5);
                            error := abs(root-guess);
                            IF error > 0.00001
                                THEN guess := root
                                ELSE BEGIN   (* Write final answer *)
                                        flag := false;
                                        writeln;
                                        write(' Root= ',root:7:5);
                                        writeln('   No. of iterations= ',count:2)
                                    END
                        END
                    ELSE BEGIN   (* Error message *)
                            flag := false;
                            writeln;
                            write(' Numbers out of range - ');
                            writeln('try again using another initial guess')
                        END
            END;
        IF (count = 50) AND (error > 0.00001) (* Error message *)
            THEN BEGIN
                    writeln;
                    writeln(' Convergence not obtained after 50 iterations')
                END
    END.
```

The program includes a number of control structures. In particular, the actual iteration is controlled by a WHILE—DO structure, though a REPEAT—UNTIL structure could have been used instead. In addition, several IF—THEN and IF—THEN—ELSE structures are included within the program. Notice the use of nested IF—THEN—ELSE structures toward the middle of the program.

Notice the statement

```
root := exp(0.2*ln(test));
```

near the middle of the program. This statement is required in order to raise the value of test to the 0.2 power. (Recall that Pascal does not include an exponentiation operator.) Thus, we obtain the natural log of test, multiply by 0.2, and then raise $e$ to a power equal to the resulting product.

The output that is generated for an initial guess of x = 1 is shown below. (The user's responses are underlined.) Notice that the computation has converged to the solution x = 1.35196 after 16 iterations. The printed output shows the successive values of x becoming closer and closer, leading to the final converged solution.

```
Initial guess= 1

Iteration number  1   x= 1.47577
Iteration number  2   x= 1.28225
Iteration number  3   x= 1.38344
Iteration number  4   x= 1.33613
Iteration number  5   x= 1.35952
Iteration number  6   x= 1.34826
Iteration number  7   x= 1.35375
Iteration number  8   x= 1.35109
Iteration number  9   x= 1.35238
Iteration number 10   x= 1.35175
Iteration number 11   x= 1.35206
Iteration number 12   x= 1.35191
Iteration number 13   x= 1.35198
Iteration number 14   x= 1.35195
Iteration number 15   x= 1.35196
Iteration number 16   x= 1.35196

Root= 1.35196   No. of iterations= 16
```

Now suppose that a value of x = 10 is selected as an initial guess. This value generates a negative value for test in the first iteration. Therefore the output would appear as follows.

```
Initial guess= 10

Numbers out of range - try again using another initial guess
```

It is interesting to see what happens when the initial guess is once again chosen as x = 1, but the maximum number of iterations is changed from 50 to 10. The reader is encouraged to try this and observe the result.

## 6.7  THE CASE STRUCTURE

The CASE structure is a conditional control structure that allows some particular group of statements to be chosen from several available groups. The selection will be based upon the current value of an expression, referred to as the *selector*.

The general form of the CASE structure is

```
CASE expression OF
    case label list 1 : statement 1;
    case label list 2 : statement 2;
        .
        .
        .
    case label list n : statement n
END
```

The expression can be any simple-type expression other than real. It often takes the form of a single simple-type variable.

Each of the case labels represents one of the permissible values of the expression. Thus, if the expression is of type integer, the case labels would represent integer values that fall within the permissible range. The case labels need not appear in any particular order, though each of the case labels must be unique. Moreover, each label can appear in only one list. (*Note*: These labels are referred to as *case labels* to distinguish them from a different type of label, which we will discuss in the next section.)

The statements can be either simple or structured. The use of compound statements is quite common. Null (empty) statements are also permitted, to indicate that no action is to be taken for certain values of the selector. The statements need not be unique (that is, the same statement may be used with two or more lists of case labels).

A statement will be executed if (and only if) one of its corresponding case labels matches the current value of the expression. Thus, the current value of the expression determines which of the statements will be executed. If the current value of the expression does not match any of the labels, then the action will be undefined. (Some versions of Pascal include an *otherwise* clause which specifies what action is to be taken if the value of the selector does not match any of the labels.)

**EXAMPLE 6.15**

A typical CASE structure is illustrated below. In this example, choice is assumed to be a char-type variable.

```
CASE choice OF
    'R' : writeln(' RED ');
    'W' : writeln(' WHITE ');
    'B' : writeln(' BLUE ')
END;
```

Thus, RED will be written out if choice is assigned the value R, WHITE will appear if W is assigned to choice and BLUE will be written out if B is assigned to choice. No output will be generated if choice is assigned some character other than R, W or B.

**EXAMPLE 6.16**

Here is another typical CASE structure.

```
CASE trunc(x/10) OF
    1   : y := y+5;
    3,5 : y := y-2;
    6   : y := 2*(y+1);
    2,4 : ;
    9   : y := 0
END;
```

In this example, x and y are real-type variables. The value of x/10 is truncated and hence converted to an integer, which will be used as the selector. If this integer equals 1, then y will be increased by 5. Similarly, y will be decreased by 2 if the selector equals either 3 or 5; y will be assigned the value of 2*(y+1) if the selector equals 6; and it will be assigned 0 if the selector equals 9. The value of y will remain unchanged if the selector equals 2 or 4. The action will be undefined for all other values of the selector; hence, no action will be taken (an error message may be generated).

In a practical sense, the CASE structure may be thought of as an alternative to the use of nested IF—THEN—ELSE structures. However, it can only replace those IF—THEN—ELSE structures that test for equalities. In such situations, the use of the CASE structure is usually more convenient.

**EXAMPLE 6.17**

**Calculating Depreciation.** Let us consider how to calculate the yearly depreciation for some depreciable item (a building, a machine, etc.). There are three commonly used methods for calculating depreciation, known as the *straight-line* method, the *double declining balance* method and the *sum-of-the-years'-digits* method. We wish to write a Pascal program that will allow us to select any one of these methods for each set of calculations.

The computation will begin by reading in the original (undepreciated) value of the item, the life of the item (i.e., the number of years over which it will be depreciated) and an integer that indicates which method will be used. The yearly depreciation and the remaining (undepreciated) value of the item will then be calculated and written out for each year.

The straight-line method is the easiest to use. In this method the original value of the item is divided by its life (total number of years). The resulting quotient will be the amount by which the item depreciates each year. For example, if an $8000 item is to be depreciated over 10 years, then the annual depreciation would be $8000/10 = $800, so that the item would decrease by $800 each year. Notice that the annual depreciation is the same each year.

When using the double declining balance method, the value of the item will decrease by a constant *percentage* each year. (Hence the actual amount of the depreciation, in dollars, will vary from one year to the next.) To obtain the depreciation factor we divide 2 by the life of the item. This factor is multiplied by the value of the item at the beginning of each year (*not the original* value of the item) to obtain the annual depreciation.

Suppose, for example, that we wish to depreciate an $8000 item over 10 years, using the double declining balance method. The depreciation factor will be 2/10 = 0.20. Hence the depreciation for the first year will be 0.20 × $8000 = $1600. The second year's depreciation will be 0.20 × ($8000 − $1600) = 0.20 × $6400 = $1280; the third year's depreciation will be 0.20 × $5120 = $1024, and so on.

In the sum-of-the-years'-digits method the value of the item will decrease by a percentage that is different each year. The depreciation factor will be a fraction whose denominator is the sum of the digits from 1 to $n$, where $n$ represents the life of the item. (For a 10-year lifetime, the denominator will be $1 + 2 + 3 + \cdots + 10 = 55$.) For the first year the numerator will be $n$, for the second year it will be $(n - 1)$, for the third year $(n - 2)$, and so on. The yearly depreciation is obtained by multiplying the depreciation factor by the *original* value of the item.

To see how the sum-of-the-years'-digits method works, we again depreciate an $8000 item over 10 years. The depreciation for the first year will be (10/55) × $8000 = $1454.55; for the second year it will be (9/55) × $8000 = $1309.09, and so on.

Now let us define the following symbols.

> val = the value of the item
>
> tag = the original value of the item (i.e., the original value of val)
>
> deprec = the annual depreciation
>
> n = the number of years over which the item will be depreciated
>
> year = a counter ranging from 1 to n
>
> choice = an integer indicating which method to use
>
> flag = a boolean variable indicating whether or not to perform another set of calculations

Our Pascal program will follow the outline presented below.

1. Declare all variables.
2. Assign the value true to flag.
3. Repeat all of the following steps, until flag becomes false.

    (*a*)  Read a value for choice (either 1, 2, 3 or 4, indicating what kind of calculation is to be carried out).

    (*b*)  If choice is not assigned a value of 4, then read values for val and n (choice = 4 will indicate the end of execution).

    (*c*)  If choice is assigned a value of 1, 2 or 3, calculate the yearly depreciation and the new value of the item by the appropriate method (determined by the value of choice) and print the results on a year-by-year basis. Otherwise (choice = 4), set flag to false, write a message and terminate the computation.

Now let's express this outline in pseudo code.

```
PROGRAM depreciation1(input,output);

(* variable declarations *)

BEGIN

(* initialize flag *)

REPEAT

    (* read choice *)

    IF choice <> 4 THEN (* read val and n *)

    CASE choice OF
        1 : BEGIN

                (* write heading: Straight-Line Method *)

                deprec := val/n;
                FOR year := 1 TO n DO
                    BEGIN
                        val := val-deprec;

                        (* write year, deprec, val *)

                    END
            END;
        2 : BEGIN

                (* write heading: Double Declining Balance Method *)

                FOR year := 1 TO n DO
                    BEGIN
                        deprec := 2*val/n;
                        val := val-deprec;

                        (* write year, deprec, val *)

                    END
            END;
        3 : BEGIN

                (* write heading: Sum-of-the-Years'-Digits Method *)

                tag := val;
                FOR year := 1 TO n DO
                    BEGIN
                        deprec := (n-year+1)*tag/(n*(n+1)/2);
                        val := val-deprec;

                        (* write year, deprec, val *)

                    END
            END;
        4 : BEGIN

                (* write message *)

                flag := false;
            END
    END
UNTIL flag = false
END.
```

Most of the pseudo code is straightforward, though a few comments are in order. First, we see that a REPEAT—UNTIL structure is used to repeat the entire set of calculations. Within this overall structure, the CASE structure is used to select a particular depreciation method. Each depreciation method uses a FOR structure to loop through the entire n-year lifetime of the item.

The calculation of the depreciation for the sum-of-the-years'-digits method appears somewhat obscure. In particular, the term (n-year+1) in the numerator requires some explanation. This quantity is used to count backward (from n down to 1), as year progresses forward (from 1 to n). These declining values are required by the sum-of-the-years'-digits method. We could, of course, have set up a backward-counting loop instead (i.e., FOR year := n DOWNTO 1 DO), but then we would have required a corresponding forward-counting loop to write out the yearly depreciations in the proper order.

At this point it is not difficult to write a complete Pascal program, as shown below.

```
PROGRAM depreciation1(input,output);

(* THIS PROGRAM CALCULATES DEPRECIATION INTERACTIVELY,
   USING ONE OF THREE POSSIBLE METHODS *)

VAR n,choice,year : integer;
    val,deprec,tag : real;
    flag : boolean;

BEGIN   (* action statements *)
   flag := true;
   REPEAT
      page;      (* Begin input routine *)
      write(' Method: (1-SL  2-DDB  3-SYD  4-End) ');
      readln(choice);
      IF choice <> 4 THEN
      BEGIN
         write(' Original value: ');
         readln(val);
         write(' Number of years: ');
         readln(n);
         writeln
      END;

      CASE choice OF

         1 : BEGIN   (* SL *)
                writeln(' Straight-Line Method');
                writeln;
                deprec := val/n;
                FOR year := 1 TO n DO
                   BEGIN
                      val := val-deprec;
                      write(' End of Year ',year:2);
                      write('   Depreciation: ',deprec:5:0);
                      writeln('   Current Value: ',val:6:0)
                   END
             END;

         2 : BEGIN   (* DDB *)
                writeln(' Double Declining Balance Method');
                writeln;
                FOR year := 1 TO n DO
```

(*Program continues on next page*)

```
                    BEGIN
                        deprec := 2*val/n;
                        val := val-deprec;
                        write(' End of Year ',year:2);
                        write('   Depreciation: ',deprec:5:0);
                        writeln('   Current Value: ',val:6:0)
                    END
                END;

        3 : BEGIN   (* SYD *)
                writeln(' Sum-of-the-Years''-Digits Method');
                writeln;
                tag := val;
                FOR year := 1 TO n DO
                    BEGIN
                        deprec := (n-year+1)*tag/(n*(n+1)/2);
                        val := val-deprec;
                        write(' End of Year ',year:2);
                        write('   Depreciation: ',deprec:5:0);
                        writeln('   Current Value: ',val:6:0)
                    END
                END;

        4 : BEGIN   (* end computation *)
                writeln(' That''s all, folks!');
                flag := false;
            END
        END   (* choice *)
    UNTIL flag = false
END.
```

The program is designed to be run interactively, with prompts for the required input data. Notice that the program generates a "menu" with four choices, to calculate the depreciation using one of the three methods or to end the computation. The computer will continue to accept new sets of input data, and carry out the appropriate calculations for each data set, until a value of 4 is selected from the menu.

Some representative output is shown below. (The user's responses are underlined.) In each case, an $8000 item is depreciated over a 10-year period, using one of the three methods. Finally, the computation is terminated in response to the last menu selection.

```
Method: (1-SL  2-DDB  3-SYD  4-End) 1
Original value: 8000
Number of years: 10

Straight-Line Method

End of Year  1   Depreciation:   800.   Current Value: 7200.
End of Year  2   Depreciation:   800.   Current Value: 6400.
End of Year  3   Depreciation:   800.   Current Value: 5600.
End of Year  4   Depreciation:   800.   Current Value: 4800.
End of Year  5   Depreciation:   800.   Current Value: 4000.
End of Year  6   Depreciation:   800.   Current Value: 3200.
End of Year  7   Depreciation:   800.   Current Value: 2400.
End of Year  8   Depreciation:   800.   Current Value: 1600.
End of Year  9   Depreciation:   800.   Current Value:  800.
End of Year 10   Depreciation:   800.   Current Value:    0.
```

*(continues on next page)*

```
Method: (1-SL  2-DDB  3-SYD  4-End) 2
Original value: 8000
Number of years: 10

Double Declining Balance Method

End of Year  1    Depreciation: 1600.    Current Value: 6400.
End of Year  2    Depreciation: 1280.    Current Value: 5120.
End of Year  3    Depreciation: 1024.    Current Value: 4096.
End of Year  4    Depreciation:  819.    Current Value: 3277.
End of Year  5    Depreciation:  655.    Current Value: 2621.
End of Year  6    Depreciation:  524.    Current Value: 2097.
End of Year  7    Depreciation:  419.    Current Value: 1678.
End of Year  8    Depreciation:  336.    Current Value: 1342.
End of Year  9    Depreciation:  268.    Current Value: 1074.
End of Year 10    Depreciation:  215.    Current Value:  859.


Method: (1-SL  2-DDB  3-SYD  4-End) 3
Original value: 8000
Number of years: 10

Sum-of-the-Years'-Digits Method

End of Year  1    Depreciation: 1455.    Current Value: 6545.
End of Year  2    Depreciation: 1309.    Current Value: 5236.
End of Year  3    Depreciation: 1164.    Current Value: 4073.
End of Year  4    Depreciation: 1018.    Current Value: 3055.
End of Year  5    Depreciation:  873.    Current Value: 2182.
End of Year  6    Depreciation:  727.    Current Value: 1455.
End of Year  7    Depreciation:  582.    Current Value:  873.
End of Year  8    Depreciation:  436.    Current Value:  436.
End of Year  9    Depreciation:  291.    Current Value:  145.
End of Year 10    Depreciation:  145.    Current Value:    0.


Method: (1-SL  2-DDB  3-SYD  4-End) 4
That's all, folks!
```

Notice that the last two methods result in a large annual depreciation during the early years, but a very small annual depreciation in the last few years of the item's lifetime. Also, we see that the item has a value of zero at the end of its lifetime when using the first and third methods, but a small value remains undepreciated when using the double declining balance method.

## 6.8  THE GOTO STATEMENT

The GOTO statement is a simple-type statement that is used to alter the sequence of program execution by transferring control (i.e., by *jumping*) to some remote part of the program. The form of the GOTO statement is

   GOTO *statement label*

where *statement label* represents a positive integer not greater than 9999.

**EXAMPLE 6.18**

Several typical GOTO statements are shown below.

```
GOTO 100;

IF flag THEN GOTO 9999;

IF sum > 100.0 THEN BEGIN
                        writeln(sum);
                        GOTO 35
                  END;
```

Each statement label must be declared before it can be utilized within a program. (Recall that the label declarations must *precede* the constant and variable declarations, as described in Secs. 1.5 and 5.2.) Label declarations are of the form

LABEL *statement label 1*, *statement label 2*, . . .

where *statement label 1*, *statement label 2*, etc. represent the individual statement labels. (Note the distinction between *statement* labels and *case* labels, discussed in the last section. In particular, note that statement labels are restricted to positive integers, whereas case labels are not so restricted, and that statement labels must be declared before they can be used whereas case labels are not declared.)

## EXAMPLE 6.19

Here is a portion of a Pascal program that contains a label declaration.

```
PROGRAM sample(input,output);
LABEL 100,200,300;
CONST factor = 0.5;
VAR a,b,c : real;
```

Notice that the label declaration follows the program statement and precedes the constant definition, as required.

Labeled statements are written in the form

*statement label* : *statement*

Such statements may precede or follow their corresponding GOTO statements.

## EXAMPLE 6.20

Several Pascal statements are shown below. Each contains a statement label.

```
10 : readln(a,b,c);

20 : FOR count := 1 TO n DO
        BEGIN
           .
           .
           .
        END;

99 : BEGIN
        writeln(sum);
        IF flag THEN writeln(x,y,z);
        writeln
     END;
```

Execution of the GOTO statement causes a transfer of control to the corresponding labeled statement. Thus, the labeled statement will be the next statement to be executed.

A program may contain several different GOTO statements that transfer control to the same place (i.e., to the same remote statement) within the program. However, each labeled statement must have its own unique label (thus, no two "target" statements can have the same label).

**EXAMPLE 6.21**

A portion of a Pascal program is shown below.

```
PROGRAM sample(input,output);
LABEL 10,20;
CONST . . .;
VAR   . . .;
BEGIN
     .
     .
     .
 10 : readln(a,b,c);
     .
     .
     .
    IF a <= 0 THEN GOTO 20;
     .
     .
     .
    GOTO 10;
     .
     .
     .
    IF flag THEN GOTO 20;
     .
     .
     .
 20 : writeln(x,y,z);
     .
     .
     .
END.
```

Notice that control can be transferred to statement 20 from two different places within the program. Both transfers are conditional, i.e., dependent upon some boolean expression being true.

In general, programs of this type should be avoided in Pascal. In fact, many of Pascal's features are specifically designed to eliminate the need for this type of program logic. (More about this later.)

Some care must be exercised when using the GOTO statement with compound statements. Control can be transferred *out of* or *within* a compound statement, and control can be transferred to the *beginning* of a compound statement. However, control cannot be transferred *into* a compound statement. Moreover, if control is transferred internally to the END of a compound statement (i.e., if the keyword END is labeled), then the label must be preceded by an empty (null) statement. This is accomplished by placing a semicolon after the statement that precedes END.

These restrictions are illustrated in the following examples.

**EXAMPLE 6.22**

Here is an example of a permissible transfer of control out of a compound statement.

```
        BEGIN
          .
          .
          .
          IF flag THEN GOTO 50;
          .
          .
          .
        END;
         .
         .
         .
   50 : writeln(answer);
```

**EXAMPLE 6.23**

Here is an example of a permissible transfer of control within a compound statement.

```
      BEGIN
        .
        .
        .
        IF flag THEN GOTO 20;
        .
        .
        .
   20 : writeln(answer);
        .
        .
        .
      END;
```

**EXAMPLE 6.24**

Now consider the following transfer of control to the END of a compound statement.

```
      BEGIN
        .
        .
        .
        IF flag THEN GOTO 30;
        .
        .
        .
        writeln(answer);
   30 : END;
```

Notice the semicolon after the writeln statement. This creates an empty (null) statement between writeln and END, as required.

**EXAMPLE 6.25**

Finally, consider the following *illegal* attempt to transfer control into a compound statement.

```
   IF flag THEN GOTO 40;
      .
      .
      .
   BEGIN
      .
      .
      .
40 : writeln(answer);
      .
      .
      .
   END;
```

If a program contains this type of structure, then a *syntax error* will be obtained during compilation.

Similar restrictions apply to the use of the GOTO statement with other control structures. In general, control can be transferred within or out of a control structure but not into a control structure. Moreover, some Pascal compilers will not accept labeled statements within WHILE, FOR or IF structures. It is therefore a good idea to avoid using the GOTO statement in such situations.

There are also restrictions on the use of the GOTO statement that relate to program *scope*. This topic will be discussed in the next chapter. In general terms, however, we will see that blocks can be nested, just as control structures can be nested within a program. In such cases control can be transferred within a block and out of a block to an enclosing block, but not into a parallel block.

Finally, it should be recognized that the use of the GOTO statement is discouraged in Pascal, since it alters the clear, sequential flow of logic that is characteristic of the language. In fact, some computer scientists advocate a total ban on the GOTO statement, though this may be a bit extreme. There is widespread agreement, however, that the GOTO statement should be used very sparingly, and only when it is awkward to use another control structure. Actually, such situations are quite rare.

In practice, the GOTO statement is sometimes included in an IF structure to transfer control (conditionally) toward the end of a program. (The WHILE—DO and REPEAT—UNTIL structures are preferred for situations that require a transfer of control toward the beginning of a program.) Usually, such moves are made in conjunction with some *global* type of strategy (e.g., jumping to the end of the program if an input quantity is negative). On the other hand, a program should not under any circumstances include a large number of *localized* jumps, as this is precisely the type of sloppy program structure that Pascal was designed to avoid.

**EXAMPLE 6.26**

**Averaging a List of Numbers.** Let us again consider the problem of averaging a list of numbers, as in Examples 6.4, 6.5 and 6.8. Now, however, suppose that the length of the list is not known in advance. Rather, we will continue to read and sum successive input quantities until a negative value is read into the computer. This negative number will be interpreted as a stopping criterion and will not be included in the average.

The calculations will be carried out in the following manner.

1.  Assign a value of 0 to the integer variable count.
2.  Assign a value of 0 to the real variable sum.
3.  Assign the value true to the boolean variable flag.
4.  Do the following steps repeatedly, while flag remains true.
    (*a*)  Read in one of the numbers in the list. (Each number will be represented by the real variable x.)
    (*b*)  If the value of x is negative, GOTO step 5 below. Otherwise, add the value of x to sum and increase the value of count by 1.

5.   Divide sum by count to obtain the desired average.

6.   Write out the values of count and average.

The corresponding Pascal program is shown below.

```
PROGRAM average5(input,output);

(* THIS PROGRAM CALCULATES THE AVERAGE OF A LIST OF NUMBERS
    USING THE WHILE - DO STRUCTURE AND A GOTO STATEMENT *)

LABEL 10;

VAR count : integer;
    x,sum,average : real;
    flag : boolean;

BEGIN   (* action statements *)
    count := 0;
    sum := 0;
    flag := true;
    WHILE flag DO
       BEGIN
           readln(x);
           IF x < 0 THEN GOTO 10;
           sum := sum+x;
           count := count+1
       END;
10 : average := sum/count;
    writeln(' The average of ',count:5,' numbers is ',average)
END.
```

Notice that flag remains true throughout this program. Thus, the repetition will continue indefinitely, until a negative value of x is entered into the computer. Once a negative value for x is detected, control is transferred out of the loop, to statement 10. The desired average is then calculated and written out.

The reader should try to program this problem without the use of the GOTO statement (see Prob. 6.45 at the end of this chapter). Such a program can be written, but it is somewhat more awkward than with the GOTO statement.

# Review Questions

**6.1**   What is meant by repetition?

**6.2**   What is conditional looping? What is unconditional looping? In what ways do conditional looping and unconditional looping differ from one another?

**6.3**   What is meant by conditional execution?

**6.4**   What is meant by selection?

**6.5**   What values can be represented by a boolean expression?

**6.6**   Summarize the rules associated with boolean expressions.

**6.7**      Summarize the differences between relational operators and logical operators. What types of operands are used with each type of operator?

**6.8**      What is the difference between simple and structured statements?

**6.9**      Name three different kinds of simple statements.

**6.10**     Summarize the syntactical rules associated with compound statements.

**6.11**     What is the purpose of the WHILE—DO structure? When is the boolean expression evaluated? What is the minimum number of times the WHILE—DO structure will be executed?

**6.12**     How is execution of the WHILE—DO structure terminated?

**6.13**     Summarize the syntactical rules associated with the WHILE—DO structure.

**6.14**     What is the purpose of the REPEAT—UNTIL structure? How does it differ from the WHILE—DO structure?

**6.15**     What is the minimum number of times the REPEAT—UNTIL structure will be executed? Compare with the WHILE—DO structure and explain the reason for the differences.

**6.16**     Summarize the syntactical rules associated with the REPEAT—UNTIL structure. Compare with the WHILE—DO structure.

**6.17**     What is the purpose of the FOR structure? How does it differ from the WHILE—DO and the REPEAT—UNTIL structures?

**6.18**     How many times will a FOR structure be executed? Compare with the WHILE—DO and the REPEAT—UNTIL structures.

**6.19**     What is the purpose of the control variable in a FOR structure? What type of variable can this be?

**6.20**     Describe the two different forms of the FOR structure. What is the purpose of each?

**6.21**     Summarize the syntactical rules associated with FOR structures.

**6.22**     What rules apply to the nesting of control structures? Can one type of control structure be embedded within another?

**6.23**     What is the purpose of the IF structure? In what way is this structure fundamentally different from WHILE—DO, REPEAT—UNTIL and FOR?

**6.24**     Describe the two different forms of the IF structure. Fundamentally, how do they differ?

**6.25**     Summarize the syntactical rules associated with IF structures.

**6.26**   How are nested IF structures interpreted? In particular, how is the structure

      IF *be1* THEN IF *be2* THEN *s1* ELSE *s2*

interpreted? Which boolean expression is associated with the ELSE clause?

**6.27**   What is the purpose of the CASE structure? How does this structure differ from the other structures described in this chapter?

**6.28**   What is a selector? What purpose does it serve?

**6.29**   What values can be assigned to the case labels?

**6.30**   What happens when the value of the selector is the same as one of the labels? What happens when the value of the selector is not the same as any of the case labels?

**6.31**   Summarize the syntactical rules associated with the CASE structure. Can two or more labels be associated with one statement?

**6.32**   Compare the use of the CASE structure with the use of nested IF—THEN—ELSE structures. Which is more convenient?

**6.33**   What is the purpose of the GOTO statement? Is this a simple or a structured statement?

**6.34**   Summarize the syntactical rules associated with statement labels. What values can be used as statement labels? How are they declared? How is a statement label associated with a remote ("target") statement?

**6.35**   Compare the syntax associated with statement labels with that of case labels. Note all differences.

**6.36**   Describe the restrictions that apply to the use of the GOTO statement with compound statements. Do these same restrictions apply when using the GOTO statement with other control structures?

**6.37**   Why is the use of the GOTO statement discouraged in Pascal? Under what conditions might the GOTO statement be helpful? What type of usage should be avoided, and why? Discuss thoroughly.

# Solved Problems

**6.38** Determine the value of each of the following boolean expressions, using the identifiers defined below.

```
CONST a = 50;
      t = 0.02;
      x = 'P';
```

| Boolean Expression | Value |
| --- | --- |
| a < 12 | false |
| abs(t) = a/2500 | appears true, but probably false because of numerical inaccuracies |
| x <> 'p' | true |
| x = a | error—mixed data types |
| (a > 6) OR (t <= 0) | true |
| (a > 6) AND (t <= 0) | false |
| ((x = 'P') AND (t = 0)) OR (x > 'A') | true |
| (t >= 0) AND (NOT (x <> 'P')) | true |

**6.39** Each of the following skeletal control structures illustrates a different way to carry out a looping operation 100 times. (Assume that count is an integer-type variable.)

(*a*)
```
count := 1;
WHILE count <= 100 DO
   BEGIN
      .
      .
      .
      count := count + 1
   END;
```

(*b*)
```
count := 1;
REPEAT
   .
   .
   .
   count := count + 1
UNTIL count > 100;
```

(*c*)
```
FOR count := 1 TO 100 DO
   BEGIN
      .
      .
      .
   END;
```

(*d*)
```
FOR count := 100 DOWNTO 1 DO
   BEGIN
      .
      .
      .
   END;
```

**6.40**  Each of the following skeletal outlines illustrates a different approach to the nesting of control
structures.

(*a*)  
```
VAR i : integer;
    flag : boolean;
    .
    .
    .
flag := true;
WHILE flag DO
    BEGIN
        FOR i := 1 TO n DO
            BEGIN
                .
                .
                .
            END;
        .
        .
        .
        IF . . . THEN flag := false
    END;
```

(*b*)  
```
VAR i : integer;
    flag : boolean;
    .
    .
    .
flag := true;
REPEAT
    .
    .
    .
    IF . . . THEN FOR i := 1 TO n DO
                    BEGIN
                        .
                        .
                        .
                    END
             ELSE FOR i := n DOWNTO 1 DO
                    BEGIN
                        .
                        .
                        .
                    END;
    IF . . . THEN flag := false
UNTIL NOT flag;
```

(*c*)  
```
VAR c : char;
    count : integer;
    .
    .
    .
IF c <> '*'
```

(*Program continues on next page*)

```
                    THEN REPEAT
                            .
                            .
                            .
                        UNTIL c = '*'
                    ELSE FOR count := 1 TO 3 DO BEGIN
                                                    .
                                                    .
                                                    .
                                                END;
```

(d)  VAR count,start,finish,test,i : integer;

```
                .
                .
                .
            FOR count := start TO finish DO
                BEGIN
                    .
                    .
                    .
                    test := 1;
                    WHILE test < 10 DO
                        FOR i := 1 TO test DO
                            BEGIN
                                .
                                .
                                .
                            END;
                    test := test + 1;
                    .
                    .
                    .
                END;
```

**6.41**  The following skeletal outlines illustrate two different ways to select one of three distinct actions. (Assume that choice is an integer-type variable.)

(a)  IF choice =1 THEN . . .
```
                    ELSE IF choice = 2 THEN . . .
                                        ELSE . . . ;
```

(b)  CASE choice OF
```
            1 : . . . ;
            2 : . . . ;
            3 : . . .
        END;
```

Note that the use of nested IF-THEN-ELSE structures, as in part (a), becomes more cumbersome as the number of choices increases.

# Supplementary Problems

**6.42**   Determine the value of each of the following boolean expressions, using the identifiers defined below.

```
CONST f = 300;
      p = -0.001;
      q = 0.001;
      c = '5';
```

(*a*)  2*f >= 500

(*b*)  abs(p) = abs(q)

(*c*)  c = 5

(*d*)  p + q > 0

(*e*)  (abs(p) = q) AND (c > '4')

(*f*)  (p = abs(q)) OR (c > 4)

(*g*)  sqr(p) < sqrt(q)

(*h*)  (q < 0) OR ((f > 0) AND (f < 100))

(*i*)  NOT (c < '7')

**6.43**   Several control structures are outlined below. Some are written incorrectly. Identify all errors.

(*a*)
```
VAR result : real;
   .
   .
   .
WHILE result > 0 DO
   BEGIN
      .
      .
      .
   END;
```

(*b*)
```
VAR a,b,c,d : integer;
   .
   .
   .
REPEAT
   .
   .
   .
UNTIL (a+b) > (2*c-d);
```

(*c*)
```
VAR x,n1,n2 : real;
   .
   .
   .
FOR x := n1 TO n2 DO
   BEGIN
      .
      .
      .
   END;
```

(*d*)
```
VAR x : char;
   .
   .
   .
FOR x := 'z' DOWNTO 'a' DO
   BEGIN
      .
      .
      .
   END;
```

(*e*)
```
VAR a,b,c : integer;
   .
   .
   .
FOR a := b TO c DO
   BEGIN
      .
      .
      .
   END;
```

(*f*)
```
VAR a,b,c,d : integer;
   .
   .
   .
FOR a := b DOWNTO d DO
   BEGIN
      .
      .
      .
      FOR c := b TO d DO
         BEGIN
            .
            .
            .
         END
   END;
```

```
(g)  VAR a,b,c,d : integer;
          .
          .
          .
     FOR b := a TO c DO
        BEGIN
          .
          .
          .
           FOR d := a TO b DO
              BEGIN
                .
                .
                .
              END
        END;


(h)  VAR flag : boolean;
         c : char;
          .
          .
          .
     flag := true;
     WHILE flag DO
        BEGIN
          .
          .
          .
           REPEAT
             .
             .
             .
             read(c);
             IF c = '*' THEN flag := false;
             .
             .
           UNTIL NOT flag
        END;


(i)  VAR i,j : integer;
         x : real;
         flag : boolean;
          .
          .
          .
     IF i < 0 THEN IF j > 10 THEN flag := true
                       ELSE flag := false ELSE x := -0.1;


(j)  VAR x,y : real;
          .
          .
          .
     CASE sqr(x) OF
          1.0 : y := x;
          4.0 : y := 2*x;
          9.0 : y := 3*x;
         16.0 : y := 4*x
     END;
```

```
(k)  LABEL 10;
     VAR c : char;
          .
          .
          .
     read(c);
     IF c = '*' THEN GOTO 10;
          .
          .
          .
     WHILE c <> '*' DO
        BEGIN
          .
          .
          .
     10 : write(c);
          .
          .
          .
        END;


(l)  LABEL 1,2,3;
     VAR i : integer;
          .
          .
          .
     CASE i OF
        1 : BEGIN . . . GOTO 3 . . . END;
        2 : BEGIN . . . GOTO 3 . . . END;
        3 : BEGIN . . . END
     END;
```

# Programming Problems

**6.44**  Compile and execute the programs given in Examples 6.4, 6.5 and 6.8, using the following 10 numbers:

| | |
|---|---|
| 27.5 | 87.0 |
| 13.4 | 39.9 |
| 53.8 | 47.7 |
| 29.2 | 8.1 |
| 74.5 | 63.2 |

**6.45**  Modify the program given in Example 6.26, which averages a list of numbers whose length is unspecified, so that the GOTO statement is eliminated. Write the new program two different ways:

(*a*)  Using a WHILE—DO structure

(*b*)  Using a REPEAT—UNTIL structure

Test each version of the program using the data presented in the last problem.

**6.46**  Rewrite the depreciation program given in Example 6.17 to use the IF—THEN—ELSE structure instead of the CASE structure. Test the program using the data given in Example 6.17. Which version do you prefer? Why?

**6.47**  The equation

$$x^5 + 3x^2 - 10 = 0$$

which was presented in Example 6.14, can be rearranged into the form

$$x = [(10 - x^5)/3]^{1/2}$$

Rewrite the Pascal program presented in Example 6.14 to make use of the above form of the equation. Run the program and compare the calculated results with those presented in Example 6.14. Why are the results different? (Do computers ever make mistakes?)

**6.48**  Modify the program given in Example 6.14, which solves for the roots of an algebraic equation, so that the WHILE—DO structure is replaced by a REPEAT—UNTIL structure. Which structure is best suited for this particular problem?

**6.49**  Modify the program given in Example 6.14, which solves for the roots of an algebraic equation, so that the WHILE—DO structure is replaced by a FOR—TO structure. Compare the use of the FOR—TO, WHILE—DO and REPEAT—UNTIL structures. Which version do you prefer, and why?

**6.50**  Write a complete Pascal program for each of the problems presented below. Use the most natural type of control structure for each problem. Begin with a detailed outline, then rewrite the outline in pseudo-code if the translation into a working Pascal program is not entirely clear. Be sure to use good programming style (comments, indentation, etc.).

(*a*)  Calculate the *weighted average* of a list of *n* numbers, using the formula

$$x_{\text{avg}} = f_1 x_1 + f_2 x_2 + \cdots + f_n x_n$$

where the *f*'s are fractional *weighting factors*, i.e.,

$$0 <= f_i < 1 \quad \text{and} \quad f_1 + f_2 + \cdots + f_n = 1$$

Test your program with the following data:

$$
\begin{array}{lll}
i = 1 & f = 0.06 & x = 27.5 \\
\phantom{i =} 2 & \phantom{f =} 0.08 & \phantom{x =} 13.4 \\
\phantom{i =} 3 & \phantom{f =} 0.08 & \phantom{x =} 53.8 \\
\phantom{i =} 4 & \phantom{f =} 0.10 & \phantom{x =} 29.2 \\
\phantom{i =} 5 & \phantom{f =} 0.10 & \phantom{x =} 74.5 \\
\phantom{i =} 6 & \phantom{f =} 0.10 & \phantom{x =} 87.0 \\
\phantom{i =} 7 & \phantom{f =} 0.12 & \phantom{x =} 39.9 \\
\phantom{i =} 8 & \phantom{f =} 0.12 & \phantom{x =} 47.7 \\
\phantom{i =} 9 & \phantom{f =} 0.12 & \phantom{x =} 8.1 \\
\phantom{i =} 10 & \phantom{f =} 0.12 & \phantom{x =} 63.2
\end{array}
$$

(b)  Calculate the cumulative product of a list of $n$ numbers. Test your program with the following set of data ($n = 6$): 6.2, 12.3, 5.0, 18.8, 7.1, 12.8.

(c)  Calculate the geometric average of a list of numbers, using the formula

$$
x_{avg} = [x_1 x_2 x_3 \cdots x_n]^{1/n}
$$

Test your program using the data given in part (b) above. Compare the results obtained with the arithmetic average of the same data. Which average is larger?

(d)  Determine the roots of the quadratic equation

$$
ax^2 + bx + c = 0
$$

using the well-known quadratic formula

$$
x = \frac{-b \pm \sqrt{b^2 - 4ac}}{2a}
$$

(see Example 5.8). Allow for the possibility that one of the constants has a value of zero, and that the quantity $b^2 - 4ac$ is less than or equal to zero. Test the program using the following sets of data:

$$
\begin{array}{lll}
a = 2 & b = \phantom{0}6 & c = \phantom{-}1 \\
\phantom{a =} 3 & \phantom{b =} 3 & \phantom{c =} \phantom{-}0 \\
\phantom{a =} 1 & \phantom{b =} 3 & \phantom{c =} \phantom{-}1 \\
\phantom{a =} 0 & \phantom{b =} 12 & \phantom{c =} -3 \\
\phantom{a =} 3 & \phantom{b =} 6 & \phantom{c =} \phantom{-}3 \\
\phantom{a =} 2 & \phantom{b =} -4 & \phantom{c =} \phantom{-}3
\end{array}
$$

(e)  The *Fibonacci numbers* form an interesting sequence in which each number is equal to the sum of the previous two numbers. In other words,

$$
F_i = F_{i-1} + F_{i-2}
$$

where $F_i$ refers to the $i$th Fibonacci number. The first two Fibonacci numbers are, by definition, equal to 1; i.e., $F_1 = F_2 = 1$.
    Hence,

$$
F_3 = F_2 + F_1 = 1 + 1 = 2
$$
$$
F_4 = F_3 + F_2 = 2 + 1 = 3
$$
$$
F_5 = F_4 + F_3 = 3 + 2 = 5
$$

and so on.
    Write a program that will determine the first $n$ Fibonacci numbers. Test the program with $n = 23$.

(f)  A *prime number* is a positive integer quantity that is evenly divisible (without a remainder) only by 1 or by itself. Calculate and tabulate the first $n$ prime numbers. (*Hint*: a number $n$ will be a prime if none of the quotients $n/2, n/3, n/4, \ldots, n/\mathrm{sqrt}(n)$ are integer-valued.) Test your program by calculating the first 100 prime numbers.

(g) Write a conversational-style program that will read in a positive integer value and determine the following:

(1) If the integer is a prime number

(2) If the integer is a Fibonacci number

Write the program in such a manner that it will execute repeatedly (loop) until a zero value is detected for the input quantity. Test the program with several integer values of your choice.

(h) Calculate the sum of the first $n$ odd integers (i.e., $1 + 3 + 5 + \cdots + 2*n - 1$). Test the program by calculating the first 100 odd integers (note that the last integer will be 199).

(i) The sine of $x$ can be calculated approximately by summing the first $n$ terms of the infinite series

$$\sin x = x - x^3/3! + x^5/5! - x^7/7! + \cdots$$

where $x$ is expressed in radians. Write a Pascal program that will read in a value for $x$ and then calculate its sine. Write the program two different ways:

(1) Sum the first $n$ terms, where $n$ is a positive integer that is read into the computer along with the numerical value for $x$.

(2) Continue adding successive terms in the series until the value of a term becomes smaller (in magnitude) than $10^{-5}$.

Test the program for $x = 1$, $x = 2$ and $x = -3$. In each case write out the number of terms used to obtain the final answer.

(j) Suppose that $P$ dollars are borrowed from a bank, with the understanding that $A$ dollars will be repaid each month until the entire loan has been repaid. Part of the monthly payment will be interest, calculated as $i$ percent of the current unpaid balance. The remainder of the monthly payment will be applied toward the unpaid balance. Write a Pascal program that will determine the following information:

(1) The amount of interest paid each month
(2) The amount of money applied toward the unpaid balance each month
(3) The cumulative amount of interest that has been paid at the end of each month
(4) The amount of the loan that is still unpaid at the end of each month
(5) The number of monthly payments required to repay the entire loan
(6) The amount of the last payment (since it will probably be less than $A$)

Test your program using the following data: $P = \$40,000$; $A = \$2000$; $i = 1$ percent per month.

(k) A class of students earned the following grades for the six examinations taken in a Pascal programming course.

| Student Number | Exam Scores (percent) | | | | | |
|---|---|---|---|---|---|---|
| 10001 | 45 | 80 | 80 | 95 | 55 | 75 |
| 10002 | 60 | 50 | 70 | 75 | 55 | 80 |
| 10003 | 40 | 30 | 10 | 45 | 60 | 55 |
| 10004 | 0 | 5 | 5 | 0 | 10 | 5 |
| 10005 | 90 | 85 | 100 | 95 | 90 | 90 |
| 10006 | 95 | 90 | 80 | 95 | 85 | 80 |
| 10007 | 35 | 50 | 55 | 65 | 45 | 70 |
| 10008 | 75 | 60 | 75 | 60 | 70 | 80 |
| 10009 | 85 | 75 | 60 | 85 | 90 | 100 |
| 10010 | 50 | 60 | 50 | 35 | 65 | 70 |
| 10011 | 70 | 60 | 75 | 70 | 55 | 75 |
| 10012 | 10 | 25 | 35 | 20 | 30 | 10 |
| 10013 | 25 | 40 | 65 | 75 | 85 | 95 |
| 10014 | 65 | 80 | 70 | 100 | 60 | 95 |

Write a conversational-style Pascal program that will accept each student's number and exam grades as input, determine an average grade for each student and then write out the student number, the individual exam grades and the calculated average. Make the program as general as possible.

(*l*)   Modify the program written for part (*k*) above to allow for unequal weighting of the individual exam grades. In particular, assume that each of the first four exams contributes 15 percent to the final score and each of the last two exams contributes 20 percent.

(*m*)   Extend the program written for part (*l*) above so that an overall class average is determined in addition to the individual student averages.

(*n*)   Write a Pascal program that will allow the computer to be used as an ordinary desk calculator. Consider only the common arithmetic operations (addition, subtraction, multiplication and division). Include a memory that can store one number.

(*o*)   Generate the following "pyramid" of digits, using nested loops.

$$
\begin{array}{c}
1 \\
232 \\
34543 \\
4567654 \\
567898765 \\
67890109876 \\
7890123210987 \\
890123454321098 \\
90123456765432109 \\
0123456789876543210
\end{array}
$$

(Do *not* simply write out 10 multidigit strings.)

(*p*)   Generate a plot of the function

$$y = e^{-0.1t} \sin (0.5t)$$

on a line printer, using an asterisk (*) for each of the points that makes up the plot. Have the plot run vertically down the page, with one point (one asterisk) per line. (*Hint*: Each line should be comprised of one asterisk, preceded by an appropriate number of blank spaces. Determine the position of the asterisk using the round function.)

(*q*)   Write an interactive Pascal program that will convert a positive integer quantity to a roman numeral. Design the program so that it will execute repeatedly, until a value of zero is read in from the keyboard.

(*r*)   Write an interactive Pascal program that will convert a date, entered in the form mm-dd-yy (example: 4-12-69) into an integer that indicates the number of days beyond January 1, 1960. To do so, make use of the following relationships:

(1)   The day of the current year can be determined approximately as

```
day := trunc(30.42*(mm-1)) + dd
```

(2)   If mm = 2 (February), increase the value of day by 1.

(3)   If mm > 2 and mm < 8 (March, April, May, June and July), decrease the value of day by 1.

(4)   If yy MOD 4 = 0 and mm > 2 (leap year), increase the value of day by 1.

(5)   Increase the value of day by 1461 for each full 4-year cycle beyond 1-1-60.

(6)   Increase day by 365 for each additional full year beyond the completion of the last full 4-year cycle, then add 1 (for the most recent leap year).

Test the program with today's date, or any other date of your choice.

# Chapter 7

# Procedures and Functions

We have already seen that Pascal programs can easily be written in a modular form, thus allowing an overall problem to be decomposed into a sequence of individual subproblems. Modularization provides two important advantages in Pascal. First, for tasks that must be accessed from more than one place within a program, modularization avoids the need for redundant (repeated) programming of essentially the same set of instructions. Rather, a program module can be defined once and then accessed from several different places within the program. A different set of data can be processed each time the module is accessed. The use of program modules can therefore reduce the length of a program appreciably.

Of even greater significance is the logical clarity resulting from the decomposition of a program into individual, concise modules, where each module represents some well-defined part of the overall problem. Such programs are easier to write and to debug, and their logical structure is more apparent than programs that lack this type of structure. This is particularly true of lengthy, complicated programs. Many Pascal programs are therefore modularized, even though they may not involve repeated execution of the same tasks. In fact the decomposition of a program into individual modules is generally considered to be an important part of good programming practice.

There are two types of program modules in Pascal—*procedures* and *functions*. These two types of program structures are similar. They are, however, accessed differently, and they each exchange information in a different manner. We have already discussed the use of standard procedures (e.g., read and write) and standard functions (e.g., sqr) in Chap. 2. Let us now consider procedures and functions in greater detail. In particular, we will see how procedures and functions are written, how they differ from one another and how each type of structure is properly used. At the end of the chapter we will consider an interesting property of Pascal known as *recursion*, in which a procedure or function can successively access itself.

## 7.1 PROCEDURES

A *procedure* is a self-contained program structure that is included within a Pascal program. In some other programming languages, this type of structure is known as a *subroutine*.

A procedure can be referenced simply by writing the procedure name, followed by an optional list of parameters. The parameters must be enclosed in parentheses and, if there are more than one, separated by commas. Procedure references are also known as procedure *accesses* or procedure *calls*.

When a procedure is referenced, control is automatically transferred to the beginning of the procedure. The action statements within the procedure are then executed, taking into account any special declarations that are unique to the procedure. When all of the action statements have been executed, control is automatically returned to the statement *immediately after* the procedure reference.

**EXAMPLE 7.1**

A Pascal program reads in three integer quantities and then determines which quantity is the largest. The program includes the procedure maximum, which determines the largest of the three quantities and then writes out the result. The action statements that read in the three quantities and then access the procedure are shown below.

```
BEGIN
    readln(a,b,c);
    WHILE a <> 0 DO
        BEGIN maximum; readln(a,b,c) END
END.
```

When the reference to the procedure maximum is encountered, control is automatically transferred to this procedure (the procedure itself is not shown in this example). The procedure determines which of the variables a, b and c has the largest value and then writes out this result. Control is then returned to the following readln statement (which is also a procedure reference).

Notice that the program reads successive sets of three integer quantities and determines the maximum of each set. The repetition, which is controlled by the WHILE—DO structure, continues until a value of 0 is assigned to the variable a.

Now let us consider how the procedure itself is written. Each procedure has its own header and its own block. The header is written as

        PROCEDURE *name*

or, if formal parameters are included,

        PROCEDURE *name*(*formal parameters*)

(We will discuss the use of formal parameters in Sec. 7.3.)

The block consists of a declarations part (which is local to the procedure) and a group of action statements, just like the Pascal program in which the procedure is included. Thus, a procedure can be thought of as a special type of Pascal program that is embedded within another Pascal program.

### EXAMPLE 7.2

Here is a procedure called maximum that finds the largest of three integer quantities, a, b and c, and writes out the result.

```
PROCEDURE maximum;

(* This procedure finds the largest
        of three integer quantities *)
VAR max : integer;
BEGIN
    IF a > b THEN max := a ELSE max := b;
    IF c > max THEN max := c;
    writeln(' The maximum is ',max)
END;
```

The first line, which contains the keyword PROCEDURE, is the procedure header. (Note the similarity to the program header.) This is followed by the procedure block, which consists of one variable declaration and several action statements.

Notice that this procedure requires that values for a, b and c be assigned before the procedure is accessed. Use of the procedure is compatible with the program segment shown in Example 7.1.

All procedure declarations, such as that shown in the preceding example, must be included within the calling block (or some other external block that surrounds the calling block). In particular, the procedure and function declarations must be the last items in the declarations section, following the variable declarations (see Secs. 1.5 and 5.2). After a procedure has been declared within a block, it can be accessed anywhere in the action part of the block.

### EXAMPLE 7.3

**Largest of Three Numbers**. Here is a complete Pascal program that combines the program segments shown in the previous two examples.

```
PROGRAM sample(input,output);

(* This program uses a procedure to determine the maximum
                in each set of three integer quantities *)

VAR a,b,c : integer;

    PROCEDURE maximum;
    (* This procedure finds the largest
            of three integer quantities *)
    VAR max : integer;
    BEGIN
       IF a > b THEN max := a ELSE max := b;
       IF c > max THEN max := c;
       writeln(' The maximum is ',max)
    END;
BEGIN   (* main action block *)
   readln(a,b,c);
   WHILE a <> 0 DO
       BEGIN maximum; readln(a,b,c) END
END.
```

This program repeatedly reads sets of three integers and determines the maximum of each set. The computer will continue to read and process successive sets of data as long as the most recent value for a is not zero.

Notice that the procedure is declared before it is accessed and that the procedure declaration follows the variable declarations. (The blank lines are included only to improve the overall readability of the program.) Also, observe that the variables a, b and c, which are defined in the main part of the program, are recognized throughout the program, including the procedure. On the other hand, max is defined only within the procedure. Thus, it is not possible to make use of the variable max within the main part of the program.

The rules that govern procedure references are actually more general than the above examples indicate. We shall see shortly that a procedure can be accessed by the main program more than once. Moreover, a procedure can also be accessed by other procedures and functions.

## 7.2  SCOPE OF IDENTIFIERS

The constants and variables that appear within the action statements of a procedure may have been declared externally, within a program block that contains the procedure declaration, or locally, within the procedure itself. Those constants and variables that are declared within a block containing the procedure declaration can be utilized anywhere within that block, whether inside of or external to the procedure. Identifiers defined in this manner are considered to be *global* to the procedure. On the other hand, *local* constants and variables are not defined outside of the procedure and therefore cannot be utilized externally.

The *scope* of an identifier refers to the region within which the identifier is declared and can hence be utilized. This concept applies to *all* types of declarations, not just constants and variables.

**EXAMPLE 7.4**

**Largest of Three Numbers**. Let us again examine the Pascal program shown in Example 7.3.

```
PROGRAM sample(input,output);

(* This program uses a procedure to determine the maximum
                in each set of three integer quantities *)

VAR a,b,c : integer;
```

(*Program continues on next page*)

```
      PROCEDURE maximum;
      (* This procedure finds the maximum
              of three integer quantities *)
      VAR max : integer;
      BEGIN
         IF a > b THEN max := a ELSE max := b;
         IF c > max THEN max := c;
         writeln(' The maximum is ',max)
      END;

BEGIN    (* main action block *)
    readln(a,b,c);
    WHILE a <> 0 DO
        BEGIN maximum; readln(a,b,c) END
END.
```

This program contains one procedure, called maximum. The variables a, b and c are declared outside of this procedure and are therefore global to the procedure. These variables can be utilized both within and outside of the procedure (as is indeed the case). However, the variable max is declared within the procedure. Thus max is local to the procedure and cannot be utilized elsewhere.

In general, local identifiers are preferrable to global identifiers, provided this is not inconsistent with the overall program logic. In particular, the use of local identifiers contributes to greater program legibility. It also minimizes the likelihood of programming errors caused by incorrect or inconsistent identifier references.

On the other hand, many programs require that certain data items be recognized both within and outside of a procedure. One way to transfer such information across procedure boundaries is to make use of global identifiers, since global identifiers can be referenced wherever necessary. (Another approach is to use *parameters*, as discussed in the next section.) Thus a program might contain both local and global identifiers, depending on the logical requirements of the problem and the corresponding program structure. It is important to recognize when to use each type of identifier.

It is possible to use the same identifier to represent different entities in different portions of a program (though it is generally considered poor programming practice to do so). Thus, an identifier that is declared locally within a procedure may have the same name as a global identifier that has been declared externally. In such situations, the local definition will take precedence within its scope. Outside of this scope, however, the local identifier will be undefined, so that the global definition will apply.

**EXAMPLE 7.5**

The skeletal portion of a Pascal program containing two procedures is shown below.

```
PROGRAM sample(input,output);
VAR a,b : integer;
    c,d : char;

    PROCEDURE one;
    VAR a,d : real;
    BEGIN
        .
        .
        .
    END;

    PROCEDURE two;
    VAR a : char;
        b : boolean;
```

(*Program continues on next page*)

```
        BEGIN
            .
            .
            .
        END;

    BEGIN   (* main program - action statements *)
        .
        .
        .
    END.
```

Notice that procedure one contains two real, local variables: a and d. This procedure can also reference two global variables: b, which is integer, and c, which is of type char.

Procedure two recognizes the local variables a and b, which are of types char and boolean, respectively. Procedure two can also reference the global variables c and d, which are of type char.

The main block contains four local variables—a and b, which are integer, and c and d, which are of type char.

Notice that several of the variable names are used differently within the procedures than in the main block. In particular, a is redefined within each procedure, and b and d are each redefined within one of the procedures. The local definitions will take precedence within their respective procedures. Within the main block, however, the variables will be interpreted as in the original declarations.

Note that the use of the local variables, within their respective scopes, will not alter the values that are assigned to the global variables. The fact that the local and global variables share the same names is immaterial.

The issue of global versus local declarations applies to procedures (and functions) as well as to constants and variables. Thus, it is possible to declare a procedure (or a function) within another procedure. This feature allows procedures to be nested one within another. In such situations it is important, of course, that a procedure not be accessed outside of the block that contains the procedure declaration.

## EXAMPLE 7.6

Here is a skeletal outline of a Pascal program that contains nested procedures. The scope of the various procedures is indicated by indentation.

```
    PROGRAM main(input,output);

    PROCEDURE one;

        PROCEDURE two;
        BEGIN   (* procedure two - action statements *)
            .
            .
            .
        END;

        PROCEDURE three;
        BEGIN   (* procedure three - action statements *)
            .
            .
            two;   (* reference to procedure two *)
            .
            .
        END;
```

(*Program continues on next page*)

```
        BEGIN     (* procedure one - action statements *)
            .
            .
            .
            two;   (* reference to procedure two *)
            three;   (* reference to procedure three *)
            .
            .
            .
        END;

    BEGIN     (* main program - action statements *)
        .
        .
        .
        one;   (* reference to procedure one *)
        .
        .
        .
    END.
```

In this example, procedure one is declared within the main program block, and procedures two and three are declared within procedure one. The scope of procedures two and three is therefore local to procedure one. Thus, procedures two and three can be accessed within procedure one, but not within the main action statements. Procedures two and three can also access each other. On the other hand, procedure one *can* be accessed by the main action statements, since it is declared within the main block.

## EXAMPLE 7.7

**Largest of Three Numbers**. We now consider a variation of the Pascal program shown in Example 7.4. In the present example we decompose the original procedure maximum into two procedures, one nested within the other (as indicated by the indentation). The outermost procedure is still called maximum, but some of the original action statements now appear in the embedded procedure findmax.

```
    PROGRAM sample(input,output);

    (* This program uses a procedure to determine the maximum
                    in each set of three integer quantities *)

    VAR a,b,c : integer;

        PROCEDURE maximum;
        (* This procedure finds the largest
                of three integer quantities *)
        VAR max : integer;

            PROCEDURE findmax;
            (* This is where the action is *)
            BEGIN
                IF a > b THEN max := a ELSE max := b;
                IF c > max THEN max := c
            END;

        BEGIN   (* back to maximum - action statements *)
            findmax;
            writeln(' The maximum is ',max)
        END;

    BEGIN   (* main action statements *)
        readln(a,b,c);
        WHILE a <> 0 DO
            BEGIN maximum; readln(a,b,c) END
    END.
```

Notice that findmax is declared within maximum and that maximum is declared within the main program block. Thus, findmax is local to maximum. Notice also that maximum is accessed in the main block, but findmax is accessed within maximum.

A similar situation is seen with respect to the variables a, b, c and max. In particular, a, b and c are global with respect to the procedures, since they are declared within the main program block. These three variables can therefore be utilized anywhere within the program. On the other hand, max is local to the procedure maximum, and can therefore be utilized only within maximum or its nested procedure, findmax.

Finally, the concept of scope must be observed with statement labels as well as with constants, variables and procedures (and functions). In particular, a statement cannot be labeled unless the statement is included within the scope of the label declaration. Also, control cannot be transferred to a labeled statement from outside the scope of the label. It is possible, however, to transfer control to a labeled statement from anywhere within the scope of the label. Thus, control can be transferred out of a procedure (or function), provided the transfer does not go beyond the scope of the label definition. This applies even to procedures that have been nested several layers deep.

### EXAMPLE 7.8

**Averaging a List of Numbers.** In Example 6.26 we saw a Pascal program that calculates the average of a list of numbers by using a GOTO statement to transfer control out of a conditional loop once a negative number is read into the computer. (The negative number is intended as a stopping condition and is not included in the average.)

Let us now rewrite this program so that the data input and data accumulation functions are handled through a procedure. We will retain the use of the GOTO statement, so that control is transferred out of the procedure once a negative number is entered into the computer. Here is the complete Pascal program.

```
PROGRAM average6(input,output);

(* THIS PROGRAM CALCULATES THE AVERAGE OF A LIST OF NUMBERS
   USING THE WHILE - DO STRUCTURE AND A GOTO STATEMENT
   WITHIN A PROCEDURE *)

LABEL 10;
VAR count : integer;
    sum,average : real;

    PROCEDURE enterdata;
    (* This procedure reads and sums
       successive real, positive quantities *)
    VAR x : real;
        flag : boolean;
    BEGIN   (* action statements *)
       flag := true;
       WHILE flag DO
          BEGIN
             read(x);
             IF x < 0 THEN GOTO 10;
             sum := sum+x;
             count := count+1
          END
    END;

BEGIN   (* main action statements *)
    count := 0;
    sum := 0;
    enterdata;
10 : average := sum/count;
    writeln(' The average of ',count:5,' numbers is ',average)
END.
```

Notice that the statement label 10 and the variables count, sum and average are declared within the main block, since these items are required both in the action part of this block and in the enclosed procedure. On the other hand, x and flag are declared locally within the procedure because these identifiers are not required outside of the procedure. Notice that control is transferred directly out of the procedure when a negative value for x is encountered.

It should be understood that this example contains several contrivances in order to illustrate certain features. In reality, this program should have been written without the GOTO statement. Moreover, the calculation of the average and the subsequent output statements could have been included within the procedure. This would have allowed all of the variables to be declared locally within the procedure—a generally better approach to the problem.

## 7.3  PARAMETERS

Many Pascal programs require that information be exchanged between a procedure (or a function) and the point at which the procedure (function) is referenced. One way to accomplish this is to utilize global variables, as discussed in the last section. We have also seen, however, that there are some potentially undesirable aspects to the use of global variables. For example, altering the value of a global variable within a procedure may inadvertently alter certain information outside of the procedure, and vice versa. Furthermore, the transfer of multiple data sets cannot easily be accommodated with global variables.

The use of parameters offers a better approach to the exchange of information between a procedure and its reference point. Each data item is transferred between an *actual parameter*, which is included within the procedure reference, and a corresponding *formal parameter*, which is defined within the procedure itself. When the procedure is accessed, the actual parameters replace the formal parameters, thus creating an information exchange mechanism between the procedure and its reference point. The manner in which the information is exchanged depends, however, on the manner in which the parameters are defined and utilized.

### EXAMPLE 7.9

The skeletal structure given below illustrates the simplest type of information exchange between a procedure reference and the procedure itself.

```
    PROGRAM sample(input,output);
    VAR a,b,c,d : real;

        PROCEDURE flash(x,y : real);
        BEGIN
           .
           .
        (* process the values of x and y *)
           .
           .
        END;

    BEGIN    (* main program action statements *)
       .
       .
       flash(a,b);
       .
       .
       flash(c,d);
       .
       .
    END.
```

In this example the variables x and y are real-type formal parameters defined within the procedure flash. The actual parameters are the real variables a, b, c and d. We will assume that a, b, c and d have been assigned values elsewhere in the program, prior to the procedure references.

The first procedure reference causes the values of the actual parameters a and b to be transferred to the formal parameters x and y. Thus, the values of a and b are passed to procedure flash, where they are then processed. (The manner in which they are processed is immaterial in this example.)

This process is then repeated in the second procedure statement, this time transferring the values of c and d to x and y. The values of c and d are thus passed to flash, where they are processed accordingly.

Notice that we have processed two different data sets simply by accessing the same procedure twice, with a different set of actual parameters each time.

There are certain rules that must be observed in order to establish a correspondence between a procedure reference and the procedure itself (i.e., when substituting actual parameters for formal parameters). They are

1. The number of actual parameters in the procedure reference must be the same as the number of formal parameters in the procedure definition.

2. Each actual parameter must be of the same type as its corresponding formal parameter.

3. Each actual parameter must be expressed in a manner which is consistent with its corresponding formal parameter, as determined by the class of the formal parameter (the class of a formal parameter is described below).

**EXAMPLE 7.10**

Consider the following skeletal program structure.

```
PROGRAM sample(input,output);
VAR a,b : integer;
    c,d : real;

    PROCEDURE flash(x : integer; y : real);
    BEGIN
         .
         .
    (* process the values of x and y *)
         .
         .
    END;

BEGIN   (* main program action statements *)
     .
     .
    flash(a,c);
     .
     .
    flash(b,d);
     .
     .
END.
```

Note that each procedure reference includes two actual parameters, since two formal parameters (x and y) are defined within the procedure. Moreover, x is declared as an integer-type variable, and y is a real-type variable. Thus, each procedure reference must include one integer variable and one real variable, in that order.

A procedure can contain four different classes of formal parameters. They are *value parameters*, *variable parameters*, *procedure parameters* and *function parameters*. We will discuss value parameters and variable parameters at this time. The two remaining parameter types will be discussed later in this chapter (see Sec. 7.5).

**Value Parameters**

Value parameters can best be thought of as *input parameters* for their respective procedures. The use of a value parameter involves a transfer of value rather than an actual parameter substitution. Thus, when information is transferred between an actual parameter and a value parameter, the value of the actual parameter is assigned to the value parameter. This value can then be processed within the procedure (by referring to the value parameter). Values that are represented by value parameters *cannot*, however, be transferred in the opposite direction, i.e., from the procedure to the calling portion of the program. This is why value parameters are regarded as input parameters.

Value parameters are very simple to use. They are declared by simply including their names and corresponding data types within the procedure header, without any prefix (such as VAR). It is the absence of such a prefix that automatically identifies this class of parameters. Examples 7.9 and 7.10 both make use of value parameters.

It should be understood that any alteration to the value of a value parameter within the procedure will not affect the value of any of the actual parameters (remember that value parameters are regarded as *input* parameters). This characteristic may limit the use of value parameters. However, such parameters are easy to use in situations that allow for a one-way transfer of information. Furthermore, since it is the *values* of the actual parameters that are transferred rather than the parameters themselves, there is considerable latitude in the manner in which the actual parameters can be written. In particular, an actual parameter may be expressed as a constant, a variable or an expression (provided the value of the parameter is of the proper data type).

**EXAMPLE 7.11**

Consider the following modification of the program outline shown in Example 7.10.

```
PROGRAM sample(input,output);
VAR a,b : integer;
    c,d : real;

    PROCEDURE flash(x : integer; y : real);
    BEGIN
       .
       .
    (* process the values of x and y *)
       .
       .
    END;

BEGIN   (* main program action statements *)
   .
   .
   flash(3,a*(c+d)/b);
   .
   .
   flash(2*(a+b),-0.5);
   .
   .
END.
```

Notice that the formal parameters x and y, declared in procedure flash, are value parameters. (This is also true in Examples 7.9 and 7.10.) The first of these (x) is of type integer, and the second (y) is real. Therefore, each reference to flash must contain two actual parameters, the first of which must be of type integer and the second real.

The main block includes two different procedure references (i.e., two different references to flash). Each procedure reference contains two actual parameters, the first of which is of type integer and the second real, as required. Notice that two of these parameters are written as constants and two are written as expressions. Thus, the first procedure reference transfers the value 3 to x, and the value of the real expression a*(c+d)/b to y.

Similarly, the second procedure reference transfers the value of the integer expression 2*(a+b) to x and the value $-0.5$ to y.


## EXAMPLE 7.12

**Calculating Depreciation**. Consider once again the problem described in Example 6.17 of calculating depreciation by one of three different methods. Let us now rewrite the program so that a separate procedure is used for each method. This approach offers us a cleaner way to organize the program into its logical components. (A detailed description of the program logic is given in Example 6.17.)

Here is the complete Pascal program.

```
PROGRAM depreciation2(input,output);

(* THIS PROGRAM USES PROCEDURES TO CALCULATE
   DEPRECIATION BY ONE OF THREE POSSIBLE METHODS *)

VAR years,choice : integer;
    value : real;
    flag : boolean;

    PROCEDURE straightline(n : integer; val : real);
    (* Calculate depreciation using the straight line method *)
    VAR year : integer;
        deprec : real;
    BEGIN
      writeln(' Straight-Line Method');
      writeln;
      deprec := val/n;
      FOR year := 1 TO n DO
         BEGIN
            val := val-deprec;
            write(' End of Year ',year:2);
            write('   Depreciation: ',deprec:5:0);
            writeln('   Current Value: ',val:6:0)
         END
    END;

    PROCEDURE decliningbalance(n : integer; val : real);
    (* Calculate depreciation using the
       double-declining balance method *)
    VAR year : integer;
        deprec : real;
    BEGIN
      writeln(' Double Declining Balance Method');
      writeln;
      FOR year := 1 TO n DO
         BEGIN
            deprec := 2*val/n;
            val := val-deprec;
            write(' End of Year ',year:2);
            write('   Depreciation: ',deprec:5:0);
            writeln('   Current Value: ',val:6:0)
         END
    END;
```

(*Program continues on next page*)

```
                        PROCEDURE sumofyears(n : integer; val : real);
                        (* Calculate depreciation using the
                           sum-of-the-years'-digits method *)
                        VAR year : integer;
                            deprec,tag : real;
                        BEGIN
                           writeln(' Sum-of-the-Years''-Digits Method');
                           writeln;
                           tag := val;
                           FOR year := 1 TO n DO
                              BEGIN
                                 deprec := (n-year+1)*tag/(n*(n+1)/2);
                                 val := val-deprec;
                                 write(' End of Year ',year:2);
                                 write('   Depreciation: ',deprec:5:0);
                                 writeln('   Current Value: ',val:6:0)
                              END
                        END;

                 BEGIN   (* main action block *)
                     flag := true;
                     REPEAT
                        page;        (* begin input routine *)
                        write(' Method: (1-SL  2-DDB  3-SYD  4-End) ');
                        readln(choice);
                        IF choice <> 4 THEN
                        BEGIN
                           write(' Original value: ');
                           readln(value);
                           write(' Number of years: ');
                           readln(years);
                           writeln
                        END;   (* input routine *)
                        CASE choice OF
                           1 : straightline(years,value);
                           2 : decliningbalance(years,value);
                           3 : sumofyears(years,value);
                           4 : BEGIN
                                  writeln(' That''s all, folks!');
                                  flag := false
                               END
                        END   (* choice *)
                     UNTIL flag = false
                 END.
```

Notice that the CASE structure is still employed, as in Example 6.17, but now the program utilizes a different procedure for each type of calculation. The procedures make use of the value parameters n and val, which represent the lifetime of the depreciated item and its original value, respectively. The corresponding actual parameters in the main block are years and value. Thus, when a procedure is referenced, the value of years is assigned to n, and the value of value is assigned to val. (We could, of course, have utilized the same variable names in both the main block and each of the procedures. This would have been simpler, though perhaps less informative.)

Notice that the use of value parameters is appropriate in this example because the procedures do not change the values of the parameters and they do not return any values to the main (calling) block.

### Variable Parameters

We have seen that value parameters are convenient to work with in situations where information is transferred only from the procedure reference to the procedure. In many applications, however, information must be transferred in both directions between the procedure and the procedure reference. In other words, the procedure must be able to accommodate both input from and output to the calling block. Variable parameters are generally used in such situations.

When a procedure containing a variable parameter is accessed, an actual parameter in the procedure reference is substituted for the formal parameter within the procedure itself. Thus, the actual parameter will be utilized during the execution of the procedure. This contrasts with the use of a value parameter, where the *value* of the actual parameter is assigned to the formal parameter (note the distinction between *assignment* and *substitution*). It is this substitution process that allows a two-way transfer of information between the procedure reference and the procedure itself.

On the other hand, it should be pointed out that only a variable can be substituted for another variable. Thus, the actual parameters that are substituted for variable parameters must themselves be variables; they cannot be constants or expressions. We therefore have somewhat less generality in the use of variable parameters than with value parameters.

Another consequence of the substitution process is the fact that any change in the value of a variable parameter within a procedure will also change the value of the corresponding actual parameter outside of the procedure. Thus, variable parameters can affect a program globally, even though their scope is local to the procedure within which they are declared.

Variable parameters are declared within the procedure header, as are value parameters. However, variable parameter declarations must be preceded by the keyword VAR, as illustrated in the next example.

**EXAMPLE 7.13**

Consider once again the skeletal program structure presented in Example 7.10. If the procedure were modified to make use of variable parameters, the skeletal structure would appear as follows.

```
    PROGRAM sample(input,output);
    VAR a,b : integer;
        c,d : real;

        PROCEDURE flash( VAR x : integer; VAR y : real);
        BEGIN
            .
            .
        (* process the values of x and y *)
            .
            .
        END;

    BEGIN   (* main program action statements *)
        .
        .
        flash(a,c);
        .
        .
        flash(b,d);
        .
        .
    END.
```

The first procedure reference causes the actual parameters a and c to be substituted for x and y. If the value of either x or y is altered within the procedure, then a corresponding alteration in the value of a or c will occur in the main block.

Similarly, the second procedure reference results in b and d being substituted for x and y. Any alteration in the value of either x or y within the procedure will therefore cause a corresponding alteration in the value of b or d in the main block.

Note that the actual parameters agree with the corresponding formal parameters in number and in type.

**EXAMPLE 7.14**

**Search for a Maximum**. Suppose we wish to find the particular value of $x$ that causes the function

$$y = x \cos (x)$$

to be maximized within the interval bounded by $x = 0$ on the left and $x = \pi$ on the right. We will require that the maximizing value of $x$ be known quite accurately. We will also require that the search scheme be relatively efficient in the sense that the function $y = x \cos (x)$ should be evaluated as few times as possible.

An obvious way to solve this problem would be to generate a large number of closely spaced trial functions (that is, evaluate the function at $x = 0$, $x = 0.0001$, $x = 0.0002, \ldots, x = 3.1415$, and $x = 3.1416$) and determine the largest of these by visual inspection. This would not be very efficient, however, and it would require human intervention to obtain the final result. Instead let us use the following *elimination scheme*, which is a highly efficient computational procedure for all functions that have only one peak within the search interval.

The computation will be carried out as follows. We begin with two search points at the center of the search interval, located a very small distance from each other, as shown in Fig. 7-1. The following notation is used.

$$a = \text{left end of the search interval}$$
$$xl = \text{left-hand interior search point}$$
$$xr = \text{right-hand interior search point}$$
$$b = \text{right end of the search interval}$$
$$sep = \text{distance between xl and xr.}$$

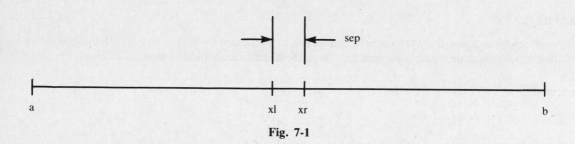

**Fig. 7-1**

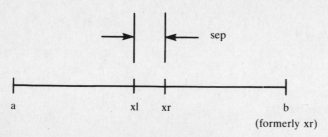

**Fig. 7-2**

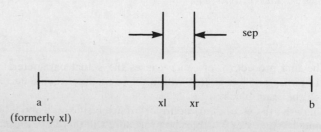

**Fig. 7-3**

If a, b and sep are known, then the interior points can be calculated as

$$xl = a + .5*(b-a-sep)$$

$$xr = a + .5*(b-a+sep) = xl + sep$$

Let us evaluate the function y = x cos (x) at xl and at xr, and let us call these values yl and yr, respectively. Suppose yl turns out to be greater than yr. Then we know that the maximum will lie somewhere between a and xr. Hence we retain only that portion of the search interval which ranges from x = a to x = xr (we will now refer to the old point xr as b, since it is now the right end of the new search interval) and generate two new search points, xl and xr. These points will be located at the center of the new search interval, a distance sep apart, as shown in Fig. 7-2.

On the other hand, suppose now that in our *original* search interval the value of yr turned out to be greater than yl. This would indicate that our new search interval should lie between xl and b. Hence we rename the point which was originally called xl to be a and we generate two new search points, xl and xr, at the center of the new search interval, as shown in Fig. 7-3.

We continue to generate a new pair of search points at the center of each new interval, compare the respective values of y, and eliminate a portion of the search interval until the search interval becomes smaller than 3*sep. Once this happens we can no longer distinguish the interior points from the boundaries. Hence the search is ended.

Each time we make a comparison between yl and yr we eliminate that portion of the search interval that contains the smaller value of y. If both interior values of y should happen to be identical (which can happen, though it is unusual), then the search procedure stops, and the maximum is assumed to occur at the center of the last two interior points.

Once the search has ended, either because the search interval has become sufficiently small or because the two interior points yield identical values of y, we can calculate the approximate location of the maximum as

$$xmax = .5*(xl + xr)$$

The corresponding maximum value of the function can then be obtained as xmax cos (xmax).

Let us consider a program outline for the general case where a and b are input quantities but sep has a fixed value of 0.0001.

1. Assign a value of sep = 0.0001.

2. Read in the values of a and b.

3. Repeat the following until either yl becomes equal to yr (the desired maximum will be at the midpoint), or the most recent value of (b-a) becomes less than or equal to 3*sep:
   (a) Generate the two interior points, xl and xr.
   (b) Calculate the corresponding values of yl and yr, and determine which is larger.
   (c) Reduce the search interval, by eliminating that portion that does not contain the larger value of y.

4. Evaluate xmax and ymax.

5. Write out the values of xmax and ymax, and stop.

Step 3 can very conveniently be packaged as a procedure. To do so, let us define the variables a, b, xl, xr, yl and yr to be variable parameters. (The values represented by these parameters will change through the course of the computation and will be transferred back and forth between the procedure and the main block.)

```
PROCEDURE reduce( VAR a,b,xl,xr,yl,yr : real);
(* Interval reduction routine *)
BEGIN
    xl := a + 0.5*(b-a-sep);
    xr := xl + sep;
    yl := xl*cos(xl);
    yr := xr*cos(xr);
    IF yl > yr THEN b := xr;    (* retain left interval *)
    IF yr > yl THEN a := xl     (* retain right interval *)
END;
```

Notice that sep is not declared as a parameter within the procedure. We will define sep as a global constant within the main block, since its value never changes. Also, notice the use of the standard function cos within the procedure; we will also utilize this function in the main block. Finally, we point out that the interval reduction will not work properly if yl and yr are equal (this is possible but unlikely). This problem can easily be corrected, by replacing one of the > operators with >=.

It is now quite easy to write the complete program. Here it is.

```
PROGRAM maximum1(input,output);

(* THIS PROGRAM FINDS THE MAXIMUM OF A
   FUNCTION WITHIN A SPECIFIED INTERVAL *)

CONST sep = 0.0001;
VAR a,b,xl,xr,xmax,yl,yr,ymax : real;

PROCEDURE reduce( VAR a,b,xl,xr,yl,yr : real);
(* Interval reduction routine *)
BEGIN
  xl := a + 0.5*(b-a-sep);
  xr := xl + sep;
  yl := xl*cos(xl);
  yr := xr*cos(xr);
  IF yl > yr THEN b := xr;   (* retain left interval *)
  IF yr > yl THEN a := xl    (* retain right interval *)
END;

BEGIN   (* main action block *)
  readln(a,b);
  REPEAT
    reduce(a,b,xl,xr,yl,yr)
  UNTIL (yl=yr) OR ( b-a <= 3*sep );
  xmax := 0.5*(xl+xr);
  ymax := xmax*cos(xmax);
  writeln(' xmax = ',xmax:8:6,'   ymax = ',ymax:8:6)
END.
```

Execution of the program, with a = 0 and b = 3.141593, results in the following output.

```
xmax = 0.860586   ymax = 0.561096
```

Thus, we have obtained the location and the value of the maximum within the given original interval.

## 7.4 FUNCTIONS

A *function* is a self-contained program structure that is in many respects similar to a procedure. (Recall our brief discussion of this topic in Sec. 2.12.) Unlike a procedure, however, a function is used to return a single simple-type value to its reference point. Moreover, a function is referenced by specifying its name within an expression as though it were an ordinary simple-type variable. The function name can be followed by one or more actual parameters, enclosed in parentheses and separated by commas. In most situations, the actual parameters will transfer information to value parameters within the function and can therefore be expressed as constants, variables or expressions.

**EXAMPLE 7.15**

Suppose that factorial is the name of a function that calculates the factorial of some integer quantity. (Recall that the factorial of a positive integer quantity $n$ is defined as $n! = 1 \times 2 \times \cdots \times n$.) Then the formula

$$f = x!/a!(x - a)!$$

could be evaluated as

```
f := factorial(x)/(factorial(a)*factorial(x-a));
```

where f, x and a are integer-type variables.

Notice the similarity between the use of this user-defined function and the use of a standard function, as described in Sec. 2.12.

The function itself consists of a function header and a block. The function header is written in the form

```
FUNCTION name : type
```

or, if parameters are included,

```
FUNCTION name(formal parameters) : type
```

The last item, *type*, specifies the data type of the result that is returned by the function.

Generally, the formal parameters will be value parameters rather than variable parameters. This allows the corresponding actual parameters to be expressed as constants, variables or expressions. (Remember that these parameters will provide only input values to the function; the single output value provided by the function will be represented by the function name rather than a parameter.)

The block is similar to that of a procedure and involves the same rules of scope as a procedure. Within the block, however, the identifier that represents the function name must be assigned a value of the appropriate type (as specified in the header). This is the value that the function returns to its reference point. Values can be assigned to the function name at two or more points within the block. Once an assignment is made, however, it cannot subsequently be altered.

**EXAMPLE 7.16**

Here is a function called factorial that calculates the factorial of a positive integer quantity. (See Example 7.15.)

```
FUNCTION factorial(n : integer) : integer;
(* Calculate the factorial of n *)
VAR factor,product : integer;
BEGIN
    IF n <= 1 THEN factorial := 1
            ELSE BEGIN
                    product := 1;
                    FOR factor := 2 TO n DO
                        product := product*factor;
                    factorial := product
                END
END;
```

The first line, which contains the keyword FUNCTION, is the function header. Notice that the header includes a declaration of the value parameter n. Also, notice the last item on the line (integer), which states that the function will return an integer-type quantity.

This function accepts a value for n and then calculates the value of n! using two local integer variables, factor and product. The final result is assigned to the identifier factorial, which is also the function name.

Note that there are two different assignments to factorial, but only one of these assignments is utilized when the function is executed. The choice depends upon the value that is assigned to n. Once factorial is assigned a value, however, it is not altered within the function.

To amplify on this last point, consider the following variation of the above function.

```
FUNCTION factorial(n : integer) : integer;
(* Calculate the factorial of n *)
VAR factor : integer;
BEGIN
    factorial := 1;
    IF n > 1 THEN FOR factor := 2 TO n DO
                    factorial := factorial*factor
END;
```

On the surface this version appears more appealing than the original, since it is simpler. This version is *not* valid, however, because the value of factorial is altered after its initial assignment when n is greater than 1.

Functions are declared in the same manner as procedures, within the calling block or some external block that surrounds the calling block. There is no particular order with respect to functions vs. procedures. (Remember, though, that the function and procedure declarations must be the *last* declarations within the block, following any label, constant, type and variable declarations.)

**EXAMPLE 7.17**

**Calculating Factorials**. Here is a complete Pascal program that determines the factorial of a given input quantity.

```
PROGRAM factorials2(input,output);

(* THIS PROGRAM USES A FUNCTION TO CALCULATE
   THE FACTORIAL OF A GIVEN INTEGER QUANTITY *)

VAR x : integer;

    FUNCTION factorial(n : integer) : integer;
    (* calculate the factorial of n *)
    VAR factor,product : integer;
    BEGIN
       IF n <= 1 THEN factorial := 1
                 ELSE BEGIN
                         product := 1;
                         FOR factor := 2 TO n DO
                             product := product*factor;
                         factorial := product
                      END
    END;

BEGIN   (* main action block *)
   write(' Enter a positive integer: ');
   readln(x);
   writeln;
   writeln(' x= ',x,'   x! = ',factorial(x))
END.
```

Notice that the function factorial is accessed only once, in the last writeln statement within the main block.

When running this program some care must be given to the value that is assigned to x since an overflow may occur if x is assigned too large a number. (Remember that factorials increase in value very quickly.) This is particularly true of small computers, where the largest permissible integer quantity may be relatively small. The value 8! = 40,320 may be too large for some small computers.

Functions can be nested, one within another, in the same manner as procedures. Moreover, the nesting of functions and procedures can be interchanged. Thus, a function can be declared within a procedure that has been declared within another function, and so on.

**EXAMPLE 7.18**

**Simulation of a Game of Chance (Shooting Craps)**. Here is an interesting programming problem that makes use of a procedure with nested functions.

Craps is a popular dice game in which you throw a pair of dice one or more times until you either win or lose. The game can be computerized by substituting the generation of random numbers for the actual throwing of the dice.

There are two ways to win in craps. You can throw the dice once and obtain a score of either 7 or 11, or you can obtain a 4, 5, 6, 8, 9 or 10 on the first throw and then repeat the same score on a subsequent throw before obtaining a 7. Conversely, there are two ways to lose. You can throw the dice once and obtain a 2, 3 or 12, or you can obtain a 4, 5, 6, 8, 9 or 10 on the first throw and then obtain a 7 on a subsequent throw before repeating your original score.

Let us computerize the game in a conversational manner, so that one throw of the dice will be simulated each time you depress the carriage return on the console. A message will then appear indicating the outcome of each throw. At the end of each game, you will be asked whether or not you want to continue to play.

Our program will require a random number generator, which produces uniformly distributed random numbers between zero and one. (By *uniformly distributed* we mean that any number between zero and one is just as likely to appear as any other number.) Some versions of Pascal include a random number generator as a standard function or a standard procedure, but many do not. Therefore we will provide our own random number generator, using a well-known technique called the *power-residue method*.

The numbers that we generate will not really be random because the *same* sequence of numbers will always be generated for a given starting value (i.e., for the same "seed"). However, the sequence of numbers will *appear* to be random and will have many of the statistical characteristics of numbers that are truly random.

We will not discuss the underlying basis of the random number generator, as it is well beyond the scope of this book, though the actual program module is quite simple. We simply present the random number generator in the form of a function called rand. This function is written specifically for a computer that utilizes 16-bit integer quantities. (Most personal computers fall into this category.)

```
FUNCTION rand : real;
(* 16-bit random number generator *)
VAR y,z : integer;
BEGIN
   z := 259*x;
   IF z >= 0 THEN y := z
             ELSE BEGIN y := z + 32767; y := y + 1 END;
   rand := 0.3051757E-4*y;
   x := y
END;
```

In order to use this function an integer value must be assigned to the global variable x each time the function is called. Initially, this will be the "seed," which can be specified as an input parameter or as a constant. Subsequent references to rand will use the previous value for y as the new value for x (note that this feature is included at the end of the function).

Let us define another function, called throw, to simulate one throw of the dice. This function will contain the random number generator. Each die will be simulated separately by generating a random integer that takes on the value 1, 2, 3, 4, 5 or 6 with equal likelihood. The two simulated values are then added together to represent one throw of the dice. In pseudocode, we can represent this function as

```
FUNCTION throw : integer;
(* Throw the dice one time *)
VAR d1,d2 : integer;

(* define the random number generator *)

BEGIN
   d1 := 1 + trunc(6*rand);
   d2 := 1 + trunc(6*rand);
   throw := d1 + d2
END;
```

This function requires some explanation. Consider, for example, the first assignment statement (d1 := . . .). The function rand will return a random number between the limits 0 and 1 (actually, between 0 and 0.9999999...). Thus the expression 6*rand will return a random value between 0 and 6 (actually, between 0 and 5.9999999...), and the expression trunc(6*rand) will return a random integer whose value can be 0, 1, 2, 3, 4 or 5 with equal likelihood. We then add 1 to obtain a random integer which can take on the values 1, 2, 3, 4, 5 or 6 with equal likelihood. Hence, this expression will simulate the throwing of one die.

Now let us define a procedure, called play, that can simulate one complete game of craps (i.e., the dice will be thrown as many times as is necessary to establish either a win or a loss). This procedure will therefore contain function throw. The complete rules of craps will also be built into this procedure. In pseudocode, we can write this function as

```
PROCEDURE play;
(* Simulate a single game of craps *)
VAR score,tag : integer;

(* define function throw *)

BEGIN

    (* instruct the user to throw the dice *)

    score := throw;
    CASE score OF
       7,11 : BEGIN   (* win on first throw *)

                 (* write a message indicating a win on the first throw *)

              END;
       2,3,12 : BEGIN   (* loss on first throw *)

                  (* write a message indicating a loss on the first throw *)

                END;
       4,5,6,8,9,10 : BEGIN   (* multiple throws *)
                         tag := score;
                         REPEAT

                         (* instruct the user to throw the dice again *)

                            score := throw;
                         UNTIL (score = tag) OR (score = 7);
                         IF score = tag
                            THEN BEGIN

                                    (* write a message indicating a win *)

                                 END
                            ELSE BEGIN

                                    (* write a message indicating a loss *)

                                 END
                      END   (* multiple throws *)
    END   (* case *)
END;
```

Finally, the main block will be used to control the execution of the game. This routine will consist of little more than some interactive input/output and a call to procedure play. (Note, however, that play will be defined within this block.) Thus, we can write the pseudocode as follows.

```
PROGRAM craps(input,output);
(* Interactive simulation of a game of craps *)
CONST seed = 12345;
VAR count,x : integer;
    n : real;
    answer : char;
    flag : boolean;

(* define procedure play *)
```

(*Program continues on next page*)

```
BEGIN
   x := seed;
   flag := true;

   (* generate a welcoming message *)

   WHILE flag DO
      BEGIN
         play;
         write(' Do you want to play AGAIN? (Y/N) ');
         readln(answer);
         IF (answer = 'N') OR (answer = 'n') THEN flag := false
      END;

   (* generate a sign-off message *)

END.
```

Note that the program will be executed repeatedly, until the player indicates a desire to stop. Here is the complete Pascal program, with some additional comments.

```
PROGRAM craps(input,output);

(* THIS PROGRAM USES SEVERAL FUNCTIONS TO SIMULATE A GAME OF CRAPS.

   IT INCLUDES A RANDOM NUMBER GENERATOR THAT IS SPECIFICALLY DESIGNED
   FOR A COMPUTER THAT UTILIZES 16-BIT (2-BYTE) INTEGER QUANTITIES. *)

CONST seed = 12345;
VAR count,x : integer;
    n : real;
    answer : char;
    flag : boolean;

PROCEDURE play;
(* This procedure simulates a single game of craps *)
VAR score,tag : integer;

      FUNCTION throw : integer;
      (* This function simulates one throw of a pair of dice *)
      VAR d1,d2 : integer;

           FUNCTION rand : real;
           (* Note: This function can only be used with a computer that
                    supports 16-bit (2-byte) integer quantities. *)
           VAR y,z : integer;
           BEGIN   (* generate a random number *)
              z := 259*x;
              IF z >= 0 THEN y := z
                       ELSE BEGIN y := z + 32767; y := y + 1 END;
              rand := 0.3051757E-4*y;
              x := y
           END;   (* rand *)

      BEGIN   (* throw the dice once *)
         d1 := 1 + trunc(6*rand);
         d2 := 1 + trunc(6*rand);
         throw := d1 + d2
      END;   (* throw *)
```

(*Program continues on next page*)

```
BEGIN   (* play one game *)
   writeln;
   writeln(' Throw the dice . . .');
   readln;
   score := throw;
   CASE score OF
      7,11 : BEGIN   (* win on first throw *)
                write(score:3,' - Congratulations!');
                writeln('  You WIN on the first throw!');
                writeln
             END;
      2,3,12 : BEGIN   (* loss on first throw *)
                write(score:3,' - Tough luck!');
                writeln('  You LOSE on the first throw!');
                writeln
             END;
      4,5,6,8,9,10 : BEGIN   (* multiple throws *)
                        tag := score;
                        REPEAT
                           write(score:3);
                           writeln(' - Throw the dice again . . .');
                           readln;
                           score := throw;
                        UNTIL (score = tag) OR (score = 7);
                        IF score = tag
                           THEN BEGIN
                                   write(score:3);
                                   write(' - You WIN by matching');
                                   writeln(' your first score');
                                   writeln
                                END
                           ELSE BEGIN
                                   write(score:3);
                                   write(' - You LOSE by failing to');
                                   writeln(' match your first score');
                                   writeln
                                END
                     END   (* multiple throws *)
   END   (* case *)
END;   (* play *)

BEGIN   (* executive routine *)
   x := seed;
   flag := true;
   page;
   writeln(' Welcome to the Game of CRAPS!');
   writeln;
   write(' Press the CARRIAGE RETURN to begin playing');
   readln;
   WHILE flag DO
      BEGIN
         play;
         write(' Do you want to play AGAIN? (Y/N) ');
         readln(answer);
         IF (answer = 'N') OR (answer = 'n') THEN flag := false
      END;
   writeln;
   writeln(' Bye, come back again!')
END.
```

It should be mentioned that the random number generator (function rand) is designed to generate deliberate integer overflows. This may be a problem for some compilers, which may generate a fatal error message and discontinue execution if such overflows are experienced. Usually, however, this problem can be overcome by adding a special command that causes the compiler to suppress the overflow check. For example, if this program were run on an IBM Personal Computer using the standard IBM (Microsoft) Pascal compiler, the special instruction $MATHCK− would have to be added as a comment. Thus, rand would appear as

```
FUNCTION rand : real;
(*$MATHCK- *)
(* Note: This function can only be used with a computer that
        supports 16-bit (2-byte) integer quantities. *)
VAR y,z : integer;
BEGIN   (* generate a random number *)
  z := 259*x;
  IF z >= 0 THEN y := z
            ELSE BEGIN y := z + 32767; y := y + 1 END;
  rand := 0.3051757E-4*y;
  x := y
END;
```

It is instructive to run this program in an interactive environment, such as on a personal computer. A typical set of output is shown below. The user's responses are underlined for clarity.

```
Welcome to the Game of CRAPS!

Press the CARRIAGE RETURN to begin playing (press carriage return)

Throw the dice . . .

 7 - Congratulations!  You WIN on the first throw!

Do you want to play AGAIN? (Y/N) y

Throw the dice . . .

 5 - Throw the dice again . . .

 6 - Throw the dice again . . .

12 - Throw the dice again . . .

 7 - You LOSE by failing to match your first score

Do you want to play AGAIN? (Y/N) y

Throw the dice . . .

 9 - Throw the dice again . . .

 4 - Throw the dice again . . .

 9 - You WIN by matching your first score

Do you want to play AGAIN? (Y/N) y

Throw the dice . . .

 2 - Tough luck!  You LOSE on the first throw!

Do you want to play AGAIN? (Y/N) n

Bye, come back again!
```

Finally, the reader is cautioned against altering the value of a global variable or a variable parameter within a function, as this may have unexpected and unwanted results outside of the function. Actions of this type are sometimes referred to as *side effects* of functions. (Note that such unwanted side effects can also be generated by a procedure. Side effects are generally more dangerous with functions, however, because programmers tend to think of a function as returning only one value.)

For example, the function rand in Example 7.18 alters the value of the global variable x each time the function is called, resulting in a different value being assigned to the variable x in the main block. This is required by the recursive nature of the random number generator. In general, however, this practice should be avoided if at all possible.

## 7.5  MORE ABOUT PARAMETERS

Sometimes it is desirable for a given procedure or function to access another procedure or function that has been defined (declared) outside the scope of the given procedure or function. For example, we may wish to have procedure A make use of function B, though function B has been defined outside of procedure A. This may be accomplished by passing the external procedure or function (e.g., function B) to the given procedure or function (e.g., procedure A) as a parameter. Thus, Pascal supports procedure parameters and function parameters as well as value parameters and variable parameters.

The formal parameter declaration for a procedure or a function parameter is written in the form of a procedure or a function header, as illustrated below.

### EXAMPLE 7.19

Suppose that the procedure process must access an externally defined real function that includes an integer-type parameter. Let us refer to this externally defined function as f. The procedure (process) might appear as follows.

```
PROCEDURE process (FUNCTION f(u : integer) : real; c1,c2 : integer);
VAR c : integer;
    x : real;
BEGIN
   FOR c := c1 TO c2 DO
      BEGIN
         x := f(c);
         writeln(' x=',x)
      END
END;
```

The main block might include the following reference to this procedure.

```
process(calc,1,100);
```

where the function calc is defined within the main block.
Here is a skeletal structure of the entire main block.

```
PROGRAM main(input,output);
   .
   .
FUNCTION calc(w : integer) : real;
   .
   .
BEGIN   (* function calc *)
   .
   .
   calc := . . .
END;   (* calc *)
```

(*Program continues on next page*)

```
      PROCEDURE process (FUNCTION f(u : integer) : real; c1,c2 : integer);
      VAR c : integer;
          x : real;
      BEGIN
         FOR c := c1 TO c2 DO
            BEGIN
               x := f(c);
               writeln(' x=',x)
            END
      END;   (* process *)

      BEGIN   (* main block *)
         .
         .
         .
         process(calc,1,100);
         .
         .
         .
      END.
```

The formal procedure and function parameters and the actual procedure and function parameters must correspond with respect to their own parameters. This correspondence must include the number, class and type of parameters.

Procedure parameters and function parameters are particularly useful when the given procedure or function accesses *different* procedures or functions (i.e., makes use of different actual parameters) at different calling points. The use of this technique is illustrated in the next two examples.

**EXAMPLE 7.20**

Consider once again the procedure process, defined in the last example. This procedure can be accessed several times in the main block, with a different function parameter included in each access. Thus, the main block might include the statements

```
      process(calc,1,100);
         .
         .
         .
      process(flag,-10,50);
```

where the functions calc and flag are defined within the main block.

**EXAMPLE 7.21**

Here is an example of a function being passed to another function.

```
      FUNCTION sum (FUNCTION f(x : real) : real; c1,c2 : integer) : real;
      VAR c : integer;
          s : real;
      BEGIN
         x := 0;
         FOR c := c1 TO c2 DO x := x + f(0.01*c);
         sum := x
      END;
```

In this example the function sum calculates the sum of several values, where each value is determined by accessing the function f which is passed to sum as a parameter.

The main block might include several statements such as

```
      value1 := sum(root(x),a,b);
         .
         .
         .
      value2 := sum(cube(x),1,n+1);
```

where root and cube are functions defined within the main block, and a, b and n are global integer-type variables. Note that sum accepts a different actual parameter (first root, then cube) each time it is accessed.

ISO Pascal does not permit standard procedures or standard functions to be passed as parameters. However, some implementations of the language do not impose this restriction.

**EXAMPLE 7.22**

**Search for a Maximum**. Let us again consider the problem of maximizing the expression

$$y = x \cos (x)$$

within the interval $x = 0$ and $x = \pi$, as described in Example 7.14. Now, however, let us use a function to evaluate the given expression.

Here is a version of the program in which the function max is passed to the procedure reduce as a parameter.

```
PROGRAM maximum2(input,output);

(* THIS PROGRAM FINDS THE MAXIMUM OF A
   FUNCTION WITHIN A SPECIFIED INTERVAL *)

CONST sep = 0.0001;
VAR a,b,xl,xr,xmax,yl,yr,ymax : real;

    FUNCTION curve(x : real) : real;
    (* Define the function f=x*cos(x) *)
    BEGIN
       curve := x*cos(x)
    END;

    PROCEDURE reduce( FUNCTION f(x : real) : real;
                              VAR a,b,xl,xr,yl,yr : real);
    (* Interval reduction routine *)
    BEGIN
       xl := a + 0.5*(b-a-sep);
       xr := xl + sep;
       yl := f(xl);
       yr := f(xr);
       IF yl > yr THEN b := xr;   (* retain left interval *)
       IF yr > yl THEN a := xl    (* retain right interval *)
    END;

BEGIN   (* main action block *)
   readln(a,b);
   REPEAT
      reduce(curve,a,b,xl,xr,yl,yr);
   UNTIL (yl=yr) OR ( b-a <= 3*sep )
   xmax := 0.5*(xl+xr);
   ymax := curve(xmax);
   writeln(' xmax = ',xmax:8:6,'   ymax = ',ymax:8:6)
END.
```

Execution of this program results in the same output shown in Example 7.14. It should be understood, however, that there is no particular advantage in passing the function to the procedure in this example, since the procedure uses the *same* function each time it is accessed. Thus, a more straightforward approach would be to access the function *without* passing it to the procedure as a parameter. A version of the program that does this is shown below.

```
PROGRAM maximum3(input,output);

(* THIS PROGRAM FINDS THE MAXIMUM OF A
   FUNCTION WITHIN A SPECIFIED INTERVAL *)

CONST sep = 0.0001;
VAR a,b,xl,xr,xmax,yl,yr,ymax : real;

    FUNCTION curve(x : real) : real;
    (* Define the function f=x*cos(x) *)
    BEGIN
       curve := x*cos(x)
    END;

    PROCEDURE reduce( VAR a,b,xl,xr,yl,yr : real);
    (* Interval reduction routine *)
    BEGIN
       xl := a + 0.5*(b-a-sep);
       xr := xl + sep;
       yl := curve(xl);
       yr := curve(xr);
       IF yl > yr THEN b := xr;    (* retain left interval *)
       IF yr > yl THEN a := xl     (* retain right interval *)
    END;

BEGIN   (* main action block *)
   readln(a,b);
   REPEAT
      reduce(a,b,xl,xr,yl,yr)
   UNTIL (yl=yr) OR ( b-a <= 3*sep );
   xmax := 0.5*(xl+xr);
   ymax := curve(xmax);
   writeln(' xmax = ',xmax:8:6,'   ymax = ',ymax:8:6)
END.
```

Execution of this program also produces the correct calculated result; namely,

```
xmax = 0.860586    ymax = 0.561096
```

We have now seen three different approaches to the solution of this problem. The question of which version is best is somewhat subjective, though the last program appears most appropriate for this particular problem.


## 7.6   RECURSION

One of the most interesting features of Pascal is the ability of a procedure or a function to call itself. This is known as *recursion*. The use of recursion is particularly convenient for those problems that can be defined in naturally recursive terms (though such problems can also be programmed using nonrecursive techniques).

When writing a recursive procedure or function, it is essential that the procedure (or function) include some terminating condition. This prevents the recursion from continuing indefinitely. While the terminating condition remains unsatisfied, however, the procedure (or function) simply calls itself at the appropriate place, just as it would call any other procedure or function.

**EXAMPLE 7.23**

**Calculating Factorials**. In Example 7.17 we saw a program for calculating the factorial of a given input quantity using a nonrecursive function to perform the actual calculations. Now let us see how this same calculation can be carried out using recursion.

First, notice that the factorial of a positive integer quantity, $n$, can be defined recursively as $n! = n \times (n-1)!$, where $1! = 1$. These equations provide the basis for the following recursive function.

```
FUNCTION factorial (n : integer) : integer;
(* Calculate the factorial of n *)
BEGIN
   IF n <= 1 THEN factorial := 1
             ELSE factorial := n*factorial(n-1)
END;
```

Notice that this function is much simpler than that presented in Example 7.17. The close correspondence between this function and the natural problem definition, in recursive terms, should be readily apparent. Also, notice that the IF—THEN clause provides a termination condition which is activated when the parameter n becomes less than or equal to 1 (n will never become less than 1 unless its original value is less than 1).

Here is the complete Pascal program. The main block is very similar to that shown in Example 7.17.

```
PROGRAM factorials3(input,output);

(* THIS PROGRAM USES A RECURSIVE FUNCTION TO CALCULATE
            THE FACTORIAL OF A GIVEN INTEGER QUANTITY *)

VAR x : integer;

    FUNCTION factorial (n : integer) : integer;
    (* Calculate the factorial of n *)
    BEGIN
       IF n <= 1 THEN factorial := 1
                 ELSE factorial := n*factorial(n-1)
    END;

BEGIN   (* main action block *)
   write(' Enter a positive integer: ');
   readln(x);
   writeln;
   writeln(' x= ',x,'   x! = ',factorial(x))
END.
```

Thus, to calculate the factorial of a single quantity n, the function factorial is now accessed repeatedly; once in the main block, and (n–1) times within itself.

In some applications, the use of recursion allows multiple data items to be stored inside the computer without the need for special data structures. This is illustrated in the next example.

**EXAMPLE 7.24**

**Printing Backward**. Suppose that we want to write a program that will read in a line of text whose length is unspecified until a carriage return (end of line) is encountered. The line of text will then be written out in reverse order (i.e., backward).

The traditional approach to this problem is to store the characters in a list as they are read in. We would then write them out in reverse order by proceeding through the list backward, after all of the characters have been entered. In order to do this, however, we would have to create a data structure (an *array*) to store the characters as they are entered. (We will see how this is done in Chap. 9.)

Another way to solve this problem is to use recursion, as shown below.

```
PROGRAM backwards(input,output);

(* THIS PROGRAM READS A LINE OF TEXT AND
   THEN WRITES IT OUT IN REVERSE ORDER. *)

   PROCEDURE flipit;
   (* Read single characters recursively,
                  then write them out. *)
      VAR c : char;
```

(*Program continues on next page*)

```
      BEGIN
         read(c);
         IF NOT eoln THEN flipit;
         write(c)
      END;

   BEGIN   (* main action block *)
      writeln(' Enter a line of text, then press RETURN');
      writeln;
      flipit
   END.
```

Procedure flipit is the key to the program. This procedure calls itself recursively, reading in successive characters until an end-of-line is encountered (until eoln is true). Notice that the recursive call precedes the write statement. Hence, *all* of the characters will be read in before any of them are written out. After all of the characters have been read in, the most recent character will be written out (because the most recent character corresponds to the most recent procedure call), followed by the second most recent character, and so on.

For example, if the program is executed with the following line of input,

    NOW IS THE TIME FOR ALL GOOD MEN TO COME TO THE AID OF THEIR COUNTRY

then the corresponding output will be

    YRTNUOC RIEHT FO DIA EHT OT EMOC OT NEM DOOG LLA ROF EMIT EHT SI WON

If a procedure or a function containing local variables is called recursively, then a *different* set of local variables will be created during each call. The names of the local variables will, of course, be the same (as declared within the procedure or function). However, a different set of values will be associated with these variable names each time the procedure or function is activated. These values will become available as the procedure or function "unwinds"; i.e., as the previous recursive calls are completed.

**EXAMPLE 7.25**

Consider the recursive procedure flipit shown in Example 7.24. This procedure includes the local char-type variable c. Each time the procedure is called a different character is read in and assigned to c. Thus, several different characters will be associated with c and stored sequentially within the computer's memory. These characters will be independent of one another. They will be written out in the proper order as the previous recursive calls are completed (which means that more recent values of c will already have been entered, stored and written out).

**EXAMPLE 7.26**

**The Towers of Hanoi**. Here is a widely used example that illustrates how recursion can be utilized to simplify the programming of a seemingly complicated problem. The problem is concerned with a popular children's game, consisting of three poles and a number of different-sized disks. Each disk has a hole in the center, allowing the disks to be stacked around the poles. Initially, the disks are stacked on the leftmost pole in the order of their size, with the largest on the bottom and the smallest on the top. (See Fig. 7-4.)

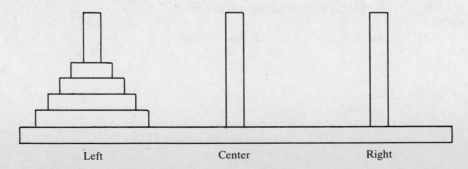

Fig. 7-4

The object of the game is to transfer the disks from the leftmost pole to the rightmost pole, without ever placing a larger disk on top of a smaller disk. Only one disk may be moved at one time, and each disk must always be placed over one of the poles.

The general strategy is to consider one of the poles to be the origin and another to be the destination. The third pole will be used for intermediate storage, thus allowing for the movement of the disks. Therefore, if $n$ disks are initially stacked on the left pole, the problem of moving all $n$ disks to the right pole can be represented in the following manner.

1.  Move the top $n-1$ disks from the left pole to the middle pole, using the right pole for intermediate storage.

2.  Move the remaining disk to the right pole.

3.  Move the $n-1$ disks on the middle pole to the right pole, using the left pole for intermediate storage.

Thus, the problem can be expressed in recursive terms which apply for any value of $n$ greater than 0. (When $n = 1$, we simply move one disk from the left pole to the right pole.)

In order to write a program for this game we first number the poles, so that left = 1, center = 2 and right = 3. We then construct a recursive procedure called transfer that will transfer $n$ disks from one pole to another. We will refer to the poles with the integer-type variables origin, destination and other. Thus, if we assign the value 1 to origin, 3 to destination and 2 to other, we will in effect be specifying the movement of $n$ disks from pole 1 (the leftmost pole) to pole 3 (the rightmost pole), using pole 2 (the center pole) for intermediate storage. With this notation, the procedure will have the following skeletal structure.

```
PROCEDURE transfer(n,origin,destination,other : integer);

IF n>0 THEN

(* transfer n-1 disks from the origin to the intermediate pole *)

(* transfer the remaining disk from the origin to the destination *)

(* transfer n-1 disks from the intermediate pole to the destination *)

END;
```

The transfer of n-1 disks can be accomplished by a recursive call to transfer. Thus, we can write

```
transfer(n-1,origin,other,destination)
```

for the first transfer, and

```
transfer(n-1,other,destination,origin)
```

for the second. (Note the order of the parameters in each call.) The movement of one disk from the origin to the destination simply requires writing out the values for origin and destination. This can be carried out by calling another procedure, called diskmove, which is defined within transfer. The complete procedure transfer can be written as follows.

```
PROCEDURE transfer(n,origin,destination,other : integer);

    PROCEDURE diskmove(origin,destination : integer);
    BEGIN
       writeln('Move ',origin:1,' to ',destination:1)
    END;

BEGIN
    IF n>0 THEN BEGIN
                transfer(n-1,origin,other,destination);
                diskmove(origin,destination);
                transfer(n-1,other,destination,origin)
            END
END;
```

It is now a simple matter to add the main block, which merely reads in a value for n and then initiates the computation by calling transfer. In this first procedure call, the actual parameters will be specified as integer numbers; i.e.,

        transfer(n,1,3,2)

This specifies the transfer of all n disks from pole 1 (the origin) to pole 3 (the destination), using pole 2 for intermediate storage.

Here is the complete program.

```
PROGRAM towersofhanoi(input,output);

(* THIS PROGRAM SOLVES A WELL-KNOWN GAME
          USING RECURSIVE PROCEDURE CALLS *)

VAR n : integer;

    PROCEDURE transfer(n,origin,destination,other : integer);
    (* Transfer n disks from the origin to the destination *)

        PROCEDURE diskmove(origin,destination : integer);
        (* Move a single disk from the origin to the destination *)
        BEGIN
            writeln('Move ',origin:1,' to ',destination:1)
        END;   (* diskmove *)

    BEGIN   (* transfer *)
        IF n>0 THEN BEGIN
                    transfer(n-1,origin,other,destination);
                    diskmove(origin,destination);
                    transfer(n-1,other,destination,origin)
                END
    END;   (* transfer *)

BEGIN   (* main action block *)
    write(' Enter the number of disks -> ');
    readln(n);
    writeln;
    transfer(n,1,3,2)
END.
```

It should be understood that a *different* set of values is defined for the value parameters n, origin, destination and other each time transfer is called. These sets of values will be stored independently of one another within the computer's memory. It is this ability to store these independent sets of values and then retrieve them at the proper time that allows the recursion to work.

When the program is executed for the case where n = 3, the following output is obtained. (Note that the user's response is underlined.)

```
Enter the number of disks -> 3

Move 1 to 3
Move 1 to 2
Move 3 to 2
Move 1 to 3
Move 2 to 1
Move 2 to 3
Move 1 to 3
```

The reader should think through this sequence of moves to verify that it is indeed correct.

The reader is urged to study this example carefully. The logic is tricky, despite the simplicity of the program.

In all of the recursive examples that we have seen so far, a single procedure or a single function has called itself. There is another form of recursion, called *mutual recursion*, in which one procedure (or function) calls another and the second procedure (or function) then calls the first. Recall, however, that a procedure or function cannot be accessed before it has been declared. Thus there is a potential problem with mutual recursion, when the first procedure (function) calls the second before it has been declared.

Pascal solves this problem by allowing a *dummy declaration* for the second procedure (or function) to precede the first procedure (or function). This dummy declaration consists of the procedure (function) header, followed by the keyword *forward*. The true declaration for the second procedure (function) is then written in the proper place, after the first procedure (function) declaration. It is written in the usual manner except that the formal parameter list is omitted from the header. (In the case of a function, the result type is also omitted.)

**EXAMPLE 7.27**

Here is a skeletal outline of a function that calls a procedure, which then recursively calls the function.

```
FUNCTION second(a,b : real) : real; forward;

PROCEDURE first(x,y : real);
VAR w : real;
BEGIN
   .
   .
   w := second(x,y);
   .
   .
END;

FUNCTION second;
VAR u,v : real;
BEGIN
   .
   .
   first(u,v);
   .
   .
   second := . . .
END;
```

Notice that the dummy declaration for second is necessary so that first can access second before second has been declared. The true declaration for second then follows the declaration for first. Note, however, that the function header is now abbreviated.

Finally, it should be understood that the use of recursion is not necessarily the best way to approach a problem, even though the problem definition may be recursive in nature. A nonrecursive implementation may be more efficient in terms of memory utilization and execution speed. Thus, the use of recursion frequently involves a trade-off between simplicity and performance degradation. Each problem should therefore be judged on its own individual merits.

# Review Questions

**7.1** What are the advantages of program modularization? What two types of program modules are available in Pascal?

**7.2** How is a procedure referenced? What other words are used to refer to a procedure reference?

**7.3** Describe the grammatical structure of a procedure. How is the procedure header written?

**7.4** In what part of a Pascal program must a procedure declaration appear?

**7.5** What is the difference between global and local identifiers? Which is preferable and why?

**7.6** What is meant by the scope of an identifier?

**7.7** What is meant by nested procedures? What restriction requires particular attention when attempting to access nested procedures?

**7.8** Does the concept of scope apply only to identifiers that represent constants and variables? Explain.

**7.9** How do the rules of scope affect transfers of control associated with the use of the GOTO statement?

**7.10** What are parameters? How are they used?

**7.11** What is the difference between actual parameters and formal parameters?

**7.12** Summarize the rules that must be observed when substituting actual parameters for formal parameters.

**7.13** What are the four different classes of formal parameters? How do they differ?

**7.14** What are value parameters? How are formal value parameters written? For what type of application are value parameters generally used?

**7.15** What are variable parameters? How are formal variable parameters written? How do variable parameters differ from value parameters, in terms of

(*a*) the way they are written

(*b*) the way they are used

**7.16** What is a function? How does a function differ from a procedure?

**7.17** How is a function referenced? Compare with a procedure reference.

**7.18** Describe the grammatical structure of a function. How is the function header written? How does this grammatical structure differ from that of a procedure?

**7.19** Where within a Pascal program must a function declaration appear? Is there any particular ordering that must be observed between procedure declarations and function declarations?

**7.20**   Can functions be nested in the same manner as procedures? Can the nesting of functions and procedures be interchanged?

**7.21**   What is meant by the side effects associated with a function? Are procedures also susceptible to side effects?

**7.22**   When is it desirable to pass a procedure or a function as a parameter?

**7.23**   When a procedure or a function is passed as a parameter, what correspondence must be maintained between formal parameters and actual parameters?

**7.24**   How are formal procedure parameters and formal function parameters written?

**7.25**   Can standard procedures or standard functions be passed as parameters?

**7.26**   What is meant by recursion? Is recursion an essential programming technique?

**7.27**   When writing a recursive procedure or function, how does one prevent the recursive process from continuing indefinitely?

**7.28**   What advantage does recursion offer with respect to the storage of multiple data items?

**7.29**   Suppose that a recursive procedure or function includes a set of local variables. As the procedure or function is accessed repeatedly, how are the local variables interpreted?

**7.30**   What is meant by mutual recursion?

**7.31**   When defining mutually recursive procedures (or functions), what potential problem is solved by the use of a dummy declaration? How is the dummy declaration written? What changes must be made to other declarations because of the dummy declaration?

# Solved Problems

**7.32**   Several illustrative procedure and function references are outlined below. (Assume that `sample`, `sample1` and `sample2` are procedures, and that `demo`, `demo1` and `demo2` are functions. Type compatibility is assumed throughout.)

(*a*)  `sample;`                            (*f*)  `z := a + 2*demo - 3;`

(*b*)  `sample1(a,b,c);`                     (*g*)  `z := demo1(a,b,c);`

(*c*)  `sample1(a+b,2*x,sqr(c));`           (*h*)  `z := y + demo1(a+b,2*x,sqr(c));`

(*d*)  `sample2(sample,demo);`              (*i*)  `z := demo2(sample,demo);`

(*e*)  `z := demo;`                         (*j*)  `IF demo1(a,b,c) < zstar THEN z := demo1(a,b,c);:`

**7.33**   Several skeletal procedure and function declarations are shown below. (These declarations correspond to the procedures and functions referred to in Prob. 7.32.)

(*a*)  PROCEDURE sample;
       VAR . . .;    (* local variables *)
       BEGIN
          .
          .
          .
       END;

(*b*)  PROCEDURE sample1(x,y,z : real);
       VAR . . .;    (* local variables *)
       BEGIN
          .
          .
          .
       END;

(*c*)  PROCEDURE sample1(VAR x,y,z : real);
       VAR . . .;    (* local variables *)
       BEGIN
          .
          .
          .
       END;

(Notice that part (*b*) makes use of value parameters, whereas part (*c*) utilizes variable parameters. Variable parameters are necessary if the parameters are altered within the procedure and the altered values are then returned to the point of access.)

(*d*)  PROCEDURE sample2(PROCEDURE sample; FUNCTION demo : real);
       VAR . . .;    (* local variables *)
       BEGIN
          .
          .
          .
       END;

(*e*)  PROCEDURE sample2(PROCEDURE sample1(x,y,z : real);
                 FUNCTION demo1(VAR a,b,c : real) : real);
       VAR . . .;    (* local variables *)
       BEGIN
          .
          .
          .
       END;

(*f*)  FUNCTION demo : real;
       VAR . . .;    (* local variables *)
       BEGIN
          .
          .
          .
          demo := . . .
       END;

(*g*)  FUNCTION demo1(x,y,z : real) : real;
       VAR . . .;    (* local variables *)
       BEGIN
          .
          .
          .
          demo1 := . . .
       END;

(*h*)  FUNCTION demo2(PROCEDURE sample; FUNCTION demo : real) : real;
       VAR . . .;   (* local variables *)
       BEGIN
          .
          .
          .
          demo2 := . . .
       END;

(*i*)  FUNCTION demo2(PROCEDURE sample1(VAR x,y,z : real);
                 FUNCTION demo1(a,b,c : real) : real) : real;
       VAR . . .;   (* local variables *)
       BEGIN
          .
          .
          .
          demo2 := . . .
       END;

**7.34**  The following skeletal outlines illustrate procedure and/or function declarations with corresponding references.

(*a*)  PROGRAM sample1(input,output);
       VAR a,b,c : integer;

          PROCEDURE  proc1(a,b,c : integer);
          VAR . . .;   (* local variables *)
          BEGIN
             .
             .
             .
          END;

          FUNCTION funct1(x,y : integer) : integer;
          VAR r,s,t : integer;
          BEGIN
             .
             .
             proc1(r,s,t);
             .
             .
             funct1 := . . .
          END;

       BEGIN   (* main action statements *)
          .
          .
          c := funct1(3,-1);
          .
          .
          proc1(a,b+c,0);
          .
          .
          proc1(a+b,funct1(0,1),c+3)
       END.

```
(b)   PROGRAM sample2(input,output);
      VAR a,b,c : integer;

          FUNCTION funct2(x,y : integer) : integer; forward;

          PROCEDURE proc2(a,b,c : integer);
          VAR p,q,r : integer;
          BEGIN
             .
             .
             r := funct2(p,q-1);
             .
             .
          END;

          FUNCTION funct2;
          VAR r,s,t : integer;
          BEGIN
             .
             .
             proc2(r,s,t);
             .
             .
             funct2 := . . .
          END;

      BEGIN    (* main action statements *)
         .
         .
         c := funct2(3,-1);
         .
         .
         proc2(a,b+c,0);
         .
         .
         proc2(abs(a+b),c,funct2(1,1))
      END.
```

Note that this example utilizes the forward feature.

```
(c)   PROGRAM sample3(input,output);
      VAR a,b,c : integer;

          FUNCTION funct3(p,q : integer) : integer;
          VAR r,s,t : integer;

             PROCEDURE proc3(VAR x,y,z : integer);
             VAR . . .;    (* local variables *)
             BEGIN
                .
                .
                .
             END;
```

(*Program continues on next page*)

```
      BEGIN   (* funct3 action statements *)
         .
         .
      proc3(r,s,t);
         .
         .
      funct3 := . . .
   END;

   BEGIN   (* main action statements *)
      .
      .
   c := funct3(1,2);
      .
      .
   a := funct3(2,0);
      .
      .
END;
```

Note that proc3 is embedded within funct3.

(d)  PROCEDURE factorial (VAR f : integer; n : integer);
```
   BEGIN
      IF n <= 1 THEN f := 1
               ELSE BEGIN
                        factorial (f,n-1);
                        f := n*f
                    END
   END;
```

This example illustrates the recursive use of a procedure. (Compare with the function shown in Example 7.23.) Note that this procedure utilizes both a variable parameter (f) and a value parameter (n).

# Supplementary Problems

**7.35**  The following skeletal outlines illustrate several different situations involving the use of procedures and/or functions. Some are written incorrectly. Identify all errors.

(a)  PROCEDURE sum(a,b,c : real);
```
   VAR sum : real;
   BEGIN
      sum := a + b + c
   END;
```

(b)  FUNCTION sum(a,b,c : real) : real;
```
   BEGIN
      sum := a + b + c
   END;
```

(c)  PROCEDURE sum1(a,b,c : real; VAR sum : real);
```
   BEGIN
      sum := a + b + c
   END;
```

```
(d)  FUNCTION sum(x : real);
     VAR sum : real;
     BEGIN
        sum := sum + x
     END;
(e)  PROGRAM sample(input,output);
     VAR a,b,c : char;

        PROCEDURE proc1(x,y : integer);
        BEGIN
           .
           .
           .
        END;

     BEGIN   (* main action statements *)
        .
        .
        proc1(a,b);
        .
        .
     END.
(f)  PROGRAM sample(input,output);
     VAR a,b : integer;
         flag : boolean;

        PROCEDURE proc1(x,y : integer);
        VAR . . .;   (* local variables *)
        BEGIN
           .
           .
           REPEAT
              .
              .
              IF . . . THEN flag := false;
              .
              .
           UNTIL flag = false
        END;

     BEGIN   (* main action statements *)
        .
        .
        flag := true;
        proc1(a,a+2);
        .
        .
        flag := true;
        proc1(abs(b-a),0);
        .
        .
     END.
(g)  PROGRAM sample(input,output);
     VAR a,b,t : integer;

        PROCEDURE proc2(VAR x,y : integer);
        VAR . . .;   (* local variables *)
```

(*Program continues on next page*)

```
               BEGIN
                  .
                  .
                  IF t > 0 THEN y := . . .
                           ELSE y := . . .;
                  .
                  .
               END;
            BEGIN   (* main action statements *)
               .
               .
               readln(n);
               .
               .
               proc2(2*a+1,b);
               .
               .
               proc2(abs(a-10),b);
               .
               .
            END.
```

(*h*)  PROGRAM sample(input,output);
```
       VAR a,b,c : char;
           t1,t2,t3 : boolean;

          FUNCTION upper(x : char) : boolean;
          BEGIN
             IF ord(x) <= 90 THEN upper := true
                             ELSE upper := false
          END;
       BEGIN   (* main action statements *)
          .
          .
          t1 := upper(a);
          .
          .
          t2 := upper(b,c);
          .
          .
          t3 := upper(a+b)
       END.
```

(*i*)  PROGRAM sample(input,output);
```
       VAR a,b : integer;

          FUNCTION smaller : integer;
          BEGIN
             IF a < b THEN smaller := a
                      ELSE smaller := b
          END;
       BEGIN   (* main action statements *)
          .
          .
          writeln(' Smallest number: ',smaller);
          .
          .
       END.
```

```
(j)   PROGRAM sample(input,output);
      VAR a,b : integer;

          PROCEDURE proc1(x,y : integer);
          VAR a,b : char;
          BEGIN
              .
              .
              .
          END;

      BEGIN   (* main action statements *)
          .
          .
          proc1(a,b);
          .
          .
      END.
```

```
(k)   PROGRAM sample(input,output);
      VAR a,b,c : integer;
          x,y : real;

          FUNCTION funct1(x,y : integer) : real;
          VAR . . .;   (* local variables *)
          BEGIN
              .
              .
              c := . . .;
              .
              .
              funct1 := . . .
          END;

      BEGIN   (* main action statements *)
          .
          .
          x := funct1(a,b);
          .
          .
          y := funct1(b,a-2);
          .
          .
      END.
```

```
(l)   PROGRAM sample(input,output);
      VAR x,y,z : real;

          FUNCTION smaller(FUNCTION f1(x : real) : real;
                           FUNCTION f2(x : real) : real) : real;
          BEGIN
              IF f1(x) < f2(x) THEN smaller := f1(x)
                              ELSE smaller := f2(x)
          END;
```

*(Program continues on next page)*

```
        BEGIN   (* main action statements *)
          .
          .
          y := smaller(sin,cos);
          .
          .
          z := smaller(log,sqrt);
          .
          .
        END.
```

(*m*)  PROGRAM sample(input,output);
       VAR a,b,c : integer;

```
        FUNCTION funct1(x,y : integer) : integer;
        VAR . . .;   (* local variables *)
        BEGIN
          .
          .
          .
          funct1 := . . .
        END;

        PROCEDURE proc1(a,b,c : integer);
        VAR r,s,t : integer;
        BEGIN
          .
          .
          r := funct1(s,t);
          .
          .
        END;

        BEGIN   (* main action statements *)
          .
          .
          c := funct1(3,-1);
          .
          .
          proc1(a,b+c,0);
          .
          .
          proc1(a+b,funct1(0,1),c+3);
          .
          .
        END.
```

(*n*)  PROGRAM sample(input,output);
       VAR a,b,c : integer;

```
        PROCEDURE proc1(a,b,c : integer);
        VAR r,s,t : integer;
        BEGIN
          .
          .
          r := funct1(s,t);
          .
          .
        END;
```

(*Program continues on next page*)

```
          FUNCTION funct1(x,y : integer) : integer;
          VAR . . .;   (* local variables *)
          BEGIN
             .
             .
             .
             funct1 := . . .
          END;
      BEGIN   (* main action statements *)
         .
         .
         c := funct1(3,-1);
         .
         .
         proc1(a,b+c,0);
         .
         .
         proc1(a+b,funct1(0,1),c+3);
         .
         .
      END.
(o)  PROGRAM sample(input,output);
     VAR a,b,c : integer;

          PROCEDURE test(VAR : x,y,z : integer);
          VAR r,s,t : integer;

              FUNCTION value(p,q : integer) : integer;
              VAR . . .;   (* local variables *)
              BEGIN
                 .
                 .
                 .
                 value := . . .
              END;
          BEGIN   (* test action statements *)
             .
             .
             r := value(s,t);
             .
             .
          END;

      BEGIN   (* main action statements *)
         .
         .
         test(a,b,c);
         .
         .
         c := value(a,b);
         .
         .
      END.
(p)  FUNCTION factorial(n : integer) : integer;
     BEGIN
         factorial := n*factorial(n-1)
     END;
```

**7.36**   Express each of the following formulas in a recursive form.

(a)   $y = (x_1 + x_2 + \cdots + x_n)$

(b)   $y = 1 - x + x^2/2 - x^3/6 + x^4/24 + \cdots + (-1)^n x^n/n!$

(c)   $p = (f_1 * f_2 * \cdots * f_t)$

# Programming Problems

**7.37**   Write a procedure that will calculate the real roots of the quadratic equation

$$ax^2 + bx + c = 0$$

using the quadratic formula

$$x = \frac{-b \pm \sqrt{b^2 - 4ac}}{2a}$$

Assume that $a$, $b$ and $c$ are parameters whose values are given, and that $x_1$ and $x_2$ are the calculated roots. Also, assume that $b^2 > 4ac$, so that the calculated roots will always be real and distinct.

**7.38**   Write a complete Pascal program that will calculate the real roots of the quadratic equation

$$ax^2 + bx + c = 0$$

using the quadratic formula, as described in the previous problem. Read the coefficients $a$, $b$ and $c$ into the computer in the main action block. Then access the procedure written for the preceding problem in order to obtain the desired solution. Finally, write out the values of the coefficients, followed by the calculated values of $x_1$ and $x_2$. Be sure that all of the output is clearly labeled.

Test the program using the following data.

|       |       |       |
|-------|-------|-------|
| $a = 2$ | $b = 6$ | $c = 1$ |
| 3     | 3     | 0     |
| 1     | 3     | 1     |

**7.39**   Modify the procedure written for Prob. 7.37 so that all roots of the quadratic equation

$$ax^2 + bx + c = 0$$

will be calculated, given the values of $a$, $b$ and $c$. Note that the roots will be repeated (i.e., there will be only one real root) if $b^2 = 4ac$. Also, the roots will be complex if $b^2 < 4ac$. In this case, the real part of each root will be determined as

$$-b/2a$$

and the imaginary parts will be calculated as

$$(\pm\sqrt{4ac - b^2})i$$

where $i$ represents $\sqrt{-1}$.

**7.40**   Modify the Pascal program written for Prob. 7.38 so that all roots of the quadratic equation

$$ax^2 + bx + c = 0$$

will be calculated, using the procedure written for Prob. 7.39. Be sure that all of the output is clearly labeled. Test the program using the following data.

| $a = 2$ | $b =$ 6 | $c =$ 1 |
|---|---|---|
| 3 | 3 | 0 |
| 1 | 3 | 1 |
| 0 | 12 | −3 |
| 3 | 6 | 3 |
| 2 | −4 | 3 |

**7.41** Write a function that will allow either a real or an integer-type number to be raised to an integer-type power. In other words, we wish to evaluate the formula

$$y = x^n$$

where $y$ and $x$ are either real or integer-type variables and $n$ is an integer-type variable. (Note that $y$ and $x$ will always be of the same type.)

**7.42** Write a complete Pascal program that will read in numerical values for $x$ and $n$, evaluate the formula

$$y = x^n$$

using the function written for Prob. 7.41, and then write out the calculated result. Test the program using the following data.

| $x =$ | 2 | $n =$ | 3 |
|---|---|---|---|
| | 2 | | 12 |
| | 2 | | −5 |
| | −3 | | 3 |
| | −3 | | 7 |
| | −3 | | −5 |
| | 1.5 | | 3 |
| | 1.5 | | 10 |
| | 1.5 | | −5 |
| | 0.2 | | 3 |
| | 0.2 | | 5 |
| | 0.2 | | −5 |

**7.43** Expand the function written for Prob. 7.41 so that positive values of $x$ can be raised to any power, either real or integer. (*Hint*: use logarithms if the exponent is of type real. The formula is $y = x^n = e^{(n \ln x)}$. Remember to include a test for inappropriate values of $x$.) Include this function in the program written for Prob. 7.42. Test the program using the data given in Prob. 7.42 and the following additional data.

| $x =$ | 2 | $n =$ | 0.2 |
|---|---|---|---|
| | 2 | | −0.8 |
| | −3 | | 0.2 |
| | −3 | | −0.8 |
| | 1.5 | | 0.2 |
| | 1.5 | | −0.8 |
| | 0.2 | | 0.2 |
| | 0.2 | | −0.8 |
| | 0.2 | | 0.0 |

**7.44** Modify the character-encoding program given in Example 6.13 so that it makes use of a procedure. Compile and execute the program to be sure that it runs correctly.

**7.45**  Modify the program for calculating the solution of an algebraic equation, given in Example 6.14, so that each iteration is carried out within a function. Compile and execute the program to be sure that it runs correctly.

**7.46**  Modify the program for averaging a list of numbers, given in Example 7.8, so that it makes use of a function. Test the program using the following 10 numbers:

| | |
|------|------|
| 27.5 | 87.0 |
| 13.4 | 39.9 |
| 53.8 | 47.7 |
| 29.2 | 8.1 |
| 74.5 | 63.2 |

**7.47**  The program given in Example 7.14 can easily be modified to *minimize* a function of *x*. Such a minimization procedure can provide us with a highly effective technique for calculating the roots of a nonlinear algebraic equation. For example, suppose we want to find the particular value of *x* that causes some function $f(x)$ to equal zero. A typical function of this nature might be

$$f(x) = x + \cos(x) - 1 - \sin(x).$$

If we let $g(x) = f(x)^2$, then the function $g(x)$ will always be positive except for those values of *x* that are roots of the given function; i.e., for which $f(x)$, and hence $g(x)$, will equal zero. Therefore any value of *x* that causes $g(x)$ to be minimized will also be a root of the equation $f(x) = 0$.

Modify the program shown in Example 7.14 to minimize a given function. Use the program to obtain the roots of the following equations:

(a)  $x + \cos(x) = 1 + \sin(x)$,        $\pi/2 < x < \pi$
(b)  $x^5 + 3x^2 = 10$,        $0 <= x <= 3$   (see Example 6.14)

**7.48**  Modify the program shown in Example 7.18 so that a sequence of craps games will be simulated automatically, in a noninteractive manner. Include an integer-type counter that will determine the total number of wins, and an integer input variable whose value will specify how many games will be simulated.

Use the program to simulate some large number of games (e.g., 1000). Estimate the probability of coming out ahead when playing craps. (This value, expressed as a decimal, is equal to the number of wins divided by the total number of games played. If the probability exceeds .500, it favors the player; otherwise it favors the house.)

**7.49**  Rewrite each of the following programs so that it includes at least one procedure or function, whichever is most appropriate. Be careful with your choice of parameters.
(a)  Calculate the weighted average of a list of numbers [see Prob. 6.50(a)].
(b)  Calculate the cumulative product of a list of numbers [see Prob. 6.50(b)].
(c)  Calculate the geometric average of a list of numbers [see Prob. 6.50(c)].
(d)  Calculate and tabulate a list of prime numbers [see Prob. 6.50(f)].
(e)  Compute the sine of *x*, using the method described in Prob. 6.50(i).
(f)  Compute the repayments on a loan [see Prob. 6.50(j)].
(g)  Determine the average exam score for each student in a class, as described in Prob. 6.50(k).

**7.50**  Write a complete Pascal program to solve each of the problems described below. Utilize procedures and/or functions wherever appropriate. Compile and execute each program using the data given in the problem description.
(a)  Suppose you place a given sum of money, *A*, into a savings account at the beginning of each year for *n* years. If the account earns interest at the rate of *i* percent annually, then the amount of money that will have accumulated after n years, *F*, is given by

$$F = A \left[(1+i/100) + (1+i/100)^2 + (1+i/100)^3 + \cdots + (1+i/100)^n\right]$$

Write a conversational-style Pascal program to determine the following.

(i)   How much money will accumulate after 30 years if $1000 is deposited at the beginning of each year and the interest rate is 6 percent per year, compounded annually?

(ii)  How much money must be deposited at the beginning of each year in order to accumulate $100,000 after 30 years, again assuming that the interest rate is 6 percent per year, with annual compounding?

In each case, first determine the unknown amount of money. Then create a table showing the total amount of money that will have accumulated at the end of each year. Use the function written for Prob. 7.41 to carry out the exponentiation.

(b)  Modify the above program to accommodate quarterly rather than annual compounding of interest. Compare the calculated results obtained for both problems. *Hint*: the proper formula is

$$F = A \left[(1 + i/100m)^m + (1 + i/100m)^{2m} + (1 + i/100m)^{3m} + \cdots + (1+i/100m)^{nm}\right]$$

where $m$ represents the number of interest periods per year.

(c)  Home mortgage costs are determined in such a manner that the borrower pays the same amount of money to the lending institution each month throughout the life of the mortgage. The fraction of the total monthly payment that is required as an interest payment on the outstanding balance of the loan varies, however, from month to month. Early in the life of the mortgage most of the monthly payment is required to pay interest, and only a small fraction of the total monthly payment is applied toward reducing the amount of the loan. Gradually, the outstanding balance becomes smaller, which causes the monthly interest payment to decrease, and the amount that is used to reduce the outstanding balance therefore increases. Hence the balance of the loan is reduced at an accelerated rate.

Typically, prospective home buyers know how much money they must borrow and the time required for repayment. They then ask a lending institution how much their monthly payment will be at the prevailing interest rate. They should also be concerned with how much of each monthly payment is charged to interest, how much total interest they have paid since they first borrowed the money, and how much money they still owe the lending institution at the end of each month.

Write a Pascal program that can be used by a lending institution to provide a potential customer with this information. Assume that the amount of the loan, the annual interest rate and the duration of the loan are specified. The amount of the monthly payment is calculated as

$$A = \frac{iP(1+i)^n}{(1+i)^n - 1}$$

where   $A$ = monthly payment, dollars
        $P$ = total amount of the loan, dollars
        $i$ = monthly interest rate, expressed as a decimal (e.g., 1/2% would be written 0.005)
        $n$ = total number of monthly payments

The monthly interest payment can then be calculated from the formula

$$I = iB$$

where $I$ = monthly interest payment in dollars and $B$ = current outstanding balance in dollars.

The current outstanding balance is simply equal to the original amount of the loan less the sum of the previous payments toward principal. The monthly payment toward principal (i.e., the amount which is used to reduce the outstanding balance) is

$$T = A - I$$

where $T$ = monthly payment toward principal.

Make use of the function written for Prob. 7.41 to carry out the exponentiation.

Use the program to calculate the cost of a 25-year, $50,000 mortgage at an annual interest rate of 8 percent. Then repeat the calculations for an annual interest rate of 8.5 percent. How significant is the additional 0.5 percent in the interest rate over the entire life of the mortgage?

(d)  The method used to calculate the cost of a home mortgage in the previous problem is known as a *constant-payment* method, since each monthly payment is the same. Suppose instead that the monthly payments were computed by the method of simple interest. That is, suppose that the same amount is applied toward reducing the loan each month. Hence

$$T = P/n$$

However, the monthly interest will depend on the amount of the outstanding balance, that is,

$$I = iB$$

Thus the total monthly payment, $A = T + I$, will decrease each month as the outstanding balance diminishes.

Write a Pascal program to calculate the cost of a home mortgage using this method of repayment. Label the output clearly. Use the program to calculate the cost of a 25-year, \$50,000 loan at 8 percent annual interest. Compare the results with those obtained in Prob. 7.50(c).

(e) Suppose we are given a number of discrete points $(x_1, y_1), (x_2, y_2), \ldots, (x_n, y_n)$ which are read from a curve $y = f(x)$, where $x$ is bounded between $x_1$ and $x_n$. We wish to approximate the area under the curve by breaking up the curve into a number of small rectangles and calculating the area of these rectangles. (This is known as the *trapezoidal rule*.) The appropriate formula is

$$A = (y_1 + y_2)(x_2 - x_1)/2 + (y_2 + y_3)(x_3 - x_2)/2 + \cdots + (y_{n-1} + y_n)(x_n - x_{n-1})/2$$

Notice that the average height of each rectangle is given by $(y_i + y_{i+1})/2$ and the width of each rectangle is equal to $(x_{i+1} - x_i)$; $i = 1, 2, \ldots, (n - 1)$.

Write a Pascal program to implement this strategy, using a function to evaluate the mathematical formula $y = f(x)$. Use the program to calculate the area under the curve $y = x^3$ between the limits $x = 1$ and $x = 4$. Solve this problem first with 16 evenly spaced points, then with 61 points, and finally with 301 points. Note that the accuracy of the solution will improve as the number of points increases. (The exact answer to this problem is 63.75.)

(f) The preceding problem describes the trapezoidal rule for calculating the area under a curve $y(x)$, where a set of tabulated values $(x_1, y_1), (x_2, y_2), \ldots, (x_n, y_n)$ is used to describe the curve. If the tabulated values of $x$ are equally spaced, then the equation given in the preceding problem can be simplified to read

$$A = (y_1 + 2y_2 + 2y_3 + 2y_4 + \cdots + 2y_{n-1} + y_n)h/2$$

where $h$ is the distance between successive values of $x$.

Another technique that applies when there is an even number of equally spaced intervals, i.e., an odd number of data points, is *Simpson's rule*. The computational equation for implementing Simpson's rule is

$$A = (y_1 + 4y_2 + 2y_3 + 4y_4 + 2y_5 + \cdots + 4y_{n-1} + y_n)h/3$$

For a given value of $h$, this method will yield a more accurate result than the trapezoidal rule. (Note that the method requires about the same amount of computation as the trapezoidal rule.)

Write a Pascal program for calculating the area under a curve using either of the above techniques, assuming an odd number of equally spaced data points. Implement each method with a separate procedure, utilizing a function to evaluate $y(x)$.

Use the program to calculate the area under the curve

$$y = e^{-x^2}$$

where $x$ ranges from 0 to 1. Calculate the area using each method, and compare the results with the correct answer of $A = 0.7468241$.

(g) Still another technique for calculating the area under a curve is to employ the *Monte Carlo* method, which makes use of randomly generated numbers. Suppose that the curve $y = f(x)$ is positive for any value of $x$ between the specified lower and upper limits $x = a$ and $x = b$. Let the largest value of $y$ within these limits be $y^*$. The Monte Carlo method proceeds as follows.

(i) Begin with a counter set equal to zero.

(ii) Generate a random number, $r_x$, whose value lies between $a$ and $b$.

(iii) Evaluate $y(r_x)$.

(iv) Generate a second random number, $r_y$, whose value lies between 0 and $y^*$.

(*v*) Compare $r_y$ with $y(r_x)$. If $r_y$ is less than or equal to $y(r_x)$, then this point will fall on or under the given curve. Hence the counter is incremented by 1.

(*vi*) Repeat steps (*ii*) through (*v*) a large number of times. Each time will be called a *cycle*.

(*vii*) When a specified number of cycles has been completed, the fraction of points which fell on or under the curve, $F$, is computed as the value of the counter divided by the total number of cycles. The area under the curve is then obtained as

$$A = Fy^*(b - a)$$

Write a Pascal program to implement this strategy. Use this program to find the area under the curve $y = e^{-x^2}$ between the limits $a = 0$ and $b = 1$. Determine how many cycles are required to obtain an answer that is accurate to three significant figures. Compare the computer time required for this problem with the time required for the preceding problem. Which method is better?

(*h*) A normally distributed random variate $x$, with mean $\mu$ and standard deviation $\sigma$, can be generated from the formula

$$x = \mu + \sigma \, \frac{\sum\limits_{i=1}^{N} r_i - N/2}{\sqrt{N/12}}$$

where $r_i$ is a uniformly distributed random number whose value lies between 0 and 1. A value of $N = 12$ is frequently selected when using this formula. The underlying basis for the formula is the *central limit theorem*, which states that a set of mean values of uniformly distributed random variates will be normally distributed.

Write a Pascal program that will generate a specified number of normally distributed random variates with a given mean and a given standard deviation. Let the number of random variates, the mean and the standard deviation be input parameters.

(*i*) Write a Pascal program that will allow a person to play a game of tic-tac-toe against the computer. Write the program in such a manner that the computer can be either the first or the second player. If the computer is to be the first player, let the first move be generated randomly. Write out the complete status of the game after each move. Have the computer acknowledge a win by either player when it occurs.

**7.51** For each of the following problems, write a complete Pascal program that includes a recursive function.

(*a*) Determine the value of the *n*th Fibonacci number, $F_n$, where $F_n = F_{n-1} + F_{n-2}$ and $F_1 = F_2 = 1$ [see Prob. 6.50(*e*)]. Let the value of $n$ be an input parameter.

(*b*) The *Legendre polynomials* can be calculated by means of the formulas $P_0 = 1$, $P_1 = x$,

$$P_n = \frac{2n - 1}{n} \, x P_{n-1} - \frac{n - 1}{n} \, P_{n-2}$$

where $n = 2, 3, 4, \ldots$ and $x$ is any real number between $-1$ and 1. (Note that the Legendre polynomials are real-type quantities.) Let the values of $n$ and $x$ be input parameters.

# Chapter 8

# User-Defined Simple-Type Data

We have already seen that there are two general categories of simple-type data in Pascal. They are *standard-type* data, and *user-defined* data (see Sec. 2.7). These two categories can be further subdivided as follows.

1. Standard-type data
   - (*a*)  integer
   - (*b*)  real
   - (*c*)  char
   - (*d*)  boolean
2. User-defined data
   - (*a*)  enumerated
   - (*b*)  subrange

The use of standard-type data has already been discussed in detail in Chap. 3. We now turn our attention to user-defined simple data types. In particular, we will consider *enumerated-type* data and *subrange-type* data. We will see how these simple data types can be declared, and how they can be utilized effectively within a Pascal program.

## 8.1  ENUMERATED-TYPE DATA

An enumerated data type consists of an ordered sequence of identifiers, where each identifier is interpreted as an individual data item. These data items will collectively be associated with a particular name which serves to identify the data type. The association between the name of the data type and the individual data items is established by the *type* definition.

In general terms, the type definition is written as

```
TYPE name = (data item 1,data item 2, . . . ,data item n)
```

where *name* is the name of the enumerated data type, and *data item 1*, *data item 2*, etc. are the actual data items.

### EXAMPLE 8.1

In this example we define an enumerated data type called days. The actual data items will be the days of the week; i.e., sunday, monday, tuesday, wednesday, thursday, friday and saturday. Thus, the type definition will be written as

```
TYPE days = (sunday,monday,tuesday,wednesday,thursday,friday,saturday);
```

Notice that the data items are enclosed in parentheses and separated by commas.

It should be understood that these are the *only* values that can be associated with type days. An error will result if any other value is assigned to an identifier (i.e., a constant or a variable) of type days.

Since enumerated-type data are defined in an ordered sequence, the relational operators may be applied to them to form boolean expressions. Also, the standard functions pred and succ may be used to determine which data items precede and succeed any particular data item.

174

**EXAMPLE 8.2**

Consider the enumerated data type days, defined in the last example. Several boolean expressions that make use of these data items, and their corresponding values, are shown below.

| Expression | Value |
|---|---|
| sunday < tuesday | true |
| wednesday >= saturday | false |
| monday <> friday | true |
| pred(friday) = thursday | true |
| succ(friday) = saturday | true |
| succ(tuesday) <> pred(thursday) | false |

The standard function ord can also be used with enumerated data. To do so, it must be understood that the first data item is assigned the ordinal number 0, the second data item is assigned the ordinal number 1, and so on. Thus, if there are $n$ data items within an enumerated data type, the ordinal values will range from 0 to $n - 1$.

**EXAMPLE 8.3**

Consider once again the enumerated data type days, defined in Example 8.1. The following relationships are all true.

| | |
|---|---|
| succ(sunday) = monday | ord(sunday) = 0 |
| pred(monday) = sunday | ord(monday) = 1 |
| succ(monday) = tuesday | ord(tuesday) = 2 |
| . | . |
| . | . |
| . | . |
| pred(friday) = thursday | ord(saturday) = 6 |
| succ(friday) = saturday | |
| pred(saturday) = friday | |

## 8.2  SUBRANGE-TYPE DATA

A *subrange* refers to some portion of the original range of an ordered, simple data type. Subrange-type data are the data items that fall within this subrange, thus forming a subset of contiguous, ordered data. The original data type is referred to as the *host* data type. Each of the data items falling within the subrange is considered to be of the host type.

The subrange concept can be applied to any set of ordered, simple data. This includes previously defined enumerated data as well as three of the standard data types, integer, char and boolean. (Note that real-type data *cannot* be used to define a subrange.)

The general form of a subrange-type definition is written as

    TYPE *name* = *first data item..last data item*

where *name* is the name of the subrange data type, *first data item* is the first of the ordered data items within the subrange, and *last data item* is the last of the ordered data items. The complete subrange will consist of all data items contained within these two bounds (including the bounds themselves). Note that two consecutive periods must separate the first and last data items.

**EXAMPLE 8.4**

Several user-defined data types are given below.

```
TYPE days = (sunday,monday,tuesday,wednesday,thursday,friday,saturday);
     weekdays = monday..friday;
     month = 1..31;
     caps = 'A'..'Z';
```

The first line repeats the enumerated type definition given in Example 8.1. In the second line we then define a subrange data type called weekdays, consisting of a subset of days (specifically, the five data items monday, tuesday, wednesday, thursday and friday). Note that the enumerated type definition of days must precede the subrange definition of weekdays.

The third line defines another subrange data type called month. This data type consists of the consecutive integers 1 through 31. Thus, the data type is a subset of the standard integer data type.

Finally, the last line defines the subrange data type caps, which consists of the uppercase letters A through Z. Notice that this last data type is a subset of the standard char-type data.

Since subrange-type data are always ordered, the individual data items may be used with the relational operators to form boolean expressions. They may also be used with the standard functions pred, succ and ord, in the same manner as other ordered simple-type data. We will see some examples illustrating the use of subrange-type data later in this chapter.

## 8.3  MORE ABOUT DECLARATIONS

Let us again review the overall structure of a Pascal program. In particular, let us examine the declarations part of the program, since we are now able to understand the meaning of all of the constituent items. (Recall that this material has been presented earlier, in Secs. 1.5 and 5.2.)

Here is the overall program outline.

1. Header
2. Block
    (*a*)  Declarations
        (*i*)    Labels
        (*ii*)   Constants
        (*iii*)  Type definitions
        (*iv*)   Variables
        (*v*)    Procedures and functions
    (*b*)  Statements

The declarations section begins with statement labels, which are used in conjunction with the GOTO statement (see Sec. 6.8). This is followed by constant definitions (Sec. 2.8), then type definitions, as discussed in Secs. 8.1 and 8.2. Then come variable declarations (Sec. 2.9), followed by procedure and function declarations (Secs. 7.1 and 7.4).

Of particular significance is the fact that the type definitions precede the variable declarations. This permits variables to be declared in terms of user-defined data types as well as the standard data types. Our ability to utilize user-defined data types is thus considerably enhanced.

It is also possible to combine a subrange-type definition with a corresponding variable declaration. This is particularly convenient if the subrange type is used with only one variable declaration.

The declaration of variables whose data types are user-defined is illustrated in the next example.

**EXAMPLE 8.5**

Consider the following type definitions and variable declarations. (The type definitions are reproduced from Example 8.4.)

```
TYPE days = (sunday,monday,tuesday,wednesday,thursday,friday,saturday);
     weekdays = monday..friday;
     month = 1..31;
     caps = 'A'..'Z';
VAR workdays,holidays : weekdays;
    dayofmonth : month;
    hoursworked : 1..24;
    grosspay,netpay : real;
    employeenumber : 1..maxint;
```

Notice that the variables workdays and holidays are of type weekdays. Hence, each of these variables can take on the values monday, tuesday, wednesday, thursday or friday. Similarly, the variable dayofmonth is of type month, and can therefore take on any of the integer values 1 through 31.

Now consider the variable hoursworked. This is a subrange-type variable, similar to dayofmonth, that can take on any of the integer values 1 through 24. Note, however, that the type definition and the variable declaration are combined in this case. We could, of course, have replaced this single declaration with

```
TYPE hour = 1..24;
VAR hoursworked : hour;
```

though this is somewhat more cumbersome.

Note that we could also have combined the definition of the type month with the declaration of the variable dayofmonth. Thus, we could have written

```
VAR dayofmonth : 1..31;
```

Finally, the last two variable declarations establish that grosspay and netpay are real-type variables and that employeenumber is a positive integer-type variable. (Note that employeenumber is actually a subrange-type variable.) Thus, we see variable declarations that involve standard data types as well as user-defined data types in this example.

## 8.4  UTILIZING USER-DEFINED DATA

Once enumerated and subrange data have been defined, they can be used just as other simple-type data items are used within a Pascal program. This includes their use as control variables in FOR structures and as selectors in CASE structures.

**EXAMPLE 8.6**

Here is an example of an enumerated data type being used as a control variable in a FOR structure.

```
FOR weekdays := monday TO friday DO
   BEGIN
      .
      .
      .
   END;
```

The control variable weekdays is defined in Example 8.5. Hence, weekdays will take on the value monday during the first pass through the loop, tuesday during the second pass, and so on, until weekdays takes on the value friday during the last (fifth) pass.

**EXAMPLE 8.7**

Now consider the use of the same enumerated variable, weekdays, as a selector in a CASE structure.

```
CASE weekdays OF
     monday    : writeln(' First workday');
     tuesday   : writeln(' Second workday');
     wednesday : writeln(' Third workday');
     thursday  : writeln(' Fourth workday');
     friday    : writeln(' Last workday')
  END;
```

Only one message will be written out each time the CASE structure is encountered, depending on the value that is currently assigned to weekdays.

We have already seen that enumerated and subrange data can be used to create boolean-type expressions. Integer-type subrange data can also appear in integer-type expressions, following essentially the same rules as for standard integer-type data.

Both enumerated and subrange-type variables can be assigned values of an appropriate (corresponding) type. Thus, an element of an enumerated type can be assigned to an enumerated variable of the same type. Similarly, an element of a subrange can be assigned to a subrange variable of the same type.

### EXAMPLE 8.8

Suppose that holidays is an enumerated variable and that hoursworked and employeenumber are subrange variables, as defined in Example 8.5. Then the following assignment statements are valid.

```
employeenumber := 12345;

holidays := thursday;

hoursworked := 8;
```

Enumerated-type data cannot be entered into the computer via a read or a readln statement. However, integer or char-type subrange data may be entered, provided the values fall within the permissible subrange. Similar restrictions apply to writing out data via the write or writeln statement.

The use of enumerated-type data allows a Pascal program to be expressed in terms of variables that are closely related to the corresponding problem definition. This practice is strongly encouraged, since it promotes clarity and logical simplicity. Program debugging is also simplified.

The advantages to the use of subrange data are similar, though perhaps less dramatic. In particular, the use of subrange data simplifies the program and enhances its readability, and it may also result in a reduction in memory requirements.

### EXAMPLE 8.9

**Number of Days Between Two Dates**. Suppose that two different dates are entered into the computer, and we wish to determine the number of days between the two dates. One way to approach this problem is to determine the number of days from each of the specified dates to some earlier, common base date. The number of days between the two dates can then be determined as the difference in these two numbers less one.

Let us choose January 1, 1960, as the base date. If each of the dates is entered in the form mm dd yy (where mm represents an integer, dd an integer and yy an integer), then the number of days from the base date to a given date can be determined in the following manner.

1. Determine the day of the current year approximately as
   n := trunc(30.42*(mm-1)) + dd
2. If mm=2 (February), increase the value of n by 1.
3. If mm $>$ 2 and mm $<$ 8 (March, April, May, June and July), decrease the value of n by 1.
4. If yy MOD 4 $= 0$ and mm $>$ 2 (leap year), increase the value of n by 1.
5. Increase the value of n by 1461 for each full 4-year cycle beyond 1-1-60.
6. Increase n by 365 for each additional full year beyond the completion of the last full 4-year cycle, then add 1 (for the most recent leap year).

Let us utilize a function, called daysbeyond1960, to determine an appropriate value for n, given the values for mm, dd and yy. We will assume that n, mm, dd and yy are integer, subrange-type variables. Here is the complete function, which is based upon the six steps described above.

```
FUNCTION daysbeyond1960(mm : month; dd : day; yy : year) : numberofdays;
(* This function converts a given date (month,day,year)
                 to the number of days beyond January 1, 1960. *)
VAR n : numberofdays;
```

*(Program continues on next page)*

```
      BEGIN
         n := trunc(30.42*(mm-1)) + dd;
         IF mm=2 THEN n := n + 1;
         IF (mm > 2) AND (mm < 8) THEN n := n - 1;
         IF (yy MOD 4 = 0) AND (mm > 2) THEN n := n + 1;
         IF (yy-1960) DIV 4 > 0 THEN n := n + 1461*((yy-1960) DIV 4);
         IF (yy-1960) MOD 4 > 0 THEN n := n + 365*((yy-1960) MOD 4) + 1;
         daysbeyond1960 := n
      END;
```

It is now a simple matter to complete the entire program. To do so, we define the integer subrange types day, month, year and numberofdays; then declare an appropriate group of subrange-type global variables (dd, mm, yy, days1 and days2). The function declaration appears next, followed by the main block which merely reads in the two dates, accesses the function for each of the dates and then writes out the final answer.

Here is the entire program.

```
      PROGRAM dates(input,output);

      (* THIS PROGRAM DETERMINES THE NUMBER OF DAYS BETWEEN TWO DATES *)

      TYPE day = 1..31;
           month = 1..12;
           year = 1960..2100;
           numberofdays = 0..maxint;
      VAR dd : day;
          mm : month;
          yy : year;
          days1,days2 : numberofdays;

      FUNCTION daysbeyond1960(mm : month; dd : day; yy : year) : numberofdays;
      (* This function converts a given date (month,day,year)
                       to the number of days beyond January 1, 1960. *)
      VAR n : numberofdays;
      BEGIN
         n := trunc(30.42*(mm-1)) + dd;
         IF mm=2 THEN n := n + 1;
         IF (mm > 2) AND (mm < 8) THEN n := n - 1;
         IF (yy MOD 4 = 0) AND (mm > 2) THEN n := n + 1;
         IF (yy-1960) DIV 4 > 0 THEN n := n + 1461*((yy-1960) DIV 4);
         IF (yy-1960) MOD 4 > 0 THEN n := n + 365*((yy-1960) MOD 4) + 1;
         daysbeyond1960 := n
      END;

      BEGIN   (* main action block *)
         write(' Enter the first date  (mm dd yyyy) :');
         readln(mm,dd,yy);
         days1 := daysbeyond1960(mm,dd,yy);
         write(' Enter the second date (mm dd yyyy) :');
         readln(mm,dd,yy);
         days2 := daysbeyond1960(mm,dd,yy);
         writeln;
         writeln(' There are ',days2-days1-1,' days between the two dates.')
      END.
```

Notice that the second date is assumed to be greater than the first date.

Execution of this program results in the following output, if the two input dates are 12 29 1963 and 3 21 1983. (The user's responses are underlined.)

```
      Enter the first date  (mm dd yyyy) :12 29 1963
      Enter the second date (mm dd yyyy) : 3 21 1983

      There are    7021 days between the two dates.
```

The above example illustrates the use of subrange-type data in a realistic programming problem. The use of enumerated-type data is illustrated in the next example.

**EXAMPLE 8.10**

**The Towers of Hanoi**. Consider once again the problem described in Example 7.26. Let us now modify the Pascal program so that enumerated-type data are used to represent the three poles. In particular, let us introduce the enumerated data type poles, whose three constituent elements are left, center and right. The complete program is shown below.

```
      PROGRAM towersofhanoi(input,output);

      (* THIS PROGRAM SOLVES A WELL-KNOWN GAME USING
         RECURSIVE PROCEDURE CALLS AND USER-DEFINED DATA *)

      TYPE poles = (left,center,right);
           disks = 0..maxint;
      VAR n : disks;

         PROCEDURE transfer(n : disks; origin,destination,other : poles);
         (* Transfer n disks from the origin to the destination *)

            PROCEDURE diskmove(origin,destination : poles);
            (* Move a single disk from the origin to the destination *)
            BEGIN
               write(' Move ');
               CASE origin OF
                  left   : IF destination = center
                              THEN writeln('left to center')
                              ELSE writeln('left to right');
                  center : IF destination = left
                              THEN writeln('center to left')
                              ELSE writeln('center to right');
                  right  : IF destination = center
                              THEN writeln('right to center')
                              ELSE writeln('right to left')
               END   (* case *)
            END;   (* diskmove *)

         BEGIN   (* transfer *)
           IF n>0 THEN BEGIN
                        transfer(n-1,origin,other,destination);
                        diskmove(origin,destination);
                        transfer(n-1,other,destination,origin)
                      END
         END;   (* transfer *)

      BEGIN   (* main action block *)
         write(' Enter the number of disks -> ');
         readln(n);
         writeln;
         transfer(n,left,right,center)
      END.
```

This version of the program is not as clean as that presented in Example 7.26 because of the restriction that enumerated data cannot appear in a write or writeln statement. In particular, notice the need for the somewhat cumbersome CASE structure in procedure diskmove. Otherwise, however, the program definition is more straightforward, since the individual poles can be referred to in more natural terms.

Execution of the program for the case of n=3 results in the following output. (The user's response is again underlined.)

```
Enter the number of disks -> 3

Move left to right
Move left to center
Move right to center
Move left to right
Move center to left
Move center to right
Move left to right
```

# *Review Questions*

**8.1** What are the two general categories of simple-type data in Pascal? How can each be further subdivided?

**8.2** How is enumerated-type data defined?

**8.3** In what sense do enumerated-type data comprise an ordered sequence?

**8.4** Which operators can be used with enumerated-type data?

**8.5** Which standard functions can be used with enumerated-type data?

**8.6** How is subrange-type data defined? Compare with enumerated-type data.

**8.7** To what types of simple data can the subrange concept be applied? What types of simple data are incompatible with the subrange concept?

**8.8** Which operators can be used with subrange-type data?

**8.9** Which standard functions can be used with subrange-type data?

**8.10** What items are included in the declarations part of a Pascal program? In what order must these items appear?

**8.11** Under what circumstances is it advantageous to combine a subrange-type definition with a corresponding variable declaration? Can this also be done with enumerated-type data?

**8.12** Can an enumerated data item be used as a control variable in a FOR structure? Can a subrange-type data item be used for this purpose?

**8.13** Can an enumerated data item be used as a selector in a CASE structure? Can a subrange-type data item be used for this purpose?

**8.14** What restrictions apply to the use of user-defined data items in an expression?

**8.15** Can a user-defined data item appear in an assignment statement? What restrictions apply?

**8.16**  What restrictions apply to the use of user-defined data items in input/output statements?

**8.17**  What advantages are there in the use of enumerated-type data in a Pascal program? What disadvantages are there? Explain.

**8.18**  What advantages are there in the use of subrange-type data in a Pascal program? What disadvantages are there? Explain.

# Solved Problems

**8.19**  Consider the following type definition.

```
TYPE notes = (do,re,mi,fa,sol,la,ti) ;
```

Several boolean expressions which involve the use of these data items are shown below. Determine the value of each expression.

| Expression | Value |
|---|---|
| re > fa | false |
| do <= ti | true |
| pred(mi) = re | true |
| mi = succ(fa) | false |
| ord(do) < 1 | true |
| 3 = ord(pred(fa)) + 1 | true |

**8.20**  The following skeletal outlines illustrate the definition and use of enumerated-type and/or subrange-type data.

```
(a)   PROGRAM sample1(input,output);
      TYPE flavors = (vanilla,chocolate,strawberry,cherry,coconut);
           sizes = (small,medium,large);
      VAR cone,dish,sundae : flavors;
          pint,quart : vanilla..strawberry;
          conesize : sizes;
      BEGIN
        .

        .
        cone := cherry;
        .

        .
        IF quart = chocolate THEN . . .
                             ELSE . . .;
        .

        .
        CASE conesize OF
           small  : . . .;
           medium : . . .;
           large  : . . .
        END;
        .

        .
      END.
```

```
(b)    PROGRAM sample2(input,output);
       TYPE primary = (yellow,cyan,magenta);
       VAR color : primary;

           PROCEDURE proc1(VAR hue : primary);
           BEGIN
               .
               .
               IF hue = cyan THEN . . .
                           ELSE . . .;
               .
               .
           END;

       BEGIN   (* main action statements *)
           .
           .
           FOR color = yellow TO magenta DO . . .;
           .
           .
       END.

(c)    PROGRAM sample3(input,output);
       TYPE digits = '0'..'9';
       VAR d1,d2 : digits;
       BEGIN
           .
           .
           REPEAT
               .
               .
           UNTIL d1 = d2;
           .
           .
       END.
```

Note that the variables d1 and d2 do not represent numerical quantities.

# Supplementary Problems

**8.21**    Consider the following type definition.

```
TYPE cities = (Boston,Miami,Pittsburgh,Chicago,Denver,Phoenix,Seattle);
```

Determine the value of each of the following expressions.

(a)  pred(Pittsburgh)          (e)  succ(ord(Chicago))

(b)  succ(Denver)              (f)  Miami < Seattle

(c)  ord(Seattle)             (g)  Chicago < Pittsburgh

(d)  ord(succ(Chicago))

**8.22**    The skeletal outlines of several Pascal programs are shown below. Some are written incorrectly. Identify all errors.

(a)
```
PROGRAM sample(input,output);
TYPE days = (sun,mon,tues,wed,thurs,fri,sat);
VAR day1 : mon..fri;
    day2 : sun..sat;
BEGIN
    .
    .
    day1 := mon;
    WHILE day1 <> day2 DO
        BEGIN
            .
            .
            day1 := succ(day1)
        END;
    .
    .
END.
```

(b)
```
PROGRAM sample(input,output);
VAR highlight,foreground,background : colors;
    main : red..blue;
CONST border = red;
TYPE colors = (red,green,blue,white,black);
BEGIN
    .
    .
    foreground := 2;
    background := pred(foreground)
    .
    .
END.
```

(c)
```
PROGRAM sample(input,output);
TYPE suits = (clubs,diamonds,hearts,spades);
     values = 1..12;
VAR cardtype : suits;
    cardvalue : values;
    count,n : 1..maxint;
BEGIN
    .
    .
    write(' How many cards? ');
    readln(n);
    .
    .
    FOR count := 1 TO n DO
        BEGIN
            .
            .
            cardtype := . . .;
            cardvalue := . . .;
            writeln(count,cardtype,cardvalue)
        END
END.
```

(*d*)   PROGRAM sample(input,output);
```
        TYPE suits = (clubs,diamonds,hearts,spades);
             values = 1..12;
        VAR cardtype : suits;
            cardvalue : values;
            count,n : 1..maxint;
        BEGIN
           .
           .
           .
           write(' How many cards? ');
           readln(n);
           .
           .
           .
           FOR count := 1 TO n DO
              IF cardvalue > 9 THEN writeln('Picture card');
           .
           .
           .
        END.
```

(*e*)   PROGRAM sample(input,output);
```
        TYPE wines = (chablis,sauterne,rose,burgundy,chianti);
        VAR dinner : wines;
            cost : real;

            FUNCTION special(cost : real) : wines;
            BEGIN
               .
               .
               .
               special := . . .
            END;

        BEGIN   (* main action statements *)
           .
           .
           readln(cost);
           dinner := special(cost);
           .
           .
           .
        END.
```

# Programming Problems

**8.23**   Modify the program shown in Example 8.9 so that it accepts the following information as input

(*a*)   today's date

(*b*)   the user's name (assume a five-letter name)

(*c*)   the user's birthdate

and then determines how many days the user has been alive. (Enter the dates in the same manner as in Example 8.9.)

**8.24**   Modify the program shown in Example 8.9 so that it accepts any date beyond January 1, 1960, as input, and then prints out the corresponding day of the week. *Hint*: January 1, 1960, was a Friday.

**8.25**　Modify the program given in Example 8.10 so that the initial stack of disks can be on any pole (not necessarily the left), and the final stack can be on any other pole (not necessarily the right). Specify the origin and destination poles as input parameters. Then print out the moves that are required to transfer the poles from the specified origin to the specified destination.

**8.26**　Modify each of the following programs to make use of enumerated and/or subrange-type data. Also, include procedures and/or functions wherever appropriate.

(*a*)　Repeated averaging of a list of numbers (see Example 6.9).

(*b*)　Calculating a list of factorials (see Example 6.10).

(*c*)　Calculating depreciation (see Example 7.12).

(*d*)　Simulation of a game of craps (see Example 7.18).

**8.27**　Solve each of the following programming problems, utilizing enumerated and/or subrange data wherever appropriate. Also, be sure to modularize each program by making proper use of procedures and/or functions.

(*a*)　Calculate the first *n* Fibonacci numbers, as described in Prob. 6.50(*e*). Then determine which of these is a prime number [see Prob. 6.50(*f*)].

(*b*)　Convert a positive integer number to a roman numeral, as described in Prob. 6.50(*q*).

(*c*)　Program an interactive game of tic-tac-toe, as described in Prob. 7.50(*i*).

# Chapter 9

# Arrays

We have already mentioned the fact that Pascal supports three different categories of data types: *simple* data, *structured* data and *pointer* data. So far, however, our discussions have been confined to simple-type data. We have seen that simple-type data include the four standard data types: *integer*, *real*, *char* and *boolean* (see Chap. 3), and the two user-defined data types: *enumerated* and *subrange* (see Chap. 8). All simple-type data have the common characteristic that each variable represents a single data item.

We now turn our attention to structured-type data. In fact, each of the next four chapters will be concerned with a different type of structured data. These chapters will cover *arrays*, *records*, *files* and *sets*, respectively. All of these data types have the common characteristic that a single identifier can represent multiple data items. The individual data items can also be accessed separately (though this is done in a different manner for each structured data type). Thus, structured-type data items can be manipulated collectively or individually, depending on the requirements of each particular application.

## 9.1 ONE-DIMENSIONAL ARRAYS

A one-dimensional array can be thought of as a list (i.e., a column) of data items, all of the same type, that are collectively referred to by the same name. Each individual array element (i.e., each of the data items) can be referred to by specifying the array name, followed by an *index* (also called a *subscript*), enclosed in square brackets. The array elements can be of any data type, as long as they are all the same. Thus, if list is a one-dimensional array containing n elements, the individual array elements will be list [1], list [2], . . . , list [n]. The entire array can then be represented as a list of the individual array elements; i.e.,

$$
list = \begin{bmatrix} list\ [1] \\ list\ [2] \\ \cdot \\ \cdot \\ \cdot \\ list\ [n] \end{bmatrix}
$$

**EXAMPLE 9.1**

A Pascal program contains a 100-element, real-type array called list. Each individual element will have a value equal to 0.01 times its index value. Thus,

$$list\ [1] = 0.01$$

$$list\ [2] = 0.02$$

$$list\ [3] = 0.03$$

. . .

etc.

The $i$th element of list can be referred to as list [i], where i is an integer-type variable. Thus, i is assigned a value of 5, then list [i] will refer to the fifth element within the array, which is list [5]. The value of this array element is 0.05.

The easiest way to define an array is to include it in a variable declaration, as follows.

```
VAR array name : ARRAY [index type] OF type
```

The index type can be an ordinal, simple type (i.e., integer, char, boolean or enumerated) or a subrange. The array itself can be of any type, including structured types (more about this later), though most elementary applications make use of simple-type arrays. (As a matter of practical interest, note that an array can be of type real, but its index cannot.)

### EXAMPLE 9.2

Suppose that a Pascal program is to include a 100-element, real-type array called list. The array declaration can be written as follows.

```
VAR list : ARRAY [1..100] OF real;
```

Alternatively, we could write

```
TYPE index = 1..100;
VAR list : ARRAY [index] OF real;
```

The first form is usually more desirable, however, because it is simpler.

Note that the array elements are of type real, but the index is a subrange of type integer.

Individual array elements can be used in expressions, assignment statements, read and write statements, etc., as though they were ordinary simple-type variables. To do so, the array element must be written as the array name, followed by an appropriate index value enclosed in square brackets. The index value can be expressed as a constant, a variable or an expression. However, the index must be of the correct type and it must fall within the correct range.

### EXAMPLE 9.3

Let us again consider the one-dimensional, real array list, described in Example 9.2. Suppose we now wish to examine the value of each element of the array and write out those values that are negative. This can be accomplished with the following loop structure.

```
FOR count := 1 TO 100 DO
    IF list [count] < 0
        THEN writeln(count:3, list [count]:4:1);
```

Notice that the value of the index (i.e., the integer-type variable count) is written out on the same line as the negative array element. Thus, if the third array element had a value of $-5.0$, the following output would be generated.

```
3 -5.0
```

In this example it is essential that the values of count do not fall outside the range 1..100, since the array index is undefined outside of this range. We could, however, work with a smaller subrange if we wish. Thus we could have written

```
FOR count := 25 TO 50 DO
    IF list [count] < 0
        THEN writeln(count:3, list [count]:4:1);
```

The use of array elements in assignment statements and in expressions must follow the same rules as with simple-type variables. Thus, if a single array element appears on either side of an assignment statement, it must be type-compatible with the other variable or expression in that statement. Also, if used within an expression, the array element must be type-compatible with the other data items that appear in the expression.

**EXAMPLE 9.4**

**Deviations About an Average.** Suppose that we want to read in a list of n real quantities and then calculate their average, as in Example 6.8. In addition to simply calculating the average, however, we will also compute the deviation of each of the numbers about the average, using the formula

$$deviation = x[i] - average$$

where x[i] represents each of the given numbers and average represents the calculated average.

Note that we are storing each of the given numbers in a one-dimensional, real-type array x. This is an essential part of this program. The reason, which must be clearly understood, is as follows.

In all of the earlier examples where we calculated the average of a list of numbers, each number was replaced by the succeeding number in the list. Hence the individual numbers were no longer available for subsequent calculations once the average had been determined. Now, however, these individual values must be retained in order to calculate the corresponding deviations after the average has been determined. We therefore store them in the one-dimensional array x.

Let us restrict the size of x to 100 elements. However, we need not make use of all 100 elements. Rather, we shall specify the actual number of elements by assigning a positive integer quantity (not exceeding 100) to the variable n.

Here is the complete Pascal program.

```pascal
PROGRAM deviations(input,output);

(* THIS PROGRAM READS IN A LIST OF n NUMBERS,
   CALCULATES THEIR AVERAGE, AND THEN COMPUTES
   THE DEVIATION OF EACH NUMBER ABOUT THE AVERAGE *)

VAR n,count : integer;
    sum,average,deviation : real;
    x : ARRAY [1..100] OF real;

BEGIN
   BEGIN (* Read in the numbers and calculate the average *)
      write(' How many numbers will be averaged? ');
      readln(n);
      writeln;
      sum := 0;
      FOR count := 1 TO n DO
         BEGIN
            write(' i= ',count:3,'     x= ');
            readln(x [count]);
            sum := sum + x [count]
         END;
      average := sum/n;
      writeln(' The average is ',average);
      writeln;
   END;   (* calculate average *)

   BEGIN (* Calculate the deviations about the average *)
      FOR count := 1 TO n DO
         BEGIN
            deviation := x [count] - average;
            write(' i= ',count:3,'     x= ',x [count]);
            writeln('     d= ',deviation)
         END
   END   (* calculate deviations *)
END.
```

Notice the manner in which this program is modularized. There are no procedures or functions in the program. Rather, the main block is comprised of two compound statements, each with its own distinct purpose. Each compound statement is identified with its own comments. This method is convenient for certain short, simple programs such as this.

Now suppose that the program is executed using the following five numerical values:

x[1] = 3.0, x[2] = -2.0, x[3] = 12.0, x[4] = 4.4, x[5] = 3.5

The interactive entering of the data will appear as follows. (The user's responses are underlined.)

```
How many numbers will be averaged? 5

i=  1      x= 3.0
i=  2      x= -2.0
i=  3      x= 12.0
i=  4      x= 4.4
i=  5      x= 3.5
```

As soon as all of the data have been entered, the following output will be generated.

```
The average is  4.1800000E+00

i=  1      x=  3.0000000E+00      d= -1.1800000E+00
i=  2      x= -2.0000000E+00      d= -6.1800000E+00
i=  3      x=  1.2000000E+01      d=  7.8200000E+00
i=  4      x=  4.4000000E+00      d=  2.2000000E-01
i=  5      x=  3.5000000E+00      d= -6.8000000E-01
```

Some applications can be enhanced through the use of an enumerated-type index, as shown in the following example.

### EXAMPLE 9.5

Here is a portion of a Pascal program which defines an integer-type one-dimensional array with an enumerated-type index.

```
TYPE color = (red,white,blue,yellow,green);
VAR index  : color;
    values : ARRAY [color] OF integer;
```

Notice that values is defined as a five-element array. Each element will represent an integer quantity.

If we wanted to write out the value of each element, we might include the following structure somewhere within the program.

```
FOR index := red TO green DO writeln(values[index]);
```

The array elements themselves can also be of an enumerated type, as illustrated in the following example.

### EXAMPLE 9.6

Here is a variation of the situation described in Example 9.5. Suppose that values is a 100-element array of type color. Then the Pascal program might include the following type definition and variable declaration.

```
TYPE color = (red,white,blue,yellow,green);
VAR values : ARRAY [1..100] OF color;
```

Now each of the array elements will take on one of the values red, white, blue, yellow or green. The index values will be integers ranging from 1 to 100.

Another type of application that arises frequently involves the use of strings. In such situations we often represent a string as a one-dimensional array of type char. The technique is illustrated in the following example.

### EXAMPLE 9.7

**Names and Addresses.** Here is a simple Pascal program that allows a name and address to be entered and stored within the computer and then written out. We will assume that each name, street address and city address does not exceed 60 characters. Hence, we will introduce three 60-element, char-type arrays, called name, street and city, respectively. Each string need not, however, contain 60 characters. Rather, we will enter successive characters into each array until an end-of-line is encountered. The standard boolean function eoln will be used for this purpose. Thus, we will continue to read characters from each line, until the function eoln returns the value true. (Note that eoln will again become false when a new line is begun.)

Also, we will count the number of characters in each array so that we will know how many characters (array elements) to write out later in the program. Let us refer to these character counters as namecount, streetcount and citycount, respectively.

Here is the entire Pascal program. Note that the program consists essentially of two procedures, readin, which causes the input data to be entered into the computer, and writeout, which then writes out the data. Observe the prompts for name, street and city that are included within readin.

```
PROGRAM namesandaddresses(input,output);

(* THIS PROGRAM READS IN AND THEN WRITES OUT
        A NAME AND ADDRESS (STREET AND CITY) *)

VAR count,namecount,streetcount,citycount : 0..60;
    name,street,city : ARRAY [1..60] OF char;

PROCEDURE readin;
(* Read a name and address into the computer *)
BEGIN
    write('Name:    ');
    count := 0;
    REPEAT
         count := count + 1;
         read(name [count])
    UNTIL eoln;
    namecount := count;
    readln;

    write('Street: ');
    count := 0;
    REPEAT
         count := count + 1;
         read(street [count])
    UNTIL eoln;
    streetcount := count;
    readln;

    write('City:    ');
    count := 0;
    REPEAT
         count := count + 1;
         read(city [count])
    UNTIL eoln;
    citycount := count;
    readln
END;   (* readin *)

PROCEDURE writeout;
(* Write a name and address out of the computer *)
BEGIN
    FOR count := 1 TO namecount DO write(name [count]);
    writeln;
    FOR count := 1 TO streetcount DO write(street [count]);
    writeln;
    FOR count := 1 TO citycount DO write(city [count])
END;    (* writeout *)
```

(*Program continues on next page*)

```
BEGIN   (* main action block *)
   readin;
   writeln;
   writeout
END.
```

Execution of the program results in the following input dialog. (The user's input is again underlined.)

```
Name:   Susan H. Gottfried
Street: 129 Old Suffolk Drive
City:   Monroeville, PA 15146
```

Once the input data have been entered, the program writes out the name, street and city, as shown below.

```
Susan H. Gottfried
129 Old Suffolk Drive
Monroeville, PA 15146
```

Finally, the reader should recognize that this program can be used as a starting point for many other more complex (and more interesting) programs. For example, many business applications (e.g., mailing lists, payrolls, accounts receivables) require that names, addresses and related data be entered into the computer, modified in some way and later written out.

## EXAMPLE 9.8

**Reordering a List of Numbers.** Consider the well-known problem of rearranging a list of n numbers into a sequence of algebraically increasing values. The program is to be written in such a manner that unnecessary storage will not be used. Therefore the program will contain only one array—a one-dimensional, real array called x—which will be reordered one element at a time.

The procedure will begin by scanning the entire array for the smallest number, and then interchanging this number with the first number in the array. (The smallest number will now be at the top of the list.) Next the remaining n – 1 numbers will be scanned for the smallest, which will be exchanged with the second number. (The second-smallest number will now be second in the list.) Then the remaining n – 2 numbers will be scanned for the smallest, which will be interchanged with the third number, and so on, until the entire array has been rearranged. This will require a total of n – 1 passes through the array, though the length of each scan will progressively become smaller with each pass.

In order to find the smallest number for each pass, we sequentially compare each number in the array, x [i], with the starting number, x [loc], where loc is an integer variable that is used to "tag" one of the array elements. If x [i] is smaller than x [loc], then we interchange the two numbers; otherwise we leave the two numbers in their original positions. Once this procedure has been applied to the entire array, the first number in the array will be the smallest. We then repeat the entire procedure n – 2 times, for a total of n – 1 passes (loc = 1, 2, . . . , n – 1).

The only remaining question is how the two numbers are interchanged. We first temporarily save the value of x [loc] for future reference. Then we assign the current value of x [i] to x [loc]. Finally, we assign the *original* value of x [loc], which had been saved, to x [i]. The interchange is now complete.

The strategy described above can be incorporated into a Pascal procedure called interchange, as shown below.

```
PROCEDURE interchange;
(* Interchange array elements from smallest to largest *)
BEGIN
   FOR loc := 1 TO n-1 DO
      FOR i := loc + 1 TO n DO
         IF x [i] < x [loc] THEN
            BEGIN
               temp := x [loc];
               x [loc] := x [i];
               x [i] := temp
            END
END;
```

In this procedure we assume that loc, i and n are integer-type variables whose values range from 1 to 100. Also, we assume that temp is a real-type variable that is used for temporary storage of x [loc]. Note that the procedure utilizes nested FOR—TO structures.

Now let us consider the overall program strategy, as shown in the following outline.

1. Read in the size of the array, n.

2. Read in the n array elements, in response to interactive prompts.

3. Rearrange the numbers within the array by accessing procedure interchange.

4. Write out the rearranged values.

Here is the entire Pascal program.

```
PROGRAM reorder(input,output);

(* THIS PROGRAM REORDERS A ONE-DIMENSIONAL ARRAY
         OF REAL NUMBERS FROM SMALLEST TO LARGEST *)

VAR n,i,loc : 1..100;
    x : ARRAY [1..100] OF real;
    temp : real;

PROCEDURE interchange;
(* Interchange array elements from smallest to largest *)
BEGIN
    FOR loc := 1 TO n-1 DO
        FOR i := loc + 1 TO n DO
            IF x [i] < x [loc] THEN
                BEGIN
                    temp := x [loc];
                    x [loc] := x [i];
                    x [i] := temp
                END
END;   (* interchange *)

BEGIN   (* main action block *)
    write('How many numbers are there? ');
    readln(n);
    writeln;
    FOR i := 1 TO n DO
        BEGIN
            write('x [',i:3,']= ? ');
            readln(x [i])
        END;
    interchange;
    writeln;
    writeln('Rearranged Data:');
    writeln;
    FOR i := 1 TO n DO
        writeln('x [',i:3,']= ',x [i]:4:1);
END.
```

Execution of the program begins with an interactive data entry session. A typical data entry session is shown below. (The user's responses are shown underlined.)

```
How many numbers are there? 5

x [   1] = ? 4.7
x [   2] = ? -2.3
x [   3] = ? 12.9
x [   4] = ? 8.8
x [   5] = ? 6.0
```

The program then rearranges the five input quantities and generates the following output.

Rearranged Data:

```
x [   1] = -2.3
x [   2] =  4.7
x [   3] =  6.0
x [   4] =  8.8
x [   5] = 12.9
```

## 9.2  MULTIDIMENSIONAL ARRAYS

The array concept need not be confined to single-dimensional arrays in Pascal. Multidimensional arrays can also be defined. In fact, such arrays are very useful in many different types of applications.

We have already seen that a one-dimensional array can be thought of as a list (i.e., a single column) of data items. The multidimensional array provides a natural extension of this idea. Thus, we can think of a two-dimensional array as a table of data items, consisting of rows and columns. The first dimension (i.e., the first index) might refer to the row number, and the second dimension (the second index) to the column number. Similarly, a three-dimensional array might be thought of as a collection of tables, like pages in a book.

Suppose, for example, that table is a two-dimensional array containing m rows and n columns. The individual array elements would be table [1,1], table [1,2], . . . , table [1, n], table [2,1], table [2,2], . . . , table [2, n], . . . , table [m, 1], table [m, 2], . . . , table [m, n]. Thus, the entire array can be visualized in the following manner.

$$
\text{table} =
\begin{bmatrix}
\text{table } [1,1] & \text{table } [1,2] & \cdots & \text{table } [1,n] \\
\text{table } [2,1] & \text{table } [2,2] & \cdots & \text{table } [2,n] \\
\text{table } [3,1] & \text{table } [3,2] & \cdots & \text{table } [3,n] \\
& \vdots & & \\
\text{table } [m,1] & \text{table } [m,2] & \cdots & \text{table } [m,n]
\end{bmatrix}
$$

Regardless of its dimensionality, an array always consists of a collection of data items of the same type. All of the data items can be collectively referred to by a single identifier (i.e., a common array name). An individual array element (i.e., a single data item) can be referred to by specifying the array name, followed by appropriate values for the indices (subscripts), enclosed in square brackets and separated by commas.

### EXAMPLE 9.9

A Pascal program contains a two-dimensional, real-type array called table. This array will represent a table of numbers containing a maximum of 60 rows and 150 columns. Therefore the first index will range from 1 to 60, and the second index from 1 to 150.

Suppose we want to access the array element in the third row and the seventh column. This data item can be referenced simply by writing table [3, 7]. Similarly, we can refer to the array element in the $i$th row and the $j$th column as table [i, j], where i and j are integer-type variables that are used as indices. Therefore, if i is assigned a value of 12 and j is assigned a value of 5, table [i, j] will refer to the array element in the fifth column of the twelfth row.

A multidimensional array definition can be included in a variable declaration, in the same manner as a one-dimensional array. However, a separate index type must be specified for each of the array dimensions. Hence an array definition can be written as

```
VAR array name : ARRAY [index 1 type, index 2 type, . . . ,

                                   index n type] OF type
```

The index types can be ordinal, simple types (i.e., integer, char, boolean or enumerated) or subranges. They need not all be of the same type. On the other hand, the array elements themselves must all be of the same type, though they can be of any type, including structured types.

### EXAMPLE 9.10

Consider once again the two-dimensional, real-type array table, described in the previous example. This array can be defined in the following manner.

```
VAR table : ARRAY [1..60, 1..150] OF real;
```

Another way to express this same definition is shown below.

```
TYPE index1 = 1..60;
     index2 = 1..150;
VAR  table : ARRAY [index1,index2] OF real;
```

Here is still another approach.

```
CONST limit1 = 60;
      limit2 = 150;
TYPE  index1 = 1..limit1;
      index2 = 1..limit2;
VAR   table : ARRAY [index1,index2] OF real;
```

Obviously, the first definition is the simplest.

Note that both indices are subranges of type integer, but the array elements themselves are of type real.

Many applications that involve the use of multidimensional arrays require nested loops, one loop for each of the dimensions. Thus, an application that is oriented toward processing the elements in a table might make use of two loops, one within another. The outer loop might be used to process each of the individual rows, and the inner loop to process the columns within each row. The manner in which this is accomplished is illustrated in the next example.

### EXAMPLE 9.11

**Table Manipulation.** Now let us write an interactive Pascal program that will read a table of real numbers into the computer and store them in a two-dimensional array, calculate the sum of the numbers in every row and every column and then write out the table along with the calculated row sums and the column sums.

Let us begin by defining the following variables.

table = the two-dimensional, real array containing the given
        table and the calculated sums

nrows = an integer variable indicating the number of rows in
        the given table

ncols = an integer variable indicating the number of columns
        in the given table

row = an integer counter that indicates the row number

col = an integer counter that indicates the column number

We will assume that the size of the table will not exceed 10 rows and 10 columns. We will add one additional row and one additional column within the array, however, so that we will have a place to store the row sums and the column sums. Thus, the row sums will be placed in the rightmost column (i.e., column number ncols + 1), and the column sums will appear in the bottom row (i.e., row nrows + 1). We will therefore define table to be two-dimensional, real array with a maximum of 11 rows and 11 columns.

Let us employ a modular structure in the development of the program. In particular, let us write separate procedures for reading in the data, calculating the row sums, calculating the column sums and writing out the final table. These procedures will be called readinput, rowsums, columnsums and writeoutput, respectively.

The logic required for each procedure is straightforward, though it should be noted that a double loop will be required within each of the procedures. For example, in order to read in the original table, we will have to provide the following double loop.

```
FOR row := 1 TO nrows DO
   BEGIN
      FOR col := 1 TO ncols DO read(table [row,col]);
      writeln
   END
```

(The writeln statement is required in order to skip to the next line.) Similarly, the following loop is required in order to calculate each of the row sums.

```
FOR row := 1 TO nrows DO
   BEGIN
      table [row,ncols+1] := 0;
      FOR col := 1 TO ncols DO
          table [row,ncols+1] := table [row,ncols+1] + table [row,col]
   END
```

Similar double-loop structures can be used to calculate the column sums and to write out the final table. Here is the complete Pascal program.

```
PROGRAM table1(input,output);

(* THIS PROGRAM READS IN A TABLE OF NUMBERS,
   SUMS THE COLUMNS WITHIN EACH ROW,
   AND THEN SUMS THE ROWS WITHIN EACH COLUMN *)

VAR row,col : 1..11;
    nrows,ncols : 1..10;
    table : ARRAY [1..11, 1..11] OF real;

PROCEDURE rowsums;
(* Add the columns within each row *)
BEGIN
   FOR row := 1 TO nrows DO
      BEGIN
         table [row,ncols+1] := 0;
         FOR col := 1 TO ncols DO
             table [row,ncols+1] := table [row,ncols+1] + table [row,col]
      END
END;   (* rowsums *)

PROCEDURE columnsums;
(* Add the rows within each column *)
BEGIN
   FOR col := 1 TO ncols DO
      BEGIN
         table [nrows+1,col] := 0;
         FOR row := 1 TO nrows DO
             table [nrows+1,col] := table [nrows+1,col] + table [row,col]
      END
END;   (* columnsums *)
```

(*Program continues on next page*)

```
      PROCEDURE readinput;
      (* Read the elements of the table *)
      BEGIN
         write(' How many rows? (1..10) ');
         readln(nrows);
         writeln;
         write(' How many columns? (1..10) ');
         readln(ncols);
         writeln;
         FOR row := 1 TO nrows DO
            BEGIN
               writeln(' Enter data for row no. ',row:2);
               FOR col := 1 TO ncols DO read(table [row,col]);
               writeln
            END
      END;   (* readinput *)

      PROCEDURE writeoutput;
      (* Write out the table and the corresponding sums *)
      BEGIN
         writeln(' Original table, with row sums and column sums:');
         writeln;
         FOR row := 1 TO nrows + 1 DO
            BEGIN
               FOR col := 1 TO ncols + 1 DO write(table [row,col]:6:1);
               writeln
            END
      END;   (* writeoutput *)

      BEGIN   (* main action block *)
         readinput;
         rowsums;
         columnsums;
         writeoutput
      END.
```

Suppose the program will be used to process the following table of numbers.

| 2.5 | −6.3 | 14.7 | 4.0 |
|-----|------|------|-----|
| 10.8 | 12.4 | −8.2 | 5.5 |
| −7.2 | 3.1 | 17.7 | −9.1 |

When the program is executed, the following dialogue will take place. (The user's responses are underlined.)

```
How many rows? (1..10) 3

How many columns? (1..10) 4

Enter data for row no.  1
2.5 −6.3 14.7 4.0

Enter data for row no.  2
10.8 12.4 −8.2 5.5

Enter data for row no.  3
−7.2 3.1 17.7 −9.1
```

The program will then calculate the row sums and the column sums, and then generate the following output.

```
Original table, with row sums and column sums:

  2.5  -6.3  14.7   4.0  14.9
 10.8  12.4  -8.2   5.5  20.5
 -7.2   3.1  17.7  -9.1   4.5
  6.1   9.2  24.2   0.4   0.0
```

From this output, we can see that the sum of the elements in the first row is 14.9 (i.e., 2.5 − 6.3 + 14.7 + 4.0 = 14.9). Similarly, the sum of the elements in the first column is 6.1 (i.e., 2.5 + 10.8 − 7.2 = 6.1), and so on.

The indices in a multidimensional array need not all be of the same type. The only restriction is that each index be of some ordinal, simple type.

**EXAMPLE 9.12**

Some additional multidimensional array declarations are shown below.

```
TYPE color = (red,white,blue,yellow,green);
     index = 1..100;
VAR sample : ARRAY [color,index] OF boolean;
```

Thus one of the elements of sample might be sample [white,25]. Another might be sample [green,66]. Since sample is a boolean array, the values assigned to the individual elements will be boolean; i.e., their values will be either false or true.

Recall that an array may be of any type, including a structured type. Therefore, it is possible to define a one-dimensional array whose elements are themselves one-dimensional arrays (all having the same dimensionality), of the same type as the first array. The result of such an array definition is equivalent to an ordinary two-dimensional array.

**EXAMPLE 9.13**

Let us define a one-dimensional, char-type array called codes, whose elements are one-dimensional, char-type arrays. We will assume that codes has a maximum of 25 elements, and that each element is a 50-element array. The array definition can be written as

```
VAR codes : ARRAY [1..25] OF ARRAY [1..50] OF char;
```

This is equivalent to defining an ordinary two-dimensional, char-type array. Thus, we can alternatively write

```
VAR codes : ARRAY [1..25, 1..50] OF char;
```

Each of these declarations defines a table having a maximum of 25 rows, with as many as 50 char-type elements within each row.

The individual array elements can also be accessed two different ways. For example, the element in row i and column j can be accessed as

```
code [i][j]
```

or as

```
code [i,j]
```

Similarly, row i can be accessed as

```
code [i]
```

Therefore, the element in row 12, column 20 can be accessed by writing either code [12][20] or code [12,20]. Also, all of the elements in row 12 (i.e., the entire row) can be accessed simply by writing code [12].

In most applications it is more convenient to utilize multidimensional array elements using the original method, as in Example 9.11, rather than the method described above.

## 9.3  OPERATIONS WITH ENTIRE ARRAYS

There are certain types of operations that can be carried out with an entire array, thus affecting all of the array elements in the same manner. In particular, we can define array types, assign arrays to one another, and pass arrays as parameters to procedures or functions. Let us consider each of these features in some detail.

Some programs make use of several different arrays of the same type and dimensionality. In such cases it is convenient to define a single array type, and then declare the individual arrays as variables of this type.

In general terms, an array type definition can be expressed as

TYPE *name* = ARRAY [*index 1 type*, *index 2 type*, . . . ,
                                        *index n type*] OF *type*

where the index types and the array data type have the same meaning as in an array-type variable declaration (see Sec. 9.2).

### EXAMPLE 9.14

Suppose that group1 and group2 are two-dimensional integer-type arrays, each having a maximum of 25 rows and 50 columns. These arrays can be defined in the following manner.

```
TYPE table = ARRAY [1..25, 1..50] OF integer;
VAR group1,group2 : table;
```

Thus, table is a user-defined structured type (specifically, an integer-type, two-dimensional array with a maximum of 25 rows and 50 columns). The variables group1 and group2 are declared to be of type table. Hence, group1 and group2 will each be an integer-type, two-dimensional array with a maximum of 25 rows and 50 columns.

The variable declarations need not have the same scope as the type definition. For example, the type might be defined within the main block, and certain of the array-type variable declarations might appear immediately thereafter. The remaining variable declarations might then appear in a procedure or a function.

Sometimes it is desirable to assign all of the elements of one array to the corresponding elements of another array, where both arrays are of the same type and the same dimensionality. This can be accomplished with a single assignment statement, thus avoiding the need to assign each element individually within some type of looping structure.

### EXAMPLE 9.15

Consider once again the two integer-type arrays, group1 and group2, defined in the previous example. Suppose that all of the elements of group1 have already been read into the computer, and we now wish to assign these elements to the corresponding elements of group2. This can be accomplished simply by writing

```
group2 := group1;
```

Note that this single assignment statement is equivalent to a nested double loop; i.e.,

```
FOR row := 1 TO 25 DO
    FOR col := 1 TO 50 DO
        group2 [row,col] := group1 [row,col];
```

Obviously, the single assignment statement is much simpler.

However, it is not possible to include entire arrays in numeric or boolean expressions. Therefore, if a, b and c are array-type variables, a statement such as

```
c := a + b;
```

would not be permitted .

Similarly, an entire array cannot be read into the computer with a single read or readln statement. Thus, a loop structure is required in order to read in multiple array elements. In general, the same restriction applies to writing an entire array with a single write or writeln statement. We shall see an important exception to this last restriction, however, in Sec. 9.5.

An entire array can be passed to a procedure or a function as an actual parameter. Note, however, that the corresponding formal parameter (within the procedure or function) must be associated with a recognized data type, in this case, an array type. Therefore, the array type must be explicitly defined within a block that encloses the procedure or function.

A convenient way to satisfy this requirement is to define a global array type, as described at the start of this section. The actual array-type parameters and the corresponding formal parameters can then be declared as members of this array type as required within the program. This approach is illustrated in the next example.

**EXAMPLE 9.16**

**Adding Two Tables of Numbers.** Suppose we want to read two tables of integers into the computer, calculate the sums of the corresponding elements, i.e.,

$$c[i,j] = a[i,j] + b[i,j]$$

and then write out the new table containing these sums. We will assume that all of the tables contain the same number of rows and columns, which do not exceed 20 rows and 30 columns.

Let us make use of the following variable definitions.

> table = a two-dimensional integer array type having a
>         maximum of 20 rows and 30 columns
>
> a,b,c = two-dimensional arrays of type table
>
> nrows = an integer variable indicating the actual number
>         of rows in each table
>
> ncols = an integer variable indicating the actual number
>         of columns in each table
>
> row = an integer counter that indicates the row number
>
> col = an integer counter that indicates the column number

We will employ a modular structure similar to that used in Example 9.11. In particular, we will define one procedure for reading the data into any table, another for summing all of the elements and a third for writing out the new table containing the calculated sums. Let us call these procedures readinput, computesums and writeoutput, respectively.

The actual program, shown below, is quite straightforward.

```
PROGRAM table2(input,output);

(* THIS PROGRAM READS IN TWO TABLES OF INTEGERS,
   CALCULATES THE SUMS OF THEIR RESPECTIVE ELEMENTS,
   AND WRITES OUT THE RESULTING TABLE CONTAINING THE SUMS *)

TYPE table = ARRAY [1..20,1..30] OF integer;
VAR  a,b,c : table;
     row,nrows : 1..20;
     col,ncols : 1..30;

PROCEDURE readinput(VAR t : table);
(* Read the elements of one table *)
BEGIN
   FOR row := 1 TO nrows DO
      BEGIN
         writeln(' Enter data for row no. ',row:2);
         FOR col := 1 TO ncols DO read(t[row,col]);
         writeln
      END
END;    (* readinput *)
```

(*Program continues on next page*)

```
      PROCEDURE computesums(t1,t2 : table; VAR t3 : table);
      (* Sum the elements of two similar tables *)
      BEGIN
         FOR row := 1 TO nrows DO
            FOR col := 1 TO ncols DO
               t3[row,col] := t1[row,col] + t2[row,col]
      END;   (* computesums *)


      PROCEDURE writeoutput(t : table);
      (* Write out the elements of a table *)
      BEGIN
         writeln(' Sums of the elements:');
         writeln;
         FOR row := 1 TO nrows DO
            BEGIN
               FOR col := 1 TO ncols DO write(t[row,col]:4);
               writeln
            END
      END;   (* writeoutput *)


      BEGIN   (* main action block *)
         write(' How many rows? (1..20) ');
         readln(nrows);
         writeln;
         write(' How many columns? (1..30) ');
         readln(ncols);
         writeln;
         writeln(' First table:');
         writeln;
         readinput(a);
         writeln(' Second table:');
         writeln;
         readinput(b);
         computesums(a,b,c);
         writeoutput(c)
      END.
```

This program contains several noteworthy characteristics. First, notice that the program contains an array type definition, called table. Three variables (a, b and c) within the main block are declared to be arrays of type table. In addition, the procedures contain array-type parameters that are also declared to be of type table.

Notice that the array-type parameter t in procedure readinput is a *variable* parameter. This allows the elements of t to be returned from the procedure to the main block. On the other hand, the array-type variable t in writeoutput is a *value* parameter, since the elements of t that are transferred to this procedure need not be returned to the main block.

The remaining procedure, computesums, utilizes both value array-type parameters and variable array-type parameters. In particular, the first two parameters (t1 and t2) are value parameters, since they represent input data to the procedure. The third parameter (t3) is a variable parameter, since it represents information that must be returned to the main block.

Now suppose that the program is used to sum the following two tables of numbers.

| First table | | | | Second table | | | |
|---|---|---|---|---|---|---|---|
| 1 | 2 | 3 | 4 | 10 | 11 | 12 | 13 |
| 5 | 6 | 7 | 8 | 14 | 15 | 16 | 17 |
| 9 | 10 | 11 | 12 | 18 | 19 | 20 | 21 |

Execution of the program will first generate the following dialogue, in order to enter the data. (Once again, the user's responses are underlined.)

```
How many rows? (1..20) 3

How many columns? (1..30) 4

First table:

Enter data for row no.  1
1 2 3 4

Enter data for row no.  2
5 6 7 8

Enter data for row no.  3
9 10 11 12

Second table:

Enter data for row no.  1
10 11 12 13

Enter data for row no.  2
14 15 16 17

Enter data for row no.  3
18 19 20 21
```

The program will then sum all of the respective elements and produce the following output.

```
Sums of the elements:

11  13  15  17
19  21  23  25
27  29  31  33
```

It is easy to verify that these are indeed the correct sums.


## 9.4  PACKED ARRAYS

Some types of arrays can be defined so that they utilize the computer's memory more efficiently by "packing" the data items close together. This feature allows a greater quantity of information to be stored in a given anount of memory.

In order to utilize array packing, we must include the reserved words PACKED ARRAY in the type specification; e.g.,

```
VAR array name : PACKED ARRAY [index 1 type,

          index 2 type, . . . , index n type] OF type
```

This feature is most effective with array elements of type char, boolean or enumerated, or with subrange-type data.

On the other hand, the storage economy gained by packing may be offset by a loss in computing speed. Thus any program that utilizes a packed array involves a potential trade-off between these two factors. For a given program, it is not clear which method is most advantageous. This distinction will generally vary from one application to another.

There are certain circumstances under which packing can be beneficial, both from a standpoint of storage economy and computing speed. This tends to be true in programs that include a large number of array assignments (i.e., assigning the elements of one array to another), or procedure or function calls in which arrays are passed as value parameters.

**EXAMPLE 9.17**

Consider once again the two-dimensional, boolean-type array called sample, which we defined in Example 9.12. If we now declare sample to be a packed array, then the array declaration will appear as follows.

```
TYPE color = (red,white,blue,yellow,green);
     index = 1..100;
VAR sample : PACKED ARRAY [color,index] OF boolean;
```

This declaration will cause the elements of sample to be packed into less memory than the corresponding declaration shown in Example 9.12.

Pascal includes two standard procedures, pack and unpack, that are used to convert unpacked arrays into packed arrays and vice versa. In particular, the standard procedure pack will transfer some or all elements of an unpacked array into a packed array. The syntax is

```
pack(unpacked array name, index, packed array name);
```

where *index* refers to the first element of the unpacked array to be transferred.

Once this procedure is accessed, the transfer operation will continue until all elements of the packed array have been filled. The unpacked array (the source array) must contain enough elements beyond element *index* so that all elements within the packed array (the target array) can be filled.

**EXAMPLE 9.18**

Consider the following two arrays.

```
VAR unpacked : ARRAY [1..20] OF char;
    packed   : PACKED ARRAY [1..20] OF char;
```

The statement

```
pack(unpacked,1,packed);
```

will cause each element of unpacked (starting at position 1) to be transferred to the corresponding location within packed. Thus,

```
packed [1] := unpacked [1];

packed [2] := unpacked [2];
```

```
                          .
                          .
                          .
```

```
packed [20] := unpacked [20];
```

The standard procedure unpack will transfer the elements of a packed array to to an unpacked array, beginning with element *index* of the unpacked array. The syntax is

```
unpack(packed array name, unpacked array name, index);
```

The transfer operation will continue until all elements of the packed array have been transferred. The unpacked array (i.e., the target array) must have enough elements beyond element *index* so that all elements within the packed array (the source array) can be transferred.

**EXAMPLE 9.19**

Consider the following two arrays.

```
VAR packed   : PACKED ARRAY [1..13] OF char;
    unpacked : ARRAY [1..20] OF char;
```

Suppose that packed contains the following 13 characters.

```
        North America
```

Then the statement

```
        unpack(packed,unpacked,5);
```

will result in the following assignments.

```
        unpacked [5] := packed [1];      (hence unpacked [5] = 'N')

        unpacked [6] := packed [2];      (hence unpacked [6] = 'o')

                   .
                   .
                   .

        unpacked [17] := packed [13];   (hence unpacked [17] = 'a')
```

The remaining elements of unpacked will be undefined.

There is one restriction that must be observed when using packed arrays, namely, that individual packed-array elements cannot be passed to a procedure or a function as actual parameters. Entire arrays can, however, be passed in the usual manner.

## 9.5   STRINGS AND STRING VARIABLES

The concept of a packed array is particularly important in conjunction with the use of strings, since an $n$-character string is actually considered to be a one-dimensional, $n$-element packed array of type char.

**EXAMPLE 9.20**

Suppose that a Pascal program contains the following constant definition.

```
        CONST title = 'The Super-Duper Computer Company';
```

The identifier title represents a 32-element packed array of type char.

The string concept extends to variables as well as constants. Thus, a variable of type

```
        PACKED ARRAY [1..n] OF char
```

is referred to as a *string variable*. Such variables can be used to represent strings of length n.

**EXAMPLE 9.21**

Suppose that a Pascal program contains the following variable declaration.

```
        VAR heading : PACKED ARRAY [1..14] OF char;
```

The identifier heading is a string variable, since it represents a 14-element packed array of type char.

Standard Pascal includes some special packed-array operations that can only be utilized with strings or string variables. For example, an $n$-element string can be assigned to an $n$-element string variable by means of an ordinary assignment statement. (Note that this single operation involves the assignment of a sequence of array elements to an entire array.)

**EXAMPLE 9.22**

Consider once again the packed array heading, defined in the previous example. Since heading is a 14-element string variable, we can assign any 14-character string to heading; e.g.,

```
        heading := 'Dallas Cowboys';
```

We can, of course, also assign one string variable to another, provided both variables contain the same number of elements. (Recall that this feature applies to *all* arrays, as described in Sec. 9.3.)

**EXAMPLE 9.23**

Now suppose that a Pascal program contains the following variable declaration.

```
VAR factory,warehouse : PACKED ARRAY [1..11] OF char;
```

The identifiers factory and warehouse are string variables, since they both represent packed arrays of type char. Also, note that both variables are defined as 11-element arrays. Hence, one array can be assigned to the other.

Now suppose that the program contains the following string assignment.

```
factory := 'Seattle, WA';
```

Then at some later point in the program we can assign this same string to another 11-element string variable; e.g.,

```
warehouse := factory;
```

Thus, warehouse will also represent the string 'Seattle, WA.'

Strings of equal length can be compared with one another by means of the relational operators. Such comparisons can be carried out between two string constants, two string variables or a string constant and a string variable. In each case, we will be creating a boolean expression which will be either true or false.

When relational operators are used to connect strings or string variables, the operators = and <> denote equivalence or lack of equivalence, respectively. The remaining four operators, < , <= , > and >= , refer to the ordering of the characters within each string, as defined by the particular character code being used.

**EXAMPLE 9.24**

Consider the following string variable declarations.

```
TYPE colors = PACKED ARRAY [1..5] OF char;
VAR  c1,c2,c3 : colors;
```

Now suppose that the string variables are assigned the following string values.

```
c1 := 'black';
c2 := 'white';
c3 := 'green';
```

Several boolean expressions involving these variables are shown below. The corresponding values of the expressions are also given.

| boolean expression | value | |
|---|---|---|
| c1 < c2 | true | (because 'b' < 'w') |
| c3 < c2 | true | (because 'g' < 'w') |
| c1 > 'brown' | false | (because 'l' < 'r') |
| 'gross' > c3 | true | (because 'o' > 'e') |

It should be understood that the use of an entire array as an operand in a boolean expression is valid only if the array represents a string variable. Such comparisons are not allowed with other types of arrays.

Another special feature associated with string variables involves the use of the write and writeln statements. String variables can be included within these statements, thus causing entire strings (i.e., all elements within the packed arrays) to be written out without the need for loop structures.

**EXAMPLE 9.25**

A portion of a Pascal program is shown below.

```
        .
        .
    VAR factory : PACKED ARRAY [1..11] OF char;
    BEGIN
        .

        .
      factory := 'Seattle, WA';
        .

        .
      writeln(' Factory Location: ',factory);
        .

        .
    END.
```

Notice that the writeln statement contains both a string constant and a string variable.
When this program is executed, the following output will be produced.

```
    Factory Location: Seattle, WA
```

It should be understood that a string variable is the *only* type of array that can be included in a write or writeln statement in this manner. Moreover, a similar capability is *not* available when using the read or readln statement, even with string variables. Therefore strings must be entered into the computer on a character-by-character basis, using some type of loop structure.

**EXAMPLE 9.26**

A portion of a Pascal program is shown below.

```
        .
        .
    VAR factory : PACKED ARRAY [1..11] OF char;
        i : 1..11;
    BEGIN
        .

        .
      FOR i := 1 TO 11 DO read(factory[i]);
      writeln;
        .

        .
      writeln(' Factory Location: ',factory);
        .

        .
    END.
```

Note the distinction between the input and the output statements in this example. Also, notice the differences between this example and the previous example.

The ability to define and manipulate string variables opens the door to a broad class of important comprehensive programming applications. Some indication is given in the following example.

**EXAMPLE 9.27**

**A Pig Latin Generator.** Pig latin is an encoded form of English that is often used by children as a game. A pig latin word is formed from an English word by transposing the first sound (usually the first letter) to the end of the word, and then adding the letter "a". Thus, the word "cat" becomes "atca," "Pascal" becomes "ascalPa," "pig latin" becomes "igpa atinla," and so on.

Let us write a Pascal program that will accept a line of English text and then print out the corresponding text in pig latin. We will assume that each textual message can be typed on one 80-column line, with a single blank space between successive words. (Actually, we will require that the pig latin message not exceed 80 characters. Therefore the original message must be somewhat less than 80 characters, since the corresponding pig latin message will be lengthened by the addition of the a's after each word.) For simplicity, we will transpose only the first letter (not the first sound) of each word. Also, we will ignore any special consideration that might be given to capital letters and to punctuation marks.

The overall computational strategy will consist of the following major steps.

1. Initialize all arrays (string variables) by assigning blank spaces to all of the elements.

2. Read in an entire line of text (several words).

3. Determine the number of words in the line (by counting the number of single blank spaces that are followed by a nonblank space).

4. Rearrange the words into pig latin, on a word-by-word basis, as follows

   (*a*)  locate the end of each word

   (*b*)  transpose the first letter to the end of the word

   (*c*)  add an "a" to the end of each modified word.

5. Write out the entire line of pig latin.

We will continue to repeat this procedure until the computer reads a line of text whose first three letters are "end."

In order to implement this strategy we will make use of two "pointers," called p1 and p2, respectively. The first pointer (p1) will indicate the position of the beginning of a particular word within the original line of text. The second pointer (p2) will indicate the end of the word. Note that the character in the column preceding column number p1 will be a blank space (except for the first word). Also, the character in the column beyond column number p2 will be a blank space.

Let us again employ a modular approach in the development of this program. Before discussing each of the modules, however, we define the following program variables.

> english = a string variable (i.e., a packed array of type
> char) that represents the original line of text
>
> latin = a string variable that represents the new line of
> text (i.e., the pig latin)
>
> flag = a boolean variable that will remain true until the
> word "end" is entered, thus allowing for
> repetitious program execution
>
> words = an integer-type variable that indicates the number
> of words in the given line of text
>
> n = an integer-type variable that is used as a word
> counter (n = 1, 2, . . . , words)
>
> count = an integer-type variable that is used as a
> character counter within each of the lines
> (count = 0, 1, 2, . . . , 80)

These variables are, of course, in addition to the integer-type variables p1 and p2 discussed earlier.

Now let us return to the overall program outline presented above. The first step, array initialization, can be carried out in a straightforward manner with the following procedure.

```
PROCEDURE initialize;
(* initialize the arrays with blank spaces *)
BEGIN
   FOR count := 1 TO 80 DO
      english [count] := ' ';
   latin := english
END;
```

Step 2 can also be carried out with a simple procedure. This procedure will contain a conditional loop (a WHILE—DO structure) that will continue to read characters from the console until an end-of-line is detected (i.e., until the function eoln becomes true). This sequence of characters will become the elements of the string variable english. Here is the entire procedure.

```
PROCEDURE readinput;
(* read one line of English *)
BEGIN
   count := 0;
   WHILE NOT eoln DO
      BEGIN
         count := count +1;
         read(english [count])
      END;
   readln
END;
```

Step 3 of the overall outline is equally straightforward. We simply scan the original line for occurrences of single blank characters followed by nonblank characters. The word counter (words) is then incremented each time such a single blank character is encountered. Here is the word-count routine.

```
PROCEDURE countwords;
(* scan the line and count the number of words *)
BEGIN
   words := 1;
   FOR count := 1 TO 79 DO
      IF (english [count] = ' ') AND (english [count + 1] <> ' ')
         THEN words := words + 1
END;
```

Now let us consider steps 4 and 5 of the overall program outline. These steps are really the heart of the program. They can easily be combined into one procedure, since step 5 requires only a single statement. On the other hand, step 4 is rather involved since it requires three separate, though related, operations.

We must first identify the end of each word, by finding the first blank space beyond p1. We then assign the characters that make up the word to latin, with the first character at the end of the word. This must be handled carefully, since the new line of text will be longer than the original line (because of the additional a's). Hence, the characters in the first pig latin word will occupy locations p1 to p2 + 1. The characters in the second word will occupy locations p1 + 1 to p2 + 2 (note that these are new values of p1 and p2), and so on. These rules can be generalized as follows.

First, for word number n, transfer all characters except the first from the original line to the new line. This can be accomplished by writing

```
FOR count := p1 TO p2 - 1 DO
   latin [count + (n - 1)] := english [count + 1];
```

Consider the statement

```
latin [count + (n - 1)] := english [count + 1];
```

Within a given word, this statement causes the second English letter to become the first pig latin letter, the third English letter to become the second pig latin letter, and so on. The quantity $(n - 1)$ is used to offset the location of each pig latin word because of the extra characters that have been added (i.e., the a's at the end of each word). Thus, the second word (n=2) will be offset (shifted to the right) one character, because of the a at the end of the first word; the third word (n=3) will be offset two characters, and so on.

After the above loop has been executed for all of the letters within a given word other than the first letter, we add the first letter followed by the letter "a." This is accomplished in the following manner.

```
latin [p2 + (n-1)] := english [p1];
latin [p2 + n] := 'a';
```

We then reset the value of p1, i.e.

```
p1 := p2 + 2
```

in preparation for the next word.

This entire group of calculations is repeated for each word in the original line. The new line, containing the pig latin equivalent of the original line, is then written out.

Here is the procedure that accomplishes all of this.

```
PROCEDURE rearrangewords;
(* rearrange each word into piglatin, then write out the entire line *)
BEGIN
   p1 := 1;
   FOR n := 1 TO words DO
      BEGIN

         (* locate end of word *)
         count := p1;
         WHILE english [count]  <> ' ' DO count := count + 1;
         p2 := count - 1;

         (* transpose first letter and add 'a' *)
         FOR count := p1 TO p2 - 1 DO
             latin [count + (n - 1)] := english [count + 1];
         latin [p2 + (n - 1)] := english [p1];
         latin [p2 + n] := 'a';
         p1 := p2 + 2
      END;
   writeln(latin)
END;
```

Now let us consider the main block. This portion of the program is nothing more than an initial message, followed by a REPEAT—UNTIL structure that allows for repetitive program execution (until the word "end" is detected as the first three letters in the English text). Specifically, we begin by assigning the value true to flag, and then change this value to false once "end" has been detected within the loop. An IF—THEN structure will be placed within the loop to test for this condition. The looping action will then terminate once flag becomes false.

The entire program is shown below. Note that several comments have been added to the procedures presented earlier.

```
PROGRAM piglatin(input,output);

(* THIS PROGRAM ACCEPTS A LINE OF ENGLISH TEXT AND CONVERTS IT TO PIGLATIN. *)

(* Word pointers: p1 -> beginning of word
                  p2 -> end of word          *)

TYPE line = PACKED ARRAY [1..80] OF char;
VAR english,latin : line;
    p1,p2,count,n,words : integer;
    flag : boolean;

PROCEDURE initialize;
(* initialize the arrays with blank spaces *)
BEGIN
   FOR count := 1 TO 80 DO
      english [count] := ' ';
   latin := english
END;   (* initialize *)

PROCEDURE readinput;
(* read one line of English *)
BEGIN
   count := 0;
   WHILE NOT eoln DO
      BEGIN
         count := count + 1;
         read(english [count])
      END;
   readln
END;   (* readinput *)
```

(*Program continues on next page*)

```
PROCEDURE countwords;
(* scan the line and count the number of words *)
BEGIN
   words := 1;
   FOR count := 1 TO 79 DO
      IF (english [count] = ' ') AND (english [count + 1] <> ' ')
         THEN words := words + 1
END;   (* countwords *)

PROCEDURE rearrangewords;
(* rearrange each word into piglatin, then write out the entire line *)
BEGIN
   p1 := 1;
   FOR n := 1 TO words DO
      BEGIN

         (* locate end of word *)
         count := p1;
         WHILE english [count]  <> ' ' DO count := count + 1;
         p2 := count - 1;

         (* transpose first letter and add 'a' *)
         FOR count := p1 TO p2 - 1 DO
             latin [count + (n - 1)] := english [count + 1];
         latin [p2 + (n - 1)] := english [p1];
         latin [p2 + n] := 'a';
         p1 := p2 + 2
      END;
   writeln(latin)
END;   (* rearrangewords *)

BEGIN   (* main action block *)
   writeln(' Piglatin generator');
   writeln;
   writeln(' Type ''end'' when finished');
   writeln;
   flag := true;
   REPEAT   (* process a line of text *)
      initialize;
      readinput;
      IF (english [1] = 'e') AND (english [2] = 'n') AND
         (english [3] = 'd') THEN flag := false;
      countwords;
      rearrangewords
   UNTIL flag = false
END.
```

Notice that this program includes the assignment of one entire array to another (in procedure initialize) as well as the assignment of individual array elements (in readinput and rearrangewords). Also, note that an entire string variable (i.e., an entire packed array) is written out with a single writeln statement in procedure rearrangewords. The corresponding input operation must, of course, be carried out on an element-by-element basis, as in procedure readinput.

Now let us consider what happens when the program is executed. Here is a typical interactive session, in which the user's responses are underlined.

```
Piglatin generator

Type 'end' when finished

Pascal is a popular structured programming language
ascalPa sia aa opularpa tructuredsa rogrammingpa anguagela
```

(*continues on next page*)

```
baseball is the great American pastime,
aseballba sia heta reatga mericanAa astime,pa

though there are many who prefer football
houghta hereta reaa anyma howa referpa ootballfa

please do not sneeze in the computer room
leasepa oda otna neezesa nia heta omputerca oomra

end
ndea
```

Observe that the program does not include any special accommodations for punctuation marks, uppercase letters, or double-letter sounds (e.g., th, sh, etc.). These refinements are left as exercises for the reader.

## 9.6  VARIABLE-LENGTH ARRAY PARAMETERS

We have already seen that entire arrays can be passed to a procedure or function provided the actual parameters and the corresponding formal parameters are of the same explicit type and hence contain the same number of elements (see Sec. 9.3, and particularly Example 9.16). In some applications, however, it may be desirable to include (within a procedure or function) a formal parameter whose maximum number of elements is unspecified in absolute terms. This feature allows the procedure or function to be accessed from several different places, with actual parameters that are of a different size at each point of access.

Formal array parameters of variable length can be included within a procedure or function provided they are declared in a special way. Such parameters are known as *formal conformant array parameters*. Their corresponding actual parameters are called *actual conformant array parameters*.

The use of conformant array parameters can enhance the generality of a Pascal program. On the other hand, the syntactical requirements associated with their use is rather complicated. Beginning programmers may therefore choose to avoid their use until they are comfortable with other forms of parameter passing. Moreover, conformant array parameters are not included in the ISO Pascal standard. Thus this feature is not supported by all Pascal compilers.

Let us first consider one-dimensional conformant array parameters. The manner in which they are defined will depend on whether they are value parameters or variable parameters, as illustrated in the following examples.

**EXAMPLE 9.28**

Suppose that sample is a procedure that makes use of a variable formal array parameter called list, which is of type real. The procedure header would then be written as follows.

```
PROCEDURE sample (VAR list : ARRAY [first..last : integer] OF real);
```

Thus we see that list is a one-dimensional real-type array whose index values will be integers ranging from first to last. The numerical values of first and last will be determined by the corresponding actual parameter, which must also be a one-dimensional real-type array with an integer-type index.

Consider, for example, the one-dimensional real-type array item, whose declaration appears in the main program block; i.e.,

```
VAR item : ARRAY [1..100] OF real;
```

Now suppose that item is an actual parameter that is passed to sample; i.e.,

```
sample(item);
```

Thus first would take on a value of 1 and last a value of 100, so that list would be treated as a 100-element real-type array during this procedure access.

If the elements of list are modified within the procedure, then these modified array elements will be returned to item, as is always the case with a variable formal parameter.

**EXAMPLE 9.29**

Here is a skeletal outline of a Pascal program which makes use of a function that counts the number of words in a line of text. For illustrative purposes, let us make use of a value conformant array parameter within the function.

```
PROGRAM dummy(input,output);
TYPE length = 1..80;
     words  = 1..20;
VAR heading : PACKED ARRAY [1..12] OF char;
    message : PACKED ARRAY [1..80] OF char;
    n1,n2   : words;

FUNCTION count(text : PACKED ARRAY [start..stop : length] OF char) : words;
BEGIN
   .
   .
   .
   count := . . .
END;

BEGIN (* main action statements *)
   .
   .
   n1 := count(heading);
   .
   .
   n2 := count(message);
   .
   .
END.
```

This example includes several features that require some explanation. First, note that text will be considered a 12-element packed array during the initial function reference and an 80-element packed array during the second function reference. In each case the function will return an integer whose value lies somewhere between 1 and 20. (This assumes that each line of text will contain at least 1 and not more than 20 words.)

Next, the packed arrays heading and message, which are used as actual parameters in the function references, are legitimate string variables. (We assume that the strings represented by these variables have been read into the computer, or otherwise assigned, prior to the function references.) However, the formal value parameter text (i.e., the value conformant array parameter) is *not* considered to be a string variable. Hence the special properties of string variables discussed in Sec. 9.5 cannot be utilized within the function. This restriction applies to all packed arrays of type char that are used as conformant array parameters.

Conformant array parameters can be multi-dimensional as well as one-dimensional. In general the same rules apply, though there is one restriction that concerns the use of packing. Specifically, only the inner-most dimension (i.e., the last dimension) can be packed. If packing is to be used in this manner, then the conformant array parameter must be defined as an array of packed arrays, as illustrated below.

**EXAMPLE 9.30**

Consider the following procedure header, which makes use of a two-dimensional conformant array parameter.

```
PROCEDURE sample (text : ARRAY [first..last : integer]

                 OF PACKED ARRAY [c1..cn : integer] OF char);
```

Notice that text is a value conformant array parameter whose elements are individual characters. It can therefore be thought of as a page of text, where the first index represents the line number and the second index represents the character position within a given line. Also, notice that both indices are of type integer, even though the array elements themselves are of type char.

There are certain restrictions that must be observed when using conformant array parameters. We have already discussed two such restrictions; namely, that a packed array of type char cannot be treated as a string variable within the procedure or function to which it has been passed (see Example 9.29), and that packing can be employed only with the innermost dimension of a multidimensional array. An additional restriction concerns the passing of a conformant array parameter to another procedure or function. In such situations the formal parameter within the secondary module must be defined as a *variable* conformant array parameter rather than a *value* formal array parameter.

**EXAMPLE 9.31**

The skeletal outline of a Pascal program is shown below.

```
PROGRAM nothing(input,output);
VAR item : ARRAY [1..100] OF real;

FUNCTION largest (VAR numbers : ARRAY [start..stop : integer] OF real) : real;
BEGIN
   .
   .
   largest := . . .
END;

PROCEDURE process (VAR list : ARRAY [first..last : integer] OF real);
VAR count : real;
BEGIN
   .
   .
   count := largest(list);
   .
   .
END;

BEGIN (* main block *)
   .
   .
   process(item);
   .
   .
END.
```

In this example the 100-element real array item is passed to procedure process. The corresponding formal parameter is a variable conformant array parameter, called list. Within process, this array is passed to the function largest. The corresponding formal parameter in largest is also a variable conformant array parameter, called numbers.

Note that the conformant array parameter within process (i.e., list) later becomes an actual parameter, when the function largest is referenced. Therefore numbers (the formal parameter within largest) must be defined as a *variable* conformant array parameter rather than a *value* conformant array parameter.

There is another restriction that must be observed when two or more conformant array parameters are defined together. In such a situation, the corresponding actual parameters in any single reference must be of the same type. Adherence to this restriction is illustrated in the next example.

**EXAMPLE 9.32**

Adding Two Tables of Numbers. Let us consider once again the program for adding two tables of numbers, originally given in Example 9.16. Now, however, let us utilize conformant array parameters to represent the tables within the program modules.

Here is the entire program.

```
PROGRAM table3(input,output);

(* THIS PROGRAM READS IN TWO TABLES OF INTEGERS,
    CALCULATES THE SUMS OF THEIR RESPECTIVE ELEMENTS,
    AND WRITES OUT THE RESULTING TABLE CONTAINING THE SUMS *)

(* THE PROGRAM MAKES USE OF CONFORMANT ARRAY PARAMETERS *)

VAR  a,b,c : ARRAY [1..20,1..30] OF integer;
     row,nrows : 1..20;
     col,ncols : 1..30;

PROCEDURE readinput (VAR t : ARRAY [firstrow..lastrow : integer;
                                    firstcol..lastcol : integer] OF integer);

(* Read the elements of one table *)


BEGIN
   FOR row := 1 TO nrows DO
      BEGIN
         writeln(' Enter data for row no. ',row:2);
         FOR col := 1 TO ncols DO read(t[row,col]);
         writeln
      END
END;   (* readinput *)

PROCEDURE computesums (VAR t1,t2,t3 : ARRAY [firstrow..lastrow : integer;
                                             firstcol..lastcol : integer] OF integer);

(* Sum the elements of two similar tables *)


BEGIN
FOR row := 1 TO nrows DO
    FOR col := 1 TO ncols DO
        t3[row,col] := t1[row,col] + t2[row,col]
END;   (* computesums *)

PROCEDURE writeoutput (t : ARRAY [firstrow..lastrow : integer;
                                  firstcol..lastcol : integer] OF integer);

(* Write out the elements of a table *)


BEGIN
   writeln(' Sums of the elements:');
   writeln;
   FOR row := 1 TO nrows DO
      BEGIN
         FOR col := 1 TO ncols DO write(t[row,col]:4);
         writeln
      END
END;   (* writeoutput *)
```

(*Program continues on next page*)

```
    BEGIN   (* main action block *)
      write(' How many rows? (1..20) ');
      readln(nrows);
      writeln;
      write(' How many columns? (1..30) ');
      readln(ncols);
      writeln;
      writeln(' First table:');
      writeln;
      readinput(a);
      writeln(' Second table:');
      writeln;
      readinput(b);
      computesums(a,b,c);
      writeoutput(c)
    END.
```

It is interesting to compare this version of the program with that given in Example 9.16. Note, for example, that a type definition is not included in the present version. Rather, the array specifications are included with the variable declarations.

Of greater significance is the fact that all of the procedures utilize conformant array parameters as formal parameters. Two of the procedures, readinput and computesums, make use of variable conformant array parameters, whereas the third procedure, writeoutput, utilizes a value conformant array parameter. Note that three conformant array parameters, t1, t2 and t3, are defined together in procedure computesums. Also note that the corresponding reference to computesums within the main block contains three actual parameters (a, b and c) that are all of the same type, as required.

Before leaving this section we again remind the reader that the use of conformant array parameters is somewhat complicated and may therefore be inappropriate for beginning programmers. Moreover, some versions of Pascal do not support the use of conformant array parameters. This is particularly true of microcomputer implementations. Even if this feature is available, however, some discretion should be exercised in its use.

## Review Questions

**9.1**  What are the four different structured data types?

**9.2**  What are the particular characteristics of an array as a structured data type?

**9.3**  Suggest a practical way to visualize a one-dimensional array.

**9.4**  What is meant by an array element? What data types can be used as array elements?

**9.5**  What is meant by an index (or subscript)? What data types can be used for an index? (Compare with the answer to the previous question.)

**9.6**  How can an individual array element be accessed?

**9.7**  Explain how an array can be defined within the variable declaration part of a program.

**9.8**   Summarize the rules for utilizing an array element within an expression, assignment statement, read/write statement, etc. How can the indices be written? What restrictions apply to the manner in which the indices are written?

**9.9**   Can enumerated data items be used as array elements?

**9.10**  Explain how an array can be used to represent a string.

**9.11**  Suggest a practical way to visualize a two-dimensional array.

**9.12**  Summarize the rules for defining a multidimensional array as a part of a variable declaration. Must the indices all be of the same data type?

**9.13**  Summarize the rules for referencing a multidimensional array element.

**9.14**  Explain why some applications of multidimensional arrays require nested loops. What is the purpose of each loop?

**9.15**  Describe how a two-dimensional array can be expressed as a one-dimensional array whose individual elements are one-dimensional arrays. Can this concept be extended to arrays of higher dimensionality?

**9.16**  Describe how several arrays of the same type can be declared by first defining an array type and then declaring the individual arrays to be variables of this type. Must all of the arrays declared in this manner have the same scope?

**9.17**  How can all of the elements of one array be collectively assigned to the corresponding elements of another array with a single assignment statement? What restrictions apply to the two arrays?

**9.18**  Can an entire array appear in a numeric or boolean expression?

**9.19**  Can an entire array be read into the computer with a single read or readln statement?

**9.20**  Can an entire array be written out of the computer with a single write or writeln statement?

**9.21**  What restrictions apply to the passing of an entire array to a procedure or a function?

**9.22**  Describe a convenient way to pass an entire array to a procedure or a function.

**9.23**  Can a single array element be passed to a procedure or a function?

**9.24**  What is a packed array? How do packed arrays differ from ordinary arrays?

**9.25**  What possible advantages and disadvantages are associated with the use of packed arrays?

**9.26**  For what types of applications are packed arrays particularly advantageous?

**9.27**  Can a packed array be unpacked? Can an unpacked array be packed? Explain.

**9.28**   Summarize the rules associated with the use of the standard procedures pack and unpack.

**9.29**   Can an entire packed array be passed to a procedure or a function?

**9.30**   Can a single packed array element be passed to a procedure or a function?

**9.31**   What is a string variable? What is the relationship between packed arrays and string variables?

**9.32**   Describe the special packed-array operations that can only be utilized with strings or string variables.

**9.33**   How are the relational operators interpreted when they are used to connect strings or string variables to form boolean expressions? In particular, how are the operators $<$, $<=$, $>$ and $>=$ interpreted?

**9.34**   What is a conformant array parameter? What purpose does it serve?

**9.35**   Summarize the rules for defining one-dimensional conformant array parameters. Distinguish between value conformant array parameters and variable conformant array parameters.

**9.36**   Summarize the rules for defining multidimensional conformant array parameters. Compare with the rules for one-dimensional conformant array parameters.

**9.37**   Can packing be utilized with a multidimensional array? Explain fully.

**9.38**   Suppose a packed array of type char is passed to a procedure or a function as a conformant array parameter. Can this array be treated as a string variable within the procedure or function?

**9.39**   Suppose that a formal conformant array parameter within a given procedure is to be passed to another procedure. (That is, the formal conformant array parameter becomes an actual conformant array parameter which is passed to the secondary procedure.) In what way must the formal conformant array parameter be defined within the secondary procedure?

**9.40**   Suppose that two or more formal conformant array parameters are defined together within a procedure header. What condition must be satisfied by the corresponding actual conformant array parameters?

**9.41**   Are conformant array parameters supported in all versions of Pascal? Explain.

# Solved Problems

**9.42**   Several illustrative array declarations are shown below.

(*a*)   VAR values : ARRAY [0..100] OF real;

(*b*)   VAR list : ARRAY [-10..10] OF real;

(*c*)   TYPE days = (sun,mon,tues,wed,thurs,fri,sat);
        VAR calories : ARRAY [days] OF integer;

(*d*)   TYPE days = (sun,mon,tues,wed,thurs,fri,sat);
        VAR sunshine : ARRAY [1..365] OF days;

(e) ```
TYPE color = (blue,brown,gray,green,black);
     size  = (small,medium,large);
VAR  coats  : ARRAY [size] OF color;
```

(f) ```
TYPE color = (blue,brown,gray,green,black);
     size  = (small,medium,large);
VAR  coats  : ARRAY [size,color] OF integer;
```

(g) ```
TYPE color = (blue,brown,gray,green,black);
     size  = (small,medium,large);
VAR  coats  : ARRAY [size] OF ARRAY [color] OF integer;
```

(h) ```
VAR parts : ARRAY ['A'..'Z', 1..10000] OF integer;
```

(i) ```
CONST max1  = 2000;
      max2  = 5000;
TYPE range1 = 1..max1;
     range2 = 1..max2;
VAR  tally  : ARRAY [range1,range2] OF char;
```

(j) ```
VAR symbol : ARRAY [1..12, 1..20, 0..5] OF boolean;
```

(k) ```
TYPE days = (sun,mon,tues,wed,thurs,fri,sat);
VAR sunshine : PACKED ARRAY [1..365] OF days;
```

(l) ```
VAR name : PACKED ARRAY [1..80] OF char;
```

(m) ```
VAR page : ARRAY [1..66] OF PACKED ARRAY [1..80] OF char;
```

**9.43** The following skeletal outlines illustrate the use of arrays and/or array elements in typical programming situations.

(a) ```
PROGRAM sample(input,output);
VAR square : ARRAY [1..100] OF integer;
    count  : 1..100;
BEGIN
   .
   .
   .
   FOR count := 1 TO 100 DO square [count] := sqr(count);
   .
   .
   .
END.
```

(b) ```
PROGRAM sample(input,output);
VAR table : ARRAY [1..20, 1..8] OF real;
    i,m : 1..20;
    j,n : 1..8;
BEGIN
   .
   .
   .
   readln(m,n);
   FOR i := 1 TO m DO
      BEGIN
         FOR j := 1 TO n DO read( table [i,j]);
         writeln
      END;
   .
   .
   .
   FOR i := 1 TO m DO
      BEGIN
         FOR j := 1 TO n DO write( table [i,j]);
         writeln
      END
END.
```
```

```
(c)  PROGRAM sample(input,output);
     VAR value : ARRAY [0..100] OF real;
         index,max : 0..100;
     BEGIN
         .
         .
         readln(max);
         .
         .
         value[0] := 0;
         FOR index := max DOWNTO 0 DO
            BEGIN
               value[index] := index MOD 8;
               IF value[index] < 5.0 THEN value[0] := value[0] + value[index]
            END;
         .
         .
     END.


(d)  PROGRAM sample(input,output);
     TYPE color = (red,white,blue,yellow,green);
     VAR foreground : PACKED ARRAY [1..5] OF color;
         background : ARRAY [1..5] OF color;
         index : 1..5;
     BEGIN
         .
         .
         FOR index := 1 TO 5 DO background[index] := . . .;
         .
         .
         pack(background,1,foreground);
         .
         .
     END.


(e)  PROGRAM sample(input,output);
     VAR city,office : PACKED ARRAY [1..3] OF char;
         order : 1..maxint;
     BEGIN
         .
         .
         city := 'CHI';
         .
         .
         readln(order);
         IF order < 100 THEN office := city
                      ELSE IF order < 1000 THEN office := 'NYC'
                                           ELSE office := 'ATL';
         .
         .
         writeln(office);
         .
         .
     END.
```

Note that city and office are string variables.

(*f*)   PROGRAM sample(input,output);
        VAR list1 : ARRAY [1..40] OF integer;
            list2 : ARRAY [1..80] OF integer;

            PROCEDURE sort(VAR items : ARRAY [first..last : integer] OF integer);
            VAR . . .;   (* local variables *)
            BEGIN
               .
               .
               (* process the elements of *items* *)
               .
               .
            END;
        BEGIN   (* main action statements *)
            .
            .
            (* read elements of *list1* *)
            .
            .
            sort(list1);
            .
            .
            (* read elements of *list2* *)
            .
            .
            sort(list2);
            .
            .
        END.

Note that list1 and list2 are integer-type arrays that differ in size.


# Supplementary Problems

**9.44**   The following skeletal outlines illustrate several different situations involving the use of arrays and/or array elements. Some are written incorrectly. Identify all errors.

(*a*)   TYPE notes = (do,re,mi,fa,sol,la,ti);
        VAR tune : ARRAY [1..256] OF notes;

(*b*)   TYPE notes = (do,re,mi,fa,sol,la,ti);
        VAR count : ARRAY [notes] OF integer;

(*c*)   TYPE notes = (do,re,mi,fa,sol,la,ti);
        TYPE chorus = PACKED ARRAY [1..256] OF notes;
        VAR first,second,trio,coda : chorus;

(*d*)   VAR demo : ARRAY [12..-5, 0..48] OF real;

(*e*)   PROGRAM sample(input,output);
        VAR list : ARRAY [1..100] OF real;
        BEGIN
            .
            .
            list [2.0] := 5.5;
            .
            .
        END.

(*f*)  ```
PROGRAM sample(input,output);
VAR list : ARRAY [1..100] OF real;
    index : 1..100;
BEGIN
   .
   .
   FOR index := -100 TO 100 DO
      IF index < 0 THEN list [index] := 0
                   ELSE list [index] := index;
   .
   .
END.
```

(*g*)  ```
PROGRAM sample(input,output);
VAR list : ARRAY [1..100] OF real;
    index : 1..100;
    max : real;
BEGIN
   .
   .
   max := 0;
   FOR index := 1 TO 100 DO
      IF list [index] > max THEN max := list [index];
   .
   .
END.
```

(*h*)  ```
PROGRAM sample(input,output);
VAR item : ARRAY ['A'..'Z', 1..50] OF integer;
BEGIN
   .
   .
   item [7] := 283;
   .
   .
END.
```

(*i*)  ```
PROGRAM sample(input,output);
VAR size : ARRAY [1..50] OF integer;
BEGIN
   .
   .
   size [12] := 41.5;
   .
   .
END.
```

(*j*)  ```
PROGRAM sample(input,output);
VAR item : ARRAY ['A'..'Z', 1..50] OF integer;
BEGIN
   .
   .
   item [7,'M'] := 283;
   .
   .
END.
```
```

(k)  PROGRAM sample(input,output);
     VAR item : ARRAY ['A'..'Z', 1..50] OF integer;
     BEGIN
        .
        .
        item ['C',9] := 60;
        .
        .
     END.

(l)  PROGRAM sample(input,output);
     TYPE list = ARRAY [1..200] OF real;
     VAR sales, costs, profits : list;
     BEGIN
        .
        .
        profits := sales - costs;
        .
        .
     END.

(m)  PROGRAM sample(input,output);
     VAR name : PACKED ARRAY [1..5] OF char;
     BEGIN
        .
        .
        IF name = 'Jones' THEN writeln(name);
        .
        .
     END.

(n)  PROGRAM sample(input,output);
     VAR table : ARRAY [1..20, 1..80] OF integer;
     BEGIN
        .
        .
        read(table);
        .
        write(table);
        .
        .
     END.

(o)  PROGRAM sample(input,output);
     VAR table : ARRAY [1..1000, 1..66, 1..132] OF integer;
        i,j,k : integer;
     BEGIN
        .
        .
        FOR i := 1 TO 1000 DO
           FOR j := 1 TO 66 DO
              FOR k := 1 TO 132 DO
                 BEGIN
                    table [i,j,k] := i + j + k - 2;
                    writeln(i:4, j:2, k:3, table[i,j,k]:4)
                 END;
        .
        .
     END.

(*p*)  PROGRAM sample(input,output);
    VAR buffer : ARRAY [1..80] OF char;
       target : PACKED ARRAY [1..80] OF char;
    BEGIN
      .
      .
      pack(buffer,target,5);
      .
      .
      unpack(target,12,buffer);
      .
      .
    END.

(*q*)  PROGRAM sample(input,output);
    VAR line : PACKED ARRAY [1..80] OF char;
      name : PACKED ARRAY [1..40] OF char;
   address : PACKED ARRAY [1..40] OF char;
    BEGIN
      .
      .
      IF name <> 'end' THEN line := name + address;
      .
      .
    END.

(*r*)  PROGRAM sample(input,output);
    VAR foreground,background : PACKED ARRAY [1..5] OF char;
      flag : boolean;
    BEGIN
      .
      .
      background := 'black';
      .
      .
      IF flag THEN foreground := background
           ELSE foreground := 'green';
      .
      .
    END.

**9.45**  Presented below are several skeletal outlines that illustrate the use of arrays or array elements with procedures or functions. Some are written incorrectly. Identify all errors.

(*a*)  PROGRAM sample(input,output);
    VAR list : ARRAY [1..100] OF integer;

      PROCEDURE process (dummy : ARRAY [1..100] OF integer);
      BEGIN
        .
        .
        .
      END;

(*Program continues on next page*)

```
        BEGIN   (* main action statements *)
          .
          .
        process(list);
          .
          .
        END.
```

(b)  ```
     PROGRAM sample(input,output);
     TYPE list = ARRAY [1..100] OF real;
     VAR list1,list2 : list;

        PROCEDURE module (VAR x : list);
        BEGIN
          .
          .
          (* process the elements of x *)
          .
        END;
     BEGIN   (* main action statements *)
          .
          .
        module(list1);
          .
          .
        module(list2);
          .
          .
     END.
     ```

(c)  ```
     PROGRAM sample(input,output);
     VAR sales : ARRAY [1..100] OF integer;
        result : integer;

        FUNCTION funct1 (x : integer) : integer;
        BEGIN
          .
          .
          .
          funct1 := . . .
        END;
     BEGIN   (* main action statements *)
          .
          .
        result := funct1 (sales [6] + sales [12]);
          .
          .
     END.
     ```

(d)  ```
     PROGRAM sample(input,output);
     VAR line : PACKED ARRAY [1..80] OF char;

        PROCEDURE proc1 (dummy : char);
        BEGIN
          .
          .
          .
        END;
     ```

(*Program continues on next page*)
     ```

```
      BEGIN    (* main action statements *)
         .
         .
      proc1(line[40]);
         .
         .
      END.
```

(e)　PROGRAM sample(input,output);
```
      VAR list  : ARRAY [1..100] OF integer;
          items : ARRAY [1..25] OF integer;

          PROCEDURE process(x : ARRAY [first..last : integer] OF integer);
          BEGIN
             .
             .
             .
          END;

      BEGIN    (* main action statements *)
         .
         .
      process(list);
         .
         .
      process(items);
         .
         .
      END.
```

(f)　PROGRAM sample(input,output);
```
      VAR stockno : ARRAY [1..100] OF integer;
          cost : ARRAY [1..100] OF real;

          PROCEDURE process(x : ARRAY [first..last : integer] OF integer);
          BEGIN
             .
             .
             .
          END;

      BEGIN    (* main action statements *)
         .
         .
      process(stockno);
         .
         .
      process(cost);
         .
         .
      END.
```

```
(g)   PROGRAM sample(input,output);
      VAR page : PACKED ARRAY [1..66, 1..80] OF char;

          FUNCTION count (text : PACKED ARRAY
             [first..last : integer; start..stop : integer]OF char) : integer;
          BEGIN
             .
             .
             .
             count := . . .
          END;

      BEGIN   (* main action statements *)
          .
          .
          (* read the elements of text *)
          .
          .
          writeln(count(text));
          .
          .
      END.


(h)   PROGRAM sample(input,output);
      VAR name : PACKED ARRAY [1..80] OF char;

          PROCEDURE proc1 (line : PACKED ARRAY [first..last : integer] OF char);
          BEGIN
             .
             .
             writeln(line);
             .
             .
          END;

      BEGIN   (* main action statements *)
          .
          .
          (* read the elements of name *)
          .
          .
          proc1(name);
          .
          .
      END.


(i)   PROGRAM sample(input,output);
      VAR item : ARRAY [1..100] OF real;

          PROCEDURE process (numbers : ARRAY [start..stop : integer] OF real);
          BEGIN
             .
             .
             .
          END;
```

(*Program continues on next page*)

```
                PROCEDURE module (x : ARRAY [start..stop :integer] OF real);
                BEGIN
                   .
                   .
                   process(x);
                   .
                   .
                END;

            BEGIN   (* main action statements *)
               .
               .
               module(item);
               .
               .
               process(item);
               .
               .
            END.
```

(*j*)    
```
        PROGRAM sample(input,output);
        VAR a : ARRAY [1..20] OF real;
            b : ARRAY [1..50] OF integer;

            PROCEDURE demo (VAR x,y : ARRAY [first..last : integer] OF real);
            BEGIN
               .
               .
               .
            END;

        BEGIN   (* main action statements *)
           .
           .
           demo(a,b);
           .
           .
        END.
```

# Programming Problems

**9.46**    Modify the program given in Example 9.8 so that the numbers are rearranged into a sequence of algebraically decreasing values (i.e., from largest to smallest). Test the program using the data given in Example 9.8.

**9.47**    Modify the program given in Example 9.8 so that any one of the following rearrangements can be carried out:

(*a*)   Smallest to largest, by magnitude

(*b*)   Smallest to largest, algebraic

(*c*)   Largest to smallest, by magnitude

(*d*)   Largest to smallest, algebraic

Include a menu that will allow the user to select which rearrangement will be used each time the program is executed. Test the program using the following 10 values.

$$
\begin{array}{rr}
4.7 & -8.0 \\
-2.3 & 11.4 \\
12.9 & 5.1 \\
8.8 & -0.2 \\
6.0 & -14.7
\end{array}
$$

**9.48** Modify the program given in Example 9.16 to calculate the differences rather than the sums of the corresponding elements in two tables of integer numbers. Test the program using the data given in Example 9.16.

**9.49** Modify the program given in Example 9.7 so that it utilizes packed arrays and variable-length array parameters. Test the program using your own name and address.

**9.50** Modify the pig latin generation program given in Example 9.27 so that it can accommodate punctuation marks, uppercase letters and double-letter sounds.

**9.51** Write a Pascal program that will enter a line of text, store it in a packed array, and then write it out backward. Allow the length of the line to be unspecified (terminated by a carriage return), but assume that it will not exceed 80 characters.

Test the program with any line of text of your own choosing. Compare with the program given in Example 7.24, which makes use of a recursive procedure rather than an array. Which approach is better?

**9.52** Presented below are several related programming problems that make use of the following set of student exam grades. (The grades are for six examinations taken by each student in a Pascal programming course.)

| Name | Exam scores, percent | | | | | |
|---|---|---|---|---|---|---|
| Adams | 45 | 80 | 80 | 95 | 55 | 75 |
| Brown | 60 | 50 | 70 | 75 | 55 | 80 |
| Davis | 40 | 30 | 10 | 45 | 60 | 55 |
| Fisher | 0 | 5 | 5 | 0 | 10 | 5 |
| Hamilton | 90 | 85 | 100 | 95 | 90 | 90 |
| Jones | 95 | 90 | 80 | 95 | 85 | 80 |
| Ludwig | 35 | 50 | 55 | 65 | 45 | 70 |
| Osborne | 75 | 60 | 75 | 60 | 70 | 80 |
| Prince | 85 | 75 | 60 | 85 | 90 | 100 |
| Richards | 50 | 60 | 50 | 35 | 65 | 70 |
| Smith | 70 | 60 | 75 | 70 | 55 | 75 |
| Thomas | 10 | 25 | 35 | 20 | 30 | 10 |
| Wolfe | 25 | 40 | 65 | 75 | 85 | 95 |
| Zorba | 65 | 80 | 70 | 100 | 60 | 95 |

(a) Write a conversational-style Pascal program that will accept each student's name and exam grades as input, determine an average grade for each student and then write out the name, the individual exam grades and the calculated average. (*Hint*: Note that each name is followed by a blank space.) Make the program as general as possible [see Prob. 6.50(*k*)].

(b) Modify the program written for the above problem to allow for unequal weighting of the individual exam grades. In particular, assume that each of the first four exams contributes 15 percent to the final score and each of the last two exams contributes 20 percent [see Prob. 6.50(*l*)].

(c) Extend the program written for the previous problem so that an overall class average is determined in addition to the individual student averages [see Prob. 6.50(m)].

(d) Extend the program written for the previous problem so that the deviation of each student's average about the overall class average will be determined. Write out the class average, followed by each each student's name, exam grades, final score and deviation about the class average. Be sure that the output is logically organized and clearly labeled.

**9.53** Write a Pascal program that will produce a table of values of the equation

$$y = 2e^{-0.1t} \sin 0.5t$$

where $t$ varies between 0 and 60. Allow the size of the $t$ increment to be entered as an input parameter. Place the calculated values in a two-dimensional array, then write out the entire array.

**9.54** Write a Pascal program that will generate a table of monthly loan repayment factors, $A/P$, where

$$A/P = \frac{i(1+i)^n}{(1+i)^n - 1}$$

In this formula $A$ represents the monthly payment, $P$ represents the original amount of the loan, $i$ represents the monthly interest rate (expressed as a decimal; e.g., $\frac{1}{2}\%$ would be written 0.005), and $n$ represents the total number of monthly payments. [See Prob. 7.50(c) for additional information.]

Let each row in the table correspond to a different value of $n$, with $n$ ranging from 1 to 60 (hence the repayment period can be as long as 60 months, i.e., 5 years). Let each column represent a different interest rate. Include the following *annual* interest rates: 4, 4.5, 5, 5.5, 6, 6.5, 7, 7.5, 8, 8.5, 9, 9.5, 10, 11, 12 and 15 percent. (The monthly interest rate is determined as the annual interest rate divided by 12.)

Place the calculated values in a two-dimensional array. Write out the array after the entire table has been generated. Be sure to label the rows and columns appropriately.

**9.55** Write a Pascal program that will rearrange a list of words into alphabetical order. To do so, enter the words into a two-dimensional packed array of type char, with each row representing one complete word. The rows can then be rearranged in the same manner that a list of numbers is rearranged from smallest to largest (see Example 9.8).

Use the program to rearrange the names given below. Be careful with the first initials.

| | | | |
|---|---|---|---|
| Washington | Polk | Arthur | Roosevelt, F. D. |
| Adams, J. | Taylor | Cleveland | Truman |
| Jefferson | Fillmore | Harrison, B. | Eisenhower |
| Madison | Pierce | McKinley | Kennedy |
| Monroe | Buchanan | Roosevelt, T. | Johnson, L. B. |
| Adams, J. Q. | Lincoln | Taft | Nixon |
| Jackson | Johnson, A. | Wilson | Ford |
| Van Buren | Grant | Harding | Carter |
| Harrison, W. H. | Hayes | Coolidge | Reagan |
| Tyler | Garfield | Hoover | |

**9.56** Consider the following list of countries and their capitals.

| | | | |
|---|---|---|---|
| Canada | Ottawa | Israel | Jerusalem |
| England | London | Italy | Rome |
| France | Paris | Japan | Tokyo |
| India | New Delhi | Mexico | Mexico City |

(continues on next page)

| People's Republic of China | Peking |
|---|---|
| United States | Washington |
| U.S.S.R. | Moscow |
| West Germany | Bonn |

Write an interactive Pascal program that will accept the name of a country as input and write out the corresponding capital, and vice versa. Design the program to continue executing until the word "end" is entered as input.

**9.57** Write a complete Pascal program for each of the problems presented below. Include the most appropriate types of arrays for each problem. Be sure to modularize each program, label the output clearly and make use of natural data types and efficient control structures.

(a) Suppose we are given a table of integers $A$, having $m$ rows and $n$ columns, and a list of integers $X$, having $n$ elements. We wish to generate a new list of integers $Y$, that is formed by carrying out the following operations.

$$Y[1] = A[1,1]*X[1] + A[1,2]*X[2] + \cdots + A[1,N]*X[N]$$
$$Y[2] = A[2,1]*X[1] + A[2,2]*X[2] + \cdots + A[2,N]*X[N]$$

.

.

.

$$Y[M] = A[M,1]*X[1] + A[M,2]*X[2] + \cdots + A[M,N]*X[N]$$

Write out the input data (i.e., the values of the elements $A$ and $X$), followed by the values of the elements of $Y$.

Use the program to process the following data.

$$A = \begin{bmatrix} 1 & 2 & 3 & 4 & 5 & 6 & 7 & 8 \\ 2 & 3 & 4 & 5 & 6 & 7 & 8 & 9 \\ 3 & 4 & 5 & 6 & 7 & 8 & 9 & 10 \\ 4 & 5 & 6 & 7 & 8 & 9 & 10 & 11 \\ 5 & 6 & 7 & 8 & 9 & 10 & 11 & 12 \\ 6 & 7 & 8 & 9 & 10 & 11 & 12 & 13 \end{bmatrix}$$

$$X = \begin{bmatrix} 1 \\ -8 \\ 3 \\ -6 \\ 5 \\ -4 \\ 7 \\ -2 \end{bmatrix}$$

(b) Suppose that $A$ is a table of real numbers having $k$ rows and $m$ columns, and $B$ is a table of real numbers having $m$ rows and $n$ columns. We wish to generate a new table, $C$, where each element of $C$ is determined by

$$C[i,j] = A[i,1]*B[1,j] + A[i,2]*B[2,j] + \cdots + A[i,m]*B[m,j]$$

where $i = 1, 2, \ldots, k$ and $j = 1, 2, \ldots, n$. Write out the elements of $A$, $B$ and $C$. Be sure that everything is clearly labeled.

Use the program to process the following set of data.

$$A = \begin{bmatrix} 2 & -1/3 & 0 & 2/3 & 4 \\ 1/2 & 3/2 & 4 & -2 & 1 \\ 0 & 3 & -9/7 & 6/7 & 4/3 \end{bmatrix}$$

$$B = \begin{bmatrix} 6/5 & 0 & -2 & 1/3 \\ 5 & 7/2 & 3/4 & -3/2 \\ 0 & -1 & 1 & 0 \\ 9/2 & 3/7 & -3 & 3 \\ 4 & -1/2 & 0 & 3/4 \end{bmatrix}$$

(c)  Consider a sequence of real numbers, $x_i$, $i = 1, 2, \ldots, m$. The mean is defined as

$$\bar{x} = \frac{(x_1 + x_2 + \cdots + x_m)}{m}$$

the deviation about the mean is

$$d_i = (x_i - \bar{x}), \qquad i = 1, 2, \ldots, m$$

and the standard deviation is

$$s = \sqrt{\frac{(d_1{}^2 + d_2{}^2 + \cdots + d_m{}^2)}{m}}$$

Read in the first $m$ elements of a one-dimensional real array. Calculate the sum of these elements, the mean, the deviations, the standard deviation, the algebraic maximum and the algebraic minimum. Use the program to process the following set of data.

| | |
|---|---|
| 27.5 | 87.0 |
| 13.4 | 39.9 |
| 53.8 | 47.7 |
| 29.2 | 8.1 |
| 74.5 | 63.2 |

Repeat the computation for $k$ different lists of numbers. Calculate the overall mean, the overall standard deviation, the absolute (largest) maximum and the absolute (algebraically smallest) minimum.

(d)  Suppose we are given a set of tabulated values for $y$ vs. $x$, i.e.,

$$\begin{array}{ccccc} y_0 & y_1 & y_2 & \ldots & y_n \\ x_0 & x_1 & x_2 & \ldots & x_n \end{array}$$

and we wish to obtain a value of $y$ at some $x$ that lies between two of the tabulated values. This problem is commonly solved by *interpolation*, i.e., by constructing a polynomial $y(x)$ that passes through $n$ points such that $y(x_0) = y_0$, $y(x_1) = y_1$, $\ldots$, $y(x_n) = y_n$ and then evaluating $y$ at the desired value of $x$.

A common way to carry out the interpolation is to use the *Lagrange form* of the interpolation polynomial. To do this we write

$$y(x) = f_0(x)*y_0 + f_1(x)*y_1 + \cdots + f_n(x)*y_n$$

where $f_i(x)$ is a polynomial such that

$$f_i(x) = \frac{(x - x_0)(x - x_1) \cdots (x - x_{i-1})(x - x_{i+1}) \cdots (x - x_n)}{(x_i - x_0)(x_i - x_1) \cdots (x_i - x_{i-1})(x_i - x_{i+1}) \cdots (x_i - x_n)}$$

Notice that $f_i(x_i) = 1$ and $f_i(x_j) = 0$, where $x_j$ is a tabulated value of $x$ different from $x_i$. Therefore we are assured that $y(x_i) = y_i$.

Write a Pascal program to read in $n$ pairs of data, where $n$ does not exceed 10, and then obtain an interpolated value of $y$ at one or more specified values of $x$. Use the program to obtain interpolated values of $y$ at $x = 13.7$, $x = 37.2$, $x = 112$ and $x = 147$ from the data listed below. Determine how many tabulated pairs of data are required in each calculation in order to obtain a reasonably accurate interpolated value for $y$.

$$y = 0.21073 \qquad x = 0$$

| $y$ | $x$ |
|---|---|
| 0.21073 | 0 |
| 0.37764 | 10 |
| 0.45482 | 20 |
| 0.49011 | 30 |
| 0.50563 | 40 |
| 0.49245 | 50 |
| 0.47220 | 60 |
| 0.43433 | 80 |
| 0.33824 | 120 |
| 0.19390 | 180 |

**9.58** The following problems are concerned with games of chance (gambling games). Each problem requires use of a random number generator, such as that described in Example 7.18. Each program requires the use of an array. In addition, the programs should be interactive and they should be modularized.

(a) Write a Pascal program that will simulate a game of blackjack between two players. Note that the computer will not be a participant in this game but will simply deal the cards to each player, provide each player with one or more "hits" (additional cards) when requested and determine the winner.

The cards are dealt in order, first one card to each player, then a second card to each player. Additional hits may then be requested.

The object of the game is to obtain 21 points, or as many points as possible without exceeding 21 points on each hand. A player is automatically disqualified if his or her hand exceeds 21 points. Picture cards count 10 points, and an ace can count either 1 point or 11 points. Thus a player can obtain 21 points (blackjack!) if he or she is dealt an ace and either a picture card or a 10. If the player has a low score with his (her) first two cards he (she) may request one or more hits, as long as his (her) total score does not exceed 21.

A random number generator should be used to simulate the dealing of the cards. Be sure to include a provision that the same card is not dealt more than once.

(b) Roulette is played with a wheel containing 38 different squares along its circumference. Two of these squares, numbered 0 and 00, are green; 18 squares are red, and 18 are black. The red and black squares alternate in color and are numbered 1 through 36 in a random order.

A small marble is spun within the wheel. The marble eventually comes to rest within a groove beneath one of the squares. The game is played by betting on the outcome of each spin, in any one of the following ways.

1. By selecting a single red or black square, at 35 to 1 odds. (Thus, if a player were to bet $1.00 and win, he or she would receive a total of $36.00; the original $1.00 plus an additional $35.00.)

2. By selecting a color, either red or black, at 1 to 1 odds. (Thus if a player chose red on a $1.00 bet, he or she would receive $2.00 if the marble came to rest beneath any red square.)

3. By selecting either the odd or the even numbers (excluding 0 and 00), at 1 to 1 odds.

4. By selecting either the low 18 (1 to 18) or the high 18 (19 to 36) numbers at 1 to 1 odds.

The player will automatically lose if the marble comes to rest beneath one of the green squares (0 or 00), no matter what was bet.

Write an interactive Pascal program that will simulate a roulette game. Allow the players to select whatever type of play they wish by choosing from a menu. Then print the outcome of each game followed by an appropriate message indicating whether each player has won or lost.

(c) Write an interactive Pascal program that will simulate a game of bingo. Print each letter-number combination as it is drawn (generated). Be sure that no combination is drawn more than once. Remember that each of the letters B-I-N-G-O corresponds to a certain range of numbers, as indicated below.

$$
\begin{array}{ll}
\text{B:} & \text{1–15} \\
\text{I:} & \text{16–30} \\
\text{N:} & \text{31–45} \\
\text{G:} & \text{46–60} \\
\text{O:} & \text{61–75}
\end{array}
$$

Each player will have a card with five columns, labeled B-I-N-G-O. Each column will contain five numbers, within the ranges indicated above. No two players will have the same card. The first player to have one entire row of numbers drawn (either vertically, horizontally or diagonally) wins. *Note*: The center position of each card is sometimes covered before the game begins ( a "free" call). Also, the game is sometimes played such that a player must have *all* of the numbers on his or her card drawn before he or she can win.

**9.59**   Write an interactive Pascal program that will encode or decode a line of text. To encode a line of text, proceed as follows.

1.   Convert each character, including blank spaces, to its ASCII equivalent.

2.   Generate a positive random integer. Add this integer to the ASCII equivalent of each character. (The same random integer will be used for the entire line of text.)

3.   Suppose that N1 represents the lowest permissible value in the ASCII code, and N2 represents the highest permissible value. If the number obtained in step 2 above (i.e., the original ASCII equivalent plus the random integer) exceeds N2, then subtract the largest possible multiple of N2 from this number and add the remainder to N1. Hence the encoded number will always fall between N1 and N2 and will therefore always represent some ASCII character.

4.   Print the characters that correspond to the encoded ASCII values.

The procedure is reversed when decoding a line of text. Be certain, however, that the same random number is used in decoding as was used in encoding.

# Chapter 10

# Records

In the last chapter we studied the array, a structured data type in which all elements must be of the same type. We now turn our attention to another important structured data type, the *record*, whose constituent elements need not be the same. Thus, we can refer collectively to a set of data items that differ among themselves in type. The individual data items are said to occupy *fields* within the record.

## 10.1 DEFINING A RECORD

The easiest way to define a record is to include the definition as part of a variable declaration. This allows us to declare an individual record-type variable, just as we declared simple-type variables and array-type variables.

The general form of a record-type variable declaration is

        VAR *record name* : RECORD *field 1*; *field 2*; . . .;*field n* END

where *field 1* represents the first field declaration, *field 2* represents the second field, and so on. Each field declaration is written in a manner that is similar to an individual variable declaration; i.e.,

        *field name* : *type*

where *field name* is an identifier that represents the name of the field, and *type* is the data type of the data item that will occupy the field.

Note that the individual fields within the record are separated by semicolons.

### EXAMPLE 10.1

Suppose that a customer record is to consist of an integer-type customer number, a customer account designation which is of type char and a customer balance which is a real number. Let us represent this record with a record-type variable called customer. The variable declaration is shown below.

```
VAR customer : RECORD
                custno : integer;
                custtype : char;
                custbalance : real
            END;
```

Notice that the record consists of an integer-type field called custno, a char-type field called custtype and a real-type field called custbalance.

The individual field declarations need not always be written on separate lines, as in this example. They are often written in this manner, however, to enhance readability.

Another way to define a record, which is frequently more useful than a variable declaration, is to define a record *type*. Then individual variables can be declared to be of this type. (Notice the analogy with the methods that are used to define arrays, described in the last chapter.) In its general form, a record type definition is written as

        TYPE *name* = RECORD *field 1*; *field 2*; . . .;*field n* END

where the meaning of the individual items is the same as described above.

**EXAMPLE 10.2**

Consider once again the customer record described in the previous example. Let us now define a record type called account, and a corresponding variable called customer, as before. This can be accomplished by writing

```
TYPE account = RECORD
                    custno : integer;
                    custtype : char;
                    custbalance : real
               END;
VAR customer : account;
```

It should be understood that this accomplishes the same thing as the variable declaration shown in Example 10.1. The present approach is more general, however, because it will allow us to introduce additional record-type variables (with this same composition) if we wish.

The individual fields can be associated with user-defined data types and subrange types as well as standard data types. Moreover, the field types can be structured as well as scalar. Hence, an individual field may be an array or another record.

**EXAMPLE 10.3**

Here is a variation of the record definition shown in Example 10.2.

```
TYPE status = (current,overdue,delinquent);
     account = RECORD
                    custno : 1..9999;
                    custtype : status;
                    custbalance : real
               END;
VAR customer : account;
```

Now the customer number (custno) is a subrange-type data item, and the customer type (custtype) is an enumerated-type data item.

Note that the enumerated data type (status) must itself be defined before it can be referenced in the record declaration.

**EXAMPLE 10.4**

Now let us add the customer's name to the above record. To do so, we define an additional field that represents a packed array of type char. Therefore, the entire record definition becomes

```
TYPE status = (current,overdue,delinquent);
     account = RECORD
                    custname : PACKED ARRAY [1..80] OF char;
                    custno : 1..9999;
                    custtype : status;
                    custbalance : real
               END;
VAR customer : account;
```

A variation of this record definition, which is somewhat more general, is given below.

```
TYPE status = (current,overdue,delinquent);
     line = PACKED ARRAY [1..80] OF char;
     account = RECORD
                    custname : line;
                    custno : 1..9999;
                    custtype : status;
                    custbalance : real
               END;
VAR customer : account;
```

This variation allows other string-type information to be defined very easily, either within the current record or in other parts of the program. Thus, if we wanted to add an address field to customer, we could write

```
TYPE status = (current,overdue,delinquent);
     line = PACKED ARRAY [1..80] OF char;
     account = RECORD
                    custname : line;
                    custaddress : line;
                    custno : 1..9999;
                    custtype : status;
                    custbalance : real
               END;
VAR customer : account;
```

**EXAMPLE 10.5**

Let us now add a last-payment date to our customer record. This can best be accomplished by representing the date as a separate record and then including this date record as one of the fields in customer. Thus, our record declaration now becomes

```
TYPE status = (current,overdue,delinquent);
     line = PACKED ARRAY [1..80] OF char;
     date = RECORD
                 month : 1..12;
                 day : 1..31;
                 year : 1900..2100
            END;
     account = RECORD
                    custname : line;
                    custaddress : line;
                    custno : 1..9999;
                    custtype : status;
                    custbalance : real;
                    lastpayment : date
               END;
VAR customer : account;
```

Notice that the record account now contains another record, lastpayment, as one of its fields. Also, we see that account contains two arrays (custname and custaddress), a subrange type (custno), an enumerated data type (custtype) and a standard data type (custbalance). This example thus illustrates the flexibility that is inherent in the definition of a record.

It should also be recognized that a record can be an individual data item in another structured data type, such as an array. Thus we can define arrays whose elements are records, records whose elements (or some of whose elements) are arrays, and so on.

**EXAMPLE 10.6**

Here is an example of an array whose elements are records. In particular, let us define an array called events, whose individual elements are dates, as defined in the previous example.

```
TYPE date = RECORD
                 month : 1..12;
                 day : 1..31;
                 year : 1900..2100
            END;
VAR events : ARRAY [1..100] OF date;
```

Thus, we have a one-dimensional array (i.e., a list) that can contain as many as 100 different dates. Notice that events is defined as a variable, not a data type.

Once a single record type has been defined, we can declare several different variables as records of that type. This feature is illustrated in the following example.

**EXAMPLE 10.7**

Consider the record account, defined in Example 10.5. We can now declare the variables preferred and regular to be records of this type. Thus,

```
TYPE status = (current,overdue,delinquent);
     line = PACKED ARRAY [1..80] OF char;
     date = RECORD
                month : 1..12;
                day : 1..31;
                year : 1900..2100
            END;
     account = RECORD
                  custname : line;
                  custaddress : line;
                  custno : 1..9999;
                  custtype : status;
                  custbalance : real;
                  lastpayment : date
              END;
VAR preferred,regular : account;
```

A record can be packed, just as arrays can be packed. This allows a record to be stored more compactly, though accessing the individual data items within the record will take longer.

Record packing is accomplished by writing PACKED RECORD instead of RECORD in the record type definition, as illustrated in the following example.

**EXAMPLE 10.8**

Let us redefine the record type account, originally shown in Example 10.2, to be a packed record.

```
TYPE account = PACKED RECORD
                  custno : integer;
                  custtype : char;
                  custbalance : real
              END;
VAR customer : account;
```

Thus, the variable customer will represent a packed record of type account.

Record packing, like array packing, involves a trade-off between execution speed and memory requirements. However, this feature is not as widely used as array packing. As a rule, it is used only in applications that emphasize the copying of entire records, rather than the more common applications where individual record elements are manipulated.

Finally, it should be mentioned that each record is considered a self-contained entity with respect to field definitions. Thus, each field within a given record must have a unique name, but the same field name can be used in different records. In other words, the scope of a field identifier is confined to the particular record within which it is defined.

**EXAMPLE 10.9**

Two different record types, one and two, are defined below.

```
TYPE one = RECORD
              a : real;
              b : integer;
              c : char
          END;
```

*(continues on next page)*

```
              two = RECORD
                      a : char;
                      b,c : real
                  END;
```

Notice that the individual field names a, b and c are duplicated between the records, but the associated data types are different. This is permissible, since the scope of each set of field definitions is confined to its respective record. Also, note that the field names are distinct within each record, as required.

## 10.2 PROCESSING A RECORD

Now that we have seen how records can be defined, let us turn our attention to the use of records, or record components, in typical programming situations.

The simplest type of record-processing operation involves the assignment of one entire record to another. This requires that both records have the same composition.

**EXAMPLE 10.10**

The skeletal outline of a Pascal program involving the assignment of one record to another is shown below. (Notice that this outline utilizes the record definitions originally presented in Example 10.7.)

```
      TYPE status = (current,overdue,delinquent);
           line = PACKED ARRAY [1..80] OF char;
           date = RECORD
                     month : 1..12;
                     day : 1..31;
                     year : 1900..2100
                  END;
           account = RECORD
                        custname : line;
                        custaddress : line;
                        custno : 1..9999;
                        custtype : status;
                        custbalance : real;
                        lastpayment : date
                     END;
      VAR preferred,regular : account;

      BEGIN
         .
         .
         .
      preferred := regular;
         .
         .
      END.
```

It is, of course, assumed that the elements of regular have been entered into the computer or otherwise defined prior to the assignment statement.

It is much more common to process record elements individually rather than processing entire records collectively. To do so, we must be able to access the individual record elements. This is accomplished by forming a *field designator*, which is a combination of a record-type variable name and a field name, i.e.,

*variable name.field name*

(Note the period between the two names.)

**EXAMPLE 10.11**

Consider once again the record-type variables `preferred` and `regular`, defined in Example 10.10. The individual data items within each of these records are referred to with field designators such as `preferred.cust-name`, `regular.custno` and `regular.lastpayment`.

For example, `preferred.custname` and `preferred.custaddress` represent 80-element string variables, preferred.custno represents an integer quantity whose value lies between 1 and 9999, and `preferred.custtype` represents one of the enumerated simple quantities `current`, `overdue` or `delinquent`. Also, `preferred.custba-lance` represents a real quantity, and `preferred.lastpayment` represents an enclosed record whose individual fields can take on the values defined by the record `date` (more about this in the next example). Similar field descriptions apply to the elements of `regular`.

If a field represents a structured data item, then the individual elements of that field can be accessed by including the structured data element in the field designator. Thus, if a field represents an array, an individual array element can be accessed by writing

> *variable name.field name* [*index values*]

Similarly, if a field represents an enclosed record, an individual element of the enclosed record can be accessed as

> *variable name.field name.sub-field name*

where *sub-field* refers to one field within the enclosed record.

**EXAMPLE 10.12**

Consider once again the record-type variables `preferred` and `regular`, defined in Example 10.10. The field designator `preferred.custname[12]` refers to the twelfth character in the first field of `preferred` (i.e., the twelfth character in the packed array `custname`).

Similarly, the field designator `regular.lastpayment.month` refers to the first integer quantity in the last field of `regular` (i.e., the quantity in the first field in the enclosed record `lastpayment`). This quantity must be an integer whose value falls within the subrange `1..12`, as defined by the record-type `date`.

The individual record elements can be utilized in the same manner as ordinary variables. The particular features (and restrictions) that apply to each element are determined by the data type of that element. Thus, if a record element represents a simple-type quantity, then it can appear in an assignment statement, within an expression, within a control structure, within an I/O statement, as a parameter within a procedure or function reference, etc., subject to the restrictions that apply to that particular data type.

Similarly, if a record element represents a structured data type (e.g., an array or another record), then it can be utilized in the same manner as other structured data items of the same type. The only special restriction is that an element of a packed record cannot be passed to a procedure or function if the corresponding formal parameter is a variable parameter.

**EXAMPLE 10.13**

Several unrelated statements that make use of individual record elements are shown below. All of the record elements conform to the record definitions and record-type variable declarations given in Example 10.10. Type compatibility is assumed throughout.

```
regular.custbalance := 0;

regular.custbalance := regular.custbalance - payment;

preferred.custname := regular.custname;

writeln(regular.custname, regular.custaddress);
```

(*continues on next page*)

```
average := (preferred.custbalance + regular.custbalance)/2;

newbalance := round(preferred.custbalance);

IF preferred.custname [1] = '*'
              THEN preferred.custtype := current;

IF regular.lastpayment.month < 6
        THEN writeln(regular.custno, regular.custbalance)
        ELSE preferred := regular;
```

Some applications require that a sequence of records be stored and processed in some particular order. In such situations it is often convenient to define a one-dimensional array whose elements are records. A particular record can then be accessed as

array name [index value]

and an individual record element as

array name [index value].field name

## EXAMPLE 10.14

Here is an example of an array (i.e., a list) containing 100 records.

```
TYPE account = RECORD
                    custno : integer;
                    custtype : char;
                    custbalance : real
                 END;
     VAR customer : ARRAY [1..100] OF account;
```

Thus, customer [23] refers to the twenty-third record. Furthermore, customer [23].custbalance refers to the third data item in the twenty-third record (i.e., the current balance for the twenty-third customer).

## EXAMPLE 10.15

Shown below is a more complicated example of several one-dimensional arrays whose elements are records.

```
TYPE status = (current,overdue,delinquent);
     line = PACKED ARRAY [1..80] OF char;
     date = RECORD
                 month : 1..12;
                 day : 1..31;
                 year : 1900..2100
             END;
     account = RECORD
                    custname : line;
                    custaddress : line;
                    custno : 1..9999;
                    custtype : status;
                    custbalance : real;
                    lastpayment : date
                 END;
     VAR preferred,regular : ARRAY [1..100] OF account;
```

In this example, preferred [5] refers to the fifth record in the first array, and regular [82].custname refers to the customer name in the eighty-second record of the second array. Similarly, regular [14].lastpayment.year refers to the year of the last payment (i.e., the third item in the enclosed record) in the fourteenth record of the second array.

**EXAMPLE 10.16**

Here are several unrelated statements that make use of individual record elements defined in the preceding example.

```
regular [82].custbalance := 0;

preferred [i].custbalance :=
                    preferred [i].custbalance - payment;

writeln(regular [15].custname, regular [15].custaddress);

IF preferred [count].custname [1] ='*'
            THEN preferred [count].custtype := current;

IF regular [i].lastpayment.month < 6
    THEN writeln(regular [i].custno, regular [i].custbalance)
    ELSE preferred [i] := regular [i];
```

In these examples the variables i and count are assumed to be integer-type variables that have been assigned appropriate values earlier in the program.

## 10.3  THE WITH STRUCTURE

Many programs require that different elements of the same record be manipulated at various places within the program. The need to specify several different field designators can become tedious, however, and may reduce the overall readability of the program. In such situations the WITH structure allows the record name to be omitted from the field designators.

The general form of the WITH structure is

```
WITH record name DO statement
```

or, if two or more records are to be included within the structure,

```
WITH record 1 name, record 2 name, . . . , record n name DO statement
```

The statement part of the structure refers to any action statement, which may itself be structured. Within this statement any reference to an element within one of the specified records need not include the record name.

**EXAMPLE 10.17**

Consider the following declarations.

```
TYPE date = RECORD
                month : 1..12;
                day : 1..31;
                year : 1900..2100
            END;
VAR birthday : date;
```

One way to update the values of birthday is to write

```
BEGIN
    birthday.month := 5;
    birthday.day := 13;
    birthday.year := 1966
END;
```

It is easier, however, to write

```
WITH birthday DO BEGIN month := 5; day := 13; year := 1966 END;
```

Both statements accomplish the same thing.

**EXAMPLE 10.18**

Here is another example that illustrates the use of the WITH structure. This example makes use of the declarations first presented in Example 10.7. These declarations are repeated in the skeletal program outline presented below.

```
TYPE status = (current,overdue,delinquent);
     line = PACKED ARRAY [1..80] OF char;
     date = RECORD
                month : 1..12;
                day : 1..31;
                year : 1900..2100
            END;
     account = RECORD
                   custname : line;
                   custaddress : line;
                   custno : 1..9999;
                   custtype : status;
                   custbalance : real;
                   lastpayment : date
               END;
VAR preferred,regular : account;

BEGIN
   .
   .
   WITH regular DO
       BEGIN
          .
          .
          custno := 1262;
          lastpayment.day := 8;
          .
          .
          IF custbalance = 0 THEN custtype := current
                             ELSE custtype := overdue;
          .
          .
       END;
   .
   .
END.
```

Note that all of the field references within the WITH structure refer to elements of regular. If it were necessary to refer to an element of preferred, then the entire field designation (e.g., preferred.custbalance) would have to be specified.

**EXAMPLE 10.19**

Now consider a skeletal program outline that makes use of the record-type array declarations given in Example 10.15.

```
TYPE status = (current,overdue,delinquent);
     line = PACKED ARRAY [1..80] OF char;
     date = RECORD
                month : 1..12;
                day : 1..31;
                year : 1900..2100
            END;
```

(*Program continues on next page*)

```
        account = RECORD
                     custname : line;
                     custaddress : line;
                     custno : 1..9999;
                     custtype : status;
                     custbalance : real;
                     lastpayment : date
                  END;
VAR i : 1..100;
    preferred,regular : ARRAY [1..100] OF account;

BEGIN
   .
   .
   FOR i := 1 TO 100 DO
      WITH regular [i] DO
          BEGIN
            .
            .
            custno := i + 1200;
            lastpayment.day := 8;
            .
            .
            IF custbalance = 0 THEN custtype := current
                              ELSE custtype := overdue;
            .
            .
          END;
   .
   .
END.
```

Compare this example with the outline shown in Example 10.18.

If the WITH statement includes two or more record-type variable names having the same field names, then a possible ambiguity arises as to which record is referred to when a field is accessed within the structure. This ambiguity is resolved as follows.

The multirecord WITH structure

WITH *record 1 name*, *record 2 name*, . . . , *record n name* DO *statement*

is equivalent to the following nested structure.

WITH *record 1 name* DO
    WITH *record 2 name* DO
        .
        .
        .
                 WITH *record n name* DO *statement*

If a field name is common to two or more of the specified records, its scope is confined to the innermost record within the nest. Any reference to a field with the same name but associated with another record must include the record name as a part of the field designation.

**EXAMPLE 10.20**

A skeletal program outline is shown below.

```
VAR first : RECORD a,b,c : integer END;
    second : RECORD c,d,e : integer END;
BEGIN
    .
    .

    WITH first, second DO
        BEGIN
            a := 1;
            b := 2;
            first.c := 3;
            c := 4;
            d := 5;
            e := 6
        END;
    .
    .

END.
```

Notice that c is a field name that is common to both records. Thus, a reference to c within the WITH structure will automatically refer to second.c, since second is the innermost record name. In order to refer to first.c within this structure, we must specify the entire field designator.

The above structure causes the following values to be assigned to the fields named c.

```
first.c := 3              second.c := 4
```

The WITH structure should be used freely in situations to which it applies. Its use contributes to overall program clarity, and in some situations may also improve the computational efficiency of the program.

**EXAMPLE 10.21**

**A Customer Billing System.** Consider a simple customer billing system in which customer records are entered into the computer, each customer's balance is updated to reflect current payments and a new balance is computed. In addition we will calculate and then display the current status of each customer, based upon the customer's previous balance and the amount of the current payment.

Suppose that each customer record contains the following items of information: name, street address, city and state, account number, account status (current, overdue or delinquent), previous balance, current payment, new balance and payment date. The record declarations are shown below.

```
TYPE status = (current,overdue,delinquent);
     line = PACKED ARRAY [1..30] OF char;
     date = RECORD
                month : 1..12;
                day : 1..31;
                year : 1900..2100
            END;
     account = RECORD
                   name : line;
                   street : line;
                   city : line;
                   custno : 1..9999;
                   custtype : status;
                   oldbalance : real;
                   newbalance : real;
                   payment : real;
                   paydate : date
               END;
```

The status of each account will be determined in the following manner: the account will be considered to be current unless

1.  The current payment is greater than zero but less than 10 percent of the previous outstanding balance. In this case the account is considered to be overdue.

2.  There is an outstanding balance and the current payment is zero, in which case the account is considered to be delinquent.

For convenience, all records will be stored as elements of a one-dimensional array. Therefore the overall program strategy will be as follows.

1.  Specify the number of accounts (i.e., the number of records) to be processed.

2.  For each record, read in the following items:

    (*a*)  name

    (*b*)  street

    (*c*)  city

    (*d*)  account number

    (*e*)  previous balance

    (*f*)  current payment

    (*g*)  payment date

3.  After all of the records have been read into the computer, process each record in the following manner:

    (*a*)  Compare the current payment with the previous balance and determine the appropriate account status.

    (*b*)  Calculate the new account balance by subtracting the current payment from the previous balance (a negative balance will indicate a credit).

4.  After all of the records have been processed, write out the following information for each record:

    (*a*)  name

    (*b*)  account number

    (*c*)  street

    (*d*)  city

    (*e*)  old balance

    (*f*)  current payment

    (*g*)  new balance

    (*h*)  account status

Let us write the program in a modular manner, with three separate procedures to read the input data, process the data and write the output, respectively. Each of these procedures is straightforward and does not require further elaboration. The main block will simply enter the number of records and then access the appropriate procedures.

Here is the entire program.

```
PROGRAM billing1(input,output);

(* THIS PROGRAM ILLUSTRATES THE USE OF RECORDS
           IN A SIMPLE CUSTOMER BILLING SYSTEM *)

TYPE status = (current,overdue,delinquent);
     line = PACKED ARRAY [1..30] OF char;
     date = RECORD
               month : 1..12;
               day : 1..31;
               year : 1900..2100
            END;
```

(*Program continues on next page*)

```
        account = RECORD
                    name : line;
                    street : line;
                    city : line;
                    custno : 1..9999;
                    custtype : status;
                    oldbalance : real;
                    newbalance : real;
                    payment : real;
                    paydate : date
                END;
VAR customer : ARRAY [1..100] OF account;
    i,n : 1..100;

PROCEDURE readinput;
(* Read input data for each record *)
VAR count : 1..30;
    slash : char;
BEGIN
   FOR i := 1 TO n DO
      WITH customer [i] DO
         BEGIN
            writeln;
            writeln('Customer no. ',i:3);
            write('   Name:    ');
            count := 1;
            REPEAT
               read(name [count]);
               count := count + 1
            UNTIL eoln;
            readln;
            write('   Street: ');
            count := 1;
            REPEAT
               read(street [count]);
               count := count + 1
            UNTIL eoln;
            readln;
            write('   City:    ');
            count := 1;
            REPEAT
               read(city [count]);
               count := count + 1
            UNTIL eoln;
            readln;
            write('   Account number: ');
            readln(custno);
            write('   Previous balance: ');
            readln(oldbalance);
            write('   Current payment: ');
            readln(payment);
            write('   Payment date (mm/dd/yyyy): ');
            WITH paydate DO
               read(month,slash,day,slash,year);
            readln
         END
END;   (* readinput *)
```

```
        PROCEDURE processdata;
        (* Determine status and calculate a new balance for each record *)
        BEGIN
           FOR i := 1 TO n DO
              WITH customer [i] DO
                 BEGIN
                    custtype := current;
                    IF (payment > 0) AND (payment < 0.1*oldbalance)
                       THEN custtype := overdue;
                    IF (oldbalance > 0) AND (payment = 0)
                       THEN custtype := delinquent;
                    newbalance := oldbalance - payment
                 END
        END;   (* processdata *)


        PROCEDURE writeoutput;
        (* Write out current information for each record *)
        BEGIN
           FOR i := 1 TO n DO
              WITH customer [i] DO
                 BEGIN
                    writeln;
                    write('Name:    ',name);
                    writeln('   Account number: ',custno:4);
                    writeln('Street: ',street);
                    writeln('City:    ',city);
                    writeln;
                    write('Old balance: ',oldbalance:7:2);
                    write('   Current payment: ',payment:7:2);
                    writeln('   New balance: ',newbalance:7:2);
                    writeln;
                    write('Account status: ');
                    CASE custtype OF
                       current    : writeln('CURRENT');
                       overdue    : writeln('OVERDUE');
                       delinquent : writeln('DELINQUENT')
                    END;
                    writeln
                 END
        END;   (* writeoutput *)


        BEGIN   (* main action statements *)
           writeln('CUSTOMER BILLING SYSTEM');
           writeln;
           write('How many customers are there? ');
           readln(n);
           readinput;
           processdata;
           writeoutput
        END.
```

Notice that a WITH structure is included in each of the procedures. In fact, readinput contains a double (nested) WITH structure to accommodate the individual elements of the enclosed record (paydate) that is contained within each customer record.

Now suppose that the program is used to process four fictitious customer records. The input dialogue is shown below, with the user's responses underlined.

CUSTOMER BILLING SYSTEM

How many customers are there? <u>4</u>

Customer no.    1
    Name:   <u>Richard L. Warren</u>
    Street: <u>123 Vistaview Drive</u>
    City:   <u>Denver, CO</u>
    Account number: <u>4208</u>
    Previus balance: <u>247.88</u>
    Current payment: <u>25.00</u>
    Payment date (mm/dd/yyyy): <u>6/14/1983</u>

Customer no.    2
    Name:   <u>Marcia Korenstein</u>
    Street: <u>4383 Affluent Avenue</u>
    City:   <u>Beechview, OH</u>
    Account number: <u>2219</u>
    Previous balance: <u>135.00</u>
    Current payment: <u>135.00</u>
    Payment date (mm/dd/yyyy): <u>8/10/1983</u>

Customer no.    3
    Name:   <u>Mark Singer</u>
    Street: <u>1787 Larynx Lane</u>
    City:   <u>Indianapolis, IN</u>
    Account number: <u>8452</u>
    Previous balance: <u>387.42</u>
    Current payment: <u>35.00</u>
    Payment date (mm/dd/yyyy): <u>7/4/1983</u>

Customer no.    4
    Name:   <u>Phyllis W. Smith</u>
    Street: <u>1000 Great White Way</u>
    City:   <u>New York, NY</u>
    Account number: <u>711</u>
    Previous balance: <u>260.00</u>
    Current payment: <u>0</u>
    Payment date (mm/dd/yyyy): <u>11/27/1983</u>

The program then generates the following output data, in response to the above input.

```
Name:   Richard L. Warren   Customer number: 4208
Street: 123 Vistaview Drive
City:   Denver, CO

Old balance:  247.88   Current payment:    25.00   New balance:  222.88

Account status: CURRENT


Name:   Marcia Korenstein   Customer number: 2219
Street: 4383 Affluent Avenue
City:   Beechview, OH

Old balance:  135.00   Current payment:   135.00   New balance:    0.00

Account status: CURRENT
```

(*continues on next page*)

```
Name:   Mark Singer    Customer number: 8452
Street: 1787 Larynx Lane
City:   Indianapolis, IN

Old balance:  387.42   Current payment:   35.00   New balance:  352.42

Account status: OVERDUE


Name:   Phyllis W. Smith   Customer number:  711
Street: 1000 Great White Way
City:   New York, NY

Old balance:  260.00   Current payment:    0.00   New balance:  260.00

Account status: DELINQUENT
```

From a practical standpoint, the nature of this example is somewhat unrealistic. In particular, it makes little sense to enter an entire customer record, perform a simple calculation and then write out the updated record without maintaining a permanent copy of the new information within the computer (or on an auxiliary storage device). In the next chapter we will see how the customer records can be permanently maintained in a data file, thus eliminating the need to reenter the data whenever an update is required.

## 10.4  VARIANT RECORDS

So far we have only considered records whose composition remains invariate throughout the program. It is also possible, however, to define a record whose composition (or a portion thereof) may vary within the program, depending upon the value that is assigned to some particular field within the record (the *tag field*). Such a variable-type record is known as a *variant record* (or the *variant part* of a record).

The general form of a record type definition containing both a fixed part and a variant part is

```
TYPE record name = RECORD
                   fixed field 1;
                   fixed field 2;

                        .
                        .
                        .

                   CASE tag field identifier : type OF
                        case label 1 : variant fieldlist 1 ;
                        case label 2 : variant fieldlist 2 ;

                             .
                             .
                             .

             END
```

Each variant fieldlist is expressed in the form of a field enumeration; i.e.,

```
(variant field 1, variant field 2, . . . , variant field n)
```

The tag field must be associated with an ordinal data type that has been previously defined. Each value of this ordinal type must appear once (and only once) as a case label, in the subsequent variant part of the record definition. The active part of the record will then consist of those fields that correspond to some particular case label, as assigned to the tag field identifier.

There can be only one variant part in any record, and it must always follow the fixed part of the record.

**EXAMPLE 10.22**

Here is an example of a record definition that contains both a fixed part and a variant part.

```
TYPE item = (stereo,tv);
     name = PACKED ARRAY [1..80] OF char;
     inventory = RECORD
                         stockno : 1..20000;
                         supplier : name;
                         quantity : integer;
                         CASE itemtype : item OF
                            stereo : (power : 1..1000);
                                  tv : (tubesize : 1..25; color : char)
                 END;
     VAR stockitem,backorder : inventory;
```

The record type is called inventory. Its fixed part consists of the fields stockno, suppplier and quantity, and its variant part will either consist of the field power or the fields tubesize and color, depending on the value that is assigned to the tag-field identifier itemtype. In particular, if stereo is assigned to itemtype, then the variant part of the record will consist of the field power, but if tv is assigned to itemtype, then the variant part will consist of the fields tubesize and color.

Note that we have included a declaration for two record-type variables—stockitem and backorder. Each of these variables represents a record of type inventory.

The individual variant record elements and the tag field identifier can be accessed in the same manner as the individual fixed record elements, by writing

    *variable name.field name*

    *variable name.field name.sub-field name*

or

    *variable name.field name [index values]*

depending upon the particular data type of the individual record element.

**EXAMPLE 10.23**

Several unrelated statements that make use of individual record elements are shown below. All of the statements refer to elements of the record-type variables defined in Example 10.22.

```
stockitem.stockno := 12345;

backorder.quantity := 15;

stockitem.itemtype := stereo;

stockitem.power := 150;

writeln(backorder.stockno,backorder.power);

IF stockitem.quantity < 24 THEN
   BEGIN
      writeln(stockitem.supplier);
      writeln(stockitem.tubesize,stockitem.color)
   END;
```

Notice that some of the statements utilize fixed fields, whereas others utilize variant fields. The last two statements include references to both fixed and variant fields. Also, note that a value is assigned to the tag-field identifier in the third statement.

Example 10.22 illustrates certain features that the programmer should be aware of. First, the field names within a record, including the variant field names, must be unique. (In some applications there is the temptation to use the same field name in two or more variant fieldlists.) Second (and more subtle), an appropriate value must be assigned to the tag-field identifier if an individual variant field is accessed. Thus, if stockitem.power is accessed in Example 10.22, then stockitem.itemtype must represent stereo.

The WITH structure can be used with variant-type records, just as with fixed-type records (see Section 10.3). This tends to reduce the likelihood of errors as well as improve the overall readability of the program.

**EXAMPLE 10.24**

Suppose we wish to update certain fields of the record stockitem, defined in Example 10.22. This can easily be accomplished using the WITH structure, as shown below.

```
WITH stockitem DO
    BEGIN
        quantity := quantity - sales;
        IF quantity < 0 THEN backorder.quantity := -quantity;
        IF itemtype = stereo THEN writeln(power)
                             ELSE writeln(tubesize,color)
    END;
```

Notice that this example includes the use of a fixed field (quantity), the tag field (itemtype) and several variable fields (power, tubesize and color). Also, notice the reference to one field within another record (backorder). This field reference is written in its complete form (i.e., as backorder.quantity), since the WITH statement does not apply to this record.

There are several variations of the general record format that should be mentioned. For example, it is possible to define a record that does not contain a fixed part. Moreover, a variant fieldlist can be empty if desired. This is indicated by an empty set of parentheses following the appropriate case label. Both of these situations are illustrated in the next example.

**EXAMPLE 10.25**

Consider the following variant record definition.

```
TYPE status = (single,married,divorced,widowed);
     background = RECORD
                      CASE maritalstatus : status OF
                          single : ();
                          married : (children : 0..10);
                          divorced,widowed : (children : 0..10;
                                              remarried : boolean)
                  END;
VAR employees : ARRAY [1..100] OF background;
```

In this example, employees is a one-dimensional array whose elements are records of type background. Notice that this particular record definition does not include a fixed part. Also, notice that the first variant field list (corresponding to the case label single) is empty.

We also see that the last variant fieldlist corresponds to two different case labels, widowed and divorced. Finally, observe that the field children is common to both the second and third variant fieldlists (i.e., case labels married and widowed,divorced).

The nature of this example suggests that a fixed record part could also be included, consisting of a name, address, employee number, etc. These fields can easily be added by the reader.

Another situation that requires some discussion is the presence of the tag-field identifier within the record definition. Strictly speaking, the presence of the tag-field identifier is not essential. If it is not present, the active variant fields will be determined implicitly by the particular variant field that is accessed. Specifically, a reference to a particular variant field will activate a particular case label; all variant fields associated with this case label will then become active. Good programming practice suggests, however, that this feature generally not be used, particularly by beginners.

**EXAMPLE 10.26**

Consider the following skeletal program outline.

```
TYPE item = (stereo,tv);
     name = PACKED ARRAY [1..80] OF char;
     inventory = RECORD
                     stockno : 1..20000;
                     supplier : name;
                     quantity : integer;
                     CASE item OF
                         stereo : (power : 1..1000);
                             tv : (tubesize : 1..25;
                                      color : char)
                 END;
VAR stockitem,backorder : inventory;
BEGIN
   WITH stockitem DO
      BEGIN
         .
         .
         .
         tubesize := 19;
         color := 'Y';
         .
         .
      END
END.
```

Notice that the record definition includes the tag-field type (i.e., item), but not the tag-field identifier. Thus, the references to tubesize and color within the main action block imply that the second variant fieldlist is active (i.e., that which corresponds to the case label tv).

Although a given record can have only one fixed part and one variant part, it is possible to include one variant definition within another. Thus we can create nested variant fields within a single record.

**EXAMPLE 10.27**

Here is a variation of the record definition shown in Example 10.22.

```
TYPE item = (stereo,tv);
     style = (portable,stationary);
     name = PACKED ARRAY [1..80] OF char;
     inventory = RECORD
                     stockno : 1..20000;
                     supplier : name;
                     quantity : integer;
                     CASE itemtype : item OF
                         stereo : (power : 1..1000);
                             tv : (tubesize : 1..25;
                                   color : char;
                                   CASE size : style OF
                                       portable : (weight : 1..100;
                                                   voltage : 1..220);
                                      stationary : ())
                 END;
VAR stockitem,backorder : inventory;
```

Notice the second variant fieldlist (corresponding to the case label tv). This fieldlist now includes another variant definition, which depends upon the value assigned to the tag-field identifier size. If size represents portable, then the variant fieldlist tv will contain the fields tubesize, color, weight and voltage. On the other hand, if size represents stationary, then tv will contain only the fields tubesize and color.

The reader should observe that the innermost variant definition has its own unique tag field (size), which is associated with its own enumerated data type (style). Also, notice the empty variant fieldlist corresponding to the nested case label stationary. And finally, note that the variant fields associated with tv follow the fixed fields, as required.

It should be understood that a new group of variant fields will become active whenever a new value is assigned to the tag-field identifier. Moreover, if the tag-field identifier is not present, then a new group of variants will become active as a result of a reference to a nonactive variant field. Any inadvertent (and unwanted) change in the active variant fields must therefore be avoided. The programmer must be particularly cautious of this potential problem in programs that employ procedures or functions.

In order to minimize the likelihood of such errors, a change of variant is not permitted under the following circumstances.

1. Within a WITH structure if a variant field name appears in the WITH statement
2. Whenever a variant field has been passed to a procedure or function as an actual variable parameter

Moreover, a tag-field identifier cannot be passed to a procedure or function as an actual variable parameter.

**EXAMPLE 10.28**

**Inventory Control.** Let us now develop a simple inventory control system, similar to the customer billing system shown in Example 10.21. Now, however, we will make use of records that contain both a fixed part and a variant part.

Specifically, consider a system that keeps track of two types of merchandise, stereos and television sets. The following information will periodically be entered into the computer: stock number (a nonnegative integer), item type ("s" for stereo, "t" for TV), the supplier's name, the original (previous) inventory level (a nonnegative integer) and the current change in inventory level (an integer that is unrestricted in sign). In addition, some descriptive information will be added for each item, the nature of which will depend on the type of item. For a stereo, the power level (an integer ranging from 1 to 1000) will be entered. For a TV, an indication of whether the set is portable ("y" or "n"), the tube size (an integer ranging from 1 to 25) and an indication of whether or not it is a color TV ("y" or "n"). Also, if the set is portable, the weight (1..100) and the voltage (1..220) will be entered.

The appropriate record declarations are shown below.

```
TYPE item = (stereo,tv);
     style = (portable,stationary);
     name = PACKED ARRAY [1..80] OF char;
     inventory = RECORD
                     stockno : 0..20000;
                     supplier : name;
                     quantity : integer;
                     CASE itemtype : item OF
                        stereo : (power : 1..1000);
                            tv : (tubesize : 1..25;
                                  color : char;
                                  CASE size : style OF
                                     portable : (weight : 1..100;
                                                 voltage : 1..220);
                                     stationary : ())
            END;
     VAR stockitem,backorder : ARRAY [1..100] OF inventory;
```

Notice that the record-type inventory contains nested variant parts. Also, notice that we have defined two different arrays—stockitem and backorder—that contain records of type inventory. The former (stockitem) will contain the inventory records as entered into the computer; backorder will contain information only for those items that are back ordered (i.e., for which there is a shortage).

The overall strategy will consist of the following two steps:

1. Read all of the input data for each record and adjust the inventory level accordingly.

2. After all of the records have been read into the computer and the inventory levels adjusted accordingly, write out the records showing the adjusted inventory levels.

Rather than specify the number of records in advance, as we did with the billing system shown in Example 10.21, let us continue to enter new records until a value of zero is entered for the stock number. Thus, the main action block will appear as follows.

```
BEGIN
    writeln('I N V E N T O R Y   C O N T R O L   S Y S T E M');
    writeln;
    writeln('          D A T A   I N P U T');
    writeln;
    writeln('  When finished, enter 0 for the stock number');
    writeln;
    i := 0;
    REPEAT
        i := succ(i);
        readinput;
    UNTIL stockitem [i].stockno = 0;
    n := pred(i);
    IF n > 0 THEN writeoutput
END.
```

Note that i is an integer record counter whose value ranges from 0 to n, where n is the total number of records entered. (The last value of i will be assigned to n.) Also, readinput and writeoutput are procedures that read data into the computer, adjust the inventory level and write the adjusted data out of the computer, respectively.

The procedure readinput will be interactive, with a number of appropriate conversational prompts. The programming is straightforward, though perhaps a bit long. Thus, we have

```
PROCEDURE readinput;
(* Enter input data for one record *)
VAR count : 1..80;
BEGIN
    WITH stockitem [i] DO
        BEGIN
            writeln;
            write('Stock no.: ');
            readln(stockno);
            IF stockno > 0 THEN
                BEGIN
                    write('Item type (s/t): ');
                    readln(designator);
                    IF (designator = 's') OR (designator = 'S')
                        THEN BEGIN (* stereo *)
                                itemtype := stereo;
                                write('Power level: ');
                                readln(power)
                            END
```

(*Program continues on next page*)

```
                    ELSE BEGIN (* tv *)
                            itemtype := tv;
                            write('Portable TV? (y/n) ');
                            readln(designator);
                            IF (designator = 'y') OR (designator = 'Y')
                               THEN BEGIN
                                        size := portable;
                                        write('Weight: ');
                                        readln(weight);
                                        write('Voltage: ');
                                        readln(voltage)
                                    END
                               ELSE size := stationary;
                            write('Tube size: ');
                            readln(tubesize);
                            write('Color: (y/n) ');
                            readln(color)
                        END;
                write('Supplier: ');
                count := 1;
                REPEAT
                   read(supplier [count]);
                   count := succ(count)
                UNTIL eoln;
                write('Original inventory level:  ');
                readln(quantity);
                write('Change in inventory level: ');
                readln(change);
                quantity := quantity + change;
                IF quantity < 0 THEN
                   BEGIN
                       backorder [i] := stockitem [i];
                       backorder [i].quantity := abs(quantity);
                       quantity := 0
                   END
            END   (* IF stockno > 0 *)
      END   (* WITH stockitem [i] *)
   END;   (* readinput *)
```

In this procedure designator is a global char-type variable that identifies the type of input, and change is a global integer-type variable that represents the change in the inventory level. Notice that change can take on values that are either positive or negative, depending on whether the inventory is being replenished or depleted. Also, notice that this procedure is written to accommodate only one record at a time (since it is not known in advance how many records will be entered into the computer).

Another noteworthy feature of readinput is the fact that the inventory is updated as soon as it has been entered. If the adjusted inventory level is negative, then the information is transferred from stockitem [i] to backorder [i], and the shortage is stored as a positive value. The use of backorder [i] is not essential and in fact adds little to the program except to suggest how such pairs of corresponding records might be maintained in a more comprehensive and realistic program (more about this later).

Now let us consider the procedure writeoutput. This procedure need not be interactive, and it can process all n records at one time. Thus, we can write

```
PROCEDURE writeoutput;
(* Write output data for all records *)
BEGIN
   writeln('I N V E N T O R Y   C O N T R O L   S Y S T E M');
   writeln;
   writeln('     C U R R E N T   I N V E N T O R Y');
   writeln;
   FOR i := 1 TO n DO
      WITH stockitem [i] DO
         BEGIN
            writeln;
            writeln('Stock no.: ',stockno:5);
            CASE itemtype OF
               stereo : writeln('Stereo: ',power:4,' watts');
                  tv : BEGIN
                          IF size = portable
                             THEN write('Portable ');
                          IF (color = 'y') OR (color = 'Y')
                             THEN write('Color TV')
                             ELSE write('B & W TV');
                          writeln('   ',tubesize:2,'-inch tube');
                          IF size = portable THEN
                             BEGIN
                                write('Weight: ',weight:3,' pounds    ');
                                writeln('Voltage: ',voltage:3,' volts')
                             END
                       END   (* tv *)
            END;   (* CASE itemtype *)
            writeln('Supplier: ',supplier);
            IF quantity > 0
               THEN writeln('Present inventory: ',quantity:3)
               ELSE writeln('Quantity backordered: ', backorder [i].quantity:3);
            writeln
         END   (* WITH stockitem [i] *)
END;   (* writeoutput *)
```

Note that one field of backorder [i] is written out in the event that the adjusted inventory indicates a shortage. Here is the entire Pascal program.

```
PROGRAM inventory1(input,output);

(* THIS PROGRAM ILLUSTRATES THE USE OF VARIANT RECORDS
                IN A SIMPLE INVENTORY CONTROL SYSTEM *)

TYPE item = (stereo,tv);
     style = (portable,stationary);
     name = PACKED ARRAY [1..80] OF char;
     inventory = RECORD
                    stockno : 0..20000;
                    supplier : name;
                    quantity : integer;
                    CASE itemtype : item OF
                       stereo : (power : 1..1000);
                          tv : (tubesize : 1..25;
                                color : char;
                                CASE size : style OF
                                   portable : (weight : 1..100;
                                               voltage : 1..220);
                                   stationary : ())
                 END;
```

*(Program continues on next page)*

```
VAR stockitem,backorder : ARRAY [1..100] OF inventory;
    designator : char;
    i,n,change : integer;

PROCEDURE readinput;
(* Read input data for one record *)
VAR count : 1..80;
BEGIN
   WITH stockitem [i] DO
      BEGIN
         writeln;
         write('Stock no.: ');
         readln(stockno);
         IF stockno > 0 THEN
            BEGIN
               write('Item type (s/t): ');
               readln(designator);
               IF (designator = 's') OR (designator = 'S')
                  THEN BEGIN (* stereo *)
                          itemtype := stereo;
                          write('Power level: ');
                          readln(power)
                       END
                  ELSE BEGIN (* tv *)
                          itemtype := tv;
                          write('Portable TV? (y/n) ');
                          readln(designator);
                          IF (designator = 'y') OR (designator = 'Y')
                             THEN BEGIN
                                     size := portable;
                                     write('Weight: ');
                                     readln(weight);
                                     write('Voltage: ');
                                     readln(voltage)
                                  END
                             ELSE size := stationary;
                          write('Tube size: ');
                          readln(tubesize);
                          write('Color: (y/n) ');
                          readln(color)
                       END;
               write('Supplier: ');
               count := 1;
               REPEAT
                  read(supplier [count]);
                  count := succ(count)
               UNTIL eoln;
               write('Original inventory level: ');
               readln(quantity);
               write('Change in inventory level: ');
               readln(change);
               quantity := quantity + change;
               IF quantity < 0 THEN
                  BEGIN
                     backorder [i] := stockitem [i];
                     backorder [i].quantity := abs(quantity);
                     quantity := 0
                  END
            END   (* IF stockno > 0 *)
      END   (* WITH stockitem [i] *)
END;   (* readinput *)
```

*(Program continues on next page)*

```
PROCEDURE writeoutput;
(* Write output data for all records *)
BEGIN
   writeln('I N V E N T O R Y   C O N T R O L   S Y S T E M');
   writeln;
   writeln('      C U R R E N T   I N V E N T O R Y');
   writeln;
   FOR i := 1 TO n DO
      WITH stockitem [i] DO
         BEGIN
            writeln;
            writeln('Stock no.: ',stockno:5);
            CASE itemtype OF
               stereo : writeln('Stereo: ',power:4,' watts');
                  tv : BEGIN
                          IF size = portable
                             THEN write('Portable ');
                          IF (color = 'y') OR (color = 'Y')
                             THEN write('Color TV')
                             ELSE write('B & W TV');
                          writeln('   ',tubesize:2,'-inch tube');
                          IF size = portable THEN
                             BEGIN
                                write('Weight: ',weight:3,' pounds   ');
                                writeln('Voltage: ',voltage:3,' volts')
                             END
                       END   (* tv *)
            END;   (* CASE itemtype *)
            writeln('Supplier: ',supplier);
            IF quantity > 0
               THEN writeln('Present inventory: ',quantity:3)
               ELSE writeln('Quantity backordered: ', backorder [i].quantity:3);
            writeln
         END   (* WITH stockitem [i] *)
END;   (* writeoutput *)

BEGIN   (* main action statements *)
   writeln('I N V E N T O R Y   C O N T R O L   S Y S T E M');
   writeln;
   writeln('            D A T A   I N P U T');
   writeln;
   writeln('  When finished, enter 0 for the stock number');
   writeln;
   i := 0;
   (* read input records *)
   REPEAT
      i := succ(i);
      readinput;
   UNTIL stockitem [i].stockno = 0;
   n := pred(i);
   (* write output records *)
   IF n > 0 THEN writeoutput
END.
```

Now suppose that the program is used to process three illustrative records. The input dialogue would appear as follows.

```
INVENTORY   CONTROL   SYSTEM

        DATA   INPUT

  When finished, enter 0 for the stock number

Stock no.: 12417
Item type (s/t): s
Power level: 150
Supplier: House of Audio
Original inventory level:  200
Change in inventory level: -12


Stock no.: 912
Item type (s/t): t
Portable TV? (y/n) n
Tube size: 23
Colour: (y/n) y
Supplier: Ace Radio & TV
Original inventory level: 8
Change in inventory level: 72


Stock no.: 644
Item type (s/t): t
Portable TV? (y/n) y
Weight: 25
Voltage: 110
Tube size: 12
Color: (y/n) n
Supplier: Crazy Harry's
Original inventory level: 12
Change in inventory level: -15


Stock no.: 0
```

In the above dialogue, the computer supplies the prompts and the user then enters the requested information (the user's responses are underlined). Notice that the input dialogue continues until a value of 0 is entered for the stock number.

The following output is generated by the program in response to the preceding input data.

```
INVENTORY   CONTROL   SYSTEM

        CURRENT   INVENTORY

Stock no.: 12417
Stereo:  150 watts
Supplier: House of Audio
Present inventory: 188

Stock no.:  912
Color TV   23-inch tube
Supplier: Ace Radio & TV
Present inventory:  80

Stock no.:  644
Portable B & W TV   12-inch tube
Weight:  25 pounds    Voltage: 110 volts
Supplier: Crazy Harry's
Quantity backordered:   3
```

The reader is again reminded that this program, like the customer billing system presented in Example 10.21, is oversimplified in the sense that it does not save the inventory records permanently within a data file. All realistic inventory control systems do, in fact, include such permanent storage capabilities. Individual records can then be retrieved from the file, modified, written out, saved, etc. We will see how this can be accomplished in the next chapter. It should be clear that the present example is intended only to show how record-type data can be processed in Pascal.

# Review Questions

**10.1**   What is the principal difference between a record and an array?

**10.2**   What is meant by a field? What is the relationship between a field and a record?

**10.3**   Summarize the rules for defining a record type.

**10.4**   Summarize the rules for defining a record-type variable. Compare with your answer to the previous problem.

**10.5**   Which data types can be associated with the individual data items within a field?

**10.6**   For what type of application would it be desirable for a record element to be an array? Explain.

**10.7**   For what type of application would it be desirable for an array element to be a record? Explain and compare with your answer to the previous problem.

**10.8**   How can a record be packed? What are the advantages and disadvantages to utilizing packed records?

**10.9**   Can two different records utilize the same field name? Explain.

**10.10**  Can an entire record be assigned to another record? What restrictions apply to this type of an assignment?

**10.11**  In what ways can individual record elements be utilized within a Pascal program?

**10.12**  What is a field designator? How is a field designator written? How is it used?

**10.13**  Suppose an individual record element is a structured data item. How can one element of that data item be accessed?

**10.14**  What is the purpose of the WITH structure?

**10.15**  Summarize the rules for using the WITH structure. Can multiple record names be included in a single WITH structure?

**10.16** Suppose that a single WITH statement includes several record-type variables with a common field name. Which record will be accessed when a field is accessed within the structure? How can a field having the same name but belonging to another record be accessed?

**10.17** Cite several advantages to using the WITH structure wherever it is appropriate to do so.

**10.18** What is meant by the variant part of a record? How does the variant part differ from the fixed part?

**10.19** Must each record have a variant part? Must it have a fixed part? Can a record have more than one variant part?

**10.20** Summarize the rules for defining a record having both a fixed part and a variant part. Contrast the variant definition with the CASE structure described in Chap. 6.

**10.21** If a record includes a variant part, where must the variant part be located?

**10.22** What is a tag field? What is its purpose?

**10.23** What data types can be associated with a tag field?

**10.24** Must a tag field be present in every variant record? Explain.

**10.25** How can individual elements within the variant part of a record be accessed? What restrictions apply to the access of such variant fields?

**10.26** Can the WITH structure be used with variant-type records?

**10.27** How can an empty variant field list be defined? Why might this be a desirable thing to do?

**10.28** How can variant parts be nested within a single record?

**10.29** Why is a change of variant not allowed within a WITH structure if a variant field name appears in the WITH statement?

**10.30** What restrictions must be observed when a variant field is passed to a procedure or function as an actual variable parameter?

**10.31** Can a tag-field identifier be passed to a procedure or function as an actual variable parameter? Explain.

**10.32** Comment on the use of variants by a beginning programmer.

# Solved Problems

**10.33** Several illustrative record declarations are shown below.

(*a*)  VAR sample : RECORD
                          first  : 1..100:
                          second : real;
                          third  : boolean
                    END;

(*b*)  TYPE demo = RECORD
                          first  : 1..100:
                          second : real;
                          third  : boolean
                    END;
        VAR sample1,sample2 : demo;

(*c*)  TYPE line = PACKED ARRAY [1..80] OF char;
              personal = RECORD
                            name,street,city : line
                          END;
        VAR employee : ARRAY [1..500] OF personal;

(*d*)  TYPE color = (red,green,blue);
              sample = PACKED RECORD
                          first  : color;
                          second : 1..132;
                          third  : char
                        END;
        VAR trial : sample;

(*e*)  TYPE color = (red,green,blue);
              sample = RECORD
                          CASE select : color OF
                            red   : (first  : 100..199;
                                      second : 200..299);
                            green : (third  : 300..399);
                            blue  : ()
                        END;
        VAR demo : ARRAY [1..500] OF sample;

   Notice that sample does not include a fixed part. Also, note the empty variant fieldlist corresponding to case label blue.

(*f*)  TYPE color   = (red,green,blue);
              texture = (coarse,fine);
              sample  = PACKED RECORD
                          first  : color;
                          second : 1..132;
                          CASE color OF
                            red   : (first  : 100..199;
                                      second : 200..299);
                            green : ();
                            blue  : (CASE texture OF
                                      coarse : (third : 300..399);
                                      fine   : ())
                        END;
        VAR demo1,demo2 : ARRAY [1..99] OF sample;

   Notice that the nested variants in sample do not include tag-field identifiers.

**10.34** The following skeletal outlines illustrate the use of records and/or record elements in typical programming situations.

(*a*)
```
PROGRAM sample(input,output);
TYPE line = PACKED ARRAY [1..80] OF char;
     personal = RECORD
                     name,street,city : line
                END;
VAR employee : personal;
BEGIN
   .
   .
   (* enter input data *)
   .

   .
   writeln(employee.name);
   writeln(employee.street);
   writeln(employee.city);
   .
   .
END.
```

(*b*)
```
PROGRAM sample(input,output);
TYPE line = PACKED ARRAY [1..80] OF char;
     personal = RECORD
                     name,street,city : line
                END;
VAR employee : ARRAY [1..500] OF personal;
    count : 1..500;
BEGIN
   .
   .
   (* enter input data *)
   .

   .
   FOR count := 1 TO 500 DO
      BEGIN
         writeln(employee [count].name);
         writeln(employee [count].street);
         writeln(employee [count].city)
      END;
   .
   .
END.
```

(*c*)
```
PROGRAM sample(input,output);
TYPE line = PACKED ARRAY [1..80] OF char;
     personal = RECORD
                     name,street,city : line
                END;
VAR employee : ARRAY [1..500] OF personal;
    count,total : 1..500;
BEGIN
   .
   .
   (* enter input data *)
   .

   .
   FOR count := 1 TO total DO
      WITH employee [count] DO
```

(*Program continues on next page*)

```
                        BEGIN
                            writeln(employee [count].name);
                            writeln(employee [count].street);
                            writeln(employee [count].city)
                        END;
            .
            .
            .
    END.
```

(d)   PROGRAM sample(input,output);
```
      TYPE line = PACKED ARRAY [1..80] OF char;
           personal = RECORD
                            name,street,city : line
                         END;
      VAR customer,employee : ARRAY [1..500] OF personal;
          i,j,total : 1..500;
      BEGIN
          .
          .
          (* enter input data *)
          .
          .
          FOR i := 1 TO total DO
              WITH customer [i] DO
                  FOR j := 1 TO total DO
                      IF name = employee [j].name THEN
                          BEGIN
                              writeln(name);
                              writeln(street);
                              writeln(city)
                          END;
          .
          .
      END.
```

Notice that the record elements which are written out are a part of customer [i], not employee [j].

(e)   PROGRAM sample(input,output);
```
      TYPE status = (single,married,divorced,widowed);
           line = PACKED ARRAY [1..80] OF char;
           background = RECORD
                            name,address : line;
                            employeeno : 1..9999;
                            CASE maritalstatus : status OF
                                single : ();
                                married : (children : 0..10);
                                divorced,widowed :
                                            (children : 0..10;
                                             remarried : boolean)
                         END;
      VAR employees : ARRAY [1..100] OF background;
          count,total : 1..100;
```

*(Program continues on next page)*

```
        BEGIN
           .
           .
           (* enter input data *)
           .
           .

        FOR count := 1 TO total DO
           WITH employees [count] DO
              BEGIN
                 writeln(name);
                 writeln(address);
                 writeln(employeeno:4);
                 IF maritalstatus <> single THEN writeln(children:2);
                 IF ((maritalstatus = divorced) OR
                      (maritalstatus = widowed)) AND
                      (remarried = true) THEN maritalstatus = married
              END;
           .
           .

     END.
```

# Supplementary Problems

**10.35** The following skeletal outlines illustrate several different situations involving the use of records and/or record elements. Some are written incorrectly. Identify all errors.

(a)
```
    CONST c1 = 12;
          c2 = 31;
          c3 = 2000;
    VAR date : RECORD
                  month : 1..c1;
                  day   : 1..c2;
                  year  : 0..c3
               END;
```

(b)
```
    TYPE months = (jan,feb,mar,apr,may,jun,
                             jul,aug,sep,oct,nov,dec);
         days   = (sun,mon,tue,wed,thu,fri,sat);
         date   = RECORD
                     name : days;
                     month : months;
                     day : 1..31;
                     year : 0..maxint
                  END;
    VAR yesterday,today : date;
```

(c)
```
    TYPE item = RECORD
                   sales : real;
                   cost : real;
                   profit : real;
                   bonus : boolean
    VAR list : ARRAY [1..1000] OF sales;
```

(*d*)  TYPE line = PACKED ARRAY [1..80] OF char;
       nameandaddress = RECORD
                        name,street,city : line
                 END;
          personal = RECORD
                    description : nameandaddress;
                    custno : 1..9999;
                    status : char;
                    balance : real
              END;
VAR customer : ARRAY [1..10000] OF personal;

(*e*)  PROGRAM sample(input,output);
TYPE date = RECORD
              month : 1..12;
              day : 1..31;
              year : 1900..2100
         END;
VAR birthday,today : date;
   count : 0..maxint;
BEGIN
   .
   .
   WITH today DO readln(month,day,year);
   .
   .
   count := 0;
   REPEAT
     WITH birthday DO
       readln(month,day,year);
     IF birthday = today THEN count := succ(count);
   UNTIL year = 0;
   writeln(count);
   .
   .
END.

(*f*)  PROGRAM sample(input,output);
TYPE line = PACKED ARRAY [1..80] OF char;
   date = PACKED RECORD
            month : 1..12;
            day : 1..31;
            year : 1900..2100
       END;
VAR total,count : 1..maxint;
   today : date;
   birthday : RECORD
           name : line;
           birthdate : date
       END;

*(Program continues on next page)*

```
        BEGIN
          .
          .
          readln(total);
          WITH today DO readln(month,day,year);
          .

          .
          FOR count := 1 TO total DO
             WITH birthday DO
                BEGIN
                   readln(name);
                   birthdate := today
                END;
          .
          .
        END.
```

(g)  ```
     TYPE item = (stereo,tv);
          name = PACKED ARRAY [1..80] OF char;
          inventory = RECORD
                          stockno : 1..20000;
                          supplier : name;
                          CASE item OF
                             stereo : (power : 1..1000);
                                 tv : (tubesize : 1..25;color : char);
                          quantity : integer
                      END;
     VAR stockitem,backorder : inventory;
     ```

(h)  ```
     PROGRAM sample(input,output);
     TYPE status = (single,married,divorced,widowed);
          background = RECORD
                          CASE maritalstatus : status OF
                             single : ();
                             married : (children : 0..10);
                             divorced,widowed :
                                     (children : 0..10;remarried : boolean)
                      END;
     VAR employees : ARRAY [1..100] OF background;
     BEGIN
        .

        .
        maritalstatus := single;
        writeln(divorced.children);
        .

        .
     END.
     ```

(i)  ```
     PROGRAM sample(input,output);
     TYPE status = (single,married,divorced,widowed);
          background = RECORD
                          CASE maritalstatus : status OF
                             single : ();
                             married : (children : 0..10);
                             divorced,widowed :
                                     (children : 0..10;remarried : boolean)
                      END;
     VAR employees : ARRAY [1..100] OF background;
              i : 1..100;
     ```

(*Program continues on next page*)
     ```

```
      PROCEDURE setup(VAR test : status);
      BEGIN
         .
         .
         IF test = widowed THEN test := single
                           ELSE test := succ(test);
         .
         .
      END;

      BEGIN   (* main action statements *)
         FOR i := 1 TO 100 DO
            WITH employees [i] DO
               BEGIN
                  .
                  .
                  setup(maritalstatus);
                  .
                  .
               END
      END.
```

# Programming Problems

**10.36** Modify the customer billing program given in Example 10.21 so that any of the following reports can be written out:

(a)   Status of all customers (now generated by the program)

(b)   Status of overdue and delinquent customers only

(c)   Status of delinquent customers only

Include a provision for generating a menu when the program is executed, from which the user may choose which report will be generated. Have the program return to the menu after printing each report, thus allowing for the possibility of generating several different reports.

**10.37** Modify the inventory control program given in Example 10.28 so that any of the following reports can be written out:

(a)   Complete inventory list (now generated by the program)

(b)   List of all backordered items

(c)   List of all stereos now in stock

(d)   List of all television sets now in stock

(e)   List of all color television sets now in stock

(f)   List of all black-and-white television sets now in stock

(g)   List of all portable television sets now in stock

Begin by generating a menu when the program is executed, allowing the user to select a particular report. Have the program return to this menu after generating each report, so that multiple reports can be generated if desired.

**10.38** Rewrite each of the following Pascal programs so that it makes use of a record-type data structure.

(a)   The depreciation program presented in Examples 6.17 and 7.12

(b)   The program given in Example 8.9, for calculating the number of days between two dates

(c)   The program for reading and writing a list of names and addresses, presented in Example 9.7

**10.39**  Modify the Pascal program given in Example 9.7 so that it reads several different names and addresses into the computer, rearranges them in alphabetical order and then writes out the alphabetized list. Include a record-type data structure within the program.

**10.40**  Modify the pig latin generator presented in Example 9.27 so that it will accept multiple lines of text. Represent each line of text with a separate record. Include the following three fields within each record:

1.  The original line of text
2.  The number of words within the line
3.  The modified line of text (i.e., the pig latin equivalent of the original text)

Include the enhancements described in Prob. 9.50 (i.e., provisions for punctuation marks, uppercase letters and double-letter sounds).

**10.41**  For each of the following programming problems, write a complete Pascal program that makes use of a record-type data structure.

(a)  The student exam score averaging problem described in Prob. 9.52(a).

(b)  The more comprehensive version of the student exam score averaging problem described in Prob. 9.52(d).

(c)  The problem that matches the names of countries with their corresponding capitals (see Prob. 9.56).

(d)  The text encoding-decoding problem as described in Prob. 9.59, but extended to accommodate multiple lines of text.

**10.42**  Write a complete Pascal program that will accept the following information for each team in a baseball or football league:

1.  Team name, including the city (e.g., Pittsburgh Steelers)
2.  Number of wins
3.  Number of losses

For a baseball team, add the following information:

1.  Number of hits (season total)
2.  Number of runs
3.  Number of errors
4.  Number of extra-inning games

Similarly, add the following information for a football team:

1.  Number of ties
2.  Number of touchdowns
3.  Number of field goals
4.  Total yards gained (season total)
5.  Total yards given up to opponents

Enter this information for all of the teams in the league. Then reorder and print the list of teams according to their won-lost records, using the reordering technique described in Example 9.8.

Be sure to utilize a record-type data structure that includes a fixed part and a variant part. These records should be maintained in an array.

Test the program using a current set of team statistics. (Ideally, the program should be tested using both baseball and football statistics.)

# Chapter 11

# Files

We now turn our attention to another important structured data type—the file. A *file*, like an array, is a collection of data items that are all of the same type. Unlike an array, however, a file can be stored on an auxiliary storage device (e.g., a magnetic tape or a disk). Thus the file structure allows us to store information permanently and access that information whenever necessary. Many important applications require this capability.

## 11.1 PRELIMINARIES

In general, there are two kinds of files that can be generated and accessed by a computer program: permanent files and temporary files. *Permanent files* are maintained on an auxiliary memory device and therefore preserved after the program has completed its execution. The contents of such files (i.e., the individual file components) can be accessed and/or modified, either by the program that created the file or some other program, at any time. In Pascal, permanent files are referred to as *external files*.

*Temporary files*, on the other hand, are stored within the computer's main memory. A temporary file is lost as soon as the the program that created the file has completed its execution. Thus, temporary files are less useful (and less common) than permanent files. Temporary files are referred to as *internal files* in Pascal.

All files, whether permanent or temporary, can be organized in one of two different ways, sequential and random (the latter is also known as a *direct-access* file, which is actually a more descriptive name). In a *sequential file* all of the file components are stored sequentially, one after the other. In order to access a particular component it is necessary to start at the beginning and search through the entire file until the desired component has been found. This type of access can be very slow, particularly if the file is large. Sequential files are relatively easy to create, however, and they are the only kind of file that can be used with certain types of storage media (e.g., magnetic tape).

In a *random-access file* any component can be accessed directly, without proceeding through the entire file from the beginning. Files of this type offer much faster access to individual file components than sequential files, though they are more difficult to create and maintain.

Standard ISO Pascal supports only sequential files, though some implementations of the language also support random access files. We will discuss only (standard) sequential files in this book.

## 11.2 DEFINING A FILE

The simplest way to define a file is to include the file definition as part of a file-type variable declaration. The general form of such a declaration is

```
VAR file name : FILE OF type
```

where *file name* is an identifier that represents the name of the file and *type* refers to the data type of the individual file components. These components must all be of the same type. They can be of any type, simple or structured, except that they cannot be file-type data. Thus, a file cannot be embedded within another file.

270

**EXAMPLE 11.1**

Shown below is a simple file definition, in which each of the file components is a simple, char-type data item.

```
VAR symbols : FILE OF char;
```

Note that the file name is symbols.

**EXAMPLE 11.2**

Now consider a file definition in which each component is a two-dimensional real array.

```
TYPE table = ARRAY [1..50,1..20] OF real;
VAR data : FILE OF table;
```

In this case, the file name is data.

**EXAMPLE 11.3**

Here is an example of a file definition in which the file components are records.

```
TYPE status = (current,overdue,delinquent);
     account = RECORD
                    custname : PACKED ARRAY [1..80] OF char;
                    custno : 1..9999;
                    custtype : status;
                    custbalance : real
               END;
VAR customers : FILE OF account;
```

Notice that each record within the file customers contains a char-type packed array (i.e., a string variable), an integer quantity, an enumerated data type and a real quantity.

Now consider a more general approach to the definition of files in which we first define a file type and then declare one or more variables to be of this type. (We have previously used this approach to define arrays and records.) The general form of this kind of file definition is

```
TYPE name = FILE OF type
```

where *type* now refers to the data type of each file component. This data type must have been defined previously.

**EXAMPLE 11.4**

Here is an example of a file definition in which two different files have the same record-type components.

```
TYPE status = (current,overdue,delinquent);
     account = RECORD
                    custname : PACKED ARRAY [1..80] OF char;
                    custno : 1..9999;
                    custtype : status;
                    custbalance : real
               END;
     customers = FILE OF account;
VAR oldcustomers,newcustomers : customers;
```

Thus, oldcustomers and newcustomers are both files of type customers. The components of each file are records of type account, as defined above.

Notice that the length of a file is never specified as a part of the file definition. This situation differs from that of other structured data types, where the number of components is either explicitly (in the case of arrays) or implicitly (as with records) specified within the data type definition. As a rule, the maximum length of a file is determined only by the physical capacity of the medium on which it is stored.

External files must be passed to a Pascal program as parameters. This is accomplished by including the names of the external files in the program header, enclosed in parentheses, and, if there are two or more files, separated by commas. This parameter specification is in addition to the required file definitions, which must be included within the main program block.

**EXAMPLE 11.5**

Suppose that a Pascal program makes use of the external file customers, described in Example 11.3. A skeletal outline of this program is shown below.

```
PROGRAM sample(customers);
    .
    .
    .
TYPE status = (current,overdue,delinquent);
     account = RECORD
                    custname : PACKED ARRAY [1..80] OF char;
                    custno : 1..9999;
                    custtype : status;
                    custbalance : real
               END;
VAR customers : FILE OF account;
    .
    .
    .
BEGIN    (* main action statements *)
    .
    .
    (* process the records within customers *)
    .
    .
    .
END.
```

Notice that the file name customers is included in the program header, enclosed in parentheses. This is followed by the file definition, which appears within the declaration part of the main block.

Pascal includes two standard (predeclared) external files, input and output, which direct character-type information from an input device and to an output device, respectively. These file names must be included in the program header if they will be accessed by a program. Since they are standard language features, however, they need not be explicitly defined within the program. In fact, we have been making use of these standard files throughout this book. We will say more about the predeclared input and output files in Sec. 11.8.

**EXAMPLE 11.6**

Now suppose that the Pascal program outlined in Example 11.5 is modified to make use of the standard files input and output. An appropriate program outline is shown below.

```
PROGRAM sample(input,output,customers);
    .
    .
    .
TYPE status = (current,overdue,delinquent);
     account = RECORD
                    custname : PACKED ARRAY [1..80] OF char;
                    custno : 1..9999;
                    custtype : status;
                    custbalance : real
               END;
```

(*Program continues on next page*)

```
        VAR customers : FILE OF account;
          .
          .
        BEGIN   (* main action statements *)
          .
          .
        (* process the records within customers *)
          .
          .
      END.
```

This outline is identical to that shown in Example 11.5 except for the inclusion of the file names input and output as parameters in the program header. Notice that input and output are not defined explicitly within the program.

It should be clear that input and output need not always appear together in the program header. Only those files that are actually required must be specified. Thus if a program generates output data but does not require any input data, the program header should include the file name output but not the file name input.

## 11.3   CREATING A FILE

We now turn our attention to the creation of a file in Pascal. First, however, we must see how to access individual data items within a file. This is accomplished by means of a *file buffer*, which allows the value (or values) associated with a single file component to be transferred between the file and its host program.

Actually, the file buffer is a special type of variable that is automatically defined whenever the corresponding file is defined. The file buffer will have the same name as the file, but will have a vertical arrow added at the end. Thus, if file name represents the name of a file, then the corresponding file buffer will be called file name↑. The file buffer will be of the same type as the file components.

### EXAMPLE 11.7

Suppose that a Pascal program includes the definition of a file called data. Then the corresponding file buffer will be called data↑. If the components of data are records, then data↑ will represent one such record.

When creating a file, the basic idea is to assign the data items that comprise one file component to the file buffer, and then transfer these values from the file buffer to the file itself. The entire file is created by repeating this procedure for each of the file components.

The first step in creating a file is to prepare the file for writing. This is accomplished with the standard procedure rewrite. Thus, we begin by writing

```
    rewrite(file name);
```

If the specified file is being created for the first time, then the rewrite statement simply establishes the beginning of the file. If a file already exists with the given name, however, then the effect of the rewrite statement is to *erase all of the information within the existing file* and then establish the beginning of the new file.

The data items that comprise a single file component are assigned to the file buffer in the same manner that any data items are assigned to their corresponding variables. If the components consist of simple-type data items, then each assignment to the file buffer will consist of a single value. These values must, of course, be compatible with the file-buffer type. (Usually, the data items will be of the same type as the file buffer.)

If the file consists of structured-type components (e.g., arrays or records), the file buffer will be a corresponding structured-type variable. Hence the buffer can be assigned the value of a corresponding structured-type variable, or the individual data items can be assigned separately. In the latter case, the individual assignments to the buffer components must follow the normal rules for assigning data items to structured data types.

After the necessary data items have been assigned to the file buffer, this information is transferred to the file by means of the standard procedure put. Thus, we can write

```
file name↑ := . . . ;
put(file name);
```

If these two statements are executed repeatedly, then a sequence of data items will be written to the file. These data items will be stored within the file in the same order as they are written. In other words, the data items associated with the current component will be appended to the end of the file, following the data items (component values) that were written earlier.

**EXAMPLE 11.8**

Here is a simple Pascal program that creates a file called data. This file will contain simple-type components (positive real numbers).

```
PROGRAM createfile1(input,output,data);
VAR data : FILE OF real;
    item : real;
    count,total : 1..maxint;
BEGIN
   write('How many values will be entered? ');
   readln(total);
   rewrite(data);
   FOR count := 1 TO total DO
      BEGIN
         readln(item);
         data↑ := item;
         put(data)
      END
END.
```

Note that this program causes data to be entered from the input device (e.g., the keyboard) and then writes this data onto the newly created file data.

The program begins by asking the user how many values (i.e., how many file components) will be entered. Once this value has been read into the computer the new file is initialized, via the rewrite statement. The program then employs a FOR—TO loop to read the value of each file component from the input device and then write it to the file.

Note that this program requires that the user know in advance how many data items (i.e., how many file components) will be added to the file. This is somewhat impractical, particularly if the file is relatively long. A better approach will be presented in the next example.

**EXAMPLE 11.9**

Here is another version of the program presented in Example 11.8. This program represents an improvement over the earlier version in the sense that the number of data items need not be known in advance. The user simply continues to enter data until a negative value is detected, which signifies the end of the data. (Note that this scheme imposes the restriction that the actual file components be nonnegative.)

```
PROGRAM createfile2(input,data);
VAR data : FILE OF real;
    item : real;
BEGIN
   rewrite(data);
   readln(item);
   WHILE item >= 0 DO
      BEGIN
         data↑ := item;
         put(data);
         readln(item)
      END
END.
```

Observe that the program header includes the file parameters input and data, but not output. This program does not require the use of the standard file output because there are no prompts written out by the program. (Compare with the program shown in Example 11.8, which generates a prompt for the total number of data items.)

If the file components are structured, it may be desirable to enter the individual data items for each component by means of a procedure. In such cases, a structured variable of the same type as the file buffer should be passed to the procedure as an actual parameter. The corresponding formal parameter will be a variable parameter, also of the same type as the file buffer. After the procedure has been accessed the data represented by the formal parameter should be assigned to the file buffer, allowing the file component to be written to the file. The details are illustrated in the following example.

**EXAMPLE 11.10**

**Creating a File for a Customer Billing System.** Now consider a program that will create a file comprised of customer billing records, as defined in Example 11.5. The program declarations will appear as follows.

```
TYPE status = (current,overdue,delinquent);
     account = RECORD
                   custname : PACKED ARRAY [1..80] OF char;
                   custno : 1..9999;
                   custtype : status;
                   custbalance : real
               END;
VAR customeracct : account;
    customers : FILE OF account;
    count : 0..80;
```

These declarations are the same as the declarations shown in Example 11.5 except for the declaration of the additional record-type variable customeracct, which will be used as a parameter, and the integer-type variable count.

Suppose we use a procedure to enter the individual data items for each file component (in this case, for each record). The procedure will read in the values for the customer name, the customer number and the customer balance. The customer type (status) can then be assigned, depending on the magnitude of the customer's balance (or whatever other criteria may be desired).

The input procedure can be written as

```
PROCEDURE readinput(VAR info : account);
(* Enter input data for one record *)
BEGIN
   WITH info DO
      BEGIN
         write('Customer number: ');
         readln(custno);
         IF custno <> 9999 THEN
            BEGIN
               write('Name: ');
               count := 0;
               WHILE NOT eoln DO
                  BEGIN
                     count := count + 1;
                     read(custname[count])
                  END;
               writeln;
               write('Current balance: ');
               readln(custbalance);
               writeln;
               custtype := current
            END
      END   (* WITH info *)
END;   (* readinput *)
```

Note that info is a formal parameter of type account. Thus, info is a record-type variable. Also, notice that the procedure first reads the customer number and then continues only if the customer number is not equal to 9999. Thus, a customer number of 9999 provides a convenient stopping criterion.

The main part of the program is quite simple. We merely initialize the new file (customers), read the first record and then repeat the following steps, as long as the customer number is not equal to 9999:

1. Assign the most recent set of data (the most recent record) to the file buffer.

2. Write the file buffer (the most recent record) to the file.

3. Read a new record.

Here is the complete program.

```
PROGRAM createfile3(input,output,customers);

(* THIS PROGRAM CREATES A FILE OF CUSTOMER RECORDS *)

TYPE status = (current,overdue,delinquent);
     account = RECORD
                      custname : PACKED ARRAY [1..80] OF char;
                      custno : 1..9999;
                      custtype : status;
                      custbalance : real
               END;
VAR customeracct : account;
    customers : FILE OF account;
    count : 0..80;

PROCEDURE readinput(VAR info : account);
(* Enter input data for one record *)
BEGIN
   WITH info DO
     BEGIN
        write('Customer number: ');
        readln(custno);
        IF custno <> 9999 THEN
           BEGIN
              write('Name: ');
              count := 0;
              WHILE NOT eoln DO
                 BEGIN
                    count := count + 1;
                    read(custname[count])
                 END;
              writeln;
              write('Current balance: ');
              readln(custbalance);
              writeln;
              custtype := current
           END
     END   (* WITH info *)
END;   (* readinput *)

BEGIN   (* main action statements *)
   rewrite(customers);
   readinput(customeracct);
   WHILE customeracct.custno < 9999 DO
      BEGIN
         customers↑ := customeracct;
         put(customers);
         readinput(customeracct)
      END
END.
```

## 11.4  MORE ABOUT THE WRITE STATEMENT

From the preceding examples we see that the statements

```
file name↑ := identifier;
put(file name);
```

are often used to write a file component onto a file. The same thing can be accomplished more easily, however, by writing

```
write(file name, identifier);
```

where *identifier* represents a variable or other identifier whose value (or values, in the case of a structured-type file buffer) is assigned to the file buffer. This alternative not only allows us to replace two statements with one but also eliminates the need for any explicit reference to the file buffer.

**EXAMPLE 11.11**

Consider once again the simple Pascal program shown in Example 11.9. This program can also be written in the following manner.

```
PROGRAM createfile4(input,data);
VAR data : FILE OF real;
    item : real;
BEGIN
   rewrite(data);
   readln(item);
   WHILE item >= 0 DO
     BEGIN
        write(data,item);
        readln(item)
     END
END.
```

Notice that we have replaced the statements

```
data↑ := item;
put(data);
```

that were present in the former example with the single write statement

```
write(data,item);
```

**EXAMPLE 11.12**

Now let us return to the billing system program presented in Example 11.10. This program can be modified to appear as

```
PROGRAM createfile5(input,output,customers);

(* THIS PROGRAM CREATES A FILE OF CUSTOMER ACCOUNTS *)

TYPE status = (current,overdue,delinquent);
     account = RECORD
                  custname : PACKED ARRAY [1..80] OF char;
                  custno : 1..9999;
                  custtype : status;
                  custbalance : real
               END;
VAR customeracct : account;
    customers : FILE OF account;
    count : 0..80;
```

(*Program continues on next page*)

```
PROCEDURE readinput(VAR info : account);
(* Enter input data for one record *)
BEGIN
    WITH info DO
        BEGIN
            write('Customer number: ');
            readln(custno);
            IF custno <> 9999 THEN
                BEGIN
                    write('Name: ');
                    count := 0;
                    WHILE NOT eoln DO
                        BEGIN
                            count := count + 1;
                            read(custname[count])
                        END;
                    writeln;
                    write('Current balance: ');
                    readln(custbalance);
                    writeln;
                    custtype := current
                END
        END   (* WITH info *)
END;   (* readinput *)

BEGIN   (* main action statements *)
    rewrite(customers);
    readinput(customeracct);
    WHILE customeracct.custno < 9999 DO
        BEGIN
            write(customers,customeracct);
            readinput(customeracct)
        END
END.
```

In this case we have replaced the pair of statements

```
customers↑ := customeracct;
put(customers);
```

in the main block with the single write statement

```
write(customers,customeracct);
```

The write statement can contain multiple identifiers if desired. In this case the write statement would appear as

```
write(file name, identifier 1, identifier 2, . . . , identifier n);
```

which is equivalent to

```
BEGIN
    write(file name, identifier 1);
    write(file name, identifier 2);
        .
        .
        .
    write(file name, identifier n)
END;
```

It should be understood, however, that the data type associated with each identifier must be either the same as, or compatible with, the file-buffer type.

Moreover, the items listed in the write statement need not necessarily be single identifiers. They can also be expressions, provided the resulting data types are compatible with the file-buffer type. Thus, the general form of the write statement can be written as

write(*file name*, *output item 1*, *output item 2*, . . . , *output item n*);

**EXAMPLE 11.13**

Here is a simple Pascal program that generates a file containing the first 100 integers, their squares and their square roots.

```
PROGRAM createfile6(data);

(* GENERATE A FILE CONTAINING THE FIRST 100 INTEGERS,
              THEIR SQUARES AND THEIR SQUARE ROOTS *)

VAR data : FILE OF real;
    value : real;
    count : 1..100;

BEGIN   (* main action statements *)
   rewrite(data);
   FOR count := 1 TO 100 DO
      BEGIN
         value := count;
         write(data,value,sqr(value),sqrt(value))
      END
END.
```

Notice that the data items are stored as real quantities. Also, note that each integer is followed by its square and its square root. And finally, notice that the program does not make use of either of the standard I/O files (input or output).

## 11.5  READING A FILE

The process of reading a file is essentially a mirror image of the process of creating a file. The first step is to prepare the file for reading by means of the standard procedure reset. This is accomplished by writing

reset(*file name*);

If the file contains one or more components, then the reset statement causes the value of the first file component to be read and assigned to the file buffer. In addition, the standard boolean function eof (end of file) will be false. If the file is empty, however, then the file buffer will remain undefined and eof will be true.

Once a file component has been read and assigned to the file buffer, the buffer contents may be processed as desired. For example, the contents of the file buffer may be assigned to a variable, printed out, written to another file, etc. The next file component can then be obtained by means of the standard procedure get. Thus, the program will typically include the following sequence of instructions:

(* statement to process the contents of *file name*↑ *);

    .

    .

    .

get(*file name*);

(Note that the first instruction is represented by a comment, since it is not clearly defined; i.e., its exact nature will vary from one program to another.) These instructions will typically be repeated until all of the file components have been read and processed, at which time the eof function will become true. The manner in which this is accomplished is illustrated in the next example.

**EXAMPLE 11.14**

Here is a simple Pascal program that will read a file containing real numbers. Each number will be written to the standard output device as soon as it is read from the file. (Note that this program can be used to process the files that were created in Examples 11.8 and 11.9.)

```
PROGRAM readfile1(output,data);

(* THIS PROGRAM READS REAL NUMBERS FROM A DATA FILE
   AND WRITES THEM TO A STANDARD OUTPUT DEVICE *)

VAR data : FILE OF real;
    item : real;

BEGIN
    reset(data);
    WHILE NOT eof(data) DO
        BEGIN
            item := data↑;
            write(item);
            get(data)
        END
END.
```

There are several noteworthy items in this example. First, notice that the program header includes the file parameters output and data, but not input (since there is no transfer of information from the standard input device). Secondly, notice the manner in which the standard identifiers reset, eof and get are utilized. Each identifier includes the file name data, enclosed in parentheses. And finally, notice that each file component is processed by first assigning the contents of the file buffer to a real-type variable and then writing the value of that variable to the standard output device.

It should also be understood that the total number of file components need not be known in advance. The components will be read sequentially, starting at the beginning of the file and continuing until the end of the file has been reached. This is a very common approach to processing the contents of a sequential file.

## 11.6  MORE ABOUT THE READ STATEMENT

When reading from a sequential file, it is quite common to assign the contents of the file buffer to a variable of the appropriate type and then get the next file component (i.e., assign the contents of the next file component to the file buffer). These two operations can be written as

```
variable name := file name↑ ;
get(file name);
```

Since this pair of statements is used so frequently, Pascal provides an easier way to accomplish the same thing, by means of the read statement. Thus, we can write

```
read(file name, variable name);
```

rather than the two statements presented earlier. Notice that the file buffer does not appear in the read statement.

**EXAMPLE 11.15**

Shown below is another version of the program given in Example 11.14. This version makes use of the read statement, rather than get preceded by an assignment statement.

```
PROGRAM readfile2(output,data);

(* THIS PROGRAM READS REAL NUMBERS FROM A DATA FILE
   AND WRITES THEM TO A STANDARD OUTPUT DEVICE *)

VAR data : FILE OF real;
    item : real;

BEGIN
   reset(data);
   WHILE NOT eof(data) DO
      BEGIN
         read(data,item);
         writeln(item)
      END
END.
```

Within the WHILE—DO loop, the read statement causes the following things to happen:

1.  The current value of the file buffer to be assigned to the real variable item.

2.  The next file component is read and assigned to the file buffer.

The write statement then causes the current value of item to be written out to the standard output device (e.g., a line printer or a timesharing console).

Multiple variables can be included in the read statement if desired. Thus, the read statement can be written as

```
read(file name, variable name 1, variable name 2, . . . , variable name n);
```

which is equivalent to

```
BEGIN
   read(file name, variable name 1);
   read(file name, variable name 2);
         .
         .
         .
   read(file name, variable name n)
END;
```

Again, it should be understood that the data type associated with each variable must either be the same as, or compatible with, the file-buffer type.

## EXAMPLE 11.16

In Example 11.13 we saw a Pascal program that generates a file containing a sequence of integers, their squares and their square roots. Let us now consider a program that will read this file. Such a program is presented below.

```
PROGRAM readfile3(output,data);

(* THIS PROGRAM READS A DATA FILE CONTAINING THE FIRST
   100 INTEGERS, THEIR SQUARES AND THEIR SQUARE ROOTS *)

VAR data : FILE OF real;
    value,square,root : real;

BEGIN   (* main action statements *)
   reset(data);
   WHILE NOT eof(data) DO
      BEGIN
         read(data,value,square,root);
         writeln(value:6:2,square:8:2,root:6:2)
      END
END.
```

Notice that this program is more general than its counterpart in Example 11.13, since it is not restricted to a file of predetermined size. Also, note the appearance of multiple variables in the read statement.

## 11.7   UPDATING A FILE

Within a single Pascal program a sequential file can be treated as either an input file or an output file, but not both. (Note, however, that a particular file can be treated as an input file in one program and an output file in another.) Thus, it is not possible to read a file component, modify the file component and then write the modified component back to the original file. Similarly, it is not possible to read a file to the end and then write additional records onto that file.

These restrictions tend to complicate the process of updating an existing file. A file can still be updated in a relatively straightforward manner, however, by utilizing *two* files within the program. One will be the original file that must be updated (the "old" file). This will be treated as an input file. The other (the "new" file) will contain the updated information, some of which will be copied from the old file and some of which will be entered from the standard input device (e.g., a timesharing terminal). The new file will therefore be treated as an output file.

To update the old file, we carry out the following steps for each component within the file.

1.  Read the file component into the computer's memory and determine whether or not this particular component must be updated. This may be accomplished by comparing some key data item, such as a customer number, with a value that has been entered from the standard input device. (The value entered from the input device will indicate the next component to be updated.)

    (*a*)  If the current file component does not require updating, then copy it directly to the new file.

    (*b*)  If updating is required, then the new information is entered from the input device and merged with the old information in an appropriate manner. The modified file component is then written to the new file. Another value is then entered from the input device, indicating which file component must be modified next.

2.  This scheme is repeated until all file components have been read from the old file (i.e., until the end of file has been reached).

3.  If additional file components must be appended to the original file, then they are entered from the input device at this time, in the proper order. Each new file component is written to the new file as it is entered.

For this scheme to work properly, the new information must be entered sequentially from the input device, in the correct order. The order must conform to that in which the file components are stored within the original file. For example, if the file components are customer records that are stored by ascending customer number, then the new information must also be entered by ascending customer number.

### EXAMPLE 11.17

**Copying a File.** The following brief program causes the components of a file called oldfile to be copied to a file called newfile.

```
PROGRAM sample(newfile,oldfile);

(* THIS PROGRAM COPIES THE CONTENTS OF ONE FILE TO ANOTHER *)

TYPE account = RECORD
                  custno : 1..9999;
                  oldbalance : real;
                  newbalance : real;
                  payment : real;
               END;
```

(*Program continues on next page*)

```
VAR newfile,oldfile : FILE OF account;
    newaccount,oldaccount : account;

BEGIN   (* main action block *)
   reset(oldfile);
   rewrite(newfile);
   WHILE NOT eof(oldfile) DO
      BEGIN
         read(oldfile,oldaccount);
         newaccount := oldaccount;
         write(newfile,newaccount)
      END
END.
```

Actually, it is not necessary to include two separate record-type variables, newaccount and oldaccount, within this program outline. One such variable would have been sufficient. Thus, the main action block could have been written

```
BEGIN   (* main action block *)
   reset(oldfile);
   rewrite(newfile);
   WHILE NOT eof(oldfile) DO
      BEGIN
         read(oldfile,newaccount);
         write(newfile,newaccount)
      END
END.
```

The use of two different variables does, however, emphasize the manner in which the individual file components are transferred from one file to another, since the contents of oldaccount could be modified in some way before being transferred to newaccount.

**EXAMPLE 11.18**

Let us now consider the process of appending one or more new components to an existing file. It will again be necessary to read all of the components from oldfile to newfile. After all of the old components have been transferred, the new components will be entered from the keyboard. This process will continue until a value of 9999 has been entered for the variable custno.

Here is the program outline.

```
PROGRAM sample(input,output,newfile,oldfile);

(* TRANSFER THE CONTENTS OF ONE FILE TO ANOTHER,
   THEN APPEND ADDITIONAL COMPONENTS TO THE NEW FILE *)

TYPE account = RECORD
                  custno : 1..9999;
                  oldbalance : real;
                  newbalance : real;
                  payment : real;
               END;
VAR newfile,oldfile : FILE OF account;
    newaccount : account;
    custno : 1..9999;

PROCEDURE readinput(VAR newaccount : account);
(* enter input data for one record *)
BEGIN
   .
   .
   (* enter input data from the keyboard for each record *)
   .
   .
END;
```

(*Program continues on next page*)

```
BEGIN  (* main action block *)
   reset(oldfile);
   rewrite(newfile);

   WHILE NOT eof(oldfile) DO   (* transfer old records *)
      BEGIN
         read(oldfile,newaccount);
         write(newfile,newaccount)
      END;   (* transfer of old records *)

   write('Customer number: ');
   readln(custno);
   WHILE custno < 9999 DO   (* enter new records *)
      BEGIN
         readinput(newaccount);
         write(newfile,newaccount);
         write('Customer number: ');
         readln(custno)
      END   (* enter new records *)
END.
```

Notice that each new file component (each new record) is passed from procedure readinput to the main part of the program as a variable-type parameter.


## EXAMPLE 11.19

Here is a skeletal Pascal program that reads successive file components from oldfile, updates them if necessary and then copies the components to newfile. The updating of various components will continue until a value of 9999 has been entered for custno. Any components remaining in oldfile will then be transferred directly to newfile, without any opportunity for updating.

Note that all of the components of oldfile will be transferred to newfile. Some will be updated, however, and some will be transferred without change.

In order for this scheme to work properly, it is essential that the successive values of custno be entered in ascending order. This will assure that the sequence of changes conforms to the order in which the corresponding components are stored in oldfile.

```
PROGRAM sample(input,output,newfile,oldfile);

(* THIS PROGRAM READS SUCCESSIVE FILE COMPONENTS FROM A
   DATA FILE, UPDATES EACH COMPONENT IF NECESSARY,
   AND THEN WRITES THE COMPONENTS TO A NEW DATA FILE *)

TYPE account = RECORD
                  custno : 1..9999;
                  oldbalance : real;
                  newbalance : real;
                  payment : real;
               END;
VAR newfile,oldfile : FILE OF account;
   newaccount,oldaccount : account;
   custno : 1..9999;

BEGIN   (* main action statements *)
   reset(oldfile);
   rewrite(newfile);
   write('Customer number: ');
   readln(custno);
```

(*Program continues on next page*)

```
                WHILE NOT eof(oldfile) DO
                    BEGIN
                        read(oldfile,oldaccount);
                        newaccount := oldaccount;
                        IF (custno < 9999) AND (oldaccount.custno = custno) THEN
                            BEGIN
                                .
                                .
                                (* accept appropriate input from the keyboard and
                                    make changes in a file component as required *)
                                .
                                .
                                write('Customer number: ');
                                readln(custno)
                            END;   (* IF custno *)
                        write(newfile,newaccount)
                    END   (* WHILE NOT eof *)
            END.
```

Sometimes it is necessary to transfer an entire file to a procedure as a parameter. In such situations, the file must always be passed as a *variable* parameter. This avoids the need to generate a copy of a lengthy file, as would be required if the file were passed as a value parameter. We will see an illustration of this in the next example.

**EXAMPLE 11.20**

**Updating a Customer Billing System.** We now consider a complete Pascal program that will allow us to update a data file that is used to maintain a customer billing system. Presumably, such an update would be carried out at regular intervals, such as once a month.

Let us examine all of the records during each update. This procedure will allow recent payments to be credited to the account of any customer with an outstanding balance. The status of the account can then be changed accordingly.

The update will include a recording of the most recent payment and the payment date, a calculation of the new balance and a determination of each customer's status.

Suppose that each customer record contains the following items of information: name, account number (i.e., customer number), account status (current, overdue or delinquent), previous balance, new balance, current payment and payment date. The appropriate record declarations are shown below.

```
        TYPE status = (current,overdue,delinquent);
             line = PACKED ARRAY [1..30] OF char;
             date = RECORD
                        month : 1..12;
                        day : 1..31;
                        year : 1900..2100
                    END;
             account = RECORD
                        name : line;
                        custno : 1..9999;
                        custtype : status;
                        oldbalance : real;
                        newbalance : real;
                        payment : real;
                        paydate : date
                    END;
```

Note that the record declarations are the same as those given in Example 10.21, except that the customer's address has been omitted for simplicity.

The status of each customer's account will be considered current unless there is an outstanding balance, in which case the status of the account will depend on the size of the most recent payment. The following rules will apply:

1. If the current payment is greater than zero but less than 10 percent of the previous outstanding balance, the account will be considered overdue.

2. If there is an outstanding balance and the current payment is zero, the account will be considered delinquent.

(This is also the same as in Example 10.21.)

The overall strategy for each file update will be as follows.

1. Write out all of the records in the old data file (thus providing a copy of the original data).

2. Proceed sequentially through the old file, updating those records for which there is an outstanding balance.

3. Write each record onto the new data file. (Note that this includes *all* records, regardless of whether or not they have been updated.) Those records that have been updated will be written in their new, modified form. The remaining records will be written as they appeared in the old file.

4. Write out all of the records in the new data file.

The overall skeletal structure of the program will appear as follows.

```
PROGRAM billing2(input,output,newfile,oldfile);

TYPE status = (current,overdue,delinquent);
     line = PACKED ARRAY [1..30] OF char;
     date = RECORD
                 month : 1..12;
                 day : 1..31;
                 year : 1900..2100
             END;
     account = RECORD
                   name : line;
                   custno : 1..9999;
                   custtype : status;
                   oldbalance : real;
                   newbalance : real;
                   payment : real;
                   paydate : date
               END;
     datafile = FILE OF account;
VAR newfile,oldfile : datafile;
    newaccount,oldaccount : account;

PROCEDURE writefile(VAR data : datafile);
VAR custaccount : account;
BEGIN
  .
  .
   (* write the contents of the file
      represented by the variable parameter data *)
  .
  .

END;

PROCEDURE update(VAR newaccount : account);
BEGIN
  .
  .
   (* accept appropriate input from the keyboard and
       make changes in a file component as required *)
  .
  .
END;
```

(*Program continues on next page*)

```
    BEGIN   (* main action block *)
       writeln('CUSTOMER BILLING SYSTEM - FILE UPDATE');
       writeln;
       writeln('OLD DATA FILE');
       writeln;
       writefile(oldfile);

       BEGIN   (* update the old file *)
          writeln;
          writeln('DATA UPDATE');
          writeln;
          reset(oldfile);
          rewrite(newfile);
          WHILE NOT eof(oldfile) DO
             BEGIN
                read(oldfile,oldaccount);
                newaccount := oldaccount;
                IF oldaccount.newbalance > 0 THEN update(newaccount);
                write(newfile,newaccount)
             END   (* WHILE NOT eof(oldfile) *)
       END;   (* file update *)

       writeln;
       writeln('NEW DATA FILE');
       writeln;
       writefile(newfile)
    END.
```

This program makes use of two procedures, writefile and update. The first of these, writefile, reads the records in a data file and writes them to an output device (e.g., a printer). Since this procedure is used with both data files we include a variable parameter, called data, within the procedure declaration. Note that data represents a file of type datafile, as defined in the main program block.

The actual procedure writefile will appear as follows.

```
PROCEDURE writefile(VAR data : datafile);

(* THIS PROCEDURE CAUSES THE CONTENTS OF A DATA FILE TO BE WRITTEN OUT *)

VAR custaccount : account;
BEGIN
   reset(data);
   WHILE NOT eof(data) DO
      BEGIN
         read(data,custaccount);
         WITH custaccount DO
            BEGIN
               writeln;
               write('Name:    ',name);
               writeln('   Customer Number: ',custno:4);
               writeln;
               write('Old balance: ',oldbalance:7:2);
               write('   Current payment: ',payment:7:2);
               writeln('   New balance: ',newbalance:7:2);
               write('Payment date: ',paydate.month:2,'/');
               writeln(paydate.day:2,'/',paydate.year:4);
               writeln;
               write('Account status: ');
```

*(Program continues on next page)*

```
                        CASE custtype OF
                            current    : writeln('CURRENT');
                            overdue    : writeln('OVERDUE');
                            delinquent : writeln('DELINQUENT')
                        END;
                        writeln
                    END   (* WITH custaccount *)
                END   (* WHILE NOT eof(data) *)
        END;
```

The logic is straightforward and does not require further discussion.

Now consider the second procedure, update. The purpose of this procedure is to enter the most recent payment for a given customer, adjust the customer's balance, and then determine the appropriate status, based upon the previous balance and the amount of the current payment.

The procedure update can be written in the following manner.

```
    PROCEDURE update(VAR newaccount : account);

    (* THIS PROCEDURE ENTERS NEW DATA FROM THE KEYBOARD
            AND THEN UPDATES EACH RECORD AS NECESSARY *)

    VAR slash : char;
    BEGIN
        WITH newaccount DO
            BEGIN
                oldbalance := newbalance;
                writeln('Customer number: ',custno:4);
                write('Current balance: ',oldbalance:7:2);
                write('   Current payment: ');
                readln(payment);
                IF payment > 0 THEN
                    BEGIN
                        write('Payment date: ');
                        WITH paydate DO
                            readln(month,slash,day,slash,year);
                    END;
                writeln;
                newbalance := oldbalance - payment;
                IF payment >= 0.1*oldbalance
                    THEN custtype := current
                    ELSE IF payment > 0 THEN custtype := overdue
                                        ELSE custtype := delinquent
            END   (* WITH newaccount *)
    END;
```

If we now put all of the pieces together, the complete program appears as shown below.

```
    PROGRAM billing2(input,output,newfile,oldfile);

    (* THIS PROGRAM UPDATES A DATA FILE BY READING AN OLD FILE,
       UPDATING EACH RECORD, AND THEN WRITING THE UPDATED
       RECORDS ONTO A NEW FILE *)

    TYPE status = (current,overdue,delinquent);
         line = PACKED ARRAY [1..30] OF char;
         date = RECORD
                    month : 1..12;
                    day : 1..31;
                    year : 1900..2100
                END;
```

*(Program continues on next page)*

```
          account = RECORD
                      name : line;
                      custno : 1..9999;
                      custtype : status;
                      oldbalance : real;
                      newbalance : real;
                      payment : real;
                      paydate : date
                    END;
        datafile = FILE OF account;
    VAR newfile,oldfile : datafile;
        newaccount,oldaccount : account;

    PROCEDURE writefile(VAR data : datafile);

    (* THIS PROCEDURE CAUSES THE CONTENTS OF A DATA FILE TO BE WRITTEN OUT *)

    VAR custaccount : account;
    BEGIN
       reset(data);
       WHILE NOT eof(data) DO
          BEGIN
             read(data,custaccount);
             WITH custaccount DO
                BEGIN
                   writeln;
                   write('Name:    ',name);
                   writeln('   Customer Number: ',custno:4);
                   writeln;
                   write('Old balance: ',oldbalance:7:2);
                   write('   Current payment: ',payment:7:2);
                   writeln('   New balance: ',newbalance:7:2);
                   write('Payment date: ',paydate.month:2,'/');
                   writeln(paydate.day:2,'/',paydate.year:4);
                   writeln;
                   write('Account status: ');
                   CASE custtype OF
                       current    : writeln('CURRENT');
                       overdue    : writeln('OVERDUE');
                       delinquent : writeln('DELINQUENT')
                   END;
                   writeln
                END   (* WITH custaccount *)
          END    (* WHILE NOT eof(data) *)
    END;   (* writefile *)


    PROCEDURE update(VAR newaccount : account);

    (* THIS PROCEDURE ENTERS NEW DATA FROM THE KEYBOARD
             AND THEN UPDATES EACH RECORD AS NECESSARY *)

    VAR slash : char;
    BEGIN
       WITH newaccount DO
          BEGIN
             oldbalance := newbalance;
             writeln('Customer number: ',custno:4);
             write('Current balance: ',oldbalance:7:2);
             write('   Current payment: ');
             readln(payment);
```

*(Program continues on next page)*

```
              IF payment > 0 THEN
                 BEGIN
                    write('Payment date: ');
                    WITH paydate DO
                       readln(month,slash,day,slash,year);
                 END;
              writeln;
              newbalance := oldbalance - payment;
              IF payment >= 0.1*oldbalance
                 THEN custtype := current
                 ELSE IF payment > 0 THEN custtype := overdue
                                     ELSE custtype := delinquent
        END   (* WITH newaccount *)
   END;  (* update *)


   BEGIN   (* main action block *)
      writeln('CUSTOMER BILLING SYSTEM - FILE UPDATE');
      writeln;
      writeln('OLD DATA FILE');
      writeln;
      writefile(oldfile);

      BEGIN   (* update the old file *)
         writeln;
         writeln('DATA UPDATE');
         writeln;
         reset(oldfile);
         rewrite(newfile);
         WHILE NOT eof(oldfile) DO
            BEGIN
               read(oldfile,oldaccount);
               newaccount := oldaccount;
               IF oldaccount.newbalance > 0 THEN update(newaccount);
               write(newfile,newaccount)
            END   (* WHILE NOT eof(oldfile) *)
      END;   (* file update *)

      writeln;
      writeln('NEW DATA FILE');
      writeln;
      writefile(newfile)
   END.
```

Now suppose that the program is used to process a small data file containing six accounts. The program will begin by printing out the contents of the original data file (oldfile), as follows.

```
CUSTOMER BILLING SYSTEM - FILE UPDATE

OLD DATA FILE


Name:   Alan B. Adams                    Customer Number:   1

Old balance: 128.32   Current Payment:  128.32   New balance:   0.00
Payment date: 11/27/1984

Account Status: CURRENT
```

*(Program continues on next page)*

```
Name:   James Brown               Customer Number:    2

Old balance:  189.00   Current Payment:  100.00  New balance:    89.00
Payment date: 11/18/1984

Account Status: CURRENT


Name:   Janet P. Davis            Customer Number:    3

Old balance:  212.18   Current Payment:    0.00  New balance:   212.18
Payment date:  9/ 4/1984

Account Status: DELINQUENT


Name:   William D. McDonald       Customer Number:    4

Old balance:  200.00   Current Payment:   65.00  New balance:   135.00
Payment date: 11/10/1984

Account Status: CURRENT


Name:   Phyllis W. Smith          Customer Number:    5

Old balance:  289.42   Current Payment:   20.00  New balance:   269.42
Payment date: 11/21/1984

Account Status: OVERDUE


Name:   Richard L. Warren         Customer Number:    6

Old balance:   70.00   Current Payment:   50.00  New balance:    20.00
Payment date: 11/15/1984

Account Status: CURRENT
```

After the contents of the old data file have been written out, the program will prompt the user to enter new data for each customer that has a nonzero outstanding balance. Thus, five of the records will be updated. The interactive data update session will appear as shown below. (Note that all user responses are underlined.)

```
DATA UPDATE

Customer number:   2
Current balance:  89.00   Current payment: 50.00
Payment date: 12/12/1984

Customer number:   3
Current balance:  212.18   Current payment: 212.18
Payment date: 12/3/1984

Customer number   4
Current balance:  135.00   Current payment: 10.00
Payment date: 12/18/1984

Customer number:   5
Current balance:  269.42   Current payment: 0

Customer number:   6
Current balance:  20.00   Current payment: 20.00
Payment date: 12/7/1984
```

Notice that the program prompts for new information only for those customers who have a current balance greater than zero. Also, note that the program will prompt for a payment date only if there is a current payment that is greater than zero.

Once the new data have been entered and the updating has been completed, the new customer file (newfile) is written out. The contents of this file will appear as follows.

```
NEW DATA FILE


Name:   Alan B. Adams              Customer Number:    1

Old balance:  128.32  Current Payment: 128.32  New balance:    0.00
Payment date: 11/27/1984

Account Status: CURRENT


Name:   James Brown                Customer Number:    2

Old balance:   89.00  Current Payment:  50.00 New balance:   39.00
Payment date: 12/12/1984

Account Status: CURRENT


Name:   Janet P. Davis             Customer Number:    3

Old balance:  212.18  Current Payment: 212.18  New balance:    0.00
Payment date:  9/ 4/1984

Account Status: CURRENT


Name:   William D. McDonald        Customer Number:    4

Old balance:  135.00  Current Payment:  10.00  New balance: 125.00
Payment date: 12/18/1984

Account Status: OVERDUE


Name:   Phyllis W. Smith           Customer Number:    5

Old balance: 269.42  Current Payment:   0.00  New balance: 269.42
Payment date: 11/21/1984

Account Status: DELINQUENT


Name:   Richard L. Warren          Customer Number:    6

Old balance:   20.00  Current Payment:  20.00  New balance:    0.00
Payment date: 12/ 7/1984

Account Status: CURRENT
```

Notice that the first record remains unchanged, since the first customer (Alan B. Adams) did not have an outstanding balance during this update period.

Once the program execution has been completed, oldfile should be deleted and newfile renamed as oldfile. This will allow the newly created data file to be updated in the future.

## 11.8  TEXT FILES

Pascal also supports another type of file, known as a *text file*. This is a file of type char, with end-of-line designations interspersed at various places to distinguish one line of text from another. (Typically, an end-of-line designation will consist of a line feed followed by a carriage return.) Thus, a text file is comprised of multiple lines of character-type data.

The characters on any given line may be grouped (i.e., separated by blank spaces), and the individual groups of characters can be interpreted in one of several different ways. For example, a group of digits can be interpreted as an integer or a real quantity. The manner in which a character group is interpreted will be determined by the associated read or write statement (more about this later).

A text file can easily be defined by declaring an identifier (i.e., a variable representing the file) to be of type text. Formally, the declaration can be expressed as

        VAR *file name* : text

where *file name* is an identifier that represents the name of the text file. Multiple file names can, of course, be included in a single declaration.

### EXAMPLE 11.21

Suppose that a Pascal program must make use of the text files oldtext and newtext. The file definitions will appear as follows.

        VAR oldtext,newtext : text;

Notice that it is not necessary to write "FILE OF text" within the declaration.

Every text file has a file buffer associated with it, just like any other file. Since a text file is a file of type char, its file buffer will represent a single character.

The standard procedures reset and rewrite can be used with text files, just as they are used with other types of files. The reset statement is used to prepare a file for reading. Thus, the statement

        reset(*file name*);

causes the first character to be assigned to the file buffer, provided the file is not empty. The standard function

        eof(*file name*)

is also set to an appropriate value when the file is reset.

Similarly, the rewrite statement prepares the file for writing. Therefore, the statement

        rewrite(*file name*);

will erase the text already in the text file (if there is any text present) and then establish the beginning of the text file.

The standard procedures get and put can also be used with text files, just as they would be used with other types of files. Hence, the statement

        get(*file name*);

will cause the next character in the text file to be assigned to the file buffer. (Normally, the preceding character will have been processed before the next character is read.)

Also, the statement

        put(*file name*);

will cause the character that is currently in the file buffer to be written to the text file. As a rule the put statement will be preceded by an assignment statement, thus placing a new character into the file buffer. It is this new character that is written to the text file as a consequence of the put statement.

Most programs that make use of text files utilize the standard procedures read, readln, write and `writeln` rather than `get` and `put`. Let us therefore reexamine these procedures, in light of our current discussion on text files.

If the statement

    read(*file name, variable name*);

is used with a text file, the action taken will depend upon the data type of the variable. If the variable is of type char, the data item will be processed in the usual manner; i.e., the character in the file buffer will be assigned to the variable, followed by a new character being read from the text file and assigned to the file buffer. If the variable is of type integer or type real, however, then a sufficient number of consecutive characters will be read to allow construction of a complete integer or real quantity. This quantity will then be assigned to the variable, and the next character in the file will be assigned to the file buffer.

Multiple variable names may appear in a single read statement. Such a statement will be interpreted as a sequence of read statements, each containing a single variable name. Thus, the statement

    read(*file name, variable name 1, variable name 2, . . . , variable name n*);

will be interpreted as

    BEGIN
        read(*file name, variable name 1*);
        read(*file name, variable name 2*);
            .
            .
            .
        read(*file name, variable name n*)
    END;

If the variables represent consecutive numerical quantities, then the separation of one such numerical quantity from another will be based upon the detection of preceding blanks or line control characters, as discussed in Chap. 4 (see Sec. 4.2).

The readln statement is similar to the read statement. In this case, however, a single readln statement will cause reading to continue until an end-of-line designation (eoln) has been encountered. Thus, any *subsequent* read or readln will begin on the next line (see Sec. 4.3).

To be more precise, the statement

    readln(*file name*);

is equivalent to

    BEGIN
        WHILE NOT eoln(*file name*) DO get(*file name*);
        get (*file name*)
    END;

(Note that the last get causes the first character on the next line to be assigned to the file buffer.) Moreover, the statement

    readln(*file name, variable name 1, variable name 2, . . . , variable name n*);

will be interpreted as

    BEGIN
        read(*file name, variable name 1, variable name 2, . . . , variable name n*);
        readln(*file name*)
    END;

Incidentally, the standard function

    eoln(*file name*)

is a standard boolean function that returns the value `false` unless the current character in the file is an end-of-line indicator. Thus, the function `eoln` remains false until an end-of-line has been detected, which causes it to become true. The function again becomes false whenever some other character is examined, after an end-of-line has been detected (see Secs. 4.4 and 9.1).

Now let us turn our attention to the write and writeln statements. If the statement

```
write(file name, output item)
```

is used with a text file, the action taken will depend upon the exact nature of the output item. If the output item is of type char (e.g., a constant or a char-type variable), then the character will be assigned to the file buffer and written to the file. If, however, the output item represents some other data type (e.g., a boolean variable or a numeric constant, variable or expression), then the value of the output item will be converted into its constituent characters. These characters will then automatically be written to the text file.

Multiple output items may appear in a single write statement. Such a statement will be interpreted as a sequence of write statements, each containing a single output item. Hence, the statement

```
write(file name, output item 1, output item 2, . . . , output item n);
```

will be interpreted as

```
BEGIN
    write(file name, output item 1);
    write(file name, output item 2);
            .
            .
            .
    write(file name, output item n)
END;
```

See Sec. 4.5.

The writeln statement

```
writeln(file name);
```

causes an end-of-line designation to be written onto the file. Hence, any subsequent output to the text file will begin on the next line. Furthermore, the statement

```
writeln(text file, output item 1, output item 2, . . . , output item n);
```

will be interpreted as

```
BEGIN
    write(file name, output item 1, output item 2, . . . , output item n);
    writeln(file name)
END;
```

thus allowing multiple output items to be placed on one line, followed by an end-of-line designation (see Sec. 4.6).

Finally, the standard procedure page can be used with any text file by including the file name as a parameter; i.e.,

```
page(file name);
```

The use of this procedure causes any new output to begin at the top of a new page, provided the output is directed to a device that can recognize distinct paging (e.g., a line printer). The page statement will otherwise be ignored (see Sec. 4.7).

**EXAMPLE 11.22**

**Transferring Text Between Text Files.** Here is a simple Pascal program that transfers the contents of oldtext to newtext, on a line-by-line basis. (Notice that oldtext and newtext are both text files.)

```
PROGRAM filetransfer(oldtext,newtext);

(* THIS PROGRAM TRANSFERS TEXT FROM ONE TEXT FILE
              TO ANOTHER ON A LINE-BY-LINE BASIS *)

VAR oldtext,newtext : text;
    x : char;

BEGIN
   reset(oldtext);
   rewrite(newtext);
   page(newtext);
   WHILE NOT eof(oldtext) DO
      BEGIN
         WHILE NOT eoln(oldtext) DO
            BEGIN   (* transfer one line of text *)
               read(oldtext,x);
               write(newtext,x)
            END;
         readln(oldtext);
         writeln(newtext)
      END
END.
```

The inner WHILE—DO loop causes the text in one line of oldtext to be read and written to newtext. The transfer takes place one character at a time, for any given line of text. Following this WHILE—DO loop is a readln statement, which prepares the program to read the next line of oldtext, and then a writeln statement, which places an end-of-line designation on the current line of newtext.

The outer WHILE—DO loop causes the action to be repeated on a line-by-line basis, until an end-of-file designation has been detected in oldtext.

There are two predeclared text files in Pascal—input and output—which are used to transfer input and output data to and from the standard input/output devices. We have, of course, been utilizing these files consistently since they were introduced in Chap. 4, though we have not specifically identified them as text files until this point.

When the standard procedures and functions described above are used with one of these predeclared text files, it is not necessary to include the file name as a parameter. If the file parameter is not specified, then either input or output is assumed, depending on the particular procedure or function. Thus, the following procedures and functions are assumed to apply to the text file input if a file parameter is not explicitly included in the procedure or function reference: read, readln, eof and eoln. Similarly, the following procedures are assumed to apply to the text file output if a file parameter is not explicitly included: write, writeln and page. Moreover, input and output are automatically initialized, so that the standard procedures reset and rewrite are not needed with these files.

**EXAMPLE 11.23**

**Entering and Saving a Text File.** Here is a program that allows several lines of text to be entered from an input device and stored in a text file called newtext. (Notice that this program is a variation of that presented in Example 11.22.)

```
PROGRAM entertext(input,newtext);

(* THIS PROGRAM ACCEPTS TEXT FROM AN INPUT DEVICE AND
      STORES IT IN A TEXT FILE ON A LINE-BY-LINE BASIS *)

VAR newtext : text;
    x : char;
```

*(Program continues on next page)*

```
      BEGIN
         rewrite(newtext);
         WHILE NOT eof DO
            BEGIN
               WHILE NOT eoln DO
                  BEGIN   (* enter and store one line of text *)
                     read(x);
                     write(newtext,x)
                  END;
               readln;
               writeln(newtext)
            END
   END.
```

When this program is executed an unspecified number of lines can be entered from the input device and stored in newtext. To terminate the execution an end-of-file designation will have to be entered from the input device. The exact nature of this designation will vary from one installation to another, though a control character is frequently used for this purpose.

### EXAMPLE 11.24

**Encoding and Decoding Text.** We now consider a more interesting application involving the use of text files. Let us develop an interactive Pascal program that will encode and decode multiple lines of text. The program will include a menu, which will allow any one of the following actions to be taken:

1.  Enter text from the keyboard, encode the text and store the encoded text in a text file.
2.  Retrieve the encoded text and display it in its encoded form.
3.  Retrieve the encoded text, decode it and then display the decoded text.
4.  End computation.

The entire body of text may consist of several lines. These lines will be preserved as the text is encoded, stored, decoded and displayed. However, the actual encoding and decoding will occur on a character-by-character basis.

In order to encode and decode the text, the user must enter a single-character "key." (The program will prompt for this if menu item 1 or 3 is selected.) Each character will be encoded by adding its numerical code to the numerical code for the key, and then determining the character represented by the sum; i.e.,

```
      z := chr(ord(x) + ord(key))
```

where z represents the encoded character that is equivalent to the original character x.

When adding the two numerical codes together, care must be taken that the sum not exceed 127, since this is the largest value for a standard character code (assuming the ASCII character set). Therefore, if the value of z exceeds 127, its value must be adjusted by subtracting 127 from the sum. Thus, we can write

```
      y := ord(x) + ord(key);
      IF y > 127 THEN y := y - 127;
      z := chr(y);
```

This scheme works well and is easy to implement. It should be understood, however, that certain of the values for z will result in unprintable characters (e.g., line feeds, carriage returns, "beeps," etc.). These characters will, of course, be placed in the encoded text. Thus, the encoded text may appear very erratic when it is displayed.

The encoded text can be decoded by reversing the above process; i.e.,

```
      y := ord(z) - ord(key);
      IF y < 0 THEN y := y + 127;
      x := chr(y);
```

When decoding the text it is, of course, essential that we use the same value of key as was used to encode the original text. Otherwise the decoded text will be garbled.

Here is a skeletal outline of the entire program, illustrating the overall computational strategy.

```
PROGRAM encode(input,output,code);

TYPE features = 1..4;

VAR code : text;
x,z,key : char;
y : -127..254;
choice : features;

PROCEDURE menu(VAR choice : features; VAR key : char);
BEGIN
   .

   .
   (* generate a menu, return the user's choice
      and a value for the key, if appropriate *)
   .

   .
END;
BEGIN   (* main action statements *)
   choice := 1;
   WHILE choice <> 4 DO
     menu(choice,key);
     CASE choice OF
       1 : BEGIN
              .

              .
              (* enter text, encode and store *)
              .

              .
           END;
       2,3 : BEGIN
              .

              .
              (* retrieve encoded text, decode
                 (if choice = 2) and display *)
              .

              .
           END;
        4 : ;

     END   (* CASE *)
   END   (* WHILE loop *)
END.
```

The overall strategy is staightforward, based upon the use of a CASE structure to implement whatever choice is returned from the menu. Upon completion of each major activity (each pass through the CASE structure), the program returns to the menu for another selection until a choice of 4 has been requested.

The complete Pascal program is shown below.

```
PROGRAM encode(input,output,code);

(* THIS IS A MENU-DRIVEN PROGRAM THAT ACCEPTS TEXT FROM AN INPUT DEVICE,
   ENCODES IT, STORES THE ENCODED TEXT IN A TEXT FILE, AND DISPLAYS THE
   TEXT, EITHER ENCODED OR DECODED *)

TYPE features = 1..4;

VAR code : text;
    x,z,key : char;
    y : -127..254;
    choice : features;
```

*(Program continues on next page)*

```
    PROCEDURE menu (VAR choice : features; VAR key : char);

    (* This procedure generates a menu and returns the user's choice *)


    BEGIN
      writeln;
      writeln('E N C O D I N G / D E C O D I N G   T E X T');
      writeln;
      writeln('Program Features:');
      writeln;
      writeln('  1 - Enter text, encode and store');
      writeln;
      writeln('  2 - Retrieve encoded text and display');
      writeln;
      writeln('  3 - Retrieve encoded text, decode and display');
      writeln;
      writeln('  4 - End computation');
      writeln;
      write('Please enter your selection (1, 2, 3 or 4) -> ');
      readln(choice);
      writeln;
      IF (choice = 1) OR (choice = 3) THEN
         BEGIN
           write('Please enter the key (one character) -> ');
           readln(key);
           writeln
         END
    END;   (* menu *)


    BEGIN   (* main action statements *)
      choice := 1;
      WHILE choice <> 4 DO
         BEGIN
           menu(choice,key);
           CASE choice OF


             1 : BEGIN   (* enter text, encode and store *)
                   rewrite(code);
                   writeln('Enter text:');
                   writeln;
                   WHILE NOT eof DO
                      BEGIN
                        WHILE NOT eoln DO
                           BEGIN
                             read(x);
                             y := ord(x) + ord(key);
                             IF y > 127 THEN y := y - 127;
                             z := chr(y);
                             write(code,z)
                           END;
                        readln;
                        writeln(code)
                      END;   (* NOT eof *)
                   reset(input)   (* eof=false *)
                 END;
```

*(Program continues on next page)*

```
          2,3 : BEGIN   (* retrieve encoded text, decode and display *)
                   reset(code);
                 WHILE NOT eof(code) DO
                   BEGIN
                     WHILE NOT eoln(code) DO
                       BEGIN
                         read(code,z);
                         IF choice = 2
                            THEN x := z
                            ELSE BEGIN
                                     y := ord(z) - ord(key);
                                     IF y < 0 THEN y := y + 127;
                                     x := chr(y)
                                  END;
                         write(x)
                       END;   (* NOT eoln *)
                     readln(code);
                     writeln
                   END   (* NOT eof *)
              END;

            4 : ;

        END   (* CASE *)
      END;   (* WHILE choice <> 4 *)
    writeln;
    writeln('That''s all, folks!')
  END.
```

Procedure menu provides the necessary input/output statements to generate the menu and, if the user chooses options 1 or 3, prompts for a single-character key. Notice that this procedure employs two variable parameters, choice, which is of type features, and key, which is of type char.

The main block consists essentially of a CASE structure with four different selections. The first selection, corresponding to choice = 1, provides the instructions for entering multiple lines of data and encoding and storing each line on a character-by-character basis. Notice that the encoded characters are written onto text file code.

The data input continues until an end-of-file marker is entered from the keyboard. (The manner with which this is accomplished will vary from one computer to another, though a control character is usually used for this purpose.) After the data entry has been completed, the text file input is reset, so that the eof condition is once again false.

If choice has a value of 2 or 3, then the text file code is reset and the encoded text is read from it on a character-by-character basis. If choice = 2, the encoded text is written directly to the output device. Otherwise (if choice = 3), the characters are decoded as they are read and then written to the output device.

When the program is executed, the following menu is generated.

```
ENCODING/DECODING  TEXT

Program Features:

  1 - Enter text, encode and store

  2 - Retrieve encoded text and display

  3 - Retrieve encoded text, decode and display

  4 - End computation

Please enter your selection (1, 2, 3 or 4) ->
```

If a value of 1 or 3 is entered for the selection, then the following prompt will be generated for the key.

```
Please enter the key (one character) ->
```

Now suppose that the user elects to enter several lines of text. The user would first enter a value of 1 for the selection. Suppose that the user then enters the character C for the key, followed by the text

```
All digital computers, regardless of their size, are
basically electronic devices that can transmit, store and
manipulate information (i.e., data).
^Z
```

(The characters ^Z at the end of the text indicate an end-of-file.) This information will be encoded, one character at a time, and then stored in text file code. Following this, the main menu will reappear.

If the user now selects the second choice, the following encoded data will be read from text file code and displayed.

```
00c(-+-8%0c'31498)67oc6)+%6(0)77c3*c8,)-6c7->)oc%6)
&%7-'%00=c)0)'8632-'c():-')7c8,%8c'%2c86%271-8oc7836)c%2(
1%2-490%8)c-2*361%8-32ck-q)qoc(%8%1q
```

This, of course, is the encoded version of the text entered above.

Now suppose that the user selects the third choice. A prompt for the key will again appear. The user must respond by entering a C, the same key that was used to encode the text. Once the key has been entered, the encoded data will again be read from text file code, decoded on a character-by-character basis and then displayed as follows.

```
All digital computers, regardless of their size, are
basically electronic devices that can transmit, store and
manipulate information (i.e., data).
```

Thus, the original text is again reconstructed.

If the incorrect key is entered in response the the prompt, the text will be decoded incorrectly and garbled text will appear. Suppose, for example, that the user entered the character B instead of C as the key. Then the following decoded text would appear.

```
Bmm!ejhjubm!dpnqvufst-!sfhbsemftt!pg!uifjs!tj{f-!bsf
cbtjdbmmz!fmfduspojd!efwjdft!uibu!dbo!usbotnju-!tupsf!boe
nbojqvmbuf!jogpsnbujpo!)j/f/-!ebub*/
```

Finally, suppose that the user elects to end the computation by choosing the last selection on the menu. Then the message

```
That's all, folks!
```

will appear and the computation will be terminated.

# Review Questions

**11.1** What are the principal characteristics of a file? How does a file differ from an array?

**11.2** What is the difference between a permanent file and a temporary file? What term is used to refer to permanent files in Pascal?

**11.3** What is the difference between an external file and an internal file?

**11.4** What is the difference between a sequential file and a random file? What are the advantages and disadvantages of each?

**11.5**    What is another name for a random access file? Which name is more descriptive? Explain.

**11.6**    What kinds of files are supported by standard ISO Pascal?

**11.7**    Summarize the rules for defining a file type.

**11.8**    Summarize the rules for defining a file-type variable. Compare with your answer to the previous problem.

**11.9**    What data types can be associated with the individual file components?

**11.10**   What restrictions apply to the maximum permissible length of a file? Do these restrictions also apply to other structured data types?

**11.11**   How are external files passed to or from a Pascal program? Syntactically, how is this accomplished?

**11.12**   What is a file buffer? How is the file buffer named? What kinds of data can it represent?

**11.13**   What is the first step when creating a new file? How is this accomplished?

**11.14**   What is the effect of the rewrite statement when preparing an existing file for writing?

**11.15**   What is the purpose of the put statement? How can this statement be used repeatedly to write multiple components onto a file?

**11.16**   Suppose a file consisting of structured components is being created. How can the individual data items for each component be entered into the computer and written to the file? Must all of these data items be of the same type?

**11.17**   How can a structured file component be passed as a parameter between a procedure and the main action block?

**11.18**   What is the purpose of the write statement? How does this statement differ from the put statement? Explain in detail.

**11.19**   What kinds of output items can be included in a write statement? Can multiple output items be included in a single write statement?

**11.20**   How can an existing file be prepared for reading?

**11.21**   What is the effect of the reset statement on a file that contains one or more components?

**11.22**   What is the effect of the reset statement on an empty file? Compare your answer with that given for the last problem.

**11.23**   What is the purpose of the get statement? How can this statement be used repeatedly to read multiple components from a file?

**11.24**   When a file is being read, how can the end of the file be detected?

**11.25**   What is the purpose of the read statement? How does this statement differ from the get statement? Explain in detail.

**11.26**   What kinds of input items can be included in a read statement? Can multiple variables be included in a single read statement?

**11.27**   Can a single Pascal program read information from a file and then append new information to that same file? Explain.

**11.28**   Summarize the steps that must be taken to update an existing file.

**11.29**   Can a file be transferred to a procedure or a function as a value parameter? Explain.

**11.30**   What is a text file? How do text files differ from other types of files?

**11.31**   How are the characters on a single line of a text file interpreted?

**11.32**   How is a text file defined?

**11.33**   Can the statements get and put be used with a text file?

**11.34**   Are the statements get and put normally used with a text file? Explain.

**11.35**   Can the standard file-oriented procedures such as reset, rewrite and eof, be utilized with a text file?

**11.36**   What is the purpose of the readln statement? How does this statement differ from the read statement? Can the readln statement be used with all types of files?

**11.37**   Suppose that a read or a readln statement contains a variable that is of type integer or real. How will the corresponding characters in the text file be interpreted?

**11.38**   What is the purpose of the standard function eoln? Compare with the standard function eof.

**11.39**   What is the purpose of the writeln statement? How does this statement differ from the write statement? Can the writeln statement be used with all types of files?

**11.40**   Suppose that a write or a writeln statement contains a variable or an expression that is of some simple type other than char. How will the corresponding characters in the text file be interpreted?

**11.41**   What is the purpose of the standard procedure page? Will this procedure be interpreted in the same manner by all output devices?

**11.42**   Outline the manner in which the contents of a text file can be transferred from one text file to another, preserving the line-by-line organization of the original file.

**11.43**  How do the predeclared text files input and output differ from other text files?

**11.44**  Describe the simplifications that are permissible when one of the predeclared text files is used with the standard file-oriented procedures and functions, such as read, write, eof and page.

**11.45**  Is the reset statement required when preparing to read an input file? Is rewrite required with an output file?

# Solved Problems

**11.46**  Several illustrative file definitions are shown below.

(*a*)  VAR data : FILE OF integer;

(*b*)  VAR sales,costs : FILE OF real;

(*c*)  TYPE acctno = 1..9999;
       VAR accounts : FILE OF acctno;

(*d*)  TYPE color = (red,green,blue);
           sample = RECORD
                          first : color;
                          second : 1..132;
                          third : char
                     END;
       VAR data : FILE OF sample;

(*e*)  TYPE color = (red,green,blue);
           sample = RECORD
                          first : color;
                          second : 1..132;
                          third : char
                     END;
           list = ARRAY [1..100] OF sample;
       VAR data : FILE OF list;

(*f*)  VAR oldstuff,newstuff : text;

**11.47**  The following brief programs illustrate typical file operations.

(*a*)  Enter a sequence of records from the keyboard and save in a file.

```
PROGRAM sample(input,data);
TYPE line = PACKED ARRAY [1..80] OF char;
     personal = RECORD
                      name : line;
                      address : line;
                      phone : line
                 END;
VAR data : FILE OF personal;
    nameandaddress : personal;

PROCEDURE readline(VAR info : line);
VAR count : 1..80;
BEGIN
   FOR count := 1 TO 80 DO read(info[count]);
   readln
END;
```

*(Program continues on next page)*

```
     BEGIN
        rewrite(data);
        WITH nameandaddress DO
           BEGIN
              readline(name);
              WHILE (name[1] <> 'e') AND (name[2] <> 'n')
                                       AND (name[3] <> 'd') DO
                 BEGIN
                    readline(address);
                    readline(phone);
                    write(data,nameandaddress);
                    readline(name)
                 END
           END
     END.
```

[See also Prob 11.47(*f*).]

(*b*)   Read a sequence of records from a file and display.

```
PROGRAM sample(output,data);
TYPE line = PACKED ARRAY [1..80] OF char;
     personal = RECORD
                      name : line;
                      address : line;
                      phone : line
                 END;
VAR data : FILE OF personal;
    nameandaddress : personal;

BEGIN
     reset(data);
     WITH nameandaddress DO
        WHILE NOT eof(data) DO
           BEGIN
              read(data,nameandaddress);
              writeln(name);
              writeln(address);
              writeln(phone);
              writeln
           END
END.
```

(*c*)   Copy a sequence of records from one file to another.

```
PROGRAM sample(data1,data2);
TYPE line = PACKED ARRAY [1..80] OF char;
     personal = RECORD
                      name : line;
                      address : line;
                      phone : line
                 END;
VAR data1,data2 : FILE OF personal;
    nameandaddress : personal;

BEGIN
     reset(data1);
     rewrite(data2);
     WHILE NOT eof(data1) DO
        BEGIN
           read(data1,nameandaddress);
           write(data2,nameandaddress)
        END
END.
```

(*d*)  Copy a sequence of records from one file to another, using get and put.

```
PROGRAM sample(data1,data2);
TYPE line = PACKED ARRAY [1..80] OF char;
     personal = RECORD
                     name : line;
                     address : line;
                     phone : line
                 END;
VAR data1,data2 : FILE OF personal;
    nameandaddress : personal;

BEGIN
   reset(data1);
   rewrite(data2);
   WHILE NOT eof(data1) DO
     BEGIN
        nameandaddress := data1↑;
        get(data1);
        data2↑ := nameandaddress;
        put(data2)
     END
END.
```

(*e*)  Enter a name from the keyboard. Then search a file for a record with the same name.

```
PROGRAM sample(input,data);
TYPE line = PACKED ARRAY [1..80] OF char;
     personal = RECORD
                     name : line;
                     address : line;
                     phone : line
                 END;
VAR count : 1..80;
    newname : line;
    data : FILE OF personal;
    nameandaddress : personal;

BEGIN
   reset(data);
   FOR count := 1 TO 80 DO read(newname[count]);
   REPEAT
      read(data,nameandaddress)
   UNTIL nameandaddress.name = newname
END.
```

(*f*)  Enter a sequence of names, addresses and phone numbers and save in a text file.

```
PROGRAM sample(input,data);
TYPE line = PACKED ARRAY [1..80] OF char;
VAR name,address,phone : line;
    data : text;

PROCEDURE readline(VAR info : line);
VAR count : 1..80;
BEGIN
   FOR count := 1 TO 80 DO read(info[count]);
   readln
END;
```

(*Program continues on next page*)

```
BEGIN
   rewrite(data);
   readline(name);
   WHILE (name[1] <> 'e') AND (name[2] <> 'n')
                           AND (name[3] <> 'd') DO
      BEGIN
         readline(address);
         readline(phone);
         write(data,name,address);
         writeln(data,phone);
         readline(name)
      END
END.
```

[See also Prob. 11.47(*a*).]

# Supplementary Problems

**11.48**  The following skeletal outlines illustrate several different situations involving the use of files. Some are written incorrectly. Identify all errors.

(*a*)  `TYPE olddata,newdata : FILE OF integer;`

(*b*)  `VAR flags : FILE OF boolean;`

(*c*)  `VAR story : FILE OF text;`

(*d*)
```
TYPE status = (current,overdue,delinquent);
     account = RECORD
                  custname : PACKED ARRAY [1..80] OF char;
                  custno : 1..9999;
                  custtype : status;
                  custbalance : real
               END;
     listing = ARRAY [1..1000] OF account;
     posting = FILE OF listing;
VAR oldposting,newposting : posting;
```

(*e*)
```
TYPE color = (red,green,blue);
     sample = RECORD
                 first : color;
                 second : 1..132;
                 third : char
              END;
     data = FILE OF sample;
VAR olddata,newdata : FILE OF data;
```

(*f*)  `VAR input,output : text;`

(*g*)
```
PROGRAM sample(input,data);
VAR data : FILE OF real;
    item : real;
    BEGIN
       readln(item);
       WHILE item <> 0 DO
          BEGIN
             writeln(data,item);
             readln(item)
          END
    END.
```

(*h*)  
```
PROGRAM sample(file1,file2);
VAR file1,file2 : text;
    byte : char;

BEGIN
   reset(file2);
   rewrite(file1);
   WHILE NOT eof(file2) DO
      BEGIN
         WHILE NOT eoln(file2) DO
            BEGIN
               read(file2,byte);
               write(file1,byte)
            END;
         readln(file2);
         writeln(file1)
      END
END.
```

(*i*)  
```
PROGRAM sample(input,output,posting);
TYPE line = PACKED ARRAY [1..80] OF char;
     account = RECORD
                  custname : line;
                  custno : 1..9999;
                  custbalance : real
               END;
VAR name : line;
    count : 1..80;
    customer : account;
    posting : FILE OF account;

BEGIN
   reset(posting);
   customer := posting;
   FOR count := 1 TO 80 DO read(name[count]);
   WHILE customer.custname <> name DO
      BEGIN
         get(posting);
         customer := posting
      END;
   WITH customer DO
      writeln(custname,custno,custbalance)
END.
```

(*j*)  
```
PROGRAM sample(input,output,oldaccts,newaccts);
TYPE line = PACKED ARRAY [1..80] OF char;
     account = RECORD
                  custname : line;
                  custno : 1..9999;
                  custbalance : real
               END;
     filetype = FILE OF account;
VAR oldaccts,newaccts : filetype;

PROCEDURE rearrange(oldfile,newfile : filetype);
BEGIN

   .

   .

   (* rearrange the records by ascending customer number *);

   .

   .

END;
```

(*Program continues on next page*)

```
BEGIN   (* main action statements *)
    .
    .
    .
    rearrange(oldaccts,newaccts);
    .
    .
END.
```

# Programming Problems

**11.49** Write a complete Pascal program that will generate the old data file shown in Example 11.20. Run the program, creating a data file for use in the next problem.

**11.50** Modify the customer billing program given in Example 11.20 by adding the following features.

(a) Specify each record to be updated by entering the customer number from the keyboard, rather than attempting to update all records for which there is a current outstanding balance. (See the program outline shown in Example 11.19.)

(b) Include a provision for increasing the outstanding balance (i.e., adding new charges) during the current billing period. Again, determine which records will be updated in this manner by entering the appropriate customer numbers from the keyboard.

Use the program to process the data file created in the last program, together with the following new charges.

| Customer | New charge |
| --- | --- |
| Alan B. Adams | 245.00 |
| William D. McDonald | 88.50 |

**11.51** Modify the encoding and decoding program given in Example 11.24 so that a multidigit key can be entered, with successive digits being used for each successive line. For example, if a three-digit key is entered, use the first digit to encode or decode the first line of text, the second digit for the second line and the third digit for the third line. If there are more lines of text than there are digits in the key, then apply the given digits repeatedly; i.e., use the first digit for the fourth line, the second digit for the fifth line, etc.

Test the program using several lines of text of your choice.

**11.52** Modify the craps game simulator given in Example 7.18 so that it simulates a specified number of games and saves the outcome of each game in a text file. At the end of the simulation, read the text file to determine the percentage of wins and losses that the player has experienced.

Test the program by simulating 100 consecutive games. Use the results to estimate the odds of winning in craps.

**11.53** Modify the pig latin generator presented in Example 9.27 so that multiple lines of text can be entered from the keyboard. Save the entire English text in a text file, and save the corresponding pig latin in another text file.

Include within the program a provision for generating a menu which will allow the user to select any one of the following features.

(a) Enter new text, convert to pig latin and save. (Save both the original text and the pig latin, as described above.)

(b) Read previously entered text from a text file and display.

(c) Read the pig latin equivalent of previously entered text and display.

(d) End computation.

Test the program using several arbitrary lines of text.

**11.54** Modify the inventory control system described in Example 10.28 so that it includes a data file containing the individual records. Include provisions for carrying out any of the following operations.

(a) Add a new record.

(b) Modify an existing record (including changes in descriptive information as well as inventory adjustments).

(c) Delete a record.

(d) Generate a complete list of all items presently in stock.

(e) End computation.

Allow the individual operations to be selected from a menu. Test the program using the sample data given in Example 10.28.

**11.55** Write a complete Pascal program that will generate a data file containing the student exam data presented in Prob. 9.52. Let each file component be a record containing the name and exam scores for a single student. Run the program, creating a data file for use in the next problem.

**11.56** Write a file-oriented Pascal program that will process the student exam scores given in Prob. 9.52. Read the data from the data file created in the previous problem. Then create a report containing the name, exam scores and average grade for each student.

**11.57** Extend the program written for Prob. 11.56 so that an overall class average is determined, followed by the deviation of each student's average about the class average. Write the output onto a new data file. Then display the output in the form of a well-labeled report.

**11.58** Write an interactive, file-oriented program that will maintain a list of names, addresses and telephone numbers in alphabetical order (by last name). Place the information associated with each name in a separate record. Include a menu that will allow the user to select any of the following features.

(a) Add a new record.

(b) Delete a record.

(c) Modify an existing record.

(d) Retrieve and display an entire record that corresponds to a given name.

(e) Generate a complete list of all names, addresses and telephone numbers.

(f) End computation.

Be sure to rearrange the records whenever a record is added or deleted so that the records are always maintained in alphabetical order.

**11.59** Write a program that will generate a data file containing the list of countries and their corresponding capitals given in Prob. 9.56. Place the name of each country and its corresponding capital in a separate record. Run the program, creating a data file for use in the next problem.

**11.60** Write an interactive, menu-driven program that will access the data file generated in the preceding problem and then allow one of the following operations to be carried out.

(a) Determine the capital of a specified country.

(b) Determine the country whose capital is specified.

(c) Terminate the computation.

**11.61**	Extend the program written for Prob. 11.60 to include the following additional features.

(*a*)	Add a new record.

(*b*)	Delete a record.

Be sure that the list of countries is maintained in alphabetical order whenever a record is added or deleted.

**11.62**	Write a complete Pascal program that can be used as a simple line-oriented text editor. This program must have the following capabilities.

(*a*)	Enter several lines of text and store in a text file.

(*b*)	List the text file.

(*c*)	Retrieve and display a particular line, determined by line number.

(*d*)	Insert *n* lines.

(*e*)	Delete *n* lines.

(*f*)	Save the newly edited text and end computation.

Each of these tasks should be carried out in response to a one-letter command, preceded by a dollar sign. The find (retrieve) command should be followed by an unsigned integer to indicate which line should be retrieved. Also, the insert and delete commands can be followed by an optional unsigned integer if several consecutive lines are to be inserted or deleted.

Each command should appear on a line by itself, thus providing a means of distinguishing commands from lines of text. (A command line will begin with a dollar sign, followed by a single-letter command, an optional unsigned integer, and an end-of-line designation.)

The following commands are recommended.

> $E—Enter new text.
> $L—List the entire text.
> $F*k*—Find (retrieve) line number *k*.
> $I*n*—Insert *n* lines after line number *k*.
> $D*n*—Delete *n* lines after line number *k*.
> $S—Save the edited text and end computation.

**11.63**	Extend the program described in Prob. 10.42 so that the team information is maintained in a data file rather than an array. Each file component should be a record containing the data for one team. Include provisions for

(*a*)	Entering new records (adding new teams)

(*b*)	Updating existing records

(*c*)	Deleting records (removing teams)

(*d*)	Generating a summary report for all of the teams in the league

# Chapter 12

# Sets

In Pascal we formally define a *set* as a collection of ordered, simple data items that are all of the same type. Thus, a set may be a collection of integers or characters or enumerated data items.

In order to utilize the set concept, we must first define a set type. We can then declare set-type variables whose individual values are elements of that set type. In fact a single set-type variable can represent any number of set elements, including none. This capability offers us a simple way to determine if an entity or an event falls into one or more predefined categories.

## 12.1 DEFINING A SET TYPE

We begin by associating a group of ordered, simple-type data items with a data type using a TYPE definition, as we have done earlier. This data type will be known as the *base type*. We can therefore establish the base type as

```
TYPE base type = (data item 1, data item 2, . . . ,data item n)
```

or

```
TYPE base type = first data item .. last data item
```

The set type that we wish to define is then introduced in terms of the base type; i.e.,

```
set type = SET OF base type
```

Thus, the set type will refer to the same collection of data items as the base type.

Once a set type has been defined we can declare a set-type variable in the following manner.

```
VAR set name : set type
```

or, if several different set-type variables are desired,

```
VAR set name 1, set name 2, . . . ,set name n : set type
```

Each of these set-type variables can represent some subset of the elements within the base type.

### EXAMPLE 12.1

Consider the following declarations.

```
TYPE sizes = (small,medium,large);
     shirtsizes = SET OF sizes;
VAR shortsleeve,longsleeve : shirtsizes;
```

In this example sizes is the base type, consisting of the enumerated data items small, medium and large. The set type is shirtsizes. (Notice that shirtsizes is defined in terms of the base type sizes.) Finally, shortsleeve and longsleeve are set-type variables of type shirtsizes.

We can, if we wish, define several different set types from the same base type. However, most simple applications do not require this much complexity.

312

**EXAMPLE 12.2**

Here is a variation of the set-type definitions given in Example 12.1.

```
TYPE sizes = (small,medium,large);
     shirtsizes,dresssizes = SET OF sizes;
VAR shortsleeve,longsleeve : shirtsizes;
     shorthem,longhem : dresssizes;
```

Notice that shirtsizes and dresssizes are both set types of base type sizes. Also, note that shortsleeve and longsleeve are set-type variables of type shirtsizes, and that shorthem and longhem are set-type variables of type dresssizes.

We can also define a set type in terms of a standard, ordered simple type (e.g., integer or char), or a subrange of a standard, ordered simple type. In such situations the standard data type, or its subrange, becomes the base type.

**EXAMPLE 12.3**

Each of the following set types is defined in terms of a standard, ordered simple type or a corresponding subrange.

```
TYPE numbers = SET OF integer;

TYPE digits = SET OF 0..9;

TYPE numchars = SET OF '0'..'9';

TYPE lowercase = SET OF 'a'..'b';
```

Notice that the second set type defines sets of integers, whereas the third defines sets of characters.


## 12.2  CONSTRUCTING A SET

Now let us turn our attention to the construction of individual sets. Such sets can then be assigned to corresponding set-type variables. They can also be used as operands in certain kinds of boolean expressions (more about this later).

A set can consist of any number of elements from the associated base set. The set is constructed by writing the individual elements consecutively, enclosed in square brackets and separated by commas. Thus, an individual set will appear as

```
[set element 1, set element 2, . . . , set element n]
```

The included elements are known as the *members* of the set.

A set can, of course, consist of only one element, and it is also possible to construct a set that does not contain any elements. This is known as an *empty* (or *null*) set. It is written as [ ].


**EXAMPLE 12.4**

Shown below are several sets that can be constructed from the base type sizes, defined in Example 12.1.

```
[small,medium,large]
[medium,large]
[large,small]
[medium]
[]
```

Notice that the set members need not be ordered, as illustrated by the third set. Also, notice that the last set is empty.

Some of the set members can be represented by variables, provided these variables represent elements of the proper base type. Moreover, if some of the set members are consecutive set elements, they may be represented as a subrange; i.e., as

        *first consecutive element .. last consecutive element*

**EXAMPLE 12.5**

Here are some additional sets that are constructed from the base type sizes and several corresponding variables.

```
TYPE sizes = (small,medium,large);
     shirtsizes = SET OF sizes;
VAR shirt,blouse : sizes;

[small..large]

[shirt]

[shirt,blouse]

[medium,large,blouse]
```

(Note that the variables used in this example are simple-type variables. They are not set-type variables, as described in the last section.)

A set element may not be included in a set more than once. It is possible, however, that a single element will indirectly (and perhaps unintentionally) be specified two or more times, particularly if the set specification includes both explicit set elements and variables. (A variable may represent a set element that has already been specified, thus resulting in unwanted duplication.) In such situations the repeated specification will be ignored.

**EXAMPLE 12.6**

Consider the set

    [medium,large,blouse]

presented in the last example. Recall that medium and large are elements of the base type sizes, but blouse is a *variable* of type sizes. If either medium or large is assigned to blouse, then that element will be repeated within the set. The set will therefore be interpreted as having only two members, medium and large. If blouse represents small, however, then the set will have three members, small, medium and large.

Similar problems can arise if some of the set elements are expressed as a subrange. If the first element and the last element in the subrange are the same, then the subrange will be interpreted as a single element. Moreover, if the first element and the last element are different but in the wrong order (i.e., if the first element comes after the last element), then the set will be considered to be empty.

**EXAMPLE 12.7**

Now consider the set

    [shirt .. blouse]

where shirt and blouse are variables of type sizes, as declared in Example 12.5. If shirt and blouse represent the same base-type element (e.g., medium), then the set will contain only one member, the element medium. Furthermore, if shirt represents an element that comes after blouse in the base type (e.g., if shirt represents large and blouse represents small), then the set will be considered to be empty.

Once a set has been constructed, it can be assigned to a set-type variable. This is accomplished in the usual manner by writing

$$variable\ name := [set\ element\ 1, set\ element\ 2, \ldots, set\ element\ n]$$

It should be understood that the set appearing on the right-hand side is regarded as a single-valued data item. This data item must be of the same set type as the variable to which it is assigned.

**EXAMPLE 12.8**

The following skeletal outline illustrates set assignment within a Pascal program.

```
PROGRAM sample(input,output);
TYPE sizes = (small,medium,large);
     shirtsizes = SET OF sizes;
VAR shortsleeve,longsleeve : shirtsizes;
BEGIN
    .
    .
    shortsleeve := [small,large];
    .
    .
    longsleeve := [small,medium,large];
    .
    .
END.
```

## 12.3   OPERATIONS WITH SETS

There are three different operations that can be carried out with sets which result in the creation of a new set. We refer to the resultants of these operations (i.e., the newly created sets) as the *union*, the *intersection* and the *set difference* of the original two sets, respectively.

Each operation requires two operands (i.e., two sets) of the same type. The resultant will then be of the same type as the operands.

The union of two sets is a new set that contains all of the members of the original two sets. The + operator is used to indicate this operation, as illustrated below.

**EXAMPLE 12.9**

This example illustrates the union of two sets.

```
PROGRAM sample(input,output);
TYPE sizes = (small,medium,large);
     shirtsizes = SET OF sizes;
VAR shortsleeve,longsleeve : shirtsizes;
BEGIN
    .
    .
    shortsleeve := [small] + [large];
    .
    .
    longsleeve := [small,medium] + [small,large];
    .
    .
END.
```

The first assignment statement causes the union of the two sets [small] and [large] to be assigned to the set-type variable shortsleeve. Therefore, shortsleeve will represent the set

```
[small,large]
```

Similarly, the second assignment statement causes the set-type variable longsleeve to represent the set

    [small,medium,large]

The intersection of two sets is a set whose members are common to both of the original sets. The operator * is used to denote this operation.

**EXAMPLE 12.10**

The intersection of two sets is illustrated below.

```
PROGRAM sample(input,output);
TYPE sizes = (small,medium,large);
     shirtsizes = SET OF sizes;
VAR shortsleeve,longsleeve : shirtsizes;
BEGIN
   .
   .
   shortsleeve := [small,medium] * [medium,large];
   .
   .
   longsleeve := [small] * [medium,large];
   .
   .
END.
```

The first assignment statement causes the intersection of the two sets [small,medium] and [medium,large] to be assigned to the set-type variable shortsleeve. Therefore, shortsleeve will represent the set

    [medium]

Similarly, the second assignment statement causes the set-type variable longsleeve to represent the empty set [], since the two operands do not contain any common members.

The set difference of two sets is a set whose members are in the first set but not in the second. This operation is denoted by the operator −, as seen below.

**EXAMPLE 12.11**

This example illustrates the operation of set difference.

```
PROGRAM sample(input,output);
TYPE sizes = (small,medium,large);
     shirtsizes = SET OF sizes;
VAR shortsleeve,longsleeve : shirtsizes;
BEGIN
   .
   .
   shortsleeve := [small,medium] - [small,large];
   .
   .
   longsleeve := [small,medium,large] - [medium];
   .
   .
END.
```

The first assignment statement causes the difference of the two sets [small,medium] and [small,large] to be assigned to the set-type variable shortsleeve. Therefore, shortsleeve will represent the set

    [medium]

Similarly, the second assignment statement causes the set

[small,large]

to be assigned to the set-type variable longsleeve.

These set operations are often combined with set assignment statements to modify the values of set-type variables. This is particularly true of the union and set difference operations.

**EXAMPLE 12.12**

Shown below are several set assignment statements that involve the use of set operations. The variables shortsleeve and longsleeve are assumed to be set-type variables, as defined in the previous examples.

```
shortsleeve := shortsleeve + [medium];

longsleeve := longsleeve - [small];

shortsleeve := longsleeve + [large];

shortsleeve := longsleeve * [small,medium];
```

The first statement causes the element medium to be added to the set represented by the set variable shortsleeve. (If medium is already a member of the set, then this statement will have no effect on the set.)

The purpose of the second statement is to remove the element small from the set represented by the variable longsleeve (unless small is not originally present, in which case the statement has no effect).

In the third statement, large is added to the set represented by longsleeve, and the new set is assigned to the variable shortsleeve. (Note that longsleeve is unchanged.)

Finally, the last statement causes the common members of the set represented by longsleeve and the set [small,medium] to be assigned to the variable shortsleeve.

## 12.4   SET COMPARISONS

Four of the seven relational operators can be used with sets to form boolean-type expressions. These four operators, and their interpretation when used with sets, are summarized below.

| Operator | Interpretation |
| --- | --- |
| = | Set equality (both operands contain the same members, in any order) |
| <> | Set inequality (the operands do not contain exactly the same members) |
| <= | Set inclusion (each member of the first set is included within the second set) |
| >= | Set inclusion (each member of the second set is included within the first set) |

When utilizing any of these operators, both operands must be of the same type.

**EXAMPLE 12.13**

Several boolean expressions involving sets are shown below. (Assume that the set members are elements of the enumerated data type

```
sizes = (small,medium,large)
```

which was first introduced in Example 12.1.)

| Expression | Value |
|---|---|
| [small,large] = [small,medium,large] | false |
| [small,large] = [large,small] | true |
| [small,medium,large] = [small..large] | true |
| [small,medium] <> [medium] | true |
| [small] <= [small..large] | true |
| [small,medium] <= [small,large] | false |
| [small..large] <= [large] | false |
| [] <= [small..large] | true |
| [small,medium,large] >= [medium,large] | true |
| [medium,large] >= [medium,large] | true |
| [medium] >= [small,medium] | false |

Note that the null set is contained in any other set. Hence, an expression such as

        [] <= [small,large]

will always be true.

The relational operators $<=$ and $>=$ have somewhat different interpretations with sets than with other types of operands. In particular, if S1 and S2 are both sets, it is possible that the expressions S1 $<=$ S2 and S1 $>=$ S2 will both be false for certain values of the operands. This cannot happen with other types of operands.

**EXAMPLE 12.14**

Suppose we have two sets that are mutually exclusive, such as [small] and [large]. Then the boolean expressions

        [small] <= [large]

and

        [small] >= [large]

will both be false.

When carrying out set comparisons, the elements within a set can be expressed as variables whose base type includes the set members. Moreover, a comparison may be carried out between a set and a set-type variable of the same base type.

**EXAMPLE 12.15**

Consider the following skeletal outline.

```
PROGRAM sample(input,output);
TYPE letters = SET OF char;
VAR used,unused : letters;
    alpha : char;
    line : PACKED ARRAY [1..80] OF char;
BEGIN
    .
    .
    FOR alpha := 'A' TO 'z' DO
        IF [alpha] <= used THEN write(alpha);
    .
    .
    WHILE NOT ([line[1]] <= ['E','e']) DO
```

(*Program continues on next page*)

```
            BEGIN
              .
              .
              .
            END;
       .
       .
   END.
```

In the first action statement (i.e., the FOR—TO statement), the set containing the value of alpha is compared with the value of used. Note that alpha is a char-type variable, so that [alpha] is a set which contains a single char-type element. Also, used is a set-type variable of base type char. Thus we are comparing sets whose elements are of the same base type (i.e., we are comparing sets whose elements are characters).

Notice that the FOR—TO loop considers all characters ranging from uppercase A (ASCII value 65, see App. G) to lowercase z (ASCII value 122). This assures that all of the characters in the alphabet will be included in the comparison.

In the second action statement (the WHILE—DO statement), the set containing the value of line[1] is compared with the the the set ['E','e']. Recall that line[1] is an element of an array of type char. Therefore [line[1]] will be a set containing a single element of type char. The set with which it is compared, ['E','e'], contains two members, also of type char. Hence we are comparing two sets whose elements are of the same base type.

The following example presents a complete Pascal program that includes the use of sets.

### EXAMPLE 12.16

**Analyzing a Line of Text.** Suppose we want to enter a line of text into the computer and then determine which letters of the alphabet are included within that line. This can easily be accomplished through the use of sets:

Our overall strategy will be to read in a line of text, analyze the line by determining which letters are present, and then write out all of the letters that have been found. We will consider both uppercase and lowercase letters, but not other kinds of characters (e.g., punctuation).

Let us introduce the following declarations.

```
TYPE letters = SET OF char;
VAR used,unused : letters;
    count : 0..80;
    alpha : char;
    line : PACKED ARRAY [1..80] OF char;
```

The set-type variables used and unused will represent the set of used and the set of unused letters, respectively. Also, line will represent the actual line of text.

Given these declarations, the main action block might appear as

```
BEGIN
    readinput;    (* read in a line of text *)
    used := [];
    unused := ['A'..'Z','a'..'z'];
    FOR count := 1 TO 80 DO
        IF [line[count]] <= unused THEN
            BEGIN
                used := used + [line[count]];
                unused := unused - [line[count]]
            END;
    writeoutput   (* write out the results of the analysis *)
END.
```

The statements readinput and writeoutput are references to procedures that read in the line of text and write out the results of the analysis, respectively.

Once the line of text has been entered, the set-type variables used and unused are initialized by assigning a null set to used, and a set containing all upper- and lowercase letters to unused. We then scan the line of text on a character-by-character basis. If the character being examined is an unused letter (i.e., if the set [line[count]] is contained within the set unused), then used and unused are updated by adding the current letter to used and removing it from unused. The updating is accomplished by writing

```
used := used + [line[count]];

unused := unused - [line[count]];
```

The results of the analysis are then written out.

This strategy will work nicely for a single line of text, but the program will have to be restarted for each new line. Let us therefore modify the main action block so that it runs repetitively, until the word "end" is entered at the start of a new line. Hence, the main action block will be modified to read

```
BEGIN
    readinput;    (* read in a line of text *)
    WHILE NOT (([line[1]] <= ['E','e']) AND
               ([line[2]] <= ['N','n']) AND
               ([line[3]] <= ['D','d'])) DO
        BEGIN
            used := [];
            unused := ['A'..'Z','a'..'z'];
            FOR count := 1 TO 80 DO
                IF [line[count]] <= unused THEN
                    BEGIN
                        used := used + [line[count]];
                        unused := unused - [line[count]]
                    END;
            writeoutput;    (* write out the results of the analysis *)
            readinput
        END
END.
```

The WHILE—DO structure allows the computation to continue until a new line of text contains an e in the first column, an n in the second column and a d in the third column. Notice that the use of set comparisons within this structure allows a convenient way to test for both upper- and lowercase letters.

The procedure used to enter a line of text, readinput, begins by initializing line so that it contains only blank spaces. It then reads the actual text, overwriting the initial blanks. The reading will continue until an end-of-line designation has been detected. Here is the complete procedure.

```
PROCEDURE readinput;
(* this procedure reads in a line of text *)
BEGIN
    FOR count := 1 TO 80 DO line[count] := ' ';
    writeln('Please enter a line of text below');
    count := 0;
    WHILE NOT eoln DO
        BEGIN
            count := count + 1;
            read(line[count])
        END;
    readln
END;
```

The output procedure, writeoutput, utilizes a somewhat different approach. Here we loop through all of the letters of the alphabet (upper- and lowercase), and write out those letters that are members of the set used. The complete procedure can be written as

```
    PROCEDURE writeoutput;
    (* this procedure writes out an analysis of a line of text *)
    BEGIN
       writeln;
       write('Letters used:');
       FOR alpha := 'A' TO 'z' DO
          IF [alpha] <= used THEN write(' ',alpha);
       writeln;
       writeln
    END;
```

(Recall that alpha is a char-type variable. Therefore [alpha] and used both represent sets whose elements are of type char.)

The complete Pascal program is shown below.

```
    PROGRAM lettersused(input,output);

    (* THIS PROGRAM READS A LINE OF TEXT AND
       DETERMINES WHICH LETTERS ARE PRESENT *)

    TYPE letters = SET OF char;
    VAR used,unused : letters;
        count : 0..80;
        alpha : char;
        line : PACKED ARRAY [1..80] OF char;

    PROCEDURE readinput;
    (* this procedure reads in a line of text *)
    BEGIN
       FOR count := 1 TO 80 DO line[count] := ' ';
       writeln('Please enter a line of text below');
       count := 0;
       WHILE NOT eoln DO
          BEGIN
             count := count + 1;
             read(line[count])
          END;
       readln
    END;

    PROCEDURE writeoutput;
    (* this procedure writes out an analysis of a line of text *)
    BEGIN
       writeln;
       write('Letters used:');
       FOR alpha := 'A' TO 'z' DO
          IF [alpha] <= used THEN write(' ',alpha);
       writeln;
       writeln
    END;

    BEGIN   (* main action block *)
       readinput;
       WHILE NOT ((([line[1]] <= ['E','e']) AND
                   ([line[2]] <= ['N','n']) AND
                   ([line[3]] <= ['D','d'])) DO
```

(*Program continues on next page*)

```
            BEGIN
               used := [];
               unused := ['A'..'Z','a'..'z'];
               FOR count := 1 TO 80 DO
                  IF [line[count]] <= unused THEN
                     BEGIN
                        used := used + [line[count]];
                        unused := unused - [line[count]]
                     END;
               writeoutput;
               readinput
            END
         END.
```

Now suppose that the program is used to process the following line of text.

```
   Pascal is a structured programming language derived from ALGOL-60
```

Execution of the program would then generate the following dialogue. (The user's responses are shown underlined.)

```
   Please enter a line of text below
   Pascal is a structured programming language derived from ALGOL-60
```

```
   Letters used: A G L O P a c d e f g i l m n o p r s t u v
```

```
   Please enter a line of text below
   end
```

## 12.5  MEMBERSHIP TESTING

Pascal also includes an additional relational operator, IN, which is used to form boolean expressions. This operator can be used only with set-type operands. It is particularly useful, since it allows us to determine whether or not a value is contained within a set (i.e., whether or not the value is a member of the set).

Formally, the IN operator must be used in the following manner to create boolean-type expressions:

> *set element* IN *set*

The expression will be true if the first operand is a member of the second, and false otherwise. Both operands must correspond to the same base type. The first operand may be an individual set element or a variable or expression representing a set element. The second operand is generally a set or a set-type variable.

### EXAMPLE 12.17

Consider the following variation on the set declarations presented in Example 12.1.

```
   TYPE sizes = (small,medium,large);
        shirtsizes = SET OF sizes;
   VAR shortsleeve,longsleeve : shirtsizes;
       mysize : sizes
```

Several boolean expressions that illustrate the use of the IN operator are shown below.

```
   medium IN [small,medium,large]
```

```
   medium IN [small,large]
```

```
   mysize IN [small,medium]
```

```
   mysize IN shortsleeve
```

The first expression is true and the second is false. The value of the third expression, however, will depend on the value that is assigned to mysize. If mysize represents small or medium, then the expression will be true. Otherwise, it will be false.

Similarly, the value of the last expression will depend on the values that are assigned to mysize and to shortsleeve. If mysize represents an element that is a member of the set represented by shortsleeve, then the expression will be true; otherwise it will be false.

For example, suppose that mysize represents the value large. The expression will be true if shortsleeve represents any of the following sets:

[small,medium,large]

[small,large]

[medium,large]

[large]

But the expression will be false for all other values of shortsleeve.

Membership testing is frequently used in conjunction with various control structures within a Pascal program. This allows us to carry out various logical operations selectively, only if certain set-type membership conditions are satisfied.

### EXAMPLE 12.18

Consider the skeletal outline shown below.

```
PROGRAM sample(input,output);
TYPE letters = SET OF char;
VAR vowels,consonants : letters;
    count,vowelcount,conscount : 0..80;
    line : PACKED ARRAY [1..80] OF char;

BEGIN
    vowels := ['A','E','I','O','U','a','e','i','o','u'];
    consonants := ['A'..'Z','a'..'z'] - vowels;
    .
    .
    .
    vowelcount := 0;
    conscount := 0;
    .
    .
    .
    FOR count := 1 TO 80 DO
        BEGIN
            IF line[count] IN vowels
                THEN vowelcount := vowelcount + 1;
            IF line[count] IN consonants
                THEN conscount := conscount + 1
        END;
    .
    .
    .
END.
```

The first two statements assign values to the set-type variables vowels and consonants. The two IF statements (within the FOR structure) then test to see if the current value of the char-type array element line[count] is a member of the sets represented by vowels and consonants.

It is instructive to compare this outline with the skeletal outline shown in Example 12.15. In the present example we are testing to see if a single data item is a member of a set. On the other hand, in the earlier example we tested to see if one set was contained within another. (Note that base-type compatibility is required in both examples.)

A complete Pascal program that makes use of membership testing is presented in the next example.

**EXAMPLE 12.19**

**Number of Vowels in a Line of Text.** Let us now develop a Pascal program that will perform the following functions:

1. Enter a line of text into the computer.
2. Determine the total number of characters (including blank spaces and punctuation) within the line.
3. Determine the total number of vowels and the total number of consonants within the line.
4. Write out the total number of characters, the number of vowels and the number of consonants.

Write the program so that it will execute repetitively, until the word "end" is entered at the beginning of a new line. Allow "end" to be entered in either uppercase or lowercase letters.

We begin by introducing the following declarations.

```
TYPE letters = SET OF char;
VAR vowels,consonants : letters;
    count,charcount,vowelcount,conscount : 0..80;
    line : PACKED ARRAY [1..80] OF char;
```

The set-type variables vowels and consonants will represent the sets of vowels and consonants, respectively. Both upper- and lowercase letters will be included in each set. The integer variables charcount, vowelcount and conscount will represent the total number of characters in the line of text (including blank spaces and punctuation), the number of vowels and the number of consonants, respectively. And finally, the char-type array line will represent the actual line of text.

Now let us consider the main action block. If we include a provision for repetitive program execution, the main block can be written as follows.

```
BEGIN
    vowels := ['A','E','I','O','U','a','e','i','o','u'];
    consonants := ['A'..'Z','a'..'z'] - vowels;
    readinput;
    WHILE NOT ((line[1] IN ['E','e']) AND
               (line[2] IN ['N','n']) AND
               (line[3] IN ['D','d'])) DO
      BEGIN
        vowelcount := 0;
        conscount := 0;
        FOR count := 1 TO 80 DO
           BEGIN
              IF line[count] IN vowels
                 THEN vowelcount := vowelcount + 1;
              IF line[count] IN consonants
                 THEN conscount := conscount + 1
           END;
        writeoutput;
        readinput
      END
END.
```

The first two statements establish the values for the set-type variables vowels and consonants, respectively. These values will be used as standards for membership testing and therefore will not change throughout the program.

Following the set assignments we see the statement readinput. This is a reference to a procedure that causes the line of text to be read into the computer and the total number of characters to be counted.

Now consider the WHILE—DO structure, which is actually the heart of the program. The structure begins by assigning an initial value of zero to the counters vowelcount and conscount. The program then examines the entire line of text on a character-by-character basis. If a given character is a vowel (more precisely, if a given character is a member of the set of characters assigned to vowels), the vowel counter (vowelcount) is incremented by 1. Similarly, if a given character is a consonant, the consonant counter (conscount) is incremented by 1.

The results of the analysis are then written out by accessing the procedure writeoutput, and a new line of text is then entered into the computer via procedure readinput. This cycle is repeated until the word "end" is entered at the beginning of a new line of text.

The procedure used to read in a new line of text and determine the total number of characters can be written as follows:

```
PROCEDURE readinput;
(* this procedure reads in a line of text *)
BEGIN
    writeln('Please enter a line of text below');
    count := 0;
    WHILE NOT eoln DO
       BEGIN
          count := count + 1;
          read(line[count])
       END;
    readln;
    charcount := count
END;
```

This procedure is straightforward and does not require further discussion.

The output procedure, writeoutput, is equally straightforward. This procedure merely writes out the final values for the three counters, charcount, vowelcount and conscount. We can therefore write this procedure as

```
PROCEDURE writeoutput;
(* this procedure writes out an analysis of a line of text *)
BEGIN
    writeln;
    writeln('Number of characters: ',charcount:2);
    writeln('Number of vowels    : ',vowelcount:2);
    writeln('Number of consonants: ',conscount:2);
    writeln
END;
```

Here is the complete program.

```
PROGRAM vowelcount(input,output);

(* THIS PROGRAM COUNTS THE TOTAL NUMBER OF CHARACTERS,
   THE NUMBER OF VOWELS AND THE NUMBER OF CONSONANTS
   APPEARING IN A LINE OF TEXT *)

TYPE letters = SET OF char;
VAR vowels,consonants : letters;
    count,charcount,vowelcount,conscount : 0..80;
    line : PACKED ARRAY [1..80] OF char;

PROCEDURE readinput;
(* this procedure reads in a line of text *)
BEGIN
    writeln('Please enter a line of text below');
    count := 0;
    WHILE NOT eoln DO
       BEGIN
          count := count + 1;
          read(line[count])
       END;
    readln;
    charcount := count
END;
```

(*Program continues on next page*)

```
PROCEDURE writeoutput;
(* this procedure writes out an analysis of a line of text *)
BEGIN
   writeln;
   writeln('Number of characters: ',charcount:2);
   writeln('Number of vowels    : ',vowelcount:2);
   writeln('Number of consonants: ',conscount:2);
   writeln
END;

BEGIN   (* main action block *)
   vowels := ['A','E','I','O','U','a','e','i','o','u'];
   consonants := ['A'..'Z','a'..'z'] - vowels;
   readinput;
   WHILE NOT ((line[1] IN ['E','e']) AND
              (line[2] IN ['N','n']) AND
              (line[3] IN ['D','d'])) DO
      BEGIN
         vowelcount := 0;
         conscount := 0;
         FOR count := 1 TO 80 DO
            BEGIN
               IF line[count] IN vowels
                  THEN vowelcount := vowelcount + 1;
               IF line[count] IN consonants
                  THEN conscount := conscount + 1
            END;
         writeoutput;
         readinput
      END
END.
```

Now consider what happens when this program is executed. Suppose, for example, that we enter the following lines of text.

```
Pascal is a structured programming language derived from ALGOL-60
end
```

Execution of the program would then result in the following dialogue. (Note that the user's responses are shown underlined.)

```
Please enter a line of text below
Pascal is a structured programming language derived from ALGOL-60

Number of characters: 65
Number of vowels    : 20
Number of consonants: 34

Please enter a line of text below
end
```

# Review Questions

**12.1**   What are the principal characteristics of a set? How does a set differ from an array? How does it differ from a record?

**12.2**   What is meant by a base type? How is a base type defined?

**12.3**   What is meant by a set type? How does a set type differ from a base type? How is a set type defined?

**12.4**   Which types of data can be included within a set?

**12.5**   Can several different set types be defined having the same base type?

**12.6**   What is the purpose of a set-type variable? What kind of data item is represented by a set-type variable?

**12.7**   Summarize the rules for constructing a set.

**12.8**   What is the minimum number of elements that must be present in a set?

**12.9**   When constructing a set, must the individual set elements be specified in any particular order?

**12.10**  What restrictions apply to the use of set-type variables when constructing a set?

**12.11**  When constructing a set, can consecutive set elements be expressed as a subrange?

**12.12**  When constructing a set, what happens if the same set element is specified more than once?

**12.13**  Suppose that a set specification consists of a single subrange, and the subrange specification is written in the wrong order. How will this be interpreted? Explain.

**12.14**  Summarize the rules for assigning a set to a set-type variable. What restrictions apply with regard to type compatibility?

**12.15**  What is meant by the union of two sets? How can this operation be carried out in Pascal? What restrictions apply to the operands?

**12.16**  What is meant by the intersection of two sets? How is this operation carried out in Pascal? What restrictions apply to the operands?

**12.17**  What is meant by the difference of two sets? How is this operation carried out in Pascal? What restrictions apply to the operands?

**12.18**  Which relational operators can be used with set-type operands? What are the relational operators used for? How is each interpreted?

**12.19**  What is meant by membership testing? How is membership testing carried out in Pascal?

**12.20**  What kinds of operands can be used with the relational operator IN? Compare with the use of other relational operators with set-type operands.

# Solved Problems

**12.21** Shown below are several illustrative set definitions and set-type variable declarations.

(*a*)  VAR vowels,consonants : SET OF char;

(*b*)  VAR caps : SET OF 'A'..'Z';

(*c*)  TYPE capitals = 'A'..'Z';
       VAR  caps : SET OF capitals;

(*d*)  TYPE capitals = 'A'..'Z';
              uppers = SET OF capitals;
       VAR  caps : uppers;

(*e*)  VAR movement : SET OF (north,south,east,west);

(*f*)  TYPE compass = (north,south,east,west);
       VAR  movement : SET OF compass;

(*g*)  TYPE compass = (north,south,east,west);
              direction = SET OF compass;
       VAR  nextmove,lastmove : direction;

**12.22** Determine which elements are included in each of the sets given below, based upon the following declarations.

TYPE weekdays = (sun,mon,tue,wed,thu,fri,sat);
       days = SET OF weekdays;

(*a*)  [mon..fri]                          (*d*)  [fri..mon] + [wed]

(*b*)  [mon..fri] + [wed]                  (*e*)  [tue] - [mon..sat]

(*c*)  [mon..fri] - [wed]                  (*f*)  [sun..wed] * [tue..sat]

(*a*)   [mon,tue,wed,thu,fri]             (*d*)   [wed]

(*b*)   [mon,tue,wed,thu,fri]             (*e*)   [ ]

(*c*)   [mon,tue,thu,fri]                 (*f*)   [tue,wed]

**12.23** Determine the outcome of each of the assignment statements shown below, based upon the following declarations.

TYPE weekdays = (sun,mon,tue,wed,thu,fri,sat);
       days = SET OF weekdays;
VAR workdays,restdays : days;
       today : weekdays;

(*a*)  workdays := [mon,wed..sat] + [sun];

(*b*)  restdays := [tue,thu];
              .
              .
              .
       workdays := [mon..sat] - restdays;

(*c*)  workdays := [ ];
       FOR today := mon TO thu DO
              workdays := workdays + [today];
       restdays := workdays * [thu..sat];

(*a*)   workdays = [sun,mon,wed,thu,fri,sat]

(*b*)   workdays = [mon,wed,fri,sat]

(*c*)   workdays = [mon,tue,wed,thu]
              restdays = [thu]

**12.24** Determine the value of each boolean expression given below, based upon the following declarations.

```
TYPE weekdays = (sun,mon,tue,wed,thu,fri,sat);
     days = SET OF weekdays;
VAR workdays,restdays : days;
    today : weekdays;
```

(a) [sun,sat] = [sun..sat]

(b) [tues,fri] >= []

(c) [mon,wed,fri] <= [mon..fri]

(d) [fri,mon..wed] = [mon,wed,fri]

(e) workdays := [mon..fri];
................................
    workdays <> [mon,tue,wed,thu,fri]

(f) today := fri;
    restdays := [fri,sat,sun];
........................
    [today] <= restdays

(g) mon IN [mon,wed,fri]

(h) sun IN [sun..sat]

(i) sat IN [mon,wed,fri]

(j) today := wed;
.................
    today IN [mon,wed,fri]

(k) today := sat;
    workdays := [mon..fri];
....................
    today IN workdays

| | | | | | |
|---|---|---|---|---|---|
|(a)|false|(e)|false|(i)|false|
|(b)|true|(f)|true|(j)|true|
|(c)|true|(g)|true|(k)|false|
|(d)|false|(h)|true| | |

## Supplementary Problems

**12.25** Determine which elements are included in each of the sets given below, based upon the following declarations.

```
TYPE notes = (do,re,mi,fa,sol,la,ti);
     song  = SET OF notes;
```

(a) [re..la]

(b) [do..fa] + [re..la]

(c) [do..fa] - [re..la]

(d) [do..fa] * [re..la]

(e) [do..fa] - [la..re]

(f) [re,fa,sol] - [re..la]

(g) [re,fa,sol] * []

(h) [do,re,mi] + [re]

**12.26** Determine the outcome of each of the assignment statements shown below, based upon the following declarations.

```
TYPE notes = (do,re,mi,fa,sol,la,ti);
     song  = SET OF notes;
VAR ballad,disco : song;
    tone : notes;
```

(a) ballad := [do..fa] * [re,fa];

(b) disco := [do..fa] - [mi];

(*continues on next page*)

(c)   tone := ti;
.
.
.
      ballad := [re..fa,la] + [tone];
(d)   disco := [do,mi,sol];
.
.
.
      ballad := disco + [re,ti];
(e)   disco := [];
      FOR tone := la DOWNTO re DO
         disco := disco + [tone];


**12.27**   Determine the value of each boolean expression given below, based upon the following declarations.

    TYPE coins = (penny,nickel,dime,quarter,half,dollar);
         change = SET OF coins;
    VAR money : coins;
        wine,whiskey,song : change;

(a)   [penny,nickel] <= [penny,quarter]

(b)   [nickel,dime,quarter] = [nickel..quarter]

(c)   [penny..dollar] = [dollar..penny]

(d)   [nickel..quarter] >= [dime,quarter]

(e)   [half..nickel] <> []

(f)   dollar IN [penny..dollar]

(g)   money := dollar;
. . . . . . . .
      [money] <= [penny..dollar]

(h)   money := dollar;
. . . . . . . .
      money IN [penny..dollar]

(i)   wine := [penny,nickel,dime];
. . . . . . . . . . . . .
      dollar IN wine

(j)   whiskey := [penny,nickel,dime];
. . . . . . . . . . . . . . .
      dime IN whiskey

(k)   wine := [penny,nickel,dime];
      song := [dime..dollar];
. . . . . . . . . . .
      dime IN wine*song

(l)   money := penny;
      song := [dime..dollar];
. . . . . . . . . . .
      money IN song


**12.28**   Shown below are several statements or groups of statements that involve sets or set members, based upon the declarations given in the previous problem. Some of the statements are incorrect. Identify all errors.

(a)   money := dime;
          .
          .
          .
      WHILE money IN [penny,nickel,dime] DO
          BEGIN
              .
              .
              .
          END;

(b)   money := dime;
          .
          .
          .
      WHILE money <= [penny,nickel,dime] DO
          BEGIN
              .
              .
              .
          END;

(c)   song := [];
          .
          .
          .
      FOR money := penny TO dollar DO
          song := song + money;

(d)   IF NOT (quarter IN wine) THEN
          wine := wine + [quarter];

(e)   IF [penny] <= song THEN song := song - [penny];

(f)   IF whiskey IN [penny..quarter] THEN
          whiskey := whiskey + [half];

# Programming Problems

**12.29**  Modify the program given in Example 12.16 in the following ways:

(a)  Utilize membership testing within the program (i.e., replace the boolean expressions with equivalent expressions that make use of the IN operator).

(b)  Determine which nonletter characters (i.e., digits, punctuation marks, etc.) are present, in addition to the characters that are present.

(c)  Write out the following four lists after analyzing each line:

1.  The letters that are included in the given line of text.

2.  The nonletter characters that are included in the given line of text.

3.  The letters that are *not* included within the text.

4.  The nonletter characters that are not included.

Test the program using several lines of input which you have chosen.

**12.30**  Extend the program given in Example 12.19 to include the following features.

(a) Count the number of times each vowel appears within the line of text.

(b) Determine the number of words within the line. (*Hint*: count the number of blank spaces within the line.)

(c) Determine the average length of each word within the line.

Test the program using several lines of your own input.

**12.31** Write an interactive Pascal program that will convert a date, entered in the form mm-dd-yy (e.g., 4-12-69) into an integer that indicates the number of days beyond January 1, 1960, using the method described in Prob. 6.50(*r*). Include error checks in the program so that an incorrectly entered date will be detected and an appropriate error message generated. Utilize a set-type data structure for the error-check routine.

**12.32** Rewrite the interactive tic-tac-toe program described in Prob. 7.50(*i*) so that it includes an error-checking routine for the input data. This routine should check for illegal moves and incorrect responses to the input prompts. Utilize a set-type data structure for this purpose.

**12.33** Write an interactive Pascal program that makes use of the set-type data structure for each of the following gambling games.

(a) The interactive blackjack game, described in Prob. 9.58(*a*).

(b) The interactive roulette game, described in Prob. 9.58(*b*).

(c) The interactive BINGO game, described in Prob. 9.58(*c*).

(*Suggestion*: The set-type data structure offers a convenient way to carry out error checking, membership testing and sampling without replacement.)

**12.34** Rewrite the pig latin generator described in Prob. 9.50 so that it makes use of a set-type data structure when testing for punctuation marks, uppercase letters and double-letter sounds. Is the use of a set the best way to implement each of these tests?

**12.35** Problem 9.52 describes a programming application in which the exam scores for each student in a Pascal programming course are averaged and an overall class average is determined. Now suppose that five numerical ranges are defined in such a way that the overall class average falls in the middle of the third category. Each student could then be given a letter grade, determined by the particular range that contains the student's average score. Thus, the first (highest) range would represent A's, the second would represent B's, etc.

One way to construct the individual numerical ranges is as follows. Let CA represent the overall class average. Calculate the quotient

$$Q = \frac{(100 - CA)}{3}$$

Then calculate the ranges as

| | | | | |
|---|---|---|---|---|
| first range | (A): | (CA + 2Q) | to | 100 |
| second range | (B): | (CA + Q) | to | (CA + 2Q) |
| third range | (C): | (CA − Q) | to | (CA + Q) |
| fourth range | (D): | (CA − 2Q) | to | (CA − Q) |
| fifth range | (F): | below (CA−2Q) | | |

Thus, if the overall class average were 70 percent, $Q$ would equal $(100 − 70)/3 = 10$, and the ranges would be

A: 90 to 100
B: 80 to 90
C: 60 to 80
D: 50 to 60
F: below 50

Write an interactive Pascal program that will implement this strategy, assuming equal weighting of all exams. Include both record-type and set-type data structures in your program. Test the program using the data given in Prob. 9.52.

**12.36** Here is an interesting technique for obtaining a list of prime numbers that fall within the interval ranging from 2 to $n$.

(a) Generate an ordered list of integers ranging from 2 to $n$.

(b) For some particular integer, $i$, within the list, carry out the following operations:

1. Write out the integer, thus adding it to the list of primes.

2. Remove all succeeding integers that are multiples of $i$.

(c) Part (b) is repeated for each successive value of $i$, beginning with $i = 2$ and ending with the last remaining integer.

This method is often referred to as the *sieve of Eratosthenes*.

Write a Pascal program that uses this method to determine the primes that are contained in a list of numbers ranging from 1 to $n$, where $n$ is an input quantity. Utilize a set-type data structure within the program.

**12.37** An employment agency wishes to maintain a computerized list of currently available positions. Within this list, each position will be described by the monthly salary and one or more attributes that characterize the position.

When the agency is approached by a person seeking a position, descriptive information about that person will be entered into the computer and compared with the attributes that characterize the available positions. A list will then be generated of all positions with a sufficiently high monthly salary and attributes that match those of the prospective employee.

The following attributes are used to characterize the required job skills:

| Attribute | Job Skill |
| --- | --- |
| A | accounting |
| B | business |
| C | computer programming |
| D | dental technology |
| E | engineering/technical |
| F | food service |
| M | medical technology |
| P | personnel administration |
| R | receptionist |
| S | sales |
| T | typing/word processing |
| U | unskilled labor |

Several attributes are also required to indicate the required educational level. They are

| Attribute | Educational Level |
| --- | --- |
| 1 | high school |
| 2 | vocational |
| 3 | college |
| 4 | postgraduate |

Write a Pascal program that can accommodate the needs of the agency. Use a set-type data structure to carry out the matching.

Test the program using the following data:

Positions Available

| Position Number | Monthly Salary, $ | Required Job Skills | Education Level |
|---|---|---|---|
| 1 | 625 | U | 1 |
| 2 | 1350 | A,T | 3 |
| 3 | 900 | S | 3 |
| 4 | 2400 | E,B | 4 |
| 5 | 450 | F | 1 |
| 6 | 1100 | P,T | 1 |
| 7 | 1700 | D,T,R | 1 |
| 8 | 200 | M | 2 |

Potential Employees

| Client Number | Minimum Req'd Salary, $ | Job Skills | Education Level |
|---|---|---|---|
| 1 | 800 | R,T | 1 |
| 2 | 1200 | A,C,T | 3 |
| 3 | 2000 | E,B,C | 4 |
| 4 | 400 | U | 1 |
| 5 | 800 | S,P,T | 3 |

**12.38** Modify the program written for the above problem so that information describing the positions available is stored in a data file. Utilize a record-type data structure to represent each of the available positions. Include provisions for adding records, deleting records, changing records and listing all records.

**12.39** A university wishes to create an automated registration procedure for its students. Each department will utilize its own small computer and its own database for this purpose. The database will contain a list of all courses that the student must take in order to graduate and the corresponding prerequisites. This list of courses will be stored in a data file.

The courses should be taken in numerical order, except that students cannot register for a course unless they have taken (and passed) all of the required prerequisites. This situation becomes somewhat complicated by the fact that some students fail a course and are therefore thrown out of sequence. Also, some students transfer into a program of study and therefore have not taken all of the prerequisites.

Write a Pascal program that will allow each student in a given department to register for three new courses each term, choosing from the courses that are listed in the data file. (Assume that all of the courses listed will be offered each term.) The courses should be selected in their proper numerical sequence, provided the student has successfully completed all of the prerequisites for each course. Use a set-type data structure to carry out the selection.

Test your program using the following sample data (the prerequisites for each course are shown in parentheses following the course number).

Courses

| | | | |
|---|---|---|---|
| 101 | 201 (101) | 301 (204) | 401 (301) |
| 102 | 202 | 302 (102,202) | 402 (302) |
| 103 | 203 (106) | 303 | 403 |
| 104 (101) | 204 (201) | 304 (301) | 404 (304) |
| 105 (102) | 205 | 305 (302) | 405 (205) |
| 106 | 206 (102,203) | 306 | 406 (102,306) |

(continues on next page)

Student Records

| Name | Courses Taken |
|------|---------------|
| Smith | 101,103 |
| Brown | 101,102,103,104,105,202 |
| Richardson | 101,102,103,104,105,106,201,203,204 |
| Davis | 101,102,104,105,201,203,204,206,301,304 |
| Thomas | 101,102,103,104,105,106,201,202,203,204, 205,206,302,303,305,306,402,405 |

# Chapter 13

# Lists and Pointers

In Chaps. 9 through 12 we were concerned with several different structured data types; namely, the array, the record, the file and the set. Though each of these data types has its own unique features, they share certain common characteristics. For example, the maximum number of components within an array, a record or a set (and hence the required amount of memory) is specified within the data declaration and remains unchanged throughout the program. Furthermore, the individual components within a particular structured data type are arranged in a fixed order with respect to one another. (This is true of all structured data types, including files.) These characteristics tend to restrict the utility of the structured data types for certain kinds of applications.

In particular, some applications require the use of lists, whose components are linked together by means of *pointers*. Such lists are therefore referred to as *linked lists*. Linked lists are used, for example, in the construction of compilers, operating systems and database management systems. Therefore, we now turn our attention to the use of linked lists within Pascal.

## 13.1 PRELIMINARIES

The basic idea of a linked list is that each individual component within the list includes a pointer that indicates where the next component can be found. Therefore, the relative order of the components can easily be changed simply by altering the pointers. In addition, individual components can easily be added to or removed from the list, again by altering the pointers. Hence a linked list is not confined to some maximum number of components. Such a list can expand and contract in size as its host program is executed.

### EXAMPLE 13.1

Figure 13-1(*a*) illustrates a linked list consisting of three components. Each component consists of two data items—an enumerated value (a color), and a pointer that references the next component within the list. Thus the first component has the value red, the second green and the third blue. The beginning of the list is indicated by a separate pointer, which is labeled start. Also, the end of the list is indicated by the value NIL (more about this later).

Now let us add another component, whose value is white, between red and green. To do so we merely change the pointers, as illustrated in Fig. 13-1(*b*).

If we now choose to delete the component whose value is green, we simply change the pointer associated with the second component, as shown in Fig. 13-1(*c*).

There are several different kinds of linked structures, including *linear* linked lists (in which the components are all linked together in some sequential manner), linked lists with multiple pointers (permitting forward and backward traversal through the list), *circular* lists (a linear list having no beginning and no ending) and *trees* (in which the components are arranged in a hierarchical structure). We have already seen an illustration of a linear linked list in Example 13.1. Some other kinds of linked lists are shown in the next example.

### EXAMPLE 13.2

In Fig. 13-2 we see a linear linked list that is similar to that shown in Fig. 13-1(*a*). Now, however, we see that there are *two* pointers associated with each component—a forward pointer and a backward pointer. This double set of pointers allows us to traverse the list in either direction; i.e., from beginning to end or from end to beginning.

336

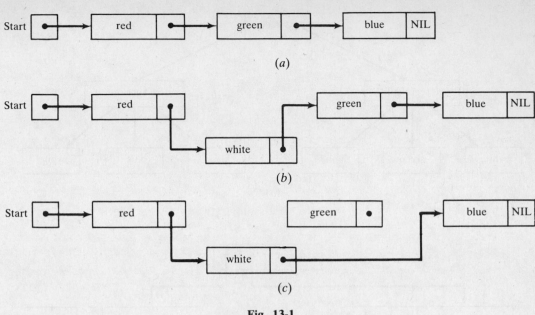

(a)

(b)

(c)

Fig. 13-1

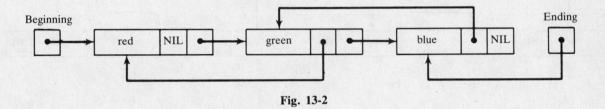

Fig. 13-2

Now consider the list shown in Fig. 13-3. This list is similar to that shown in Fig. 13-1(a), except that the last data item (blue) points to the first data item (red). Hence, this list has no beginning and no ending. Such lists are referred to as circular lists.

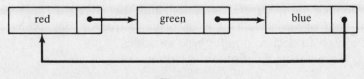

Fig. 13-3

Finally, in Fig. 13-4(a) we see an example of a tree. Trees consist of nodes and branches, arranged in some hierarchical manner which indicates a corresponding hierarchical structuring of the data. (A *binary tree* is a tree in which every node has no more than two branches.)

In Fig. 13-4(a) the root node has the value screen, and the associated branches lead to the nodes whose values are foreground and background, respectively. Similarly, the branches associated with foreground lead to the nodes whose values are white, green and amber, and the branches associated with background lead to the nodes whose values are black, blue and white.

Figure 13-4(b) illustrates the manner in which pointers are used to construct the tree.

Pascal does not include each linked structure as a separate data type. Rather, Pascal supports a single data type—the *pointer*—which allows various kinds of linked structures to be constructed from a common set of rules.

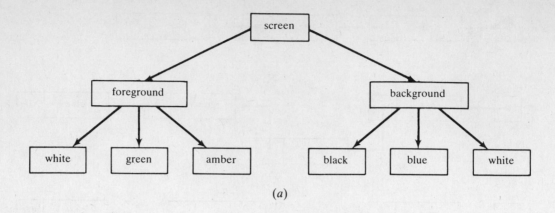

(a)

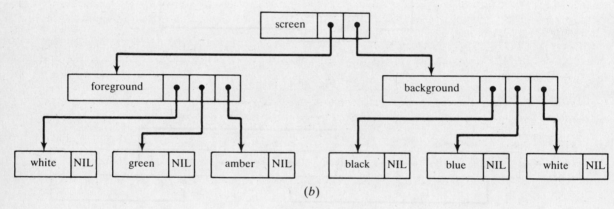

(b)

**Fig. 13-4**

## 13.2  TYPE DEFINITIONS

In applications that involve linked lists, we must work with two different kinds of variables: *pointer variables* (i.e., variables whose values point to other variables) and *referenced variables* (i.e., variables that are "pointed to"). Careful attention must be given to the type definition that is associated with each kind of variable. This is particularly true of the *pointer type*; i.e., the type definition that will be used to declare pointer-type variables.

In general terms, a pointer-type definition is written as

TYPE *pointer type* = ↑*type identifier*

where *type identifier* (without the arrow) refers to the type of the corresponding referenced variable. (This type definition will appear later in the program, *after* the pointer-type definition.) Thus a pointer type is specifically associated with the type of a referenced variable.

The basic idea behind the pointer-type definition is as follows: the value of a pointer-type variable will reference (i.e., point to) some other variable whose type is specified by the type identifier. This idea is illustrated in Fig. 13-5, where we see a pointer-type variable *p*, whose value points to a corresponding referenced variable. The value of this referenced variable is represented by *v*. The referenced variable will be of the type specified by the type identifier.

The referenced variable is usually defined as a record whose fields comprise a component within

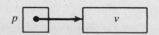

**Fig. 13-5**

the linked list. The last field will generally be a pointer-type data item that indicates the location of the next component. This field represents the link between the current component and its successor.

**EXAMPLE 13.3**

Consider the following type definitions.

```
TYPE primary = (red,green,blue);
     pointer = ↑hue;
     hue = RECORD
               color : primary;
               nextcolor : pointer
           END;
```

The first line specifies that red, green and blue are enumerated data items of type primary. In the second line, pointer is defined as a pointer type that is associated with the referenced variable of type hue. (Note that this referenced variable will be used to represent a component in a linked list.) Finally, we define hue to be a record consisting of two fields: color, which is of type primary, and nextcolor, which is a pointer to the next component in the linked list.

Notice that the referenced-variable type hue is not defined until *after* its appearance in the definition of pointer. This differs from other type definitions in Pascal, in which an identifier must be defined before it can appear in another type definition.

Since a pointer type can only be defined in terms of a corresponding referenced-variable type, we say that the pointer type is *bound* to its referenced-variable type.

## 13.3  VARIABLE DECLARATIONS

Pointer-type variables are declared in the conventional manner; i.e.,

```
VAR pointer name : type
```

where *pointer name* refers to a pointer-type variable and *type* is a pointer type. This declaration will create a *static* (conventional) variable whose value will point to a referenced variable (i.e., a component within a linked list).

*Referenced* variables, however, are *not* declared in the conventional manner, since these variables are created and destroyed dynamically; i.e., as the program is being executed. Thus, the referenced variables must be declared within those portions of the program that contain the action statements. Such declarations are carried out differently from the variable declarations that we have encountered previously.

To create a referenced variable, we utilize the standard procedure new, by writing

```
new(pointer name)
```

This statement creates a new variable (i.e., a referenced variable) whose type is defined in the formal type definitions. The pointer whose name appears in the new statement will automatically point to this new variable. The referenced variable will have the same name as the pointer variable. However, the referenced variable is written with a vertical arrow after its name so that it can be distinguished from the corresponding pointer variable.

**EXAMPLE 13.4**

Consider the following skeletal outline of a Pascal program.

```
PROGRAM sample(input,output);
TYPE primary = (red,green,blue);
     pointer = ↑hue;
     hue = RECORD
               color : primary;
               nextcolor : pointer
           END;
VAR foreground,background : pointer;
```
*(Program continues on next page)*

```
        BEGIN   (* main action block *)
              .
              .
           new(foreground);
              .
              .
        END.
```

The type definitions are repeated from Example 13.3. Following these type definitions, the variables foreground and background are declared to be pointer-type variables.

Note that these are conventional variable declarations. Therefore foreground and background will be static variables whose values can be assigned in the conventional manner.

On the other hand, the new statement within the main action block creates a referenced variable of type hue, which will be called foreground↑. Moreover, the corresponding pointer variable foreground will automatically point to foreground↑.

Note that the referenced variable foreground↑ is a record-type variable comprised of two fields. Hence, foreground↑.color will represent an enumerated value of type primary, and foreground↑.nextcolor will represent a pointer that can be assigned to the next referenced variable.

## 13.4  OPERATIONS WITH POINTER VARIABLES AND REFERENCED VARIABLES

There are two kinds of operations that can be carried out with pointer variables and referenced variables. These are *assignment* and *comparison*. Both kinds of operations must be carried out with like operands; i.e., pointers must be assigned to or compared with other pointers, and referenced variables must be assigned to or compared with other referenced variables.

Let us first consider assignment. Suppose that p1 and p2 are both pointer variables of the same type. Then we can assign the value of p1 to p2 by writing

```
    p2 := p1
```

Similarly, suppose that p1↑ and p2↑ are both referenced variables containing a pointer-type field called next. Then we can write

```
    p2 := p1↑.next

    p2↑.next := p1

    p2↑.next := p1↑.next
```

and so on. In each case, we are assigning the value of one pointer variable to another pointer variable (provided, of course, that the referenced variables have been created in each case).

A pointer variable can also be made to point to nothing, by assigning the special value NIL to the variable. (Note that NIL is a reserved word in Pascal.) Hence, if we did not want p1 to point to anything, we would write

```
    p1 := NIL
```

We will see uses for this feature later in this chapter.

Observe that we have now seen two different ways to assign values to pointer variables. One way is to use the traditional assignment statement, as we have done above. The other is to make use of the standard procedure new, as described in the last section. (Remember that a value is automatically assigned to a pointer variable when a corresponding referenced variable is created via the new statement.)

Referenced variables can also be assigned to one another, provided they are of the same type. Thus, we can write

```
    p2↑ := p1↑
```

This will cause the value of each field within p1↑ to be assigned to the corresponding field within p2↑.

Such assignments can be carried out with individual fields of referenced variables as well as entire referenced variables.

**EXAMPLE 13.5**

Consider the following declarations, which are repeated from the previous example.

```
TYPE primary = (red,green,blue);
     pointer = ↑hue;
     hue = RECORD
              color : primary;
              nextcolor : pointer
           END;
VAR foreground,background : pointer;
```

If the referenced variables foreground↑ and background↑ have both been created (via the new statement), then all of the following will be valid pointer assignments.

```
foreground := background

background := NIL

foreground := background↑.nextcolor

foreground↑.nextcolor := background

foreground↑.nextcolor := background↑.nextcolor
```

Also, we can assign some or all values of foreground↑ to background↑. Thus, we can write

```
background↑ := foreground↑

background↑.color := foreground↑.color
```

And finally, we can assign an enumerated value to a field of the same type in one of the referenced variables. For example,

```
foreground↑.color := green
```

The reader should clearly understand the difference between assignments involving pointers and assignments involving referenced variables. To illustrate this point, suppose that the pointers p1 and p2 point to their respective referenced variables, as illustrated in Fig. 13-6(*a*). Then the assignment

```
p2 := p1
```

will cause both pointers to point to the referenced variable p1↑, as shown in Fig. 13-6(*b*). On the other hand, the assignment

```
p2↑ := p1↑
```

will cause the values of the referenced variable p1↑ to be assigned to the referenced variable p2↑. This is illustrated in Fig. 13-6(*c*).

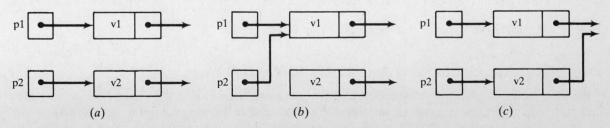

(*a*)                              (*b*)                              (*c*)

**Fig. 13-6**

Pointer variables can be compared by means of the two relational operators = and <>. This feature allows us to determine whether or not two pointer variables have the same value or if a pointer variable has been assigned the value NIL.

**EXAMPLE 13.6**

Consider once again the declarations given in Examples 13.4 and 13.5; i.e.,

```
TYPE primary = (red,green,blue);
     pointer = ↑hue;
     hue = RECORD
                color : primary;
                nextcolor : pointer
           END;
VAR foreground,background : pointer;
```

Shown below are several statements that involve comparisons among the pointer variables foreground and background. (These examples are intended to illustrate syntax; they do not have any particular logical meaning.)

```
IF foreground = background THEN foreground := NIL

WHILE foreground <> background DO

REPEAT
     .
     .
     .
UNTIL background = foreground↑.nextcolor

IF background = NIL THEN foreground↑.color := red
```

Referenced variables can also be compared for equality provided they are of the same type. Such comparisons can involve entire variables or individual fields. If individual fields are compared, then they must also be of the same type.

**EXAMPLE 13.7**

Here are some examples of comparisons among referenced variables or individual fields within referenced variables. We again make use of the declarations provided in the earlier examples; i.e.,

```
TYPE primary = (red,green,blue);
     pointer = ↑hue;
     hue = RECORD
                color : primary;
                nextcolor : pointer
           END;
VAR foreground,background : pointer;
```

Some valid comparisons are shown below.

```
IF foreground↑ = background↑ THEN foreground := NIL

IF foreground↑.color <> blue THEN foreground↑.color := blue

WHILE background↑.color <> foreground↑.color DO
```

## 13.5 CREATING AND DESTROYING DYNAMIC VARIABLES

We now turn our attention to some typical programming situations that require pointer variables and their corresponding referenced variables. We will see that the use of pointer variables allows us to create and destroy referenced variables dynamically; i.e., as the program is being executed.

In order to illustrate the manner in which referenced variables are created and destroyed dynamically, we will work with a common type of linked list in which each component points to its predecessor. Thus, the second component points to the first, the third points to the second, and so on, as illustrated in Fig. 13-7. This scheme is called *last-in*, *first-out* (LIFO), since the last component to enter the list will be the first to leave.

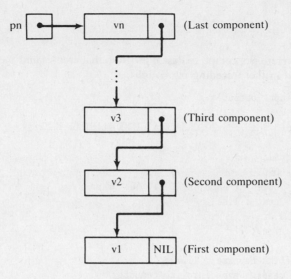

**Fig. 13-7**

The linked list will be created by reading in each new component and then linking that component to its predecessor. Suppose, for example, that item is a pointer-type variable, and that its corresponding referenced variable, item↑, contains two fields, a string variable called item↑.name, and a pointer called item↑.next. The pointer will provide a link to the previously entered component, whose location will be indicated by the pointer-type variable pointer.

In order to create the first component, we generate a dynamic variable (item), read in a value for item↑.name and set item↑.next to NIL. This will represent the component at the bottom of the list. The variable pointer is then made to point to this component (so that a predecessor can be identified when the next component is entered). Thus, the first component is created by writing

```
new(item);
readname(item↑.name);
item↑.next := NIL;
pointer := item;
```

where readname is a procedure that reads in the elements of item↑.name on a character-by-character basis.

These steps are then repeated for each successive component, except that item↑.next is made to point to its predecessor by assigning to it the current value of pointer. Thus,

```
new(item);
readname(item↑.name);
item↑.next := pointer;
pointer := item;
```

This group of statements must be placed within some type of loop (e.g., a WHILE—DO structure) so that it can be repeated for each successive component within the list.

The list can be displayed by traversing from top to bottom (last component to first). Initially, pointer will indicate the location of the last (most recent) component. Therefore we can display the entire list simply by repeating the following three statements for each component in the list.

```
            item := pointer;
          writeln(item↑.name);
          pointer := item↑.next;
```

These statements must be placed within a loop that continues to execute until the value of pointer becomes NIL.

**EXAMPLE 13.8**

**Creating a Linked List.** Here is a complete Pascal program that creates and then displays a LIFO linked list, using the methods described in the preceding paragraphs.

```
          PROGRAM makelist(input,output);

          (* THIS PROGRAM USES POINTERS TO CREATE A LINKED LIST OF NAMES *)

          TYPE link = ↑personal;
              personal = RECORD
                              name : PACKED ARRAY [1..40] OF char;
                              next : link
                          END;
          VAR item,pointer : link;

          PROCEDURE readname(VAR newname : link);
          (* this procedure reads a name into the computer *)
          VAR count : 0..40;
          BEGIN
            FOR count := 1 TO 40 DO newname↑.name[count] := ' ';
            write('New name: ');
            count := 0;
            WHILE NOT eoln DO
              BEGIN
                 count := count + 1;
                 read(newname↑.name[count])
              END;
            readln
          END;

          BEGIN    (* main action block *)

            BEGIN   (* create the list *)
              new(item);
              readname(item);
              item↑.next := NIL;
              pointer := item;
              WHILE NOT ((item↑.name[1] IN ['E','e'])
                     AND (item↑.name[2] IN ['N','n'])
                     AND (item↑.name[3] IN ['D','d'])) DO
                        BEGIN
                           new(item);
                           readname(item);
                           item↑.next := pointer;
                           pointer := item
                        END;
               pointer := item↑.next
            END;   (* create list *)
```

(*Program continues on next page*)

```
      BEGIN   (* display the list *)
         writeln;
         WHILE pointer <> NIL DO
            BEGIN
               item := pointer;
               writeln(item↑.name);
               pointer := item↑.next
            END;
      END   (* display list *)
   END.
```

This program contains a procedure called readname, which is used to read in a name containing up to 40 characters. The procedure begins by assigning blank spaces to all of the characters within the name. The actual name is then entered into the computer on a character-by-character basis until an end-of-line (eoln) is detected, in response to a carriage return.

Notice that readname makes use of a variable parameter called newname, which is of type link. Thus the parameter is a pointer-type variable. The value that is returned by this procedure is not a pointer, however, but is one of the items within the corresponding referenced variable (namely, newname↑.name). Thus, we see that a referenced variable can implicitly be utilized within a procedure by transferring the associated pointer-type variable into (or out of) the procedure.

The main action block consists of two compound statements that create the linked list and display the list, respectively. The logic that is utilized within each of these statements is straightforward, in view of the discussion that preceded this example. Note, however, the WHILE—DO loop in the first compound statement. This loop causes new names to be entered repeatedly, until the word "end" is entered as a new name (in either upper- or lowercase). Also, note that the pointer-type variable item is passed to the procedure readname.

Now suppose that the program is utilized to create a linked list containing the following names:

Sharon, Gail, Susan, Marla, Marc, Amy, Megan

The input/output dialogue is shown below, with the user's responses underlined.

```
New name: Sharon
New name: Gail
New name: Susan
New name: Marla
New name: Marc
New name: Amy
New name: Megan
New name: end
```

```
Megan
Amy
Marc
Marla
Susan
Gail
Sharon
```

Notice that the names are printed in reverse order; i.e., last-in first-out.

An additional component can easily be inserted into some designated location within a linked list that has already been created. To do so we must enter the new component, determine its intended location within the list and then adjust a few pointers. In particular, suppose that item now represents the component to be added, and pointer indicates the component above (behind) the new component. The following two statements will allow the new component to be entered (again assumed to be item↑.name).

```
new(item);
readname(item↑.name);
```

The intended location of the new component can be determined by writing

```
readname(itemname);
pointer := last;
WHILE (pointer↑.name <> itemname) AND
      (pointer↑.next <> NIL) DO pointer := pointer↑.next;
```

where itemname is a string variable that represents the new component's intended successor, and last is a pointer to the last component within the list.

Finally, the pointer adjustment proceeds as follows. If the new item is to be inserted at the *end* of the list, we write

```
item↑.next := last;
last := item;
```

Otherwise, we write

```
item↑.next := pointer↑.next;
pointer↑.next := item;
```

In each case, the pointer part of the new component is directed to its predecessor, and the (old) component that succeeds the newly added component is correctly readjusted.

The deletion of a component proceeds in much the same manner as an insertion. The actual deletion is carried out by means of the dispose statement; i.e.,

```
dispose(pointer name)
```

This statement is analogous to the new statement. Thus, dispose is a standard procedure that accepts a pointer-type variable as a parameter. Use of this procedure causes the referenced variable associated with the given pointer to be destroyed. Any subsequent reference to this variable (via another pointer) will then be undefined.

The overall strategy is as follows. We first locate the component to be deleted, then readjust a few pointers and finally dispose of the component that is to be deleted. Thus,

```
readname(itemname);
IF last↑.name = itemname
   THEN BEGIN   (* delete last item *)
           item := last;
           last := item↑.next;
           dispose(item)
        END
   ELSE BEGIN   (* find item, then delete *)
           pointer := last;
           item := last↑.next;
           WHILE (item↑.name <> itemname) AND
                 (item↑.next <> NIL) DO
              BEGIN
                 pointer := item;
                 item := item↑.next
              END;
           IF item↑.name = itemname THEN
              BEGIN
                 pointer↑.next := item↑.next;
                 dispose(item)
              END
        END;
```

These statements can accommodate two different situations: deletion of the last component and deletion of some other component. If the last component is to be deleted, then the pointer to the end of the list (last) is adjusted so that it points to the next component in the list; i.e.,

```
last := item↑.next;
```

If some other component is to be deleted, then its successor is made to point to the next component in the list; i.e.,

```
pointer↑.next := item↑.next;
```

**EXAMPLE 13.9**

**Processing a Linked List.** In this example we expand on some of the ideas that were presented in Example 13.8. Specifically, we now present an interactive Pascal program that allows us to create a linked list, add a new component or delete any component. The program will be menu-driven to facilitate its use by a nonprogrammer. We will include a provision to display the list in reverse order (last component to first) after the selection of any menu item.

The program begins with the following type definitions and variable declarations.

```
TYPE line = PACKED ARRAY [1..40] OF char;
     link = ↑personal;
     personal = RECORD
                      name : line;
                      next : link
                 END;
VAR item,pointer,last : link;
    choice : 1..4;
    count : 0..40;
    itemname : line;
```

These definitions and declarations are similar to those presented in Example 13.8, though we have expanded them somewhat to accommodate the additional features in the present program.

Now consider the main action block. If we place the generation of the menu and the action statements associated with each of the menu choices within separate procedures, then the main action block will consist of little more than a group of references to these procedures. Thus, we can write

```
BEGIN   (* main action block *)
   REPEAT
      menu;
      CASE choice OF
          1 : create;
          2 : add;
          3 : delete;
          4 :
      END
   UNTIL choice = 4
END.
```

Notice that we first access procedure menu, which causes a value of choice to be entered from the keyboard (choice can only take on the integer values 1, 2, 3 or 4). We then access an additional procedure, the choice of which depends upon the value that has been assigned to choice. This process is repeated until choice is assigned a value of 4, which indicates a stopping condition.

Now let us examine procedure menu. This is a very simple procedure, consisting only of input/output statements.

```
PROCEDURE menu;

(* this procedure displays the main menu *)
```

(*Program continues on next page*)

```
      BEGIN
         page;
         writeln('Main menu:');
         writeln;
         writeln('  1 - Create the linked list');
         writeln;
         writeln('  2 - Add a component');
         writeln;
         writeln('  3 - Delete a component');
         writeln;
         writeln('  4 - End');
         writeln;
         write('Enter your choice (1, 2, 3 or 4) -> ');
         readln(choice);
         writeln
      END;
```

(These statements could just as easily have been placed within the main action block. They were placed in a separate procedure in order to simplify the organization of the overall program logic.)

The procedures that are used to create a new list, enter a name from the keyboard and display the current list utilize essentially the same logic as the Pascal program given in Example 13.8. (Note, however, that the groups of statements required to create the list and to display the list have been moved from the main action block to individual subroutines.) Thus, the list can be created by accessing the following procedure.

```
   PROCEDURE create;

   (* this procedure creates the linked list

       item    -> the new (most recent) component
       pointer -> the preceding component

                 ('item' points to 'pointer')        *)
   BEGIN
      new(item);
      write('New name: ');
      readname(item↑.name);
      item↑.next := NIL;
      pointer := item;
      WHILE NOT ((item↑.name[1] IN ['E','e'])
              AND (item↑.name[2] IN ['N','n'])
              AND (item↑.name[3] IN ['D','d'])) DO
                 BEGIN
                    new(item);
                    write('New name: ');
                    readname(item↑.name);
                    item↑.next := pointer;
                    pointer := item
                 END;
      last := item↑.next;
      display
   END;
```

Notice that the last component in the list is tagged with the pointer last. This will enable us to find the end of the list whenever we wish to display the list, add a new component or delete a component. Also, note that the new list will automatically be displayed after it has been created.

Procedure readname, which is accessed by the above procedure (and others as well), is written as

```
   PROCEDURE readname(VAR name : line);

   (* this procedure reads a name into the computer *)
```

(*Program continues on next page*)

```
        BEGIN
           FOR count := 1 TO 40 DO name[count] := ' ';
           count := 0;
           WHILE NOT eoln DO
              BEGIN
                 count := count + 1;
                 read(name[count])
              END;
           readln
        END;
```

This procedure is very similar to a procedure with the same name in Example 13.8. Note, however, that the present procedure utilizes a string variable as a variable-type parameter, whereas the previous version employed a pointer as a variable parameter. The present treatment of the variable parameter provides more generality and therefore allows this procedure to be accessed by several other procedures (namely, create, add and delete).

The procedure used to display the list can be written as

```
        PROCEDURE display;

        (* this procedure displays the complete list

           item    -> the current component to be displayed
           pointer -> the preceding component

                    ('item' points to 'pointer')               *)

        BEGIN
           writeln;
           pointer := last;
           WHILE pointer <> NIL DO
              BEGIN
                 item := pointer;
                 writeln(item↑.name);
                 pointer := item↑.next
              END
        END;
```

This procedure begins by locating the end of the list (pointer := last;), and then proceeds in the same manner as the program shown in Example 13.8.

The following procedure allows a component to be added to a linked list that has already been created.

```
        PROCEDURE add;

        (* this procedure allows one component
           to be added to the linked list

           item    -> the component to be added
           pointer -> component below (i.e., pointing to) the new component

                    ('pointer' points to 'item')                         *)

        BEGIN
           new(item);
           writeln;
           write('New name: ');
           readname(item↑.name);
           write('Place ahead of: (press RETURN if new item is last) ');
           readname(itemname);
           IF itemname[1] = ' '
              THEN BEGIN    (* insert at end *)
                      item↑.next := last;
                      last := item
                   END
```

(*Program continues on next page*)

```
      ELSE BEGIN   (* find location, then insert *)
            pointer := last;
            WHILE (pointer↑.name <> itemname) AND
                  (pointer↑.next <> NIL) DO pointer := pointer↑.next;
            item↑.next := pointer↑.next;
            pointer↑.next := item
         END;
   display
END;
```

This procedure first causes the new name, and then its location, to be entered from the keyboard. The procedure then follows the logic described earlier in this chapter, which allows an insertion either at the end of the list (i.e., at the top) or else at an appropriate place within the list. Notice that the new list is automatically displayed after an insertion has been made.

Now consider the procedure that is used to delete a component from some specified place within the list. This procedure can be written as

```
PROCEDURE delete;

(* this procedure causes one component
   to be deleted from the linked list

   item    -> the component to be deleted
   pointer -> component above (i.e., pointing to)
                       the component to be deleted

              ('pointer' points to 'item')              *)

BEGIN
   writeln;
   write ('Name to be deleted: ');
   readname(itemname);
   IF last↑.name = itemname
      THEN BEGIN   (* delete last item *)
            item := last;
            last := item↑.next;
            dispose(item)
         END
      ELSE BEGIN   (* find item, then delete *)
            pointer := last;
            item := last↑.next;
            WHILE (item↑.name <> itemname) AND
                  (item↑.next <> NIL) DO
               BEGIN
                  pointer := item;
                  item := item↑.next;
               END;
            IF item↑.name = itemname THEN
               BEGIN
                  pointer↑.next := item↑.next;
                  dispose(item)
               END
         END;
   display
END;
```

The logical details of this procedure have already been described earlier in this chapter. Note that the new list is automatically displayed after the deletion has been carried out.

The complete program is presented below.

```
PROGRAM linklist(input,output);

(* THIS IS A MENU-DRIVEN PROGRAM THAT USES POINTERS
   TO PROCESS A LINKED LIST OF NAMES *)

TYPE line = PACKED ARRAY [1..40] OF char;
     link = ↑personal;
     personal = RECORD
                     name : line;
                     next : link
                END;
VAR item,pointer,last : link;
    choice : 1..4;
    count : 0..40;
    itemname : line;

PROCEDURE readname(VAR name : line);

(* this procedure reads a name into the computer *)

BEGIN
   FOR count := 1 TO 40 DO name[count] := ' ';
   count := 0;
   WHILE NOT eoln DO
      BEGIN
         count := count + 1;
         read(name[count])
      END;
   readln
END;

PROCEDURE display;

(* this procedure displays the complete list

   item    -> the current component to be displayed
   pointer -> the preceding component

            ('item' points to 'pointer')               *)

BEGIN
   writeln;
   pointer := last;
   WHILE pointer <> NIL DO
      BEGIN
         item := pointer;
         writeln(item↑.name);
         pointer := item↑.next
      END
END;

PROCEDURE create;

(* this procedure creates the linked list

   item    -> the new (most recent) component
   pointer -> the preceding component

            ('item' points to 'pointer')          *)
```

(*Program continues on next page*)

```
BEGIN
   new(item);
   write('New name: ');
   readname(item↑.name);
   item↑.next := NIL;
   pointer := item;
   WHILE NOT ((item↑.name[1] IN ['E','e'])
           AND (item↑.name[2] IN ['N','n'])
           AND (item↑.name[3] IN ['D','d'])) DO
              BEGIN
                   new(item);
                 write('New name: ');
                 readname(item↑.name);
                 item↑.next := pointer;
                 pointer := item
              END;
   last := item↑.next;
   display
END;

PROCEDURE add;

(* this procedure allows one component
   to be added to the linked list

   item    -> the component to be added
   pointer -> component below (i.e., pointing to) the new component

           ('pointer' points to 'item')                      *)

BEGIN
   new(item);
   writeln;
   write('New name: ');
   readname(item↑.name);
   write('Place ahead of: (press RETURN if new item is last) ');
   readname(itemname);
   IF itemname[1] = ' '
      THEN BEGIN   (* insert at end *)
             item↑.next := last;
             last := item
           END
      ELSE BEGIN   (* find location, then insert *)
             pointer := last;
             WHILE (pointer↑.name <> itemname) AND
                   (pointer↑.next <> NIL) DO pointer := pointer↑.next;
             item↑.next := pointer↑.next;
             pointer↑.next := item
           END;
   display
END;

PROCEDURE delete;

(* this procedure causes one component
   to be deleted from the linked list

   item    -> the component to be deleted
   pointer -> component above (i.e., pointing to)
                       the component to be deleted

           ('pointer' points to 'item')          *)
```

(*Program continues on next page*)

```
BEGIN
   writeln;
   write ('Name to be deleted: ');
   readname(itemname);
   IF last↑.name = itemname
      THEN BEGIN   (* delete last item *)
              item := last;
              last := item↑.next;
              dispose(item)
           END
      ELSE BEGIN   (* find item, then delete *)
              pointer := last;
              item := last↑.next;
              WHILE (item↑.name <> itemname) AND
                    (item↑.next <> NIL) DO
                 BEGIN
                    pointer := item;
                    item := item↑.next;
                 END;
              IF item↑.name = itemname THEN
                 BEGIN
                    pointer↑.next := item↑.next;
                    dispose(item)
                 END
           END;
   display
END;

PROCEDURE menu;

(* this procedure displays the main menu *)

BEGIN
   page;
   writeln('Main menu:');
   writeln;
   writeln('  1 - Create the linked list');
   writeln;
   writeln('  2 - Add a component');
   writeln;
   writeln('  3 - Delete a component');
   writeln;
   writeln('  4 - End');
   writeln;
   write('Enter your choice (1, 2, 3 or 4) -> ');
   readln(choice);
   writeln
END;

BEGIN   (* main action block *)
   REPEAT
      menu;
      CASE choice OF
         1 : create;
         2 : add;
         3 : delete;
         4 :
      END
   UNTIL choice = 4
END.
```

Now let us utilize this program to create a linked list containing the following cities: Boston, Chicago, Denver, New York, Pittsburgh, San Francisco. We will then add several additional cities and delete several cities, thus illustrating all of the features of the program. We will maintain the list of cities in alphabetical order throughout the exercise. Therefore, we will enter the initial list backward so that the cities will print out in the correct order. (Note that San Francisco will actually be at the beginning of the list and Boston at the end.)

The entire interactive session is shown below. As usual, the user's responses are underlined.

```
Main menu:

    1 - Create the linked list

    2 - Add a component

    3 - Delete a component

    4 - End

Enter your choice (1, 2, 3 or 4) -> 1

New name: San Francisco
New name: Pittsburgh
New name: New York
New name: Denver
New name: Chicago
New name: Boston
New name: end

Boston
Chicago
Denver
New York
Pittsburgh
San Francisco


Main menu:

    1 - Create the linked list

    2 - Add a component

    3 - Delete a component

    4 - End

Enter your choice (1, 2, 3 or 4) -> 2


New name: Atlanta
Enter ahead of (press RETURN if last item): _

Atlanta
Boston
Chicago
Denver
New York
Pittsburgh
San Francisco
```

(*continues on next page*)

Main menu:

   1 - Create the linked list

   2 - Add a component

   3 - Delete a component

   4 - End

Enter your choice (1, 2, 3 or 4) -> 2

New name: Seattle
Enter ahead of (press RETURN if last item): San Francisco

Atlanta
Boston
Chicago
Denver
New York
Pittsburgh
San Francisco
Seattle

Main menu:

   1 - Create the linked list

   2 - Add a component

   3 - Delete a component

   4 - End

Enter your choice (1, 2, 3 or 4) -> 3

Name to be deleted: New York

Atlanta
Boston
Chicago
Denver
Pittsburgh
San Francisco
Seattle

Main menu:

   1 - Create the linked list

   2 - Add a component

   3 - Delete a component

   4 - End

*(continues on next page)*

```
Enter your choice (1, 2, 3 or 4) -> 2

New name: Washington
Enter ahead of (press RETURN if last item): Seattle

Atlanta
Boston
Chicago
Denver
Pittsburgh
San Francisco
Seattle
Washington

Main menu:

   1 - Create the linked list

   2 - Add a component

   3 - Delete a component

   4 - End

Enter your choice (1, 2, 3 or 4) -> 3

Name to be deleted: Atlanta

Boston
Chicago
Denver
Pittsburgh
San Francisco
Seattle
Washington

Main menu:

   1 - Create the linked list

   2 - Add a component

   3 - Delete a component

   4 - End

Enter your choice (1, 2, 3 or 4) -> 2

New name: Dallas
Enter ahead of (press RETURN if last item): Chicago

Boston
Chicago
Dallas
Denver
Pittsburgh
San Francisco
Seattle
Washington
```

(continues on next page)

```
Main menu:

    1 - Create the linked list

    2 - Add a component

    3 - Delete a component

    4 - End

Enter your choice (1, 2, 3 or 4) -> 3

Name to be deleted: Washington

Boston
Chicago
Dallas
Denver
Pittsburgh
San Francisco
Seattle


Main menu:

    1 - Create the linked list

    2 - Add a component

    3 - Delete a component

    4 - End

Enter your choice (1, 2, 3 or 4) -> 4
```

# Review Questions

**13.1**    What is meant by a linked list?

**13.2**    What is a pointer? What is the relationship between pointers and linked lists?

**13.3**    How does a linked list differ from a sequential list as, for example, is found in a one-dimensional array? What advantages does the linked list offer?

**13.4**    How is the beginning of a linked list identified?

**13.5**    (a) What is a linear linked list? (b) What is a circular linked list? How does a circular linked list differ from a linear linked list?

**13.6**    (a) What is a tree? How do trees differ from linear linked lists? (b) What is a binary tree? How does a binary tree differ from other types of trees?

**13.7**   What are nodes and branches? With what type of data structure are nodes and branches associated?

**13.8**   What type of data structure is used to create linked structures in Pascal?

**13.9**   How is a pointer type defined in Pascal?

**13.10**  What structured data type is generally used to define a referenced variable? What is the reason for this choice?

**13.11**  Describe the manner in which pointer types and referenced variable types are related (bound) to one another.

**13.12**  How are pointer-type variables declared? In what part of a Pascal program do these declarations appear?

**13.13**  In general terms, how are referenced variables declared? Conceptually, how do referenced variable declarations differ from other kinds of variable declarations?

**13.14**  In what part of a Pascal program do referenced variable declarations appear? Compare with other types of variable declarations and cite reasons for the differences.

**13.15**  What is the purpose of the new statement? What type of parameter is required?

**13.16**  Explain the relationship that is established between a referenced variable and its corresponding pointer variable.

**13.17**  How can the names of a referenced variable and its corresponding pointer variable be distinguished from one another?

**13.18**  Summarize the rules that apply to the assignment of one pointer variable to another.

**13.19**  How can a pointer variable be made to point to nothing?

**13.20**  Describe two different ways to assign values to pointer variables. What is the purpose of each type of assignment?

**13.21**  Summarize the rules that apply to the assignment of one referenced variable to another.

**13.22**  Can the individual fields within two different referenced variables be assigned to one another? What restrictions apply to this type of assignment?

**13.23**  Conceptually, how does the assignment of one pointer variable to another differ from the assignment of one referenced variable to another?

**13.24**  What kinds of comparisons can be carried out between pointer variables? Which operators can be used for this purpose?

**13.25**  What kinds of comparisons can be carried out between referenced variables? Can such comparisons be carried out with entire variables? Can they be carried out with individual fields? What restrictions apply to such comparisons?

**13.26** How are the individual items within a LIFO list linked to one other?

**13.27** Summarize the logic that is used to create new components within a LIFO list. In what order are the components entered? How are they linked?

**13.28** Summarize the logic that is used to display the components within a LIFO list. In what order are the components displayed?

**13.29** Summarize the logic that is used to insert a component into some designated location within a LIFO list. How are the pointers readjusted?

**13.30** What is the purpose of the dispose statement? What type of parameter is required? Contrast with the new statement.

**13.31** Summarize the logic that is used to delete a component from a LIFO list. How are the pointers readjusted?

# Solved Problems

**13.32** Shown below are some definitions of pointer types and their corresponding referenced-variable types.

```
(a)  TYPE next = ↑stockitem;
        stockitem = RECORD
                        stockno  : 1..9999;
                        quantity : integer;
                        nextitem : next
                    END;
(b)  TYPE line = PACKED ARRAY [1..25] OF char;
        pointer = ↑customer;
        customer = RECORD
                        name   : line;
                        street : line;
                        city   : line;
                        next   : pointer
                    END;
(c)  TYPE next = ↑part;
        part = RECORD
                    length   : real;
                    width    : real;
                    depth    : real;
                    nextpart : next
                END;
(d)  TYPE values = ARRAY [1..3] OF real;
        pointer = ↑part;
        part = RECORD
                    dimension : values;
                    next : pointer
                END;
```

**13.33** Shown below are several type definitions and associated variable declarations involving pointers and their corresponding referenced variables.

(*a*)
```
TYPE next = ↑stockitem;
     stockitem = RECORD
                       stockno  : 1..9999;
                       quantity : integer;
                       nextitem : next
                 END;
VAR firstitem,lastitem,thisitem : next;

BEGIN
   .
   .
   new(thisitem);
   .
   .
END.
```

(*b*)
```
TYPE values = ARRAY [1..3] OF real;
     pointer = ↑part;
     part = RECORD
                 dimension : values;
                 next : pointer
            END;
VAR workpart : pointer;

BEGIN   (* main action part *)
   .
   .
   new(workpart);
   .
   .
END.
```

**13.34** Shown below are skeletal outlines of several Pascal programs. Each involves the use of pointers and referenced variables.

(*a*)
```
PROGRAM sample(input,output);
TYPE line = PACKED ARRAY [1..25] OF char;
     pointer = ↑customer;
     customer = RECORD
                      name   : line;
                      street : line;
                      city   : line;
                      next   : pointer
                END;
VAR nameandaddress : pointer;

PROCEDURE readinput (VAR item : line);
(* read a 25-character string *)
BEGIN
   .
   .
   .
END;
```

(*Program continues on next page*)

```
      BEGIN   (* main action block *)
        new(nameandaddress);

          .
          .

        WITH nameandaddress ↑ DO
          BEGIN
            readinput(name);
            readinput(street);
            readinput(city)
          END;
          .
          .

    END.
```

Notice the use of the WITH—DO structure to facilitate the reading of the referenced variable components (see Chap. 10). Also, notice that the actual parameters used with readinput are string variables, as required by the procedure definition.

(b)
```
      PROGRAM sample(input,output);
      TYPE line = PACKED ARRAY [1..25] OF char;
           pointer = ↑customer;
           customer = RECORD
                          name   : line;
                          street : line;
                          city   : line;
                          next   : pointer
                      END;
      VAR nameandaddress : pointer;

      PROCEDURE readinput (VAR personal : pointer);
      (* read the name, street and city *)
      BEGIN
          .
          .
          .
      END;

      PROCEDURE writeoutput (personal : pointer);
      (* display the name, street and city *)
      BEGIN
          .
          .
          .
      END;

      BEGIN   (* main action block *)
        new(nameandaddress);

          .
          .

        readinput(nameandaddress);
          .
          .

        writeoutput(nameandaddress);
          .
          .

        dispose(nameandaddress);
          .
          .

      END.
```

Notice that the actual parameters are now pointer-type variables (compare with the preceding example). Also, notice that readinput utilizes a variable parameter, whereas writeoutput makes use of a value parameter (both are pointer-type parameters).

(c)
```
PROGRAM sample(input,output);
TYPE values = ARRAY [1..3] OF real;
     pointer = ↑part;
     part = RECORD
                  dimension : values;
                  next : pointer
              END;
VAR firstpart,nextpart : pointer;
    area,volume : real;

BEGIN   (* main action statements *)
   new(nextpart);
   .

   nextpart↑.dimension[1] := 1.0;
   nextpart↑.dimension[2] := 2.5;
   nextpart↑.dimension[3] := 0.3;
   .

   .
   nextpart↑.next := firstpart;
   .

   .
   WITH nextpart↑ DO
     BEGIN
        area := dimension[1] * dimension[2];
        volume := area * dimension[3];
        IF dimension[1] <> dimension[3] THEN . . .
                                    ELSE . . .
     END;
   .
   .
   IF nextpart↑.next = NIL THEN . . .
                       ELSE . . . ;
   .
   .
   dispose(nextpart);
   .
   .
END.
```

The statements in this example are not logically related. They are simply intended to illustrate various assignments and comparisons with pointer variables and elements of referenced variables.

# Supplementary Problems

**13.35**  Write appropriate type definitions or variable declarations for each of the situations described below.

(*a*)  Define a pointer type called link whose corresponding referenced variable, called customer, contains the following fields:

(*i*)  name (20 characters)

(*ii*)  acctno (an integer ranging from 1 to 9999)

(*iii*)  balance (a real quantity)

(*iv*)  next (a pointer to the next record)

(*b*)  Declare two pointer-type variables each of type link. Name them nextcustomer and lastcustomer, respectively.

(*c*)  Create and then destroy a dynamic variable corresponding to nextcustomer. Note that nextcustomer is a pointer-type variable.

**13.36**  The following problems refer to the pointer-type variables, and their corresponding referenced variables, defined in the preceding problem.

(*a*)  Assign the value of the pointer in nextcustomer↑ to the pointer variable lastcustomer.

(*b*)  Have the value of the pointer in nextcustomer↑ point to nothing.

(*c*)  Assign each element of nextcustomer↑ to its corresponding element in lastcustomer↑.

(*d*)  Assign a balance of $287.55 to the nextcustomer whose account number is 1330.

(*e*)  Obtain a value of nextcustomer↑.name by accessing a procedure called readinput. (Include an outline of readinput in your solution.)

(*f*)  Outline a WHILE—DO structure that continues to execute as long as the value of nextcustomer is not NIL.

**13.37**  Shown below are several skeletal outlines of programs that involve the use of pointers and their corresponding referenced variables. Some statements are written incorrectly. Identify all errors.

(*a*)
```
PROGRAM sample(input,output);
TYPE textline = PACKED ARRAY [1..80] OF char;
     link = ↑pointer;
     stockitem = RECORD
                      stockno : 1..9999;
                      stocktype : textline;
                      next : pointer
                 END;
VAR newitem,olditem : stockitem;

BEGIN
     .
     .
     .
END.
```

(*b*)
```
PROGRAM sample(input,output);
TYPE link = ↑player;
     player = RECORD
                   ssn : PACKED ARRAY [1..9] OF char;
                   position : PACKED ARRAY [1..12] OF char;
                   age : 1..99;
                   height : real;
                   weight : real
              END;
VAR nextplayer,lastplayer : link;
```

(*Program continues on next page*)

```
        BEGIN
           new(player);
              .
              .
           IF player↑.age < 40 THEN . . . ;
              .
              .
           IF nextplayer <> NIL THEN . . . ;
              .
              .
        END.
```

```
(c)   PROGRAM sample(input,output);
      TYPE textline = PACKED ARRAY [1..30] OF char;
           link = ↑student;
           student = RECORD
                         name : textline;
                         next : link
                     END;
      VAR point,tag : link;

      PROCEDURE readtext (VAR line : textline);
      VAR count : 1..30;
      BEGIN
         FOR count := 1 TO 30 DO line[count] := ' ';
         count := 1;
         REPEAT
            read(line[count]);
            count := succ(count)
         UNTIL eoln;
         readln
      END;

      BEGIN   (* main action block *)
         new(point);
         readtext(point↑.name);
         point↑.next := NIL;
         tag := point;
         REPEAT
            new(point);
            readtext(point↑.name);
            point↑.next := tag;
            tag := point
         UNTIL point↑.name[1] = '*';
         tag := point↑.next
      END.
```

# Programming Problems

**13.38**  Modify the program given in Example 13.8 so that each component within the list (i.e., each record) contains a name, street address, and city/state/ZIP code. Place the name on one line, the street address on another line and the city/state ZIP code on a third line.

　　　Let the record consist of two fields. The first will be a two-dimensional array, with 3 rows and 80 columns, where each row represents a line of text. The second field will be a pointer to the next record.

**13.39**  Modify the program given in Example 13.9 so that it applies to each of the following linked structures.

   (*a*)   A linear linked list with two sets of pointers (one set pointing in the forward direction, the other set pointing backwards).

   (*b*)   A circular linked list. (Use a pointer variable to identify the beginning of the list.)

   (*c*)   A *first-in*, *first out* (FIFO) linear linked list, as illustrated in Fig. 13-8.

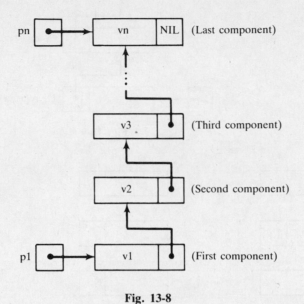

**Fig. 13-8**

   (*d*)   A binary tree with a specified number of levels. (Note that a systematic method for traversing the tree will be required.)

**13.40**  Write a complete Pascal program that will allow you to enter and maintain a computerized version of your family tree. Begin by specifying the number of generations (i.e., the number of levels). Then enter the names and nationalities in a hierarchical fashion. Include capabilities for modifying the tree and for adding new names (new nodes) to the tree. Also, include a provision for displaying the entire tree automatically after each update.

   Test the program, beginning with one pair of your grandparents or, if known, one pair of great-grandparents.

**13.41**  An RPN calculator utilizes a scheme whereby each new numerical value is followed by the operation that is to be performed between the new value and its predecessor. (RPN stands for "reverse Polish notation.") Thus, adding two numbers, say 3.3 + 4.8, would require the following keystrokes:

$$3.3 \quad \langle \text{enter} \rangle$$
$$4.8 \quad +$$

The sum, 8.1, would then be displayed in the calculator's single visible register.

   RPN calculators make use of a *stack*, typically containing four registers (four components), as illustrated in Fig. 13-9. Each new number is entered into the X register, causing all previously entered values to be pushed up in the stack. If the T register was previously occupied, then the old number will be lost (it will be overwritten by the value that is pushed up from the Z register).

   Arithmetic operations are always carried out between the numbers in the X and Y registers. The result of such an operation will always be displayed in the X register, causing everything in the upper registers to drop down one level (thus "popping" the stack). This procedure is illustrated in Figs. 13-10(*a*) to 13-10(*c*) for the addition of the two numbers described above.

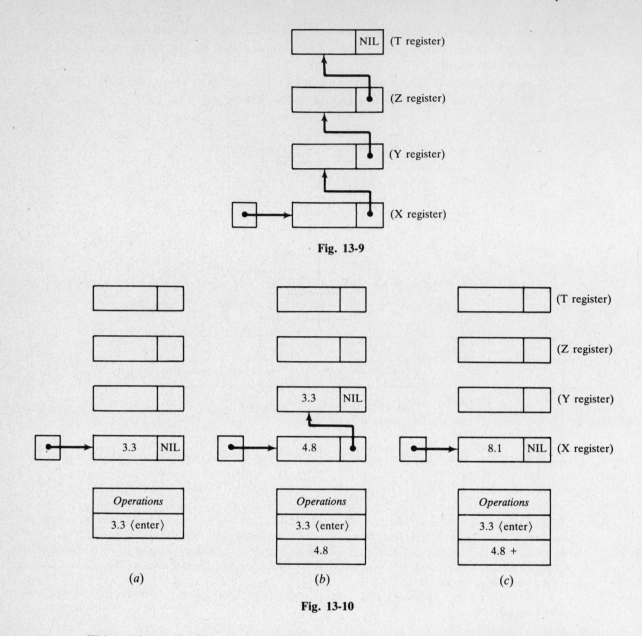

**Fig. 13-9**

**Fig. 13-10**

Write an interactive Pascal program that will simulate an RPN calculator. Display the contents of the stack after each operation, as in Figs. 13-10(a) to 13-10(c). Include a provision for carrying out each of the following operations.

| Operation | Keystrokes |
|---|---|
| enter new data | (value)⟨enter⟩ |
| addition | (value)    + |
| subtraction | (value)    − |
| multiplication | (value)    * |
| division | (value)    / |

Test the program using any numerical data of your choice.

## Reserved Words

| | | | |
|---|---|---|---|
| AND | END | NIL | SET |
| ARRAY | FILE | NOT | THEN |
| BEGIN | FOR | OF | TO |
| CASE | FUNCTION | OR | TYPE |
| CONST | GOTO | PACKED | UNTIL |
| DIV | IF | PROCEDURE | VAR |
| DO | IN | PROGRAM | WHILE |
| DOWNTO | LABEL | RECORD | WITH |
| ELSE | MOD | REPEAT | |

# Standard Identifiers

| | | | |
|---|---|---|---|
| abs | false | pack | sin |
| arctan | get | page | sqr |
| boolean | input | pred | sqrt |
| char | integer | put | succ |
| chr | ln | read | text |
| cos | maxint | readln | true |
| dispose | new | real | trunc |
| eof | odd | reset | unpack |
| eoln | ord | rewrite | write |
| exp | output | round | writeln |

# Appendix C

## Standard Procedures

| Procedure | Purpose | Reference |
|---|---|---|
| dispose | Delete a dynamic variable; i.e., a component in a linked list. | Sec. 13.5 |
| get | Transfer data items from an input file to the file buffer. | Sec. 11.5 |
| new | Create a dynamic variable; i.e., a component in a linked list. | Sec. 13.3 |
| pack | Create dense storage of data items within the computer's memory | Sec. 9.4 |
| page | Cause new output to begin at the top of a new page. | Sec. 4.7 |
| put | Transfer data items from the file buffer to an output file. | Sec. 11.3 |
| read | Read data items from an input file. | Secs. 4.2, 11.6 |
| readln | Read data items from an input file, then skip to the next line. | Sec. 4.3 |
| reset | Prepare a file for reading. | Sec. 11.5 |
| rewrite | Prepare a file for writing. | Sec. 11.3 |
| unpack | Restore sparse storage of data items within the computer's memory. | Sec. 9.4 |
| write | Write data items to an output file. | Secs. 4.5, 11.4 |
| writeln | Write data items to an output file, then skip to the next line. | Sec. 4.6 |

## Standard Functions

| Function | Purpose | Type of Parameter (x) | Type of Result |
|---|---|---|---|
| abs(x) | Compute the absolute value of x. | integer or real | same as x |
| arctan(x) | Compute the arctangent of x. | integer or real | real |
| chr(x) | Determine the character represented by x. | integer | char |
| cos(x) | Compute the cosine of x (x in radians). | integer or real | real |
| eof(x) | Determine if an end-of-file has been detected. | file | boolean |
| eoln(x) | Determine if an end-of-line has been detected. | file | boolean |
| exp(x) | Compute $e^x$, where $e=2.7182818...$ is the base of the natural (Naperian) system of logarithms. | integer or real | real |
| ln(x) | Compute the natural logarithm of x $(x > 0)$. | integer or real | real |
| odd(x) | Determine if x is odd or even. (Return a value of true if x is odd, false otherwise.) | integer | boolean |
| ord(x) | Determine the (decimal) integer that is used to encode the character x. | char | integer |
| pred(x) | Determine the predecessor of x. | integer, char or boolean | same as x |
| round(x) | Round the value of x to the nearest integer. | real | integer |
| sin(x) | Compute the sine of x (x in radians). | integer or real | real |

(*continues on next page*)

| Function | Purpose | Type of Parameter (x) | Type of Result |
|---|---|---|---|
| sqr(x) | Compute the square of x. | integer or real | same as x |
| sqrt(x) | Compute the square root of x (x > = 0). | integer or real | real |
| succ(x) | Determine the successor to x. | integer, char or boolean | same as x |
| trunc(x) | Truncate x (i.e., drop the decimal part of x). | real | integer |

# Appendix E

## Operators

The Pascal operators are summarized below, in their natural precedence (highest to lowest).

| Precedence | Operator(s) |
|---|---|
| 1 (highest) | NOT |
| 2 | * / DIV MOD AND |
| 3 | + - OR |
| 4 (lowest) | = <> < <= > >= IN |

Successive operations within the same precedence group are carried out from left to right.

# Syntax Diagrams

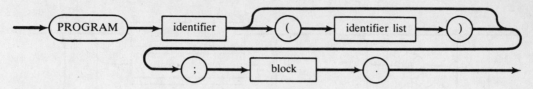

**Fig. F-1** Program.

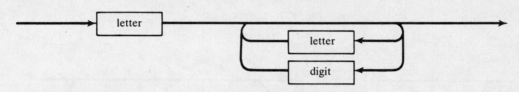

**Fig. F-2** Identifier.

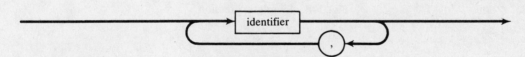

**Fig. F-3** Identifier list.

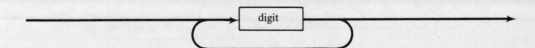

**Fig. F-4** Unsigned integer.

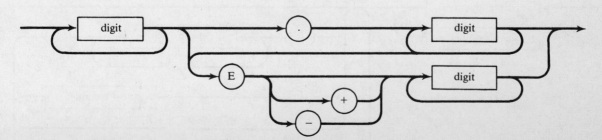

**Fig. F-5** Unsigned real.

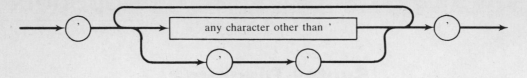

**Fig. F-6**  String.

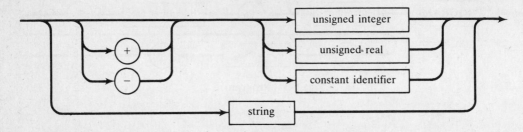

**Fig. F-7**  Constant.

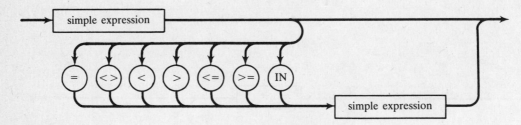

**Fig. F-8**  Simple expression.

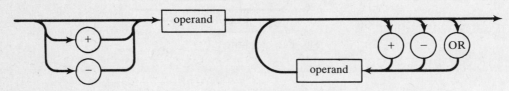

**Fig. F-9**  Expression.

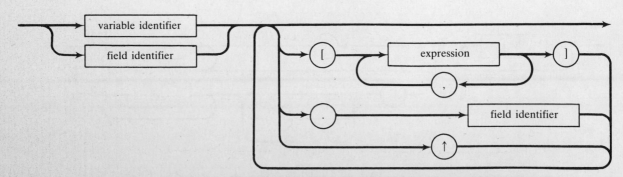

**Fig. F-10**  Variable.

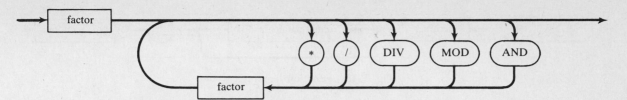

**Fig. F-11**  Operand.

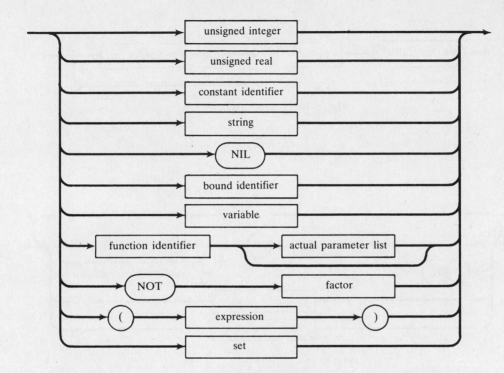

**Fig. F-12**  Factor.

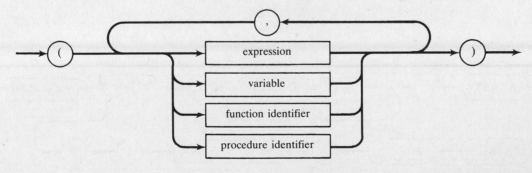

**Fig. F-13**  Actual parameter list.

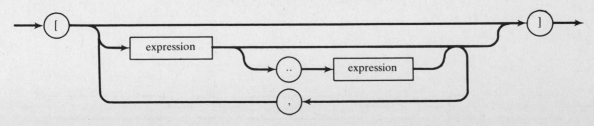

**Fig. F-14**  Set.

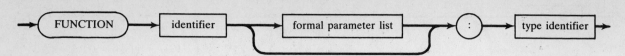

**Fig. F-15** Function heading.

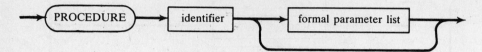

**Fig. F-16** Procedure heading.

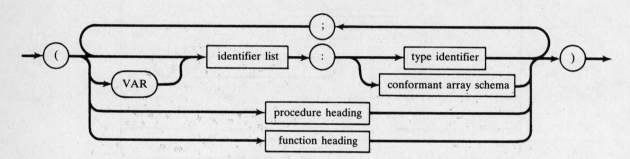

**Fig. F-17** Formal parameter list.

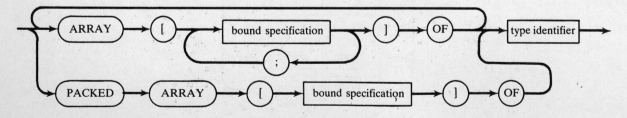

**Fig. F-18** Conformant array schema.

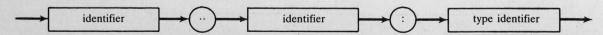

**Fig. F-19** Bound specification.

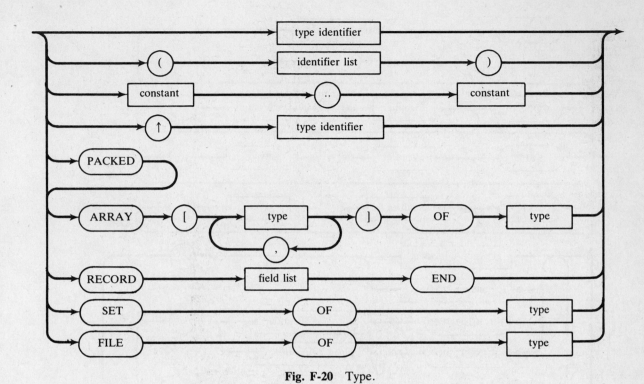

**Fig. F-20**   Type.

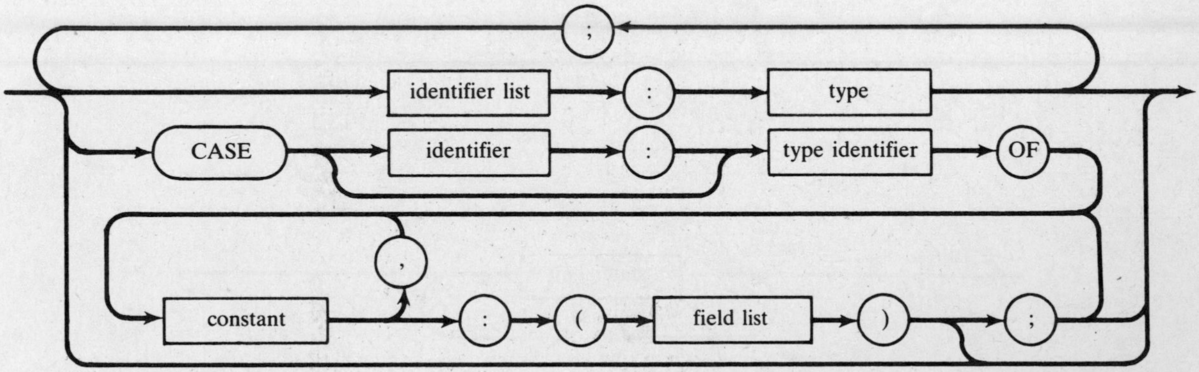

**Fig. F-21**   Field list.

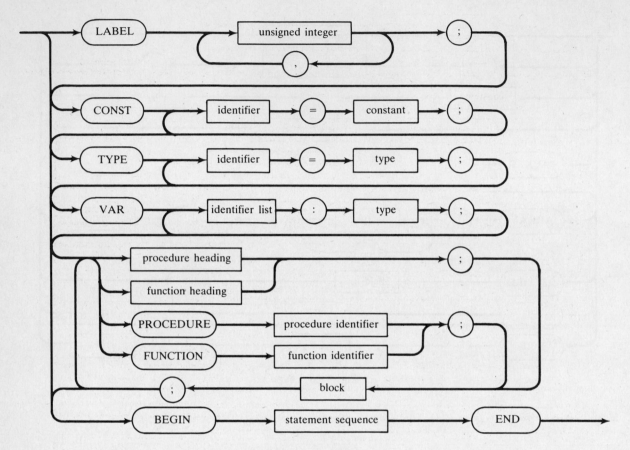

**Fig. F-22** Block.

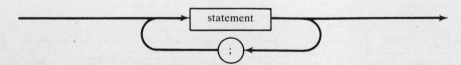

**Fig. F-23** Statement sequence.

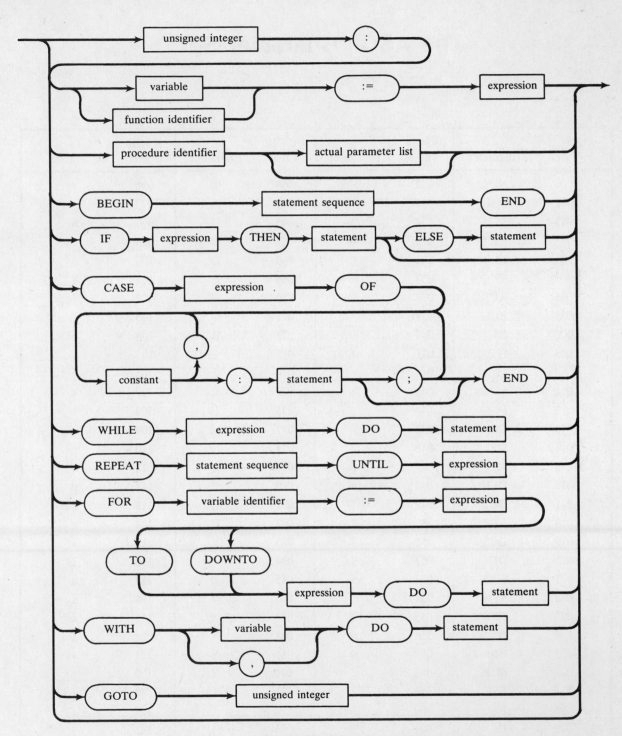

**Fig. F-24** Statement.

# Appendix G

## The ASCII Character Set

| ASCII Value | Character | ASCII Value | Character | ASCII Value | Character | ASCII Value | Character |
|---|---|---|---|---|---|---|---|
| 000 | NUL | 032 | blank | 064 | @ | 096 | ` |
| 001 | SOH | 033 | ! | 065 | A | 097 | a |
| 002 | STX | 034 | " | 066 | B | 098 | b |
| 003 | ETX | 035 | # | 067 | C | 099 | c |
| 004 | EOT | 036 | $ | 068 | D | 100 | d |
| 005 | ENQ | 037 | % | 069 | E | 101 | e |
| 006 | ACK | 038 | & | 070 | F | 102 | f |
| 007 | BEL | 039 | ' | 071 | G | 103 | g |
| 008 | BS | 040 | ( | 072 | H | 104 | h |
| 009 | HT | 041 | ) | 073 | I | 105 | i |
| 010 | LF | 042 | * | 074 | J | 106 | j |
| 011 | VT | 043 | + | 075 | K | 107 | k |
| 012 | FF | 044 | , | 076 | L | 108 | l |
| 013 | CR | 045 | - | 077 | M | 109 | m |
| 014 | SO | 046 | . | 078 | N | 110 | n |
| 015 | SI | 047 | / | 079 | O | 111 | o |
| 016 | DLE | 048 | 0 | 080 | P | 112 | p |
| 017 | DC1 | 049 | 1 | 081 | Q | 113 | q |
| 018 | DC2 | 050 | 2 | 082 | R | 114 | r |
| 019 | DC3 | 051 | 3 | 083 | S | 115 | s |
| 020 | DC4 | 052 | 4 | 084 | T | 116 | t |
| 021 | NAK | 053 | 5 | 085 | U | 117 | u |
| 022 | SYN | 054 | 6 | 086 | V | 118 | v |
| 023 | ETB | 055 | 7 | 087 | W | 119 | w |
| 024 | CAN | 056 | 8 | 088 | X | 120 | x |
| 025 | EM | 057 | 9 | 089 | Y | 121 | y |
| 026 | SUB | 058 | : | 090 | Z | 122 | z |
| 027 | ESC | 059 | ; | 091 | [ | 123 | { |
| 028 | FS | 060 | < | 092 | \ | 124 | | |
| 029 | GS | 061 | = | 093 | ] | 125 | } |
| 030 | RS | 062 | > | 094 | ↑ | 126 | ~ |
| 031 | US | 063 | ? | 095 | — | 127 | DEL |

*Note*: The first 32 characters and the last character are control characters; they cannot be printed.

# Appendix H

## Use of Turbo Pascal

Turbo Pascal, developed by Borland International, Inc., has become very popular among personal computer users. Most of the programs in this book can be compiled and executed by Turbo Pascal without any modification. Of the remaining programs, most will run under Turbo Pascal provided they are modified slightly. A few programs utilize features that are not supported by Turbo Pascal and therefore will not run at all.

### Required Modifications

1. Early versions of Turbo Pascal (version 3 and earlier) handle the standard function eoln in an unusual manner, resulting in an error when a program utilizing this function is compiled. This problem can be removed, however, if the compiler directive {B−} is included at the beginning of the program. Specific programs requiring this modification are found in Examples 7.24, 9.7, 9.11, 9.16, 9.27, 10.28, 12.16, 12.19, 13.8 and 13.9.

   Later versions of Turbo Pascal handle the eoln function in the conventional manner. Hence, the modification described above is not required.

2. Turbo Pascal opens data files differently than other versions of Pascal. Therefore, programs which make use of data files must include the assign statement. This change must be made to all of the programming examples in Chapter 11. However, some of these programs still will not run under Turbo Pascal because they make use of the unsupported features get and put, as discussed below.

3. When executing the programs shown in Examples 10.21 and 11.20, entering payment dates as shown in the text will result in an execution error. To avoid this error, separate the month, day and year with blank spaces rather than slashes.

### Unsupported Features

1. Turbo Pascal does not permit GOTO's out of a block. Therefore the program in Example 7.8 will not run.

2. Turbo Pascal does not allow procedures and functions to be passed as parameters. Hence, the first program in Example 7.22 cannot be run.

3. Conformant array parameters are not supported by Turbo Pascal. The program shown in Example 9.32 will therefore not run.

4. Turbo Pascal does not support get and put. Therefore the programs in Examples 11.8, 11.9, 11.10 and 11.14 will not run.

5. The page command is not recognized by Turbo Pascal. The programs shown in Examples 6.17, 7.12, 7.18, 11.22 and 13.9 include this command. These programs will run if the page command is removed.

Consult the Turbo Pascal manual for other differences between Turbo Pascal and standard Pascal.

# Answers to Supplementary Problems

**2.50**   (*a*)   Valid

    (*b*)   Valid

    (*c*)   file is a reserved word.

    (*d*)   Valid

    (*e*)   Blank spaces are not allowed.

    (*f*)   Characters other than letters and digits are not allowed. (Some versions of Pascal do allow underscore characters.)

    (*g*)   The first character must be a letter. Also, hyphens are not allowed.


**2.51**   (*a*)   Valid, real

    (*b*)   Commas are not allowed.

    (*c*)   Valid, real

    (*d*)   The magnitude of the exponent may be too large.

    (*e*)   A digit must appear on each side of the decimal point.

    (*f*)   Illegal character.

    (*g*)   Valid, real

    (*h*)   Valid, integer (may be too large in magnitude for some computers)

    (*i*)   Valid, real


**2.52**   (*a*)   Valid

    (*b*)   Double quotes cannot be used to surround a string.

    (*c*)   The right-hand apostrophe is missing.

    (*d*)   Valid

    (*e*)   Valid

    (*f*)   Valid


**2.53**  
```
CONST month = 'july';
      fica = '123-45-6789';
      price = '$95.00';        (or price = 95.00;)
      gross = 2500.00;
      partno = 48837;
      bound = 0.00391;
```


**2.54**  
```
VAR period,status : char;
    terminal : boolean;
    index,row : integer;
    clearance : real;
```


**2.55**   (*a*)   This is an assignment statement, not an expression.

    (*b*)   Numeric or boolean, depending on the data type associated with value

    (*c*)   Numeric

    (*d*)   Boolean

    (*e*)   Two successive operators are not permitted.

    (*f*)   Numeric

    (*g*)   Boolean

**2.56**  (a)  Simple (assignment statement)        (e)  Simple (assignment)
          (b)  Structured (compound)                (f)  Simple (procedure access)
          (c)  Structured (repetitive)              (g)  Simple (unconditional transfer)
          (d)  Structured (conditional)             (h)  Simple (assignment)


**2.57**  Procedures are accessed in Probs. 2.56(c) and 2.56(f). A function is referenced in Prob. 2.56(e).


**2.58**  (a)  A Pascal program begins with the the reserved word PROGRAM, followed by an identifier, then an optional list of identifiers enclosed in parentheses, then a semicolon. Following these items is a program block.

          (b)  This diagram shows several different ways to write an unsigned real number. They are

               (i)    One or more digits, followed by a decimal point, then one or more digits.

               (ii)   One or more digits, followed by the letter E, then one or more digits. A + or − sign may appear between the letter E and the succeeding digits. (This is the exponential form.)

               (iii)  A combination of the above; i.e., one or more digits, then a decimal point, then one or more digits, following these items, the letter E, then an optional + or − sign, then one or more digits.

          (c)  This diagram shows several different ways to write a string. They are

               (i)    An unsigned integer, preceded by an optional + or − sign

               (ii)   An unsigned real number, preceded by an optional + or − sign

               (iii)  A constant identifier, preceded by an optional + or − sign

               (iv)   A string


**3.40**  (a)  Real      −0.3333333        (d)  Integer    −14
          (b)  Integer   −2                (e)  Real       0.03
          (c)  Real      0.3333333         (f)  Integer    3


**3.41**  (a)  False        (e)  True
          (b)  True         (f)  False
          (c)  True         (g)  False
          (d)  True         (h)  True


**3.42**  (a)  4.667        (i)  True       (p)  2
          (b)  C            (j)  False      (q)  2
          (c)  101          (k)  True       (r)  −2
          (d)  9            (l)  2          (s)  −2
          (e)  d            (m)  3          (t)  <
          (f)  False        (n)  −2         (u)  64
          (g)  11           (o)  −3         (v)  g
          (h)  f


**3.43**  (b)  The character corresponding to EBCDIC 67 is not shown in Table 3.2.
          (c)  133
          (t)  The character corresponding to EBCDIC 252 is not shown in Table 3.2.
          (u)  192

**3.44**  (*a*)  DIV requires integer operands.

     (*b*)  Correct.

     (*c*)  Arithmetic operations cannot be performed on string operands.

     (*d*)  Correct.

     (*e*)  An operator is missing in the denominator.

     (*f*)  Correct.

     (*g*)  The boolean operands must be enclosed in parentheses.

     (*h*)  Correct.

     (*i*)  The operands are incompatible.

     (*j*)  The parentheses are not balanced.

     (*k*)  This expression will result in a value that exceeds maxint.

     (*l*)  Consecutive operators are not allowed.

     (*m*)  The odd function requires an integer parameter.

     (*n*)  Correct.

**3.45**
```
VAR gross,net,tax : real;
    employee : integer;
    status,sex : char;
    exempt : boolean;
```

**4.40**  The input data will be entered on two lines, with three integer and two real quantities on the first line, and four consecutive characters on the second line.

    The output will consist of three lines, double spaced. The first line will contain the values of the two constants flag and factor. The second line of text will contain the current values of the three integer variables and the two real variables. The third line will contain the current values of the four char-type variables and the two boolean variables.

    All of the individual output items will be separated from one another except the four consecutive char-type values on the second line.

**4.41**  (*a*)  $i1=1$    $i2=2$    $i3=3$    $r1=4.0$    $r2=5.0$
             $c1=b$    $c2=l$    $c3=u$    $c4=e$

     (*b*)  $i1=1$    $i2=2$    $i3=3$    $r1=4.0$    $r2=5.0$
             $c1=b$    $c2=$(blank)    $c3=$(blank)    $c4=$(blank)

     (*c*)  $i1=1$    $i2=2$    $i3=3$    $r1=4.0$    $r2=5.0$
             c1, c2, c3 and c4 will be undefined

     (*d*)  $i1=1$    $i2=2$    $i3=3$    $r1=4.0$    $r2=5.0$
             $c1=g$    $c2=r$    $c3=e$    $c4=e$

**4.42**
```
red 0.5000000E-02
(blank line)
     100    -200    -300 0.4004440E+03-0.5005550E+03
(blank line)
PINK  true false
```

**4.43**
```
flag=red factor= 0.005
(blank line)
i1= 100 i2=-200 i3=-300 r1= 400.4 r2=-500.6
(blank line)
color=PINK b1= true b2=false
```

**4.44**
```
-------------------------------------------
flag=red factor= 0.005        (top of page)
(blank line)
i1=  100 i2= -200 i3= -350
r1=  400.44 r2= -500.56

-------------------------------------------
color=PINK                    (top of page)
(blank line)
b1=  true b2= false
```

**4.45** (*a*) `readln(i1,i2,i3,r1,r2,c1,c2,c3,c4);`

(*b*) `readln(i1,r2,c3,c4);`

(*c*) `readln(i1,i2,i3);`
`readln(r1,r2);`
`readln(c1,c2,c3,c4);`

(*d*) `readln(i1);`
`readln(i2);`
`readln(i3);`
`readln(r1);`
`readln(r2);`
`readln(c1);`
`readln(c2);`
`readln(c3);`
`readln(c4);`

(*e*) `write(flag,factor:6:3,i1:5,i2:5,i3:5,r1:9:3,r2:9:3);`
`writeln(' ',c1,' ',c2,' ',c3,' ',c4,b1,b2);`

(Other solutions are also possible.)

(*f*) `write(flag,factor:8:2,i1:4,i2:4,i3:4,r1:8:2,r2:8:2);`
`writeln(' ',c1,' ',c2,' ',c3,' ',c4,b1:6,b2:6);`

(*g*) `writeln(flag,factor:6);`
`writeln;`
`writeln(c1,' ',c2,' ',c3,' ',c4,b1:6,b2:6);`
`writeln;`
`writeln(i1:5,i2:5,i3:5,r1:9:3,r2:9:3);`

(*h*) `writeln('flag=',flag,' factor=',factor);`
`writeln;`
`writeln('color=',c1,c2,c3,c4,' b1=',b1,' b2=',b2);`
`writeln;`
`write('i1=',i1:4,' i2=',i2:4,' i3=',i3:4);`
`writeln(' r1=',r1:8:3,' r2=',r2:8:3);`

(*i*) `page;`
`writeln(flag,i1:5,r1:9:3,' ',c1,' ',c2,b1:6);`
`writeln;`
`writeln;`
`writeln(factor,i2:5,i3:5,r2:9:3,' ',c3,' ',c4,b2:6);`

or

`writeln('1',flag,i1:5,r1:9:3,' ',c1,' ',c2,b1:6);`
`writeln;`
`writeln('0',factor,i2:5,i3:5,r2:9:3,' ',c3,' ',c4,b2:6);`

(*j*) `page;`
`writeln(flag,i1:5,r1:7:2,' ',c1,' ',c2,b1:7);`
`writeln;`
`writeln;`
`writeln(factor:7:2,i2:5,i3:5,r2:7:2,' ',c3,' ',c4,b2:7);`

```
(k)  page;
     writeln('flag=',flag);
     writeln('factor=',factor:12);
     writeln('i1=',i1:4);
     writeln('i2=',i2:4);
     writeln('i3=',i3:4);
     writeln('r1=',r1:12);
     writeln('r2=',r2:12);
     writeln('c1=',c1);
     writeln('c2=',c2);
     writeln('c3=',c3);
     writeln('c4=',c4);
     writeln('b1=',b1:5);
     writeln('b2=',b2:5);
```

**4.46**   SUM= 60 PRODUCT=  6000

(Note that there is one blank space before 60, two before 6000.)

**5.34**   (a)  
```
PROGRAM hello(output);
(* print HELLO! at the beginning of a line *)
BEGIN
    writeln('HELLO!')
END.
```

(b)  
```
PROGRAM friends(input,output);

(* interactive HELLO program *)

VAR c1,c2,c3,c4,c5,c6 : char;
BEGIN
    write('HI, WHAT''S YOUR NAME? ');
    readln(c1,c2,c3,c4,c5,c6);
    writeln;
    writeln;
    writeln('WELCOME ',c1,c2,c3,c4,c5,c6);
    writeln('LET''S BE FRIENDS!')
END.
```

(c)  Noninteractive version:

```
PROGRAM celsius(input,output);

(* convert temperature from Fahrenheit to Celsius *)

VAR f,c : real;
BEGIN
    readln(f);
    c := (5/9)*(f-32);
    writeln('F=',f:7:2,'   C=',c:7:2)
END.
```

Interactive version:

```
PROGRAM celsius2(input,output);

(* convert temperature from Fahrenheit to Celsius *)

(* interactive version *)

VAR f,c : real;
BEGIN
    write('F= ');
    readln(f);
    c := (5/9)*(f-32);
    writeln('C=',c:7:2)
END.
```

(d)  Noninteractive version:

```
PROGRAM piggybank(input,output);

(* piggy-bank problem *)

VAR n1,n2,n3,n4,n5 : integer;
    dollars : real;
BEGIN
   readln(n1,n2,n3,n4,n5);
   dollars := 0.5*n1 + 0.25*n2 + 0.1*n3 + 0.05*n4 + 0.01*n5;
   writeln;
   writeln('Half-dollars: ',n1:3);
   writeln('Quarters: ',n2:3);
   writeln('Dimes: ',n3:3);
   writeln('Nickels: ',n4:3);
   writeln('Pennies: ',n5:3);
   writeln;
   writeln('The piggy bank contains ',dollars:6:2,' dollars')
END.
```

Interactive version:

```
PROGRAM piggybank(input,output);

(* interactive piggy-bank problem *)

VAR n1,n2,n3,n4,n5 : integer;
    dollars : real;
BEGIN
   write('How many half-dollars? ');
   readln(n1);
   write('How many quarters? ');
   readln(n2);
   write('How many dimes? ');
   readln(n3);
   write('How many nickels? ');
   readln(n4);
   write('How many pennies? ');
   readln(n5);
   dollars := 0.5*n1 + 0.25*n2 + 0.1*n3 + 0.05*n4 + 0.01*n5;
   writeln;
   writeln('The piggy bank contains ',dollars:6:2,' dollars')
END.
```

(e)
```
PROGRAM sphere(input,output);

(* This program calculates the volume and area of a sphere, given the radius *)

CONST   pi = 3.14159;
VAR     radius,vol,area : real;

BEGIN
        writeln;
        writeln(' This program calculates the volume and area of a sphere.');
        writeln;
        write(' What is the radius?');
        readln(radius);

        (* Calculations.. *)

        area := 4.0*pi*sqr(radius);
        vol := area*radius/3.0;

        writeln;
        writeln(' The area is: ',area:8:2,' ,and the volume is: ',vol:7:2)
END.
```

(*f*)   PROGRAM mass(input,output);

```
        (* This program calculates the mass of air in a tire *)

        VAR     P,V,m,T : real;

        BEGIN
                writeln;
                write(' This program calculates the mass of air in a tire');
                writeln(' using English units.');
                writeln;
                write(' What is the Pressure, in psi? ');
                readln(P);
                writeln;
                write(' What is the Volume, in Cubic Feet? ');
                readln(V);
                writeln;
                write(' What is the Temperature, in degrees Fahrenheit? ');
                readln(T);

                (* The calculations *)

                m := (P*V)/(0.37*(T+460.0));

                (* Write out the answer *)

                writeln;
                writeln(' The Mass of air, in Pounds, is: ',m:7:2)
        END.

        PROGRAM encode(input,output);

        (* This program will encode a five-letter word. *)

        VAR     a,b,c,d,e,a1,b1,c1,d1,e1 : char;

        BEGIN
                writeln(' This program will encode a five-letter word.');
                writeln;
                write(' What word would you like encoded? ');
                readln(a,b,c,d,e);

                (* calculations *)

                a1 := chr(ord(a)-30);
                b1 := chr(ord(b)-30);
                c1 := chr(ord(c)-30);
                d1 := chr(ord(d)-30);
                e1 := chr(ord(e)-30);

                writeln;
                writeln(' The encoded word is: ',a1,b1,c1,d1,e1)
        END.
```

(*h*)   PROGRAM decode(input,output);

```
        (* This program decodes a five-letter word. *)

        VAR     a,b,c,d,e,a1,b1,c1,d1,e1 : char;
```

(*Program continues on next page*)

```
        BEGIN
                writeln(' This program will decode a five-letter word.');
                writeln;
                write(' What word would you like decoded? ');
                readln(a,b,c,d,e);

                (* calculations *)

                a1 := chr(ord(a)+30);
                b1 := chr(ord(b)+30);
                c1 := chr(ord(c)+30);
                d1 := chr(ord(d)+30);
                e1 := chr(ord(e)+30);

                writeln;
                writeln(' The decoded word is: ',a1,b1,c1,d1,e1)
        END.
```

**6.42**  (*a*)  True                    (*f*)  Error (mixed data types)
          (*b*)  True                    (*g*)  True
          (*c*)  Error (mixed data types) (*h*)  False
          (*d*)  False                   (*i*)  False
          (*e*)  True

**6.43**  (*a*)  A real-type variable cannot appear in a boolean expression.
          (*b*)  Correct.
          (*c*)  A real-type variable cannot be used as a control variable.
          (*d*)  Correct.
          (*e*)  Correct, provided b < c.
          (*f*)  The relative values of b and d are inconsistent.
          (*g*)  Correct.
          (*h*)  If flag remains true the REPEAT—UNTIL loop will continue indefinitely; otherwise, the WHILE—DO loop will execute only once, making it unnecessary.
          (*i*)  Correct.
          (*j*)  The selector cannot be a real-type expression; the labels cannot be real.
          (*k*)  Control cannot be transferred into a compound statement.
          (*l*)  Statement labels and case labels cannot be used interchangeably.

**6.50**  (*j*)  
```
PROGRAM loan(input,output);

(* This program generates a monthly payment schedule for a loan *)

VAR principal,rate,interest,monthly_interest,payment,ipart,itot,ppart : real;
    month : integer;
```

(*Program continues on next page*)

```
BEGIN

   (* Read the input data *)

   writeln(' This program generates a monthly payment schedule for a loan.');
   writeln;
   writeln;
   write(' What is the amount of the loan? ');
   readln(principal);
   write(' What is the yearly interest rate, expressed as a percentage? ');
   readln(rate);
   interest := 0.01*rate;
   monthly_interest := interest/12.0;
   write(' What is the monthly payment? ');
   readln(payment);

   (* Carry out the calculations and write the results,
                                       on a month-by-month basis *)

   month := 1;
   writeln(' Payment   Interest   Principal   Unpaid Balance   Total Interest');
   WHILE principal*(1.0 + monthly_interest) >= payment DO
      BEGIN
         ipart := principal*monthly_interest;
         ppart := payment - ipart;
         principal := principal - ppart;
         itot := itot + ipart;
         write(' ',month:5,'        ',ipart:8:2,'    ',ppart:9:2,'        ',principal:9:2);
         writeln('            ',itot:9:2);
         month := month + 1
      END;
   ipart := principal*monthly_interest;
   ppart := ipart + principal;
   principal := 0.0;
   itot := itot + ipart;
   write(' ',month:5,'        ',ipart:8:2,'    ',ppart:9:2,'        ',principal:9:2);
   writeln('            ',itot:9:2)
END.
```

(k)   
```
PROGRAM test(input,output);

(* This program averages sets of student examination scores *)

VAR avgtest,tottest,test : real;
    i,j,n,ntest,studid : integer;

BEGIN
   writeln(' This program averages n sets of student examination scores');
   writeln;

   REPEAT
      write(' How many students are there? ');
      readln(n);
      IF n < 0 THEN writeln(' Illegal value, please try again..')
   UNTIL n >= 0;
```

(*Program continues on next page*)

```
          REPEAT
             write(' How many exams for each student? ');
             readln(ntest);
             IF ntest < 0 THEN writeln(' Illegal value, please try again..')
          UNTIL ntest >= 0;
          writeln;

          FOR i := 1 TO n DO
             BEGIN
                writeln(' Student no. ',i:2);
                writeln;
                write(' Enter the student''s id: ');
                readln(studid);
                writeln;
                tottest := 0.0;
                writeln(' Enter the exam scores for this student');

                FOR j := 1 TO ntest DO
                   BEGIN   (* enter and sum the exam scores *)
                      REPEAT
                         write(' Test No. ',j:2,': ');
                         readln(test);
                         IF (test < 0.0) OR (test > 100.0) THEN
                            writeln('Illegal score, please try again..');
                      UNTIL (test >= 0.0) AND (test <= 100.0);
                      tottest := tottest + test
                   END;

                (* calculate and write out the average *)
                avgtest := tottest/ntest;
                writeln;
                writeln(' Average score: ',avgtest:6:2);
                writeln
             END
       END.
```

(*o*)   PROGRAM pyramid(output);

```
(* This program creates a pyramid of numbers in an interesting pattern *)

VAR       a,b,c,d,e,f,g,val : integer;

BEGIN
   FOR a := -9 TO 0 DO
      BEGIN
         b := (-1)*a;          (* Change counter to positive values *)
         c := a + 10;
         write('                          ');

         FOR d := 1 TO b DO write(' ');
         val := c + c - 1;

         FOR e := c TO val DO
            BEGIN   (* Print left half of line, including center *)
               IF (e >= 10) THEN f := e - 10 ELSE f := e;
               write(f:1);
            END;
         val := c+c-2;
```

(*Program continues on next page*)

```
               FOR g := val DOWNTO c DO
                  BEGIN    (* Print right half of line *)
                     IF (g >= 10) THEN f := g - 10 ELSE f := g;
                     write(f:1);
                  END;
               writeln
            END
      END.
```

(*p*)  ```
       PROGRAM plot(input,output);

       (* This program generates a plot of a damped sinusoidal function *)

       CONST star = '*';
             blank = ' ';
             dash = '-';
             line = '¦';
             linelength = 78;
       VAR time,y,i,j,half : integer;


       BEGIN
          writeln(' Generate a plot of the function exp(-0.1t) * sin(0.5t)');
          writeln;
          half := (linelength DIV 2);     (* Build a scale for the graph. *)

          FOR time := 0 TO 50 DO          (* Time 't' in seconds.  *)
             BEGIN
                y := ROUND((exp((-0.1)*(time)))*(sin(0.5*time))*(half DIV 1)) + half;
                IF time = 0 THEN          (* Plot the vertical axis *)
                            FOR i := 1 to linelength DO
                               IF i = y THEN write(star)
                                        ELSE write(dash)
                            ELSE          (* Plot the function *)
                               BEGIN
                                  IF half > y THEN j := half
                                              ELSE j := y;
                                  FOR i := 1 TO j DO
                                     IF i = y THEN write(star)
                                              ELSE IF i = half THEN write(line)
                                                              ELSE write(blank)
                               END;
                writeln
             END
       END.
```

**7.35**  (*a*)  The procedure name cannot be used as a variable.

(*b*)  Correct.

(*c*)  Correct.

(*d*)  This example contains several errors.

  (*i*)  The function is not given a data type.

  (*ii*)  The function name cannot appear in an internal VAR declaration.

  (*iii*)  The identifier representing the function name cannot be reassigned a new value.

(*e*)  The actual parameters are of a different type than the formal parameters.

(*f*)  Correct.

(*g*)  The actual parameters corresponding to the formal variable parameters cannot be expressions. (Note that the reference to the global variable t within the procedure is permissible.)
```

(h)   The actual parameters and the corresponding formal parameters do not agree in number. Also, char-type variables cannot be added together.

(i)   Correct. (Note that the function utilizes global variables.)

(j)   Correct.

(k)   The global variable c is altered each time the function is accessed (side effect).

(l)   Standard functions cannot be passed as parameters in standard (ISO) Pascal.

(m)   Correct.

(n)   funct1 is accessed (within proc1) before it is declared.

(o)   value is accessed (within the main block) outside of its declared scope.

(p)   The recursive function does not contain a termination condition.

**7.36**   (a)   $y = x_n + \sum_{i=1}^{n-1} x_i$   or   $y_n = x_n + y_{n-1}$

(b)   $y = \dfrac{(-1)^n x^n}{n!} + \sum_{i=0}^{n-1} \dfrac{(-1)^i x^i}{i!}$   or   $y_n = \dfrac{(-1)^n x^n}{n!} + y_{n-1}$

(c)   $p = f_t * \prod_{j=1}^{t-1} f_j$   or   $p_t = f_t * p_{t-1}$

**7.42**   PROGRAM powerfunction(input,output);

```
(* This program calculates the power of a number.
   The function is y = x to the nth power, where n is an integer. *)

VAR answer : char;

FUNCTION y(x : real; n : integer) : real;

(* this function raises x to the nth power *)

VAR product : real;
    count : integer;

BEGIN
   (* form the product *)
      IF n = 0 THEN product := 1.0
               ELSE BEGIN
                        product := x;
                        IF abs(n) <> 1 THEN
                            FOR count := 2 TO abs(n) DO
                                product := product * x
                    END;

   (* test for negative exponent *)
      IF n >= 0 THEN y := product ELSE y := 1.0/product
END;

PROCEDURE exponent;

(* this procedure evaluates the power function and writes out the result *)

VAR power,x : real;
    n : integer;
```

(*Program continues on next page*)

```
BEGIN
   writeln;
   write(' What is the base value? ');
   readln(x);
   write(' What is the value of the exponent? ');
   readln(n);
   power := y(x,n);
   writeln;
   writeln(' ',x:6:2,' Raised to the ',n:3,' power is ',power:10:4)
END;

BEGIN   (* main action block *)
   REPEAT
      exponent;
      writeln;
      write(' Again (Y/N)? ');
      readln(answer)
   UNTIL ((answer = 'n') OR (answer = 'N'))
END.
```

7.43    PROGRAM powerfunction(input,output);

```
(* This program calculates the power of a number.
   The function is y = x to the nth power.          *)

VAR answer : char;

FUNCTION y(x,n : real) : real;

(* this function raises x to the nth power *)

BEGIN
   y := exp(n*(ln(x)))
END;

PROCEDURE exponent;

(* this procedure evaluates the power function and writes out the result *)

VAR power,x,n : real;

BEGIN
   REPEAT
      writeln;
      write(' What is the base value? ');
      readln(x);
      IF (x < 0.0) THEN   (* write error message *)
         BEGIN
            writeln;
            writeln(' ERROR: The base value is negative.  Try again');
            writeln
         END
   UNTIL x >= 0.0;
   write(' What is the value of the exponent? ');
   readln(n);
   power := y(x,n);
   writeln;
   writeln(' ',x:6:2,' Raised to the ',n:6:2,' power is ',power:10:4)
END;
```

(*Program continues on next page*)

```
BEGIN   (* main action block *)
   REPEAT
      exponent;
      writeln;
      write(' Again (Y/N)? ');
      readln(answer)
   UNTIL ((answer = 'n') OR (answer = 'N'))
END.
```

**7.49**   (g)  
```
PROGRAM test(input,output);

   (* This program averages sets of student examination scores *)

   VAR avgtest,tottest : real;
       i,n,ntest : integer;


   PROCEDURE readinput(n,ntest : integer; VAR tottest : real);

   (* this procedure enters the input data for each student *)

   VAR test : real;
       j,studid : integer;

   BEGIN
      writeln(' Student no. ',i:2);
      writeln;
      write(' Enter the student''s id: ');
      readln(studid);
      writeln;
      tottest := 0.0;
      writeln(' Enter the exam scores for this student');

      (* enter and sum the exam scores for each student *)

      FOR j := 1 TO ntest DO
         BEGIN
            REPEAT
               write(' Test No. ',j:2,': ');
               readln(test);
               IF (test < 0.0) OR (test > 100.0)
                  THEN writeln('Illegal score, please try again..')
            UNTIL (test >= 0.0) AND (test <= 100.0);
            tottest := tottest + test
         END
   END;


   FUNCTION average(total : real; m : integer) : real;

   (* this function determines an average from a total of m numbers *)

   BEGIN
      average := total/m
   END;
```

*(Program continues on next page)*

```
PROCEDURE writeanswer(avg : real);

(* this procedure writes out the average exam score for a particular student *)

BEGIN
   writeln;
   writeln(' Average score: ',avg:6:2);
   writeln
END;

BEGIN   (* main action block *)
   writeln(' This program averages n sets of student examination scores');
   writeln;

   REPEAT
      write(' How many students are there? ');
      readln(n);
      IF n < 0 THEN writeln(' Illegal value, please try again..')
   UNTIL n >= 0;

   REPEAT
      write(' How many exams for each student? ');
      readln(ntest);
      IF ntest < 0 THEN writeln(' Illegal value, please try again..')
   UNTIL ntest >= 0;
   writeln;

   FOR i := 1 TO n DO
      BEGIN
         readinput(n,ntest,tottest);
         avgtest := average(tottest,ntest);
         writeanswer(avgtest)
      END
END.
```

**7.50**   (c)
```
PROGRAM loan(input,output);

(* This program generates a monthly payment schedule for a loan *)

VAR principal,rate,interest,monthly_interest,amount : real;
    month,months : integer;

FUNCTION POWER(y : real; x : integer) : real;

(* this function raises y to the x power *)

BEGIN
   power := exp(x*(ln(y)))
END;

FUNCTION payment(principal,monthly_interest : real;
                                    months : integer) : real;

(* this function determines the monthly payment *)

VAR quantity : real;
```

*(Program continues on next page)*

```pascal
BEGIN
   quantity := power((1 + monthly_interest),months);
   payment := principal * monthly_interest * quantity / (quantity - 1)
END;

PROCEDURE readinput(VAR principal,monthly_interest : real;
                                              VAR months : integer);
(* this procedure reads the input data *)
VAR rate,interest : real;
    years : integer;
BEGIN
   writeln;
   write(' What is the amount of the loan? ');
   readln(principal);
   write(' What is the yearly interest rate, expressed as a percentage? ');
   readln(rate);
   interest := 0.01*rate;
   monthly_interest := interest/12.0;
   write(' What is the duration of the loan, in years? ');
   readln(years);
   months := 12*years
END;

PROCEDURE writeoutput(principal,monthly_interest,amount : real;
                                              months : integer);

(* this procedure generates and writes out a
                         month-by-month payment schedule *)

VAR ipart,itot,ppart : real;
    month : integer;

BEGIN
   write(' Payment   Interest   Principal   Unpaid Balance');
   writeln('   Total Interest');
   FOR month := 1 TO months DO
      BEGIN
         ipart := principal * monthly_interest;
         ppart := amount - ipart;
         principal := principal - ppart;
         itot := itot + ipart;
         write(' ',month:5,'     ',ipart:8:2,'    ',ppart:9:2);
         writeln('       ',principal:9:2,'         ',itot:9:2)
      END
END;

BEGIN   (* main action block *)
   writeln(' This program generates a monthly payment schedule for a loan.');
   writeln;

   (* read the input data *)

   readinput(principal,monthly_interest,months);

   (* calculate the monthly payment *)

   amount := payment(principal,monthly_interest,months);
   write(' Monthly payment: ',amount:9:2);
   writeln;

   (* write the month-by-month payment schedule *)

   writeoutput(principal,monthly_interest,amount,months)
END.
```

**8.21**  (*a*)  Miami          (*e*)  4

       (*b*)  Phoenix        (*f*)  True

       (*c*)  6             (*g*)  False

       (*d*)  4


**8.22**  (*a*)  Correct.

       (*b*)  Declarations are in the wrong order; inconsistent data types in the first assignment statement.

       (*c*)  Enumerated data cannot be included in a read or a write statement.

       (*d*)  Correct.

       (*e*)  Correct.


**8.23**
```pascal
PROGRAM dates(input,output);

(* This program determines the number of days a person has been alive *)

TYPE day = 1..31;
     month = 1..12;
     year = 1960..2100;
     numberofdays = 0..maxint;

VAR dd : day;
    mm : month;
    yy : year;
    birthday,today,days : numberofdays;
    n,a,m,e,s : char;

FUNCTION daysbeyond1960(mm : month; dd : day; yy : year) : numberofdays;

(* This function counts the days from January 1, 1960 to a given date *)

VAR n : numberofdays;
BEGIN
  n := trunc(30.42*(mm - 1)) + dd;
  IF mm = 2 THEN n := n + 1;
  IF (mm > 2) AND (mm < 8) THEN n := n - 1;
  IF (yy MOD 4 = 0) AND (mm > 2) THEN n := n + 1;
  IF (yy-1960) DIV 4 > 0 THEN n := n + 1461*((yy-1960) DIV 4);
  IF (yy-1960) MOD 4 > 0 THEN n := n + 365*((yy-1960) MOD 4) + 1;
  daysbeyond1960 := n
END;


PROCEDURE header(VAR n,a,m,e,s : char);

(* This procedure generates the conversational input *)

BEGIN
  write(' Please enter your first name (5 letters): ');
  readln(n,a,m,e,s);
  writeln;
  writeln(' Hello, ',n:1,a:1,m:1,e:1,s:1);
  write(' This program will calculate the number of days ');
  writeln(' you have been alive');
  writeln
END;
```

*(Program continues on next page)*

```
      BEGIN   (* main action block *)
         header(n,a,m,e,s);
         write(' When were you born, ',n:1,a:1,m:1,e:1,s:1,'? (mm dd yyyy) ');
         readln(mm,dd,yy);
         birthday := daysbeyond1960(mm,dd,yy);
         writeln;
         write(' What is today''s date? (mm dd yyyy) ');
         readln(mm,dd,yy);
         today := daysbeyond1960(mm,dd,yy);
         days := today - birthday + 1;
         writeln;
         writeln(' ',n:1,a:1,m:1,e:1,s:1,', you have been alive ',days:5,' days.')
      END.
```

**8.24**

```
      PROGRAM dayoftheweek(input,output);

      (* This program determines the day of the week for any given date *)

      TYPE day = 1..31;
           month = 1..12;
           year = 1960..2100;
           numberofdays = 0..maxint;

      VAR dd : day;
          mm : month;
          yy : year;
          n,a,m,e,s : char;

      FUNCTION daysbeyond1960(mm : month; dd : day; yy : year) : numberofdays;

      (* This function counts the days from January 1, 1960 to a given date *)

      VAR n : numberofdays;
      BEGIN
         n := trunc(30.42*(mm - 1)) + dd;
         IF mm = 2 THEN n := n + 1;
         IF (mm > 2) AND (mm < 8) THEN n := n - 1;
         IF (yy MOD 4 = 0) AND (mm > 2) THEN n := n + 1;
         IF (yy-1960) DIV 4 > 0 THEN n := n + 1461*((yy-1960) DIV 4);
         IF (yy-1960) MOD 4 > 0 THEN n := n + 365*((yy-1960) MOD 4) + 1;
         daysbeyond1960 := n
      END;

      PROCEDURE readinput(VAR mm : month; VAR dd : day;
                          VAR yy : year;  VAR n,a,m,e,s : char);

      (* This procedure generates the conversational input *)

      BEGIN
         write(' Please enter your first name (5 letters): ');
         readln(n,a,m,e,s);
         writeln;
         writeln(' Hello, ',n:1,a:1,m:1,e:1,s:1);
         writeln(' This program will calculate the day of the week');
         writeln(' for any given date beyond January 1, 1960');
         writeln;
         write(' ',n:1,a:1,m:1,e:1,s:1,', please enter the date (mm dd yyyy) : ');
         readln(mm,dd,yy)
      END;
```

*(Program continues on next page)*

```
PROCEDURE writeoutput(mm : month; dd : day; yy : year;  n,a,m,e,s : char);

(* This procedure determines the day of the week and then writes it out *)

VAR today : numberofdays;
    dayval : 0..6;

BEGIN
    today := daysbeyond1960(mm,dd,yy) - 1;
    dayval := today MOD 7;
    writeln;
    write(' ',n:1,a:1,m:1,e:1,s:1,': The day is ');
    CASE dayval OF
        0 : writeln('Friday');
        1 : writeln('Saturday');
        2 : writeln('Sunday');
        3 : writeln('Monday');
        4 : writeln('Tuesday');
        5 : writeln('Wednesday');
        6 : writeln('Thursday')
    END;
    writeln
END;


BEGIN   (* main action block *)
    readinput(mm,dd,yy,n,a,m,e,s);
    writeoutput(mm,dd,yy,n,a,m,e,s)
END.
```

**9.44**  (a)  Correct.

(b)  Correct.

(c)  Correct.

(d)  The lower and upper limits of the first index are in the wrong order.

(e)  An index cannot be real.

(f)  Index out of range.

(g)  Correct.

(h)  The index specification in the assignment statement is inconsistent with the array declaration.

(i)  The data item assigned to the array element is of the wrong type.

(j)  The indices in the assignment statement are of the wrong data type.

(k)  Correct.

(l)  Entire arrays cannot appear as elements within a numeric expression.

(m)  Correct (because name is a string variable).

(n)  Entire arrays cannot appear in read or write statements (the appearance of a string variable in a write statement is an exception).

(o)  Correct.

(p)  Incorrect syntax for pack and unpack statements (the indices are written incorrectly, and their values are too large).

(q)  Strings of unequal length cannot be compared; string variables cannot be combined ("added").

(r)  Correct.

**9.45**  (*a*)  The formal parameter (dummy) must be of a predefined data type.

(*b*)  Correct.

(*c*)  Correct.

(*d*)  An element of a packed array cannot be passed to a procedure or a function as an actual parameter.

(*e*)  Correct.

(*f*)  The second actual parameter (cost) is of a different type than the corresponding formal parameter.

(*g*)  Only the last dimension of a multidimensional conformant array parameter can be packed.

(*h*)  A packed array of type char is not treated as a string variable within a procedure or a function to which it has been passed.

(*i*)  The formal parameter in process must be a variable conformant array parameter, not a value conformant array parameter.

(*j*)  The actual parameters must both be real-type arrays of the same dimensionality.

**10.35**  (*a*)  Correct.

(*b*)  Correct.

(*c*)  The record definition does not include END. Also, the array type definition (sales) is incorrect.

(*d*)  Correct.

(*e*)  This problem contains several errors.

　(*i*)  Entire records cannot appear in a boolean expression (birthday = today).

　(*ii*)  The reference to year in the stopping criterion (UNTIL year = 0) must be preceded by the record name.

　(*iii*)  The final value expected in the stopping criterion (year = 0) is out of range.

(*f*)  A single readln statement cannot read an entire packed array (name).

(*g*)  The variant-part of the record must follow the fixed part (i.e., quantity : integer is out of place).

(*h*)  The references to record field names must be preceded by the record name (e.g., employees [i].maritalstatus, or employees [i].divorced.children). Also, the writeln statement is incorrect because divorced is not an active variant field.

(*i*)  A tag-field identifier cannot be passed to a procedure as a variable parameter.

**11.48**  (*a*)  The statement should be a variable declaration rather than a type definition.

(*b*)  Correct.

(*c*)  FILE OF should not appear in a text file declaration.

(*d*)  Correct.

(*e*)  A file component cannot be another file.

(*f*)  The declaration is correct though unnecessary, since input and output are predeclared text files.

(*g*)  The file being written to (data) is not initialized (via rewrite). Also, writeln cannot be used, since data is not a text file.

(*h*)  Correct.

(*i*)  Correct, provided a match is found (customer.custname = name) before an end-of-file is encountered.

(*j*)  A file cannot be passed to a procedure as a value parameter.

**12.25**  (*a*)  [re,mi,fa,sol,la]　　　　(*e*)  [do,re,mi,fa]

(*b*)  [do,re,mi,fa,sol,la]　　　(*f*)  [ ]

(*c*)  [do]　　　　　　　　　　(*g*)  [ ]

(*d*)  [re,mi,fa]　　　　　　　(*h*)  [do,re,mi]

**12.26** (a)  [re,fa]                    (d)  [do,re,mi,sol,ti]

    (b)  [do,re,fa]              (e)  [re,mi,fa,sol,la]

    (c)  [re,mi,fa,la,ti]


**12.27** (a)  False        (e)  False        (i)  False

    (b)  True         (f)  True         (j)  True

    (c)  False        (g)  True         (k)  True

    (d)  True         (h)  True         (l)  False


**12.28** (a)  Correct.

    (b)  The boolean expression must be written

$$[money] <= [penny,nickel,dime]$$

    (c)  The assignment statement must be written

$$song := song + [money]$$

    (d)  Correct.

    (e)  Correct.

    (f)  The first operand in the boolean expression (whiskey) cannot be a set-type variable.


**13.35** (a)
```
TYPE link = ↑customer;
     customer = RECORD
                    name : PACKED ARRAY [1..20] OF char;
                    acctno : 1..9999;
                    balance : real;
                    next : link
                END;
```
    (b)  `VAR nextcustomer,lastcustomer : link;`

    (c)
```
new(nextcustomer);

   .
   .
   .

dispose(nextcustomer);
```

**13.36** (a)  `lastcustomer := nextcustomer↑.next;`

    (b)  `nextcustomer↑.next := NIL;`

    (c)  `lastcustomer↑ := nextcustomer↑;`

    (d)
```
IF nextcustomer↑.acctno = 1330 THEN
   nextcustomer↑.balance := 287.55;
```
    or
```
WITH nextcustomer↑ DO
    IF acctno = 1330 THEN balance := 287.55;
```
    (e)
```
PROCEDURE readinput (VAR customer : link);
VAR count : 1..20;
BEGIN

   .
   .

   count := 1;
   WHILE NOT eoln DO
```

(*Program continues on next page*)

```
        BEGIN
           read(customer↑ .name);
           count := succ(count);
        END;
        .
        .
    END;

    BEGIN   (* main action block *)
        .

        .
        readinput(nextcustomer);
        .

        .
    END.
```

(f) WHILE nextcustomer <> NIL DO

```
        BEGIN
        .
        .
        .
        END;
```

**13.37** (a) This program outline contains three errors:

(i) The pointer-type identifier does not agree with the referenced-variable name.

(ii) The pointer field within the referenced variable has an incorrect type designation.

(iii) The variable declarations have incorrect type designations.

(b) This program outline contains two errors:

(i) The referenced-variable definition does not include a pointer.

(ii) The parameter appearing in the new statement is incorrect.

(c) Correct. (This program creates a list of names.)

# Index